The Gathering of Voices

The Twentieth-Century Poetry of Latin America

MIKE GONZALEZ
and
DAVID TREECE

D0062216

V

VERSO

London · New York

First published by Verso 1992
© Verso 1992
All rights reserved

Verso
UK: 6 Meard Street, London W1V 3HR
USA: 29 West 35th Street, New York, NY 10001-2291

Verso is the imprint of New Left Books

ISBN 0-86091-369-4
ISBN 0-86091-581-6 (pbk)

British Library Cataloguing in Publication Data
A catalogue record for this book is available from the British Library

Library of Congress Cataloging-in-Publication Data
A catalogue record for this book is available from the Library of Congress

Typeset by York House Typographic Ltd, London
Printed and bound in Great Britain by
Biddles Ltd, Guildford and Kings Lynn

The
Gathering of Voices

CRITICAL STUDIES IN
LATIN AMERICAN CULTURE

SERIES EDITORS:

James Dunkerley
Jean Franco
John King

This major series – the first of its kind to appear in English – is designed to map the field of contemporary Latin American culture, which has enjoyed increasing popularity in Britain and the United States in recent years.

Six titles will offer a critical introduction to twentieth-century developments in painting, poetry, music, fiction, cinema and 'popular culture'. Further volumes will explore more specialized areas of interest within the field.

The series aims to broaden the scope of criticism of Latin American culture, which tends to extol the virtues of a few established 'master' works and to examine cultural production within the context of twentieth-century history. These clear, accessible studies are aimed at those who wish to know more about some of the most important and influential cultural works and movements of our time.

Other Titles in the Series

Drawing the Line: Art and Cultural Identity in Contemporary Latin America
Oriana Baddeley and *Valerie Fraser*

Plotting Women: Gender and Representation in Mexico
Jean Franco

Journeys Through the Labyrinth: Latin American Fiction in the Twentieth Century
Gerald Martin

Magical Reels: A History of Cinema in Latin America
John King

Memory and Modernity: Popular Culture in Latin America
William Rowe and *Vivian Schelling*

Misplaced Ideas: Essays on Brazilian Culture
Roberto Schwarz

Contents

Introduction

What Poetry Is

It is a condition of survival of a book concerned with poetry not to attempt a definition of poetry itself. The principles of selection that in practice guide what we understand to be poetry often take us beyond narrow frontiers. In a sense, poetry defines itself, yet it is also song; its form may sometimes be its definitive feature, though much contemporary Latin American poetry has burst the bounds of acknowledged poetic form. Within the broad arena of the lyric, poetry is private emotion, conceived in isolation even if not in tranquillity. Yet the overpowering presence of an external world constantly impinges upon private anguish. If it is neither form nor content that distinguishes poetry, then is it perhaps language – that 'something that is always there' to which Octavio Paz refers in one of his many attempts to define poetry? Yet the language of poetry is as diverse as the language of speech – indeed it often *is* the language of speech.

The poetry that comes out of Latin America provides a geography of social and political experience. If it goes beyond description, narrative or definition, it is because it is a field of *response* to that history. In that sense it is always complex, often paradoxical, and as invariably creative as the range of that experience. The particular mediation is the lyric mode, the poetic form, where the resonance of reality encounters the individual self, or the collective identity. But the encounter is a clash, a dialogue conducted at first in whispers and later at the top of the voice.

That dialogue is not directly with the real. Poetry has no sharp edge with which to cut a swathe through the real world. But it can and does engage with the ideas and ideologies which shape the world we see. In confronting the myths and representations with which we make sense of our lives, the poems also evoke an otherness, an alternative vision and an alternative potentiality which lie particularly within the gift of poetry. The Formalists spoke of the specific quality of poetic language as its capacity to 'make strange' or 'defamiliarize' the object of its discourse. That has frequently been taken to indicate the 'otherness' of poetry itself:

> Poetry lies at the centre of the literary experience because it is the form that most clearly asserts the specificity of literature, its difference from ordinary discourse by an empirical individual about the world.[1]

Yet the whole trajectory described in this volume is one of constant challenge and re-engagement, and ultimately of a celebratory return to 'ordinary' discourse and 'ordinary' experience. It is our view that Latin American poetry is defined not by a process of withdrawal into the poetic, but rather by a constant dialectical engagement with the shaping ideas and myths of the real. This is not to suggest for a moment an endless dialogue between intellectuals. On the contrary, it is one of the features of the most exciting and innovative poetry of contemporary Latin America that it seeks, paradoxically for the form always regarded as most esoteric, to speak directly through and with popular traditions and popular culture.

This has had many different consequences. In the eighties, the external reader gained access to the poetry of Central America as the region became a central political motive for the West. What this encounter revealed was how vital still was the oral tradition, and how far its poetry, particularly that of Nicaragua, for example, represented an encounter between the sharpest reactions of an expanding imperialism and the intransigent material of the resistance of a rural world, despite its migrations and transformations.[2] It was poetry, it seemed, which could sustain intercourse with the different levels of development and culture, cross the divisions that were the consequence of uneven economic development. On the other hand, it was the poets too who wrestled constantly with a metropolis that had given them both the seminal components of their intellectual universe and the technology of a modern world whose effects in Latin America seemed less creative than destructive – as ecological devastation and economic indebtedness combined to keep an optimistic modernism at bay. The relationship with that metropolitan discourse has been tense and ambiguous throughout. Jean Franco has described what occurs as the

'confrontation between metropolitan discourse and the utopian pro-
ject of an autonomous society'.[3]

The complex dialogue with the cultural metropolis is a central
feature of the poetry discussed here. That may often be an antagonistic
conversation – it may also be the anxious plaint of a subordinate
culture seeking to complete itself by *assimilation* into the prevailing
culture. That too may often be implicit – expressed in the announce-
ment of cultural values which represent the triumph of Western
universalism rather than the recognition of any authentic global truth.
It is in this context that poetry is endowed with an existence outside
history, in a realm of culture defined by Octavio Paz[4] to which poetry
provides access. Such a concept seems closest to Plato. Yet it has been
eagerly seized upon by critics as well as poets as the basis of a
hierarchy of achievement in Latin American poetry. The implication,
of course, is that the value of Latin American poetry, its 'achievement',
is to be measured in proportion to its absorption of the methods and
insights of Western writing. And if it does achieve equity with the
West, then the evidence it provides is twofold. On the one hand, it
confirms the suggestion that there is a single route to development
and that the Latin Americans are travelling it late. This is a version of
that 'anthropological' understanding of culture as the universal sign of
human maturity, a global insight into the identity of men and women
outside time. The second implication is that national cultures or any
questioning of the single universal culture are earlier stages in the road
to fulfilment and infected still by the twin misdemeanours of localism
and historicism.

It would therefore be understandable if the critical response to
Western bourgeois ideology were simply to reverse the coin and take
refuge in regionalisms and nostalgia. The worst of such writing may
do so. That does not invalidate its charge of protest or critique – but it
leaves its exploration of the paradoxes and conflicts of the colonial
experience open to an accusation of triviality or sentimentalism. Yet as
the following text shows, the Latin American poetry worthy of the
name takes its roots in a local experience as a mode of contesting the
arrogant expansionism of the colonial power. But in turn and at the
same time it seeks another sense of wholeness and completeness. It
contests and renders problematic the dominant universal, not always
in the name of another grand truth, but always in the context of a
search for completion. It may be that that completion is achieved
through multiplicity, through diversity as value and hope; or it may be
through an alternative all-embracing concept like *mestizaje*, or *latin-
ismo*, or the totalizing notion of a world proletariat. What is certain is

that the literature that addresses the Latin American experience as a search for self-emancipation shares the conviction that there is another totality.

The Other Utopias

That in itself says little. That totality, for example, has often spoken through a network of metaphors of nostalgia and loss – a chain of meaning anchored in a pre-Columbian world. Ironically, the evoked world was one with little correspondence to the brutal realities of Aztec and Inca authoritarianism. Indeed it led back to the harmonious pre-class world of the *European* imagination – and the conservative imagination at that. Yet even that vision bears a burden of discontent, of despair, of *rejection*; it thus belongs to that body of writing that calls into question the universality of human experience and the linear concept of history that underpins it. It seems to have no credentials for being located within the writing whose contribution is to the *transformation* of the colonial world. Indeed that exoticist writing is embedded in the aristocratic critique of bourgeois society, of its optimistic historical teleology. And curiously there are echoes of that very atavism in the work of the generation whose work in Spanish America heralds what is described as the beginning of modern poetry. Manuel José Othón turns back to the provincial immobility of Mexico; Rubén Darío himself recreates the European pastoral in his refusal to enter the modern experience.[5]

The additional dimension here, however, is that these voices speak without the accents of ancestral power; on the contrary, they speak from the outer margins of the world system and from a position of exclusion. Is this then merely a case of the poets mimicking their more powerful mentors, or is there here some element of pastiche? In Spanish America, at least, the answer to the question is itself a paradox – there *are* claims here to entry into an undifferentiated artistic Parnassus, yet it is one that is defined by its refusal to admit those it has defined as barbarians, outsiders – or any of the modern versions of the same contemptuous devaluation of the experience of the dominated. Clamouring for entry is a demeaning posture, even when it is couched in the terms of a shared nostalgia. And it is particularly humiliating when the restriction is upon entry to a world itself subject to destruction and collapse.

That contradiction explains the elision of Spanish American Modernismo, moving as it does from withdrawal into conservative utopia to a radical rejection of such nostalgia, with the poetry of the avant garde which rehearses the dismembering of all the central columns of the prevailing order. There is here no alternative order, only perhaps disorder and chaos. But it is a chaos which gives the sense of a fluid world in formation, as in some of the poems of Pablo Neruda's *Residencia en la tierra* (Residence on Earth), set against a world without issue, and which leads only to infinite regression towards the dismembered final words of Vicente Huidobro's *Altazor* or the babbling *jitanjáfora* (a nonsense word) of Cuba's Mariano Brull.

The unifying factor is the perception of a double alienation. In Europe, the division of labour between creative and repetitive, mechanical labour produced a practice and a group of practitioners asserting the inviolability of the imaginative act[6] – even if that act of conservation in turn meant isolation and withdrawal. In Latin America, such a gesture could only seem hollow where the revolutionizing of the contemporary world, the manifestation of the terrible creative power of capitalism itself, was no more than a reflected illusion. It was as if the active assertion of creative freedom rang hollow in a world where freedom from necessity itself was a mirage.

For the most advanced and insightful intellectuals of a dependent bourgeoisie the irony came home with a terrible jolt. César Vallejo remains the most ravaging exponent of that despair, but it had many expressions – some experimental and radical in form, others nationalistic and provincial in content. Their common thread was the anguished experience of the colonized imagination, often inhabiting the metropolitan utopia yet without any possibility of control over that environment. Within the context of art and poetry as defined in Western culture there were no further options. 'Making strange' thus involved the contradictory process of emphasizing the alienation of self, since there was no alternative universe available within the realm of poetry. Few options remained: one was assimilation into the problematic universal, with the questionable compensation of finding an intellectual world of equality outside the frame of history. The other was what Frantz Fanon described[7] as 'the wilful narcissism of the colonial bourgeoisie', a self-absorption which in some cases became identified with a freedom synonymous with withdrawal from the real – the poetic act an act of voluntary exile.[8]

Were this all there was to say, then the most successful of Latin American poetry would belong within a universal anthology, and the accident of origin would be no more than anecdotal. The problem of asserting the reverse proposition, however, is to enter the realm of nationalism/regionalism, with its voluntary renunciation of global impact or sense of totality. In this form, a new and different mode of renunciation is the result.

A Universal Exploitation

There is another direction and this narrative sets out to illustrate it. If the counter-universal exists it is in the common experience of alienation, of exploitation, of exclusion itself. It may have many manifestations, and may be exacerbated by other marginalities. Race and gender reinforce and repeat the alienation – and the alienation may prove overwhelming or provide the locus for a resolute resistance. The local and the specific are in many instances the necessary site of resistance.[9] On the other hand, to raise defences around that wall is to accept that the world is incapable of transformation. Is that localism or specificity the site of resistance or the originating point of a critique rooted in a common experience seeking a language, and pursuing a systematic and collective expression? Breaking the silence of isolation the poet of exclusion may appropriate his exclusion as a source not only of rebellion but of a new and authentic experience – the rediscovery of totality to which Lukács refers throughout his work.[10] In our view, Latin American poetry has found a voice not in imitation of the West and its despairs, but in an echo of public dissent, of common language. It has broken its isolation not by occupying a subordinate place on the Elysian fields of cultural tradition, but rather in the rediscovery of a collective voice and a collective experience found at times in popular culture, at times in shared ritual or song, at times in folk memory. What is important is that poetry has opened its frontiers to all those possible components, has excluded none, and in Ernesto Cardenal's words has sought the community of the shadows to be its voice.[11]

The name this new work has been given is 'conversational' or 'public poetry'. Its theorists and exponents would lay no claim to uniqueness or even to historical originality; rather the work is an act of rediscovery in the specific circumstances of contemporary Latin America. And to this extent the poetry of public utterance and the poetry of private insight grow separate. The most conscious of introspective poets, of writers absorbed with the survival of the self, must make acknowledgement of these changes. Some, of course, do not; rather, they denounce such breaking of bounds as a new form of cultural barbarism. The awarding of a Nobel Prize to Octavio Paz is a specific act of partisanship in this discussion, a resurrection of the conservative myth. The alternative history of Latin American contemporary poetry is given here in its constant and deepening engagement with the real. In this sense it is an explicit counter to the views of Paz, to the concept of universality as the sole response to solitude.[12] There is another response in our view – and that is the search for solidarity, for a communal voice or a voice within the community. It need not represent only an average; on the contrary it can and must address the complex specificity of historical experience, the individual as the field of conflict of such forces, and thus – and above all – the dynamics of change and transformation.

Nevertheless, this volume is not devoted entirely to a poetry of public utterance, nor is its criterion of selection a concern with political events or collective speech alone. It *is* concerned, however, with the centrality of historical experience in the discussion of poetry – not as a motive of evasion but as the core *material* of poetry. This yields not only a confident poetry of utopian or optimistic stripe. The appalling experiences of the late seventies in Latin America, and the imposition of brutal military dictatorships, produced a different and more insecure voice – a voice of exile, an overpowering sense of loss, particularly for example in Chile. On the broad canvas it was matched by the millennial optimism of the poetry of a Central America locked in struggle with the North American monolith. The difference from earlier times, however, is that the most poignant explorations of the sense of wandering and exclusion through those terrible times are still developed in the realm of public confession and shared utterance. Even the most private experience is offered in a form of democratic speech, and the withdrawal into hermetic privacy remains an uncharacteristic response. There can be few more moving accounts of exile than Patricio Manns's 'Cuando me acuerdo de mi país'; yet for all its sealed and often obscure metaphors it is expressed in song, and in full view of a material public.

The structure of the account of Latin American poetry that follows, therefore, is driven by that encounter of poetry and public experience. It is an encounter mediated and full of tensions – often it is a clash, or a meeting of unwilling participants. Yet it is the inescapable direction of creative activity. For it is in that resolute push out of otherness and marginality that self-consciousness begins. And poetry is not simply a locus of regret and imaginative explorations of other fictions; it is increasingly the site of a rehearsal of new relationships, new possibilities, new forms of struggle and often, at its best, a moving exhortation to find the self in the reconstruction of the world.

Te quiero porque sos
Mi amor mi cómplice y todo
Y en la marcha codo a codo
Somos mucho más que dos

(I love you because you are/My love, my accomplice and everything/
And in the march, marching shoulder to shoulder/We are many more
than two)[13]

A Method

The account of Latin American poetry that we have developed here
sets out to avoid certain problems in the discussion of poetry. Such
volumes often emerge as endless lists of schools and groups, most
ending with the suffix 'ism'. Others become catalogues of personal
likes and dislikes with nothing other than a tenuous link of unspeci-
fied taste; we are asked to accept without question the validity of a
selection based on such fragile assumptions by implicit reference to
the authority of the critic. None of these methods adds anything to our
understanding at all. On the other hand, there is a bewildering
quantity of poems to choose from. We have tried to avoid producing
the kind of book which is actually a collection of essays on individual
poets, and instead try to identify seminal writings without excluding
others. Nonetheless each chapter, in presenting a central issue or
relationship, the drama of poetry in its circumstance, has focused on
one or two key texts. But they are intended to be representative, to be
'typical' in the Lukácsian sense of enshrining the central tensions of a
historical moment.[14] The statement we are intending to make is not
that this is the greatest poem of an era, but perhaps that it is the most
revealing.

Naturally, this method produces multiple exclusions, and there will
be argument as to whether we have chosen well, or unearthed the best
or most significant poems or poets. The dialogue itself will produce
new criteria and new texts, and we shall have succeeded in the
enterprise if we provoke just such a discussion. But we are prepared to
assert that the central questions in poetry's reappropriation of its
public role are those we have attested to.

There is a palpable imbalance between men and women writers,
both within our own text and in the general literature on the poetry of
Latin America. In some sense, that visible absence of women precisely
illustrates the issue of exclusion which is central to our concerns. The
very *definition* of poetry as the form most persistently engaged in
exploring the grand issues of philosophical debate has specifically

colluded in the marginalization of women writers who would necess-
arily reflect the constraints placed upon women in the defining areas
of social activity more generally. In the critical and poetic writing of
Octavio Paz, for example, women assume a key symbolic function; but
they are the objects of creative activity and imprisoned in their role as
the vehicles of sensual liberation.[15] The writing of Alfonsina Storni,
Gabriela Mistral and Rosario Castellanos baulks at the exasperating
restraints that women face. Insofar as we have tried to explore the
body of Latin American poetry in search of resistances to marginality
and otherness, women should figure largely, or far more largely than
they do. Yet they are almost invisible in the collections and antholo-
gies, absent from the canon of 'great' writing, and passed over in much
of the supporting literature.

One response has been to produce separate anthologies of women's
writing,[16] and the active accumulation of the neglected and rejected
work of women writers is to be celebrated. Paradoxically, the detective
work appears to yield more women poets than novelists or play-
wrights. Yet the paradox is only apparent; if *lyric* poetry is the area of
intimate exploration par excellence, then the restriction of women to
the private sphere is echoed in the privacy of the lyric. On the other
hand, the attempt to return from that journey into the self, with its
implication of a refuge from oppression in a kind of self-imposed exile,
is much more difficult. The move from the private to the public is one
that appears to involve few women writers, at least until the Nicara-
guan Revolution brought women into a central position in the trans-
formation of material circumstances.

Even there, as the writing of Gioconda Belli and Rosario Murillo
make clear, the oppression of women is not necessarily or automati-
cally overcome. It remains to be fought at every level; and because it is
an impediment to the development of a poetry of public communica-
tion, that oppression remains a central topic of such work. This is not
to suggest that this is in any way a 'proper' or 'necessary' province for
women's writing; it is the product of a *historical* exclusion to which we
have referred. Nonetheless, it is an aspect of the wider experience of
marginality which is the recurrent preoccupation of much of the
poetry which we discuss. The move into the public realm is an exercise
in reclaiming the arena of social communication and social transfor-
mation; that act is not gender-specific, not an exercise in male aggres-
sion, but the most creative form of engagement with the world. The
issues of discrimination and oppression addressed by women writers
will not suddenly cease to be significant as the symbolic and real
return from exile takes place. On the contrary, they cease to be local

problems, and become instead a component of the general struggle for transformation.

This may explain the complex phenomenon of a poetry of the eighties which for the first time enjoys a significant and core representation of women. Partly, of course, this is a consequence of the growth and development of feminist literary criticism and its exploration of the 'other' which has focused so sharply on women from 'marginalized cultures', within and outside the core societies of the world system. Undoubtedly this has given confidence and encouragement to writers and critics in Latin America and generated a double response: the discovery of existing but unknown women writers, and the encouragement of women to write from a world which can no longer exclude them. That is one reason why the final chapter on the eighties has a greater representation of women. There may also be other more complex reasons. The key experiences of Latin America in the last decade have been exile, internal and external, the Central American resistance, and the extraordinary upsurge of popular struggle in Brazil. In each, for quite different reasons, women have opened a space for themselves.

Women have borne the material and psychic burden of exile; their prior experience has provided, too, a language and a source of understanding of exile. Thus the experience of women became more globally significant. In Central America, the role of women in the revolutions of the region has been central, yet the struggle against oppression has also been a battle waged *within* the revolution.[17] In Brazil the working-class movement has grown in a context of generalized social struggle, itself a response to far-reaching economic and social changes through the previous decade which have directly affected the position of women and drawn them into a variety of social and political struggles.

Brazil

Unusually, the present account embraces both Brazil and Spanish America. We have tried to avoid false parallels or analogies. While the whole of Latin America (embracing Brazil) shares a historical development and a relationship with the other components of the world system, the specificities of their development have been very different. Brazilian Modernism, for example, represented in many senses a more radical rupture with the Brazilian past. The Modernista period in the Spanish-speaking part of the continent suggested an engagement with the dramatic transformations of Europe in the late nineteenth century – though in a sense by identification alone. The aristocratic component of Latin American Modernism has its expression in the Brazil of the same era – but it is not Modernism. For European and Spanish American Modernism coincided with a moment of cultural and political *reaction* in Brazil. The 1898 Campos Sales government re-established the political control of the traditional landowning and coffee-growing oligarchy; this was the context of Brazil's 'belle épo-que', with its emphasis on continuity with the pre-Republican colonial order. There were individuals who attempted to respond to the changes heralded in the brief Jacobin interregnum of 1889–98. Joaquim de Sousândrade's extraordinary Indianist epic *O Guesa* (an incomplete version of which was published in 1888) exposed the brutality of Conquest and juxtaposed it with the actions of North American capitalism, its contemporary counterpart. Its earlier discursive epic form later breaks down into a stream of surrealist images whose linguistic violence emphasizes the frustration of an artist attempting to make sense of the 'inferno' of modernization from the perspective of contemporary Brazil. But Sousândrade and his contemporaries Cruz e Sousa or Augusto de Anjos were marginalized or absorbed by the society of the turn of the century.

In this light Brazilian Modernism was a rupture with the past. The cultural establishment that had found a temporary haven in political and economic stagnation as the century ended produced the Parnas-sianism of Bilac et al., on the one hand, and on the other a 'caboclismo' which made the *mestiço* peasant the representative of a rural order stable and secure in the face of change. Thus the regional poetry or *caipirismo* of Cornélio Pires folklorized local speech and the way of life of the peasant of the São Paulo interior, while in Menotta del Picchia's *Juca Mulato* (1917) it is the 'somnolence' of the caboclo that persuades him to end his romantic quest for the hand of the landowner's daughter. There is a clear thread of continuity between this celebration of a telluric integration of the rural Brazilian and the mystical neo-Indianism of the Verdeamarelistas of the 1920s; their conservatism and defence of the old order met the resistance of Oswald and Mário de Andrade who were prepared to confront the possibilities, challenges and contradictions of Brazilian modernization.

The theoretical and creative conflicts within Brazilian Modernism seem in many ways to have set the terms for almost all subsequent debates in Brazilian literature. The same could not be said of Spanish America, where Modernism seems simply not to survive the impact of the modern. Instead the avant-garde movements obliquely address those contradictions and dilemmas, while at the same time addressing the issue of whether poetry should be a participant at all in the public argument about social transformation. The Spanish Civil War is a watershed in those discussions. Yet in some senses they remain abstract and philosophical – an exploration not so much of categories of the real as of ideology itself. Yet the most powerful poetry 'of the world', or 'political writing' (in the broadest sense), arises from the painful irruption of the concrete world into the poetic universe. The key is whether that irruption is envisaged as creative and productive, enriching in a word, or threatening to that 'emotion recollected in tranquillity' that is, for some critics, poetry's essential quality. Writing here, it will be clear that for us poetry's entry into the arena of shared experience is a wholly positive movement, and that the reintegration of poetry with its sources and social origins, as well as its expansion into other areas of struggle and debate, is above all an act of completion. It is that 'gathering of voices' which we document and celebrate, in the hope that from the rising clamour a new and deeply transformed world will emerge in which public and private expression need not suffer such painful separation.

We have been helped and supported by many people; the list is in no particular order of priority – we are indebted to them all. To John King, James Dunkerley, Robert Pring-Mill, John Gledson, Glen Dawkins, Rachel Boyd, Mae Boyd, Newman Smith, Catherine Boyle, Suzanne Jeffery, Elmar Pereira de Mello, Hilda White Rössle and Rui Kureda, to Augusto de Campos, Mário Chamie, Armando Freitas Filho, Sebastião Uchoa Leite, Luis Costa Lima and Affonso Romano de Sant'Anna for interviews in July and August 1988, to the British Academy for funding research in Brazil in 1988, and to all those who in some way or another have indulged us in the course of writing. We hope they all feel it was worth the wait.

How to Strangle a Swan: Contradictions of Modernity in Latin America

A Refuge from the World

The modern experience in Latin America rests on a series of paradoxes. The processes of transformation and change that in Europe bore the name of modernization touched Latin America in a very different way. Powerless to affect or control matters, the liberation of the productive forces in the metropolis yielded only new forms of alienation on the periphery. Far from generating that sense of harnessing the enormous powers of nature to human purposes, modernity produced only a greater feeling of impotence and helplessness. Appearances belied the changes that were taking place, and rendered them all the more perplexing for the Latin American middle class. The continuing power of priest and landowner might suggest a continuity from colonial times; yet both priest and landowner were quite likely to be agents of an international company or an expanding section of new capital.[1] The resistance to the new encroachments began in the late 1880s to take the form of a nostalgic backward glance to communal, pre-Hispanic forms, yet the inheritors of those pre-Columbian communities were quite probably in thrall to the very proprietors who now resisted modernization in their name.[2]

The cultural paradox therefore rode astride unresolved economic contradictions, as an uneven process of development combined a deepening backwardness with the growth of industry. Few of the artists and writers of late-nineteenth century Latin America seem to have identified with the emergent bourgeoisie; from several perspectives they renounced its materialism and vulgarity. Yet at the same time the characteristic note of the Modernista school of writers with whom this study begins was their renunciation of things Spanish and their enthusiasm for the innovatory artistic activity of France. Some, like the Colombian Eduardo Caballero Calderón, wrote in French; and all either visited or dreamt of visiting Paris. At the formal level, the introduction of the new freer metres and forms of French poetry marked a 'modernization' of poetry in Spanish; yet Modernismo,[3] as the movement was called, expressed a deeply sceptical view of the benefits of modernity in general.

The Modernistas undoubtedly were innovators and critics of the conservative structures that persisted from the colonial period – structures enshrined in and sustained by the Catholic Church. Yet that did not lead them to a progressive vision of human affairs. They shared the suspicion and the ambiguity of their European mentors in the face of economic progress, for it brought with it a devaluation of the creative act, and the transformation of Art into commodity.[4] In a similar way, capitalism transformed relations between persons into a relationship between things; the Modernistas offered a defence of humanism and a resistance to that reification of human products. The paradox is that defence of humanism often took the form of a reappropriation of a European Classical culture in which they found no resonance of the specificity of their Latin American experience. On the contrary, the heroic individuality of the poets, that 'aristocracy of the spirit' that embraced all those who refused to assume their allotted position in the marketplace, led them most often to deny that particularity.[5] Nonetheless, very different conclusions were drawn and different forms evolved. Under the rubric of Modernismo huddled writers whose persona was closest to Baudelaire's *flaneur* – the wanderer in the city streets; there were others for whom Classical Greece provided a cultural home. There were the radicals of rejection, whose poetry explored and reproduced the process of disintegration, personal and social, which they saw as the consequence of change.

What then did they share? What is it that has led critics from all directions to denote Modernismo a school, or in that irritatingly imprecise term so often used in the context of poetry, a 'generation'?[6] What united them was the central place of modernity in their concerns; the pervasive issue of transformation, however, was an *unacknowledged* presence in this world of words, where what was most often evoked was order, culture, timelessness, a world of insular personal emotion. In this first generation of Modernistas the opposite – disorder, barbarism, history as turbulent change – were implicit threats. The integrity of the world of the past offered an alternative to a fragmented and mysterious present in which change appeared only as

2

destruction, as collapse. And there were none among them who manifested even that ambivalence which might make them 'simultaneously enthusiasts and enemies of modern life'.[7] As the intellectuals of a subaltern bourgeoisie, arriving at the modern experience late and as passive consumers, they experienced the process as a loss of autonomy, as alienation. For that reason they turned to a remembered totality of the past, since they could envisage no future world of promise.

The Modernistas vacillated between Palladian visions of a world of culture outside time, in which the inequities of the actual world of Latin America were lost in the equality of artistic values, and a withdrawal into a despairing and enclosed self, which would ultimately be drained by its lack of renewal, its failure to draw any sustenance from the world of change. So this aristocracy of the spirit defined itself, in part, by its sceptical response to the optimistic historicism of the Positivists; for many different reasons they called into question the assumption that modernization and progress would be universally beneficial.[8]

If Modernismo can be described as the first Latin American school of poetry, it is perhaps in the negative sense of a common rejection of modernity as a hopeful possibility for the continent. Change appeared not as the monstrous act of will identified by Nietzsche, nor as the product of the dynamics of class struggle analysed by Marx, but as a historical fatality – a destiny. And if no future class could carry the critique they offered into the world of actual human relations, then the irony was that the Modernistas found their collective identity in a re-evocation of an alternative *past*, not the Hispanic past of an imitative and trivial colonial nature,[9] but the strong European Classical past with its resulting contemporary tradition.

There *was* an alternative regional tradition – that is, a history whose social and cultural projections remained as living alternatives in the present. It was to be found in an oral culture of poetry and song, in popular ritual and myth. There were those among the Modernistas – José Martí in particular – who identified with *that* past; others, like Leopoldo Lugones, had an uncomfortable relationship with it, but little lasting sympathy with those whose life and experience were enshrined there.[10] The voice of a living oral culture was largely absent from a Modernismo which found its identity in an aristocratic concept of culture.

Modernity can be said to unite all mankind. But it is a paradoxical unity;

it pours us all into a maelstrom of perpetual disintegration and renewal, of struggle and contradiction, of ambiguity and anguish.[11]

In Latin America, the paradox is particularly poignant and painful. The experience of modernity, of that extraordinary transformation that Marshall Berman addresses in his *All That Is Solid Melts Into Air*,[12] is indirect and exasperating. In Europe, the contradiction lay in the explosive and exciting possibilities that modernity brought, set against the sense of loss, fragmentation and powerlessness that the sheer force of these powers for change generated in those who were its witnesses. The literature of the period bears testimony to that unresolved tension – in Baudelaire, Nietzsche, Marx. The nineteenth-century writers 'were simultaneously enthusiasts and enemies of modern life, wrestling inexhaustibly with its ambiguities and contradictions; their self-ironies and inner tensions were a primary source of their creative power'.[13]

For the writers of Latin America the ambiguity was even deeper. As Europe saw the structures of social and intellectual life transformed and constantly renewed, in Latin America the echoes of that process entered a world where renewal and change coexisted with immobility.

José Asunción Silva (1864–96)[14] was born and brought up in Colombia. Like others of his class and age, he travelled to Paris to acquire civilization and culture, and returned imbued with Baudelairean *spleen*, a bitter despair born of the anonymous urban landscapes of late-nineteenth-century Europe. His 'Nocturnos' (of which there are three) are simple and conversational in language, plaintive and nostalgic, evoking through the memory of his sister Elvira a remembered world of childhood and harmony. Their free verse form owes much to the work of Poe, and the plaintive repetitions of 'Nocturno' recall the haunting refrain of 'The Bells'.

> . . . una noche
> en que ardían en la sombra ñupcial y húmeda las luciérnagas
>   fantásticas
> a mi lado lentamente, contra mí ceñida toda, muda y pálida,
> como si un presentimiento de amarguras infinitas
> hasta el más secreto fondo de las fibras te agitara,
> por la senda florecida que atraviesa la llanura
> caminabas;
> . . .
> y tu sombra
> fina y lánguida
> y mi sombra

4

por los rayos de la luna proyectadas sobre las arenas tristes
de la senda se juntaban
y eran una
y eran una
y eran una sola sombra larga.

. . .

Sentí frío
. . . Era el frío del sepulcro, era el hielo de la muerte,
era el frío de la nada.

. . .

(one night/when the fantastic glowworms glowed in the warm nuptial
shadows/by my side, slowly, tight against me, silent and pale,/as if a
presentiment of infinite bitterness/had penetrated to your most secret
depths,/you were walking then;/. . ./and your shadow/delicate and lan-
guid/and my shadow/reflected by the moon on to the sad sands of the
path/drew together/and they were one/they were one/they were one
long shadow./. . ./I felt cold/the cold of the tomb/the cold of death/the
cold of nothingness.)

In 'Mal de Siglo' (Mal de siècle), Silva generalized that experience of
loss into a social vision, a sense of loss shared and relived as personal
anguish and isolation. Undoubtedly Silva, one of the first of the
Modernista generation, is closest to Baudelaire, and to the sense of
isolation and marginality that Baudelaire's poetry confirms.[15] The
shock of the new city renders all experience immediate and simulta-
neous; there is no sense that its accumulation leads to knowledge.
Death, therefore, is absolute loss, and all feeling becomes sensation,
immediate and transitory. 'The inner interests of men do not of
themselves possess that irredeemably private character; they acquire
it when for external reasons the possibility of their incorporation into
experience is progressively diminished.'[16] The sought-after harmony
is unattainable in the fearsome process of disintegration to which
Baudelaire and Silva allude. When Silva dreams ('Sueños de media-
noche' – 'Midnight dreams') it is of

La fragancia indecisa de un olor olvidado,
Llegó como un fantasma y me habló del pasado

Vi caras que la tumba desde hace tiempo esconde,
Y oí voces oídas ya no recuerdo dónde

Los sueños se acercaron y me vieron dormido . . .
Y fueron deshaciéndose y hundiéndose en la sombra

5

(The vague fragrance of a forgotten love,/Came like a ghost and spoke to me of the past//I saw faces that the tomb has long since concealed,/And heard voices last heard I know not where//Dreams came and saw me sleeping . . ./And fell apart and were lost in the shadows)

Memory serves only to underline the enduring sense of loss – and it is a loss without compensation in any future, real or imagined. Hence the bitter tone of the collection called *Gotas Amargas* (Bitter Drops), where Silva makes his own that anguish and unease called by Baudelaire 'le mal de siècle'.

> Un cansancio de todo, un absoluto
> desprecio por todo lo humano . . . un incesante
> renegar de lo vil de la existencia
> digno de mi maestro Schopenhauer;
> un malestar profundo que se aumenta
> con todas las torturas del análisis . . .

(A weariness at everything, an absolute/contempt for everything human . . . an incessant/complaint at the misery of existence/worthy of my master Schopenhauer;/a deep unease that grows/through all the tortures of analysis . . .)

The Doctor in the poem replies that he should eat and drink well because 'lo que Usted tiene es hambre' – your problem is hunger. The brief poem is tantalizing in its range of interpretative possibilities. Either the hunger is spiritual and inorganic, or the Doctor is himself the voice of a society too materialistic and instrumental to understand the deep unease that material progress can bring with it.

Henríquez Ureña describes Silva as 'el más alto representante del pesimismo contemporáneo' – 'the highest representative of contemporary pressimism'.[17] Yet what was it that was lost? For the European intellectual undoubtedly[18] it was that 'creative integrity' that allowed the poet to cast his vision across a whole world. Now, in the division of labour that an expanding and confident capitalism had produced, the spiritual and productive functions had been definitely separated. The artist faced now a dual demand – or a dual possibility – to serve the market with products of consumption, with art as object,[19] or to refuse that relation with the audience and the public. That refusal implied withdrawal, rejection – the world against nature of Huysmans,[20] whose protagonist turned nature against itself in a parody of a man-made world. Night became day, day night – and art was the reversal of the social world. Baudelaire denounced his 'hypocritical reader' for requiring of him both originality and creativity, and obedience to the spiritual requirements of commodity exchange. Then he embarked on that journey ('Le Voyage') to a landscape of human creation. That idealized landscape[21] provided a pastoral refuge, a contrast to the monstrous and consuming created nature of the new industrial cities. But is is crucial to remember too that that roaring monster of the modern city was also the repository of a promise of liberation in the industrial world, a promise it did *not* offer in Latin America, where the burgeoning city coexisted with anachronistic and repressive structures from the past.

Throughout the modern experience, it was that paradox that moved to fury – not at the creative time when an insurgent capitalism challenged and swept aside the conservative structures of the past, but at a later period of establishment and consolidation. But still there is fury, rage, a living sense of what was made possible by this 'constant revolutionizing of society' of which Marx wrote with such passion.[22] In that context, the revolution in the person, the full flowering of the potential of all human beings, is the fellow traveller of this revolutionizing of the material world.

Mexico City, for example, was the acknowledged centre of the Modernista movement. In the last twenty years of the nineteenth century, it was growing into a self-conscious Europeanism; its new buildings, shops and boulevards, and the patterns of consumption that they signalled echoed the Paris of Haussman. It signalled too the integration of the Mexican economy into the expansionist strategies of a European capital seeking to compete for domination of the world market.[23] The Mexican bourgeoisie assumed the style and appearance of its imperial patrons, and mimicked its historical purposes as embedded in the Positivist philosophy officially adopted by the Mexican state after 1891.[24] Yet the dictator Díaz's rural police still crushed the slightest protest by the debt-ridden serfs on the great estates[25] at the same time as beautiful art nouveau shops sprang up in the streets of the old city centre. After Darío, the Mexican Modernistas grouped around the *Revista Azul* gave particular voice to the new pleasure-seeking middle class.[26]

The Landscapes of Darío

That Latin American writers should have taken up the message of Montparnasse or Montmartre may at first sight be surprising. Why should the young poet son of a provincial Nicaraguan family, Rubén

Darío, absorb so thoroughly the Classical scholarship of Europe? What is problematic is the wilful blindness that seems to accompany that absorption of European style. If Silva adopts the spleen of his Parisian predecessor, he does so in the context of an uneven modernity in Latin America. The acknowledged leader of the Modernista movement, Rubén Darío (1867–1916),[27] began to write in the most remote of urban environments – his native León – though he later found more congenial milieux in Buenos Aires and Santiago de Chile, which could sustain a professional writer and his growing entourage.

What was the impact of the curious relationship between the Modernistas and their own reality? What did it mean when a generation of Latin American writers refuted the assumptions of a conservative and backward-looking Hispanic culture, and turned instead to the rest of Europe, assimilating the utopias of that world? Ricardo Jaimes Freyre (1868–1933), for example, set his poetry in a mythical Norse land; Juan José Tablada (1871–1945), the most important link with the avant garde of the 1920s, explored the reservoirs of Japanese culture. Darío set out in the Preface to *Prosas Profanas* (Profane Prose) what has come to be accepted as the manifesto of Modernismo.

> . . . he aquí que veréis en mis versos princesas, reyes, cosas imperiales, visiones de países lejanos o imposibles; ¡qué queréis!, yo detesto la vida y el tiempo en que me tocó nacer . . . Si hay poesía en nuestra América, ella está en las cosas viejas; en Palenque y Utatlán, en el indio legendario y el inca sensual y fino, y en el gran Moctezuma en su silla de oro . . .[28]

> (. . . you will see in my verses princesses, kings, imperial objects, visions of distant or impossible countries; what do you want! I detest life and the times I have to live in. . . . If there is any poetry in our America it is in the old things; in Palenque and Utatlan, in the Indian of legend and the fine and sensual Inca, and in the great Montezuma on his golden throne . . .)

> > ¿Fue en ese buen tiempo de duques pastores,
> > de amantes princesas y tiernos galanes,
> > cuando entre sonrisas y perlas y flores
> > iban las casacas de los chambelanes?
> >
> > ¿Fue acaso en el Norte o en el mediodía?
> > Yo el tiempo y el día y el país ignoro;
> > pero sé que Eulalia ríe todavía
> > y ¡es cruel y eterna su risa do oro!
> > ('Era un aire suave' – 'It was a gentle breeze')

> (Was it as in the good time of the shepherds/of lovers, princesses and tender suitors,/when among smiles and pearls and flowers/the chamber-

lains cloaks passed by?//Was it in the North or the South?/I do not know the time or the day or the country;/but I know that Eulalia is still laughing/and that her golden smile is cruel and eternal)

His utopia was a Greek landscape after Gauthier – cold, perfect, filled with mythical creatures, and above all outside time.

> Y en la copa luminosa
> está venus Citérea
> tendida cerca de Adonis
> que sus caricias desdeña
> No quiero el vino de Naxos
> ni el ánfora de asas bellas . . .
> ('Primaveral' – Spring Song)

(The luminous chalice/shows Venus Cithera/lying beside Adonis/and disdaining his caresses./I do not want the wine of Naxos/nor the vase with the beautiful handles . . .)

There is nothing here of a particular Latin American experience; the Classical utopia offers an imaginative refuge securely set in universal values. What rebellion or unease was expressed found its language or image in European Romanticism and its inheritors. The reaction against materialism that Darío set out in his *Prosas Profanas*, the denunciation of the mediocrity of the petty bourgeoisie,

Celui-qui-ne-comprend-pas es entre nosotros profesor, académico correspondiente de la real Academia Española, periodista, abogado, poeta, rastaqouère[29]

(He-who-understands-nothing in our world is a teacher, corresponding academic member of the Royal Spanish Academy, journalist, lawyer, poet, freebooter)

referred above all to the market whose reification of art threatened the creativity of the artists, their freedom and autonomy. In Latin America, the market embraced only a tiny minority whose patterns of consumption derived from Europe and the metropolis. Sharing its perspective and its history, it shared too its vision of its *own* reality.

Darío's contribution, and his impact, was undoubtedly derived from his introduction of the refinements of French poetry into Spanish. As Noe Jitrik insists, Darío made conscious and radical use of metrical schemes new to the language, exploiting accent and rhythm. Many of the rhetorical devices he used were quite consciously anachronistic; in some sense, Darío made play of their historical associations – the alexandrine, the sonnet – at times to emphasize the universal, at times to ironize that rhetoric by introducing into the

9

patterns sudden faults or 'spaces'. In this sense, however, his references were always internal – it was the poem itself that was its own referent, an object where a quality of sound complemented the printed word.[30] Beyond language, however, was the perception of the poet's role as guardian of values both eternal and timeless. Darío was scornful of the political intellectuals, so willing to set their ideas at the service of pragmatic demands. The poet was the exemplar of the professional writer, the representative of that wilful self-exclusion from history which was precisely what these writers found most reassuring in European culture. For it was the historical progress celebrated by the spokespeople of the new bourgeoisie that had made Latin America its object and victim and reinforced its inequalities. This is not to say that the Modernistas were radical democrats – some were, but most were conservative in their elitism and their celebration of an imagined pre-modern harmony and unity. That is the key quality of the worlds evoked in the work of Herrera y Reissig or Jaimes Freyre. The utopia is either an artificial paradise or it is a consciousness of the universality of despair; both these utopias represented in Europe a voluntary withdrawal from historical optimism and a return to a past still *imaginable* in Europe.

The Modernistas shared the need to respond to a 'sudden transformation which was weak and uneven in Latin America'.[31] 'Their starting point is dissatisfaction with the present, that feeling of emptiness and solitude which took possession of the artists of the period and which in large part implied an explicit or tacit critique of the new bourgeois society that was creating the contemporary universe.[32] The imperialist expansionism of the age brought with it too an explanation of backwardness which ascribed it to a set of racial deficiencies. Many of the poets of the period echoed those essentially racist explanations, since they offered a convenient understanding both of their own isolation and the lack of an audience. They served too to reinforce a cosmopolitanism which, despite their critique of progress, the Modernistas set against the contemptible provincialism of the emerging bourgeoisie. Darío's 'El Porvenir' ('The Future') is a good example, setting out three phases of human development, from the ancient religious world through a democratic material world still viewed with scepticism to the superior realization of the Spirit in the harmony of peoples, a state where Hugo and Rabelais, Aeschylus and Dante, meet. In a sense, that universal order envisaged in a Classical mould is a counterpoint to the globalization of the world market itself. The paradox seems embedded in the cosmopolitanism of Darío and his contemporaries.

10

The contradiction is present to some degree in all the poets – but most often suppressed and unacknowledged. Salvador Díaz Mirón (1853–1928), for example, was an exemplary Romantic whose 'Los parías' ('The pariahs') is a bitter social satire. Darío too displayed a critical spirit which from time to time became explicit, particularly in his *Cantos de vida y esperanza* (*Songs of life and hope*) of 1906. 'Wherever he looks, the poet takes note of the disorder of the universe, the injustice in society, the subversion of values and a general lack of harmony which seems to rule over nature and which will permit judgement even of God.[33]

Azul (*Blue*),[34] for example, confronts the love of gold with the spiritual emptiness that it brings. The stories, based on the stylish 'contes parisiens' of Catulle Mendès, are more perceptive than the poems, particularly 'El rey burgués' (The bourgeois king), where king and poet exchange qualities. And that pursuit of the material is experienced as rupture and disintegration. There is no alternative totality, or wholeness, present within this constant movement; in Peru, Abraham Valdelomar (1888–1919) experienced the new city as restlessness, as aimless traffic. In Mexico, Manuel Gutiérrez Nájera (1859–95) spoke for the new Bohemia of artists adrift in, but not part of the crowd. The rebellion of the poets was a reassertion of wholeness, of integrity in an alternative landscape – a landscape at times created in mythic imagery, at times in Bohemia. The landscape was the self, the person of the poet. But in either case, it was against nature, where nature was the site of the restless, unceasing process of change and transformation. Thus Darío was engaged in 'a vast and complex operation; the methodical construction of a poetic artifice outside nature.'[35] Faced with the deepening division of labour, the Modernista protest took the form of a call for the unity of man.[36] In Darío, that unity was realized in a created nature which he called his 'selva sagrada' (sacred jungle), or what Amado Nervo (1870–1919) called a 'cultural landscape'. Where the bourgeoisie substituted for nature the concept of an 'interior', an internal space filled with purchases and displays, the Modernistas offered an inner life without equivalence in the external reality. If Beauty was eternal and innate, it was also untranslatable into commodity terms:

> Dentro el amor que abrasa
> fuera, la noche fría
> (Darío: 'Invernal' – Winter)

(Within, a burning love/without, the cold night)

11

Where pleasure replaces love, and sensation the accumulation of experience, everything is ephemeral and a function of exchange – hence Darío's 'horror de sentirse pasajero' (horror of the transient).

> [Darío] transfers to heaven what he sees in the reality of his time, in the operations of bourgeois society and I think that that illustrates clearly his place at the margins of society, in a Latin America which was living painfully through the conflict between a traditional economy-aesthetics and another impetuously modern one imposed by the cosmopolitan metropolis.[37]

But for the completely cosmopolitan intellectuals of the Latin American middle class, the alternatives were varieties of alienation – exclusion from history, time, and the future. There could be no return except to the indigenous world, the pre-Hispanic past, or the popular culture hidden in the silent world of the oral. The Romantics and moderns of Europe confronted both the promise and the threat of the burgeoning forces of production and change. Latin America experienced that growth only as exploitation and loss, as the raw materials and minerals of the continent provided the clay from which this newness would be moulded. Yet they had no sense of an alternative, no means of grasping and controlling these enormous forces for other and different purposes.

What possibilities were then available? For Darío, the object was the attainment of a refinement and perfection of vision that could be outside time and thus accessible from Chile or Argentina where he worked as a journalist and correspondent. The philosophical quest was expressed in his famous 'Yo persigo una forma' (I seek a form):

> Y no hallo sino la palabra que huye,
> la iniciación melódica que de la flauta fluye
> y la barca del sueño que en el espacio boga;
>
> y bajo la ventana de mi bella durmiente,
> el sollozo contínuo del chorro de la fuente
> y el cuello del gran cisne blanco que me interroga

(All I can find is the fleeting word,/the melodic introduction flowing from the flute/and the ship of dreams floating in space;//and underneath the window of my Sleeping Beauty,/the continuous sobbing of the fountain's stream/and the neck of the swan that questions me)

Yet the word is fleeting and the fulfilment transient. Is this an observation on the general condition? Is the fleeting eroticism of so much of his poetry all that is available to the sensual seeker after truth? True, Darío pursues a Platonic ideal enshrined in the Swan. But that other painter of Leda and the Swan – Yeats – sought out perfection against the background of an imminent disintegration of worlds set in time. His pursuit of Leda was a race against time. But if for Darío Helen and Venus and the Swan encapsulate his ideal, then there is a flaw at the heart of perfection – these marks of the ideal belong to a symbolic universe that has denied the very culture and society from which Darío comes. Thus his cosmopolitanism is irredeemably a self-denial, and his pastoral vision a voluntary exile. This is not to say simply that only a nationalistic alternative is authentic – but the uncritical assimilation of the eternal truths of Classical art and culture implies not an escape from alienation so much as a voluntary embrace with it.

There is a rare sense of a consciousness of the paradox in his poem 'Lo Fatal' (Fatality):

> Dichoso el árbol que es apenas sensitivo,
> y más la piedra dura, porque ésta ya no siente,
> pues no hay dolor más grande que el dolor de ser vivo,
> ni mayor pesadumbre que la vida consciente.
>
> Ser, y no saber nada, y ser sin rumbo cierto,
> y el temor de haber sido y un futuro terror. . .
> Y el espanto seguro de estar mañana muerto,
> y sufrir por la vida y por la sombra y por
>
> lo que no conocemos y apenas sospechamos,
> y la carne que tienta con sus frescos racimos
> y la tumba que aguarda con sus fúnebres ramos,
> ¡y no saber adónde vamos,
> ni de dónde venimos!

(Happy the tree that is without sensitivity,/more so the hard stone, which feels nothing,/for there is no pain greater than the pain of living/ nor any greater burden than consciousness.//To be, and to know nothing, and to have no clear direction,/and the fear of having been and a future of terror. . ./and the fear of certain death tomorrow,/and suffering in life and the shadows and because of//what we do not know and scarcely yet suspect/and the flesh that tempts us with its fresh buds,/and the tomb that awaits with its funereal sprays/and not to know where we are going/nor from where we have come!)

This is perhaps Darío's most truly modern poem. The incompleteness of its form, the elision that hangs between verse and verse (of/what we do not know . . .) is an openness of form impermissible in his earlier work. In its catastrophic loss of confidence it is naked, in a fear unprotected by the order of the sonnet or the alexandrine it is genuinely despairing. It points to the loss of youth, and with it the loss

13

of the refuge of sensation; it ends with a sudden loss of certainty that for the first time points on to the Vallejo of *Los heraldos negros* (The black heralds), and to those poets who were to form an avant garde immersed in the experience of the modern.[38] The pervasive sense in the poem is of dread and shattering loss.

Darío and Silva belong, as Ángel Rama sees it,[39] to the first Modernista generation, whose perception of harmony and fulfilment turns upon the survival or the re-evocation of Classical order. Here poetry retains the role of providing access to such truths and essences – that 'forma que busca ser la rosa' (the form that seeks to be the rose) of which Darío wrote. In this group there was no contradiction in an adherence to Catholicism, or a nostalgia for the colonial world, with its stability and order, and the practice of Modernismo. Here the renewal of Spanish poetics served to reinvigorate a dying classicism. In Darío this can and did coexist with the Romantic agony of withdrawal and isolation, of self-marginalization in defence of the creative truth of art and poetry. This rejection of the market in closed and symbolic poetic universes often created a deeply subjective and even obscure poetry – and an ideology of purity that referred not so much to the practice of poetry as to the relationship with a contaminated world of shallow mercantile values.

Seeking Bohemia

Darío and his contemporaries scorn the mediocre and the materialistic, even where their society offers such immersion in economic progress to only a very few. They find a Bohemian refuge in rejection, Parnassianism, and eroticism – but an erotic always youthful and transitory. Ultimately such refuges are shallow and unsafe and produce a predominant note of despair. If Silva's despair is rooted in a sense of loss, it is isolated and set in a personal biography. For the poets of the second wave of Modernismo, however, that despair had a location far more specific than the private world. Where Darío made explicit his social critique in the artificial universe he called his 'selva sagrada', and others like the Uruguayan Julio Herrera y Reissig (1875–1910) created similar utopias defined by their anti-Modernism,[40] what was still absent was the contradictory reality of Latin America at the close of the nineteenth century.

For only a recognition of that contradictory reality could inject into Modernismo an authentic sense of the paradox of modernity. Otherwise, the defence of a tradition could only confront the promises of modernity as a defender of a deeply conservative past still extant in

Latin America; then Modernismo offered a defence of an alternative provincial *present*, Catholic, colonial and unmoved from the forms of economic colonialism of the past. In Mexico, the Modernistas proved to be bitter enemies of the Mexican Revolution, both because of their contempt for the new class that led or emerged from the movement, but also in the name of a continuity from the past.

Two currents therefore met within Modernismo, and even within the work of several Modernista poets. In a sense, they corresponded to different class experiences. The first spoke through the nostalgia of an artistic or rather a cultural aristocracy accustomed to a privileged relationship with the cultural metropolis. But the philistinism of those who in the nineteenth century still identified with the sclerotic culture of Spain, differed profoundly from the critical response to the emergent bourgeoisie delivered by the new aristocracy of the spirit.

The new bourgeoisie, arising in the new urban centres of consumption and exchange like Santiago, Buenos Aires and Mexico City, also produced its own critical intellectuals. These were the wanderers through the city streets, severed now from the conservative cultures of the past for reasons both social and philosophical, recently arrived from the provinces, ill at ease yet fascinated by the slowly promenading crowds of purchasers. Manuel Gutiérrez Nájera's 'La Duquesa Job' (The Duchess Job)[41] expresses the contradictions of that experience at whose heart is an insoluble contradiction; a fascination with this world of the modern, but also a sense of deep loss within it.

For Francisco González León (1862–1945),[42] the domestic interior provided an alternative to those safe urban streets and arcades that were the constructed nature of the new cities. But that essentially provincial interior was part of a disappearing world.

> Casas de mi lugar, que tienden a desaparecer:
> raras casas que aún suelo yo encontrar.
>
> Es de ver
> la amplitud de los patios empedrados,
> el brocal con arcadas de ladrillo,
> los arriates adosados a los muros
> altos muros patinados y sin brillo
> y la parra que se afianza entre sus grietas,
> y macetas, y macetas, y macetas . . .
> ('Antiguallas' – Antiques)

(Houses of my town that are beginning to disappear:/rare houses that I still sometimes come across//You should see their wide stone patios, the borders nestling against the walls/high dull slippery walls/and the ivy

15

wedged into its cracks,/and the potted plants, the plant pots, the potted plants . . .)

> Aunque la mañana está soleada,
> tiene algo de una celda abandonada.
> . . .
> Palabras sin sentido;
> ecos de quién sabe qué ruido
> que repiten las cámaras desiertas
> de la desierta casa en el olvido.
> > ('Palabras sin sentido' –
> > Words without meaning)

(Although the morning is sunny,/ it is like an abandoned cell./. . . Words without meaning;/echoes of some undefined sound/echoing through the empty chambers/of the deserted and forgotten house.)

Contrast this sense of words that have no echo or permanence, landscapes nostalgic and full of sadness, and a powerful sense of longing for what is already no more than a distant memory with the conservative provincialism of Manuel José Othón (1858–1906),[43] who remained outside the ambience of the new city, and died in 1906 before its major expansion. His provincial world was explored in an extended metaphor of barren deserted lands in 'Idilio Salvaje' (Savage idyll).

> En tus aras quemé mi último incienso
> y deshojé mis postrimeras rosas.
> Do se alzaban los templos de mis diosas,
> ya sólo queda el arenal inmenso . . .
>
> ¡Pasó! ¿Que resta ya de tanto y tanto
> deliquio? En ti ni la moral dolencia
> ni el dejo impuro, ni el sabor del llanto.
>
> Y en mí ¡qué hondo y tremendo cataclismo!
> ¡qué sombra y qué pavor en la conciencia
> y qué horrible disgusto de mí mismo!

(On you I burned my last incense/and tore the petals from my final rose./ Where the temples of my goddesses once were/now there is only endless desert.//It has passed! What remains now of so much illusion? In you not the moral pain/nor the impure aftertaste, nor the taste of tears.// In me what a deep and far-reaching cataclysm!/What shadows and what conscious terror/and what self-loathing!)

There is much more than nostalgia here – there is rage and an apportioning of responsibility, although it is not clear to whom. There is little here of the 'idyll' of Darío's Japanese gardens. This is not the artificial paradise of the conservative urban dream but the decay and abandonment of a provincial world now given metaphorical location in a barren steppe. The refuge of the domestic interior, recreated anxiously by González León, is itself a fragile and transitory dream.[44] For that timeless interior where animals and people meet belongs, albeit at the level of metaphor, to the realm of idealization. The provincial middle class rested on an uneasy pastoral memory enshrined in the language of a class of free farmers and universal shepherds. But that world had long since yielded to the pressures of a world market which had already penetrated the material reality, if not the consciousness of those who still spoke of the timeless contentment of the rural world in the costumbrista evocations of Manuel Payno (1810–94) or Vicente Riva Palacio (1832–96) in Mexico.[45]

Here then is the tension within Modernismo. The backward glance yields up a utopian landscape locked in a colonial past – not Spain, but the Hellenic landscapes of European imaginings. There is safety in these artificial paradises, but they are in their inwardness temporary phenomena – functions of youth and love that tarnishes and grows old as cynicism or despair take hold of the dream. For the colonial intellectual, even these paradises are alien, and they are subordinate within them. To enter them they must employ another language, a strange and emblematic language of Art in the tradition of Europe. If France is the alternative in the late nineteenth century to the burgeoning imperialism of the Anglo Saxon worlds, then it is an equally alien world. In a sense José Enrique Rodó's *Ariel*[46] expressed most clearly the nature of that dilemma. For there was none of the excitement and sense of autonomy that informed the entry into the modern world for the first generation of European intellectuals. On the contrary, the Modernistas of Latin America entered into the modern era at a moment of disillusionment, of a despair that contained no sense of progress or democracy. It is no accident, for example, that the Modernista poet with the most emphatic and combative sense of democracy, and of the struggle for change should be José Martí (1853–95).[47]

Martí's utopia was in a paradoxical sense more directly accessible; there was no failed independence project to suggest the futility of the struggle for emancipation. His utopian vision, therefore, found expression in an unrealized nationalist project mingled and interwoven with the models of Classical antiquity. It would be to misrepresent Martí to suggest that his poetry is agitational in a direct sense. It is visionary and utopian, an assertion that the harmony of human affairs will be rediscovered and re-established, and that ordinary emotion will again govern their conduct.

17

Yo soy un hombre sincero
De donde crece la palma,
Y antes de morirme quiero
Echar mis versos del alma . . .

Yo sé los nombres extraños
De las yerbas y las flores,
Y de mortales engaños,
Y de sublimes dolores . . .

Oculto en mi pecho bravo
La pena que me lo hiere:
El hijo de un pueblo esclavo
Vive por él, calla y muere.

(I am an honest man/from where the palm trees grow,/and before I die I want/to pour the verses from my soul. . .//I know the strange names of herbs and flowers,/I know life's treacheries/and sublime pain . . .//In my brave breast I hide/the sorrow that wounds my heart/The son of a people enslaved/lives, falls silent and dies for them)

Martí was a tireless organizer of the independence struggle, a fighter for the rights of workers, a poet who took up the sword and was killed in the war against imperialism. Yet the bulk of his writing was Classical in reference and European in tone. Where he differed throughout from Darío was in his denial of rhetoric, the closeness of his writing to the patterns of speech and song. His *Versos sencillos* (Simple verses) (1891), from which this most famous of his verses comes, stays firmly within the frame of traditional popular song and metre; rhyme here is an element of musicality rather than a completion of sculptured form. There is a *felt* quality in his work which is unusual in a moment when poetry was a means of creating inner distance from experience, as his 'Dos patrias' (Two motherlands) so clearly shows.

Dos patrias tengo yo: Cuba y la noche.
¿o son una las dos? No bien retira
Su majestad el sol, con largos velos
Y un clavel en la mano, silenciosa
Cuba cual viuda triste me aparece.
¡Yo sé cuál es ese clavel sangriento
Que en la mano le tiembla! Está vacío
Mi pecho, destrozado está y vacío
En donde estaba el corazón . . .

(I have two motherlands: Cuba and the night./Or are they one and the same? As soon as the sun withdraws/Its majesty, with long veils/And a

18

carnation in her hand, silently/Cuba appears to me like a sad widow./I
know what that bloody carnation is/that trembles in her hand! Empty/
my breast, destroyed and empty/Where once was my heart . . .)

The inner self feels its separation from an external world where
completion is to be found. As he looks out into the night the poet sees
the guttering candle 'red-flamed like a battle flag'. Thus Martí's
evocation of the simple and the new is interwoven with a strong sense
of nationalism and of social criticism. Curiously, that Cuban voice was
distinct from the rest of Latin American Modernismo precisely
because, as a colony still, Cuba did not confront the dilemma of the
modern in the same way as the rest of the continent. For Martí, Latin
America must be repossessed; for the Modernistas of Mexico or Chile,
it was a place where they felt already exiled and estranged – and they
wandered in a world of exiled selfhood or in the artificial constructed
nature of their Parnassianism. They are not two easily distinguished
stages, but two currents running through Modernismo in parallel,
though the note of lyrical despair became increasingly the predomi-
nant voice of the later Modernistas. From the grand manner of Herrera
y Reissig or the Darío of *Prosas Profanas*, the spectrum spread to the
prosaic quality of Ramón López Velarde (1888–1921), the personal and
insecure wanderer through the city of Gutiérrez Nájera, the fragile and
fleeting tenderness of Amado Nervo. These latter are the poets of
Bohemia, expressing themselves through the pages of Gutiérrez
Nájera's *Revista Azul*.

The Shock of the New

Poetic movements do not begin or end with any particular pronounce-
ment or manifesto. Nonetheless it is possible to say that the prevailing
mood and register among poets changes in response to material
movements and transformations. The precise structure of that rela-
tionship is a vexed and imprecise process. But we have noted a change
in the Modernista movement, from the first, confidently aristocratic
response to the modernity of the late nineteenth century, to the
increasing personalization of that experience. There is not so much an
end to the Modernista movement as an elision, or a renunciation, and
a slow, playful though ultimately tragic stroll towards Bohemia.

In this new lyrical refuge, the poets renounced their legislative role[48]
and instead celebrated experience in its most immediate sense – that

'shock' of modern urban life in which the fragmentation of daily life mirrors the division of labour.[49] Briefly, there was a period of frivolity, eroticism, a delight in the immediacy of experience and the removal of sensation from ritual, from connection with past or future. Poetry could thus celebrate the transitory and the immediate. Brief though its tenancy may be, the poem or indeed the life of the poet thus escaped the commodity relations, the objectifications, that undermined the nature of creativity itself. There was no other *world* to allude to, only the absence of any alternative worlds and a hedonism devoted to the present. Since the public and collective realm had been assimilated into the market, where all relations were expressed as relations between things, and quantified, quality (that is, intensity) could be found only in the lyrical, the personal, the distinguishing individuality. And when that was gone, there was no available return to the public realm but only the poignant emptiness and impotent rage of the fragmentary self recorded, for example, by Gutiérrez Nájera:[50]

> ¡Inmenso abismo es el dolor humano!
> ¿Quién vió jamás su tenebroso fondo?
> Aplicad el oído a la abra oscura
> de los pasados tiempos . . . Dentro cae
> lágrima eterna . . .
>
> La vida es el dolor. Y es vida oscura
> pero vida también la del sepulcro . . .
> ¡Y ruede el mundo cual planeta muerto
> por los mares sin olas del vacío!
>
> ('To Be')

(Human pain is an immense abyss!/Has anyone ever reached its murky depths?/Put your ear to the dark crack/of past times . . . Within falls/an eternal tear . . .//Life is pain, and it is obscurity/but life in the tomb is life still . . ./Let the world turn like a dead planet/through the waveless seas of emptiness!)

Gutiérrez Nájera's epicureanism, his immersion in a life without a past, turns into despair in the work of Amado Nervo:

> Pasas por el abismo de mis tristezas
> como un rayo de luna sobre los mares,
> ungiendo lo inifinito de mis pesares
> con el nardo y la mirra de tus ternezas . . .

No más en la tersura de mis cantares
dejará el desencanto sus asperezas;
pues Diós, que dió a los cielos sus luminares,
quiso que atravesaras por mis tristezas
como un rayo de luna sobre los mares.
      ('Pasas por el abismo de mis tristezas' –
'You pass through the abyss of my sadness')

(You pass through the abyss of my sadness/like a shaft of moonlight on
the sea,/anointing my infinite sorrows/with the lily and myrrh of your
tender embraces . . .//Only in the abrupt verses I write/will disenchant-
ment leave its bitter taste;/for God, who gave the sky its brightness/
chose to have you wander through my sadness/like moonlight on the
sea).

Tengo el peor de todos los cansancios;
¡el terrible cansancio de mi mismo!
¿Dónde ir que a mí propio no me lleve,
con el necio gritar de mis sentidos
y el vano abejear de mis deseos
y el tedio insoportable de lo visto . . .?

¡. . .Dormir, dormir!
¡Toda una eternidad estar dormido!
      ('Tedio' – Tedium)

(I feel the worst kind of fatigue;/the terrible exhaustion with myself!/
Where can I go where I need not take myself,/the stupid moaning of my
senses/the futile buzzing of my desire/the unbearable tedium of all that I
have seen?//To sleep, to sleep!/A whole eternity of sleeping!)

By the first decade of the twentieth century, the centre of the Moder-
nista movement was firmly established in Mexico, where the two main
journals, *Revista Azul* and *Revista Moderna*, published the work of poets
from both the capital and the provinces. Among the provincials was
López Velarde,[51] whose work represented a transition to another more
allusive and intensely personal verse. 'Mi prima Agueda' (My cousin
Agueda) for example captures with tantalizing economy the erotic
excitement of a young man bound by the conventions of provincial
society. In 'Día 13' (Day 13) that *frisson* was reproduced in the hermetic
language of a poetry that concealed more that it revealed, that spoke
through what was not said. The preoccupation with death was now a
deeply personal fear rather than a reflection on mortality, and a
presence that threatened the most intimate of emotions – as in
'Hormigas' (Ants).

Mas luego mis hormigas me negarán su abrazo
y han de huir de mis pobres y trabajados dedos
cual se olvida en la arena un gélido bagazo;
y tu boca, que es cifra de eróticos denuedos,
tu boca, que es mi rúbrica, mi manjar y mi adorno,
tu boca, en que la lengua vibra asomada al mundo
como réproba llama saliéndose de un horno . . .

(But later my ants will deny me their embrace/and they will flee from poor and overworked fingers/like a frozen weed is forgotten in the sand;/and your mouth, that is a measure of erotic boldness,/your mouth, that is my rubric, my sweet and my jewel,/your mouth, in which a tongue trembles reaching out to the world/like a mischievous flame emerging from a furnace . . .)

The sharp erotic charge of the poem is set against the transience of experience and the imminence of death. In 'Todo' (Everything) the unresolved ambivalences express themselves in impenetrable poetic paradoxes:

Si digo carne o espíritu
paréceme que el diablo
se ríe del vocablo;
mas nunca vaciló
mi fe si dije 'yo'

. . .

A pesar del moralista
que la asedia
y sobre la comedia
que la traiciona,
es santa mi persona
santa en el fuego lento
con que dora el altar
y en el remordimiento
del día que se me fue
sin oficiar.

Aunque toca al poeta
roerse los codos
vivo la formidable
vida de todas y todos . . .

(If I say flesh or spirit/it seems to me that the devil/laughs at the word;/ but my faith never wavered/if I said 'I'/. . ./Despite the moralist/besieging it/and above the comedy/that betrays it,/my person is sacred/sacred in the slow fire/which gilds the altar/and in the remorse/of the day that it left me/without ceremony.//Even though the poet is left/to bite his nails/I live the wonderful life/of everyone and everything . . .)

Perhaps López Velarde can be said to have responded to the command enshrined in Enrique González Martínez's (1871–1952) famous epitaph to Modernismo, 'Tuércele el cuello al cisne' (Strangle the swan).

> Tuércele el cuello al cisne de engañoso plumajé,
> que da su nota blanca al azul de la fuente;
> él pasea su gracia no más, pero no siente
> el alma de las cosas ni la voz del paisaje.
>
> Huye de toda forma y de todo lenguaje
> que no vayan acordes con el ritmo latente
> de la vida profunda . . . y adora intensamente
> la vida, y que la vida comprenda tu homenaje.
>
> Mira al sapiente buho cómo tiende las alas
> desde el Olimpo. Deja el regazo de Palas
> y posa en aquel árbol el vuelo taciturno . . .
>
> Él no tiene la gracia del cisne, mas su inquieta
> pupila, que se clava en la sombra, interpreta
> el misterioso libro del silencio nocturno.[52]

(Then twist the neck of this delusive swan/white stress upon the fountain's overflow;/that merely drifts in grace and cannot know/the reeds' green soul and the mute cry of stone.//Avoid all form, all speech, that does not go/shifting its beat in secret unison/with life . . . Love life to adoration!/Let life accept the homage you bestow.//See how the sapient owl, winging the gap/from high Olympus, even from Pallas's lap,/closes upon that tree its noiseless flight . . .//Here is no swan's grace. But an unquiet stare/interprets, as it stares through the shadows,/the inscrutable book of the silent night).

What is González Martínez asking here in his final word on Modernismo? Clearly he is accusing the movement of triviality, of superficiality, of an excessive concern with form and surface. And in consequence, he sees another and more far-reaching purpose for poetry – 'sentir el alma de las cosas' (to feel the soul of things). Is that the essence to which Darío alluded in 'Yo persigo una forma'? Or is it rather a sensitivity to the complexities of personal experience such as he might have discerned in López Velarde? To some, González Martínez's exigencies require an immersion in social and collective experience, to others the poetry is an instrument of consciousness, beyond and above experience.

For Rubén Darío, as age approached and as the capitals of Europe

23

entered the period of self-destruction and internal conflict that pre-saged the great battle for markets of the First World War, the Moder-nista movement increasingly sheltered an insoluble paradox at its heart. On the one hand is the cosmopolitanism of Darío's *Cantos de vida y esperanza* (Songs of love and hope), the appeal to a partnership with the emerging Anglo-Saxon imperialism expressed ambiguously in the 'Canto a Roosevelt' (Song to Roosevelt); on the other a kind of return to the landscape of Latin America – if only to its remoter history in the writings devoted to Cuauhtémoc, leader of the last Aztec resistance to the Spanish conquest ('Oda a Cuauhtémoc').

It is perhaps too simple to speak of withdrawal. But the material changes that took place in Latin America are only rarely referred to in the poetry of the time. The social fact, the processes of change, are never the subject of this poetry. Yet they are presented, refracted through a process of negation, as an absence or a threat. The home-land of López Velarde's 'Suave Patria' (Gentle Motherland) is the same as González León's – a place of nostalgic evocation, of personal experience and individual biography.

The trajectory of Leopoldo Lugones (1874–1938), in his life and his work, traces a double direction. At the heart of both was an insoluble paradox. His early commitment to socialism seemed always ill at ease with his embedded belief in the superiority of the visionary caste to which poets belonged by right and vocation. For Lugones, socialism had little to do with the involvement of the mass of people in the construction of their destiny; rather it was the certainty of a march towards perfection. And as the century ended, it was that certainty which began to falter. In his writing, a bizarre mixture of convention and surprise kept him on a knife edge between innovation and parody. Formally, Lugones was insistent upon archaic spellings and the precision of rhyme; yet his references and models were multiple and eclectic. In his anxiety to *accumulate* and assimilate all the products of the past, Lugones cloaked himself in 'culture' as a hedge against a future whose depradations he already envisaged. Later, Lugones became the singer of a conservative epic, recalling a national past lost in the flurry of change and modernity. It is that for which he is remembered and in some sense revered in official cultural circles.

Yet what Borges and Paz identify in Lugones, and what wins him his central place in their view in the development of Latin American poetry, is the iconoclastic thrust of *Lunario sentimental* (Sentimental moon journey) (1909). At first, Lugones's insistence on the heroic separation of the poet suggested that he had much in common with the spiritual aristocracy gathered around Darío. He absorbed and

24

imitated the classical models and references of the literary Parnassus. And yet his work betrays a tension at its core, a desire to both revere and reject the urgent modernity that he symbolizes in the firework display with which *Lunario* ends. This work is perhaps the only truly modernist expression that Lugones left behind; yet it is powerful in its chaotic quality. While Lugones evoked the constant renewal of language, that very transformation threatened the stability of tradition which he also revered. While, like Ezra Pound, Lugones embraced in his work all and every experience, and invited in all the objects of the modern world, he lamented at the same time the brief and insubstantial nature of the experience. In some ways he is closer, at this moment, to López Velarde and the hedonists of the new Bohemia; yet in all his subsequent work he returned to the ponderous evocations of a provincial world elevated into the repository of those very universals he had in one way or another always defended.

'Los fuegos artificiales' (Fireworks), from Lugones's extraordinary *Lunario sentimental*, could refer to poetic creation itself, so often parodied in the poem in the sudden fragments of doggerel that intercept the descriptive flow. Or the fireworks could be the momentary pleasures and inventions, the technologies of a modern world, which promise so much yet between each display plunge the world back into the melancholy grey light of the moon. More significantly, these virtuoso displays neither improve nor develop their audience, but rather evoke a kind of barbaric frenzy.

> Evocando pirotécnicas Gomorras,
> Ráfagas de silbidos sancionan la proeza.
> Abandonan más de una cabeza
> La cordura y las gorras.
> El ímpetu bellaco
> Encanalla acritudes de tabaco;
> Y casi musical como un solfeo,
> Chillan aspavientos de jóvenes criadas,
> Dichosamente frotadas
> Por aquel enorme escarceo.
> Con su reproche más acre,
> Una vieja,
> Se queja
> Desde el fondo de su fiacre . . .

(Evoking pyrotechnical Gomorrahs,/Flashes of whistles welcome the great event./Sense and hats/Leave more than one head./The villainous impulse/Besmirches sour tobacco smoke;/And almost musical, like a scale,/There are screams of fright from young maids,/Happily rubbed

25

against/By that huge wave./With her bitterest reproach,/A crone/moans/
from deep within her carriage. . .)

The old language is mercilessly assaulted here; the old world comes apart in this celebration. So the models and values that Lugones has defended are here subjected to the constantly changing, constantly reborn world of modernity. There is a barbarism at work here which Lugones clearly fears; but he like others is a helpless observer of this endless firework display. Leaving it behind in his own work, perhaps afraid of its terrifying implications for change, Lugones returned to the reactionary utopia of a re-evoked provincial Argentina, abandoning the city. More than a celebrant or a fighter, Lugones has been witness despite himself to the transformation of the modern world.[53]

Lugones's later evocation of the gaucho belongs to that metaphor of harmony by contrast with which the modern world is satirized. The whole social experience of change is mediated through metaphors which become increasingly personal and despairing on the one hand, and nostalgic on the other. Why is there so little commentary on social change? Why are the Modernistas the dominant school of writing through a period of social upheaval in Mexico, the birth of fire of the Mexican trade-union movement, the growth and emergence of radical movements in both the cities and the rural areas?[54] It is not true, of course, that no social poetry was written in that period. José Guadalupe Posada (1852–1913),[55] for example, was a contemporary of the contributors to *Revista Azul* and *Revista Moderna*, and his newspapers and broadsides were set in the vital tradition of the popular poets, in whose couplets biting satire did seem to be appropriate. What may perhaps be most interesting here is the absence of the popular tradition from Modernismo (with Martí again as an exception).

Clearly, the experience of the modern in Latin America is reflected and indirect; its sources of change seem impossible to identify, and change comes in a mysterious and inexplicable way, without rational structure or historical process. The absence of popular culture, or the myths that it enshrines, marks the lack of response of any visible or invisible alternative history. And without an alternative future or past, the response to modernity can only take two other forms – the celebration of experience and sensation as immediacy and simultaneity, or the elaboration of an alternative cultural universe whose boundaries are language itself. In a sense, the practice of poetry thus becomes an alternative to social action, and the language of poetry is freed from history in a symbolist direction.

The idealist substratum of Symbolism was the belief that the world

26

transmitted by the senses. . .should be understood as revealing a *spiritual* universe. The Symbolist poem would then be an enabling form of such revelation, a mode of realized *correspondence* in Baudelaire's sense, in which the 'poetic word' becomes a verbal symbol at once material in embodiment and metaphysical in its revelation of a spiritual but still sensual reality.[56]

By definition, such freeing of language from social practice also frees poetry itself from constraints or conventions of language or meaning. Shared meaning, the communication of the known, is the casualty. Modernismo gives way to the range of movements that are collectively called the avant garde, though in Modernista poets, the urge to communicate to however restricted a public is powerful – and the absence of communication is a source of pain and anxiety.

> Y el espanto seguro de estar mañana muerto,
> y sufrir por la vida y por la sombra y por
>
> lo que no conocemos y apenas sospechamos . . .
> (Darío: 'Lo Fatal')

(And the certain horror of being dead tomorrow/and to suffer for life and the shadow and for//what we know nothing of and barely suspect . . .)

Poetry records the striving to be heard and to hear. The increasing difficulty in breaking out of the personal, the lyric, and into a world of speech and exchange, became in its turn the condition of Modernista poetry. While critics debate the precise date at which Modernismo ends, it would seem more accurate to suggest that the immersion in form and language takes Modernismo imperceptibly into the avant garde. J.O. Jiménez[57] makes the distinction between Modernistas and 'contemporáneos', where the latter represent a move away from communication, towards a language whose internal organisation is the sole source of its communicability. The move towards a 'pure poetry' is a move away from lyricism, from communication, from imagery – and towards the irrational and the extralogical.

The Art of Despair

The new schools of poetry that emerged from the demise of the Parnassian dream of Modernismo, and which responded to the despair and the sense of loss that followed in Nervo and López Velarde, for example, embraced the modern in a new and different way. The proliferation of schools of poetry has led many critics to contort themselves in search of an all-embracing definition. There is no such definition that takes its lead from the manifestos or proclamations of the time; they were largely short-lived, proud of their transitory quality, and experimental by definition. More important, their very number and diversity attested to the enormous value the avant garde placed upon concepts like uniqueness, novelty, difference and diversity. For what these schools and currents did have in common – those, that is, that placed themselves within the avant garde – was precisely their rejection of a concept of social or historical location. We will discuss below whether it is possible to speak as the Formalists did of the 'self-sufficiency of the word'. What is clear here is that in one form or another the autonomy of the literary act and the text that derived from it was a recurrent theme in avant-garde writings. These linguistic developments, of course, shared a source, but that source was refracted and obscured within the rhetoric of free association. Its primary quality was rejection – but a rejection which implied at the same time an acceptance.

The modernity they rejected was that of an emerging Latin American city embraced once again within universals (growth, development, progress, etc.) deriving from the new metropolises. But where the schools of Darío and Silva could turn with greater or lesser justification to the artificial paradises of past and exotic worlds, or to the grand cultures enshrined in that symbol of the continuity of Judeo-Christian culture – the Parnassus – the post-world-war shock of the new made such retrenchment impossible. Further, there was the ambiguity of these writers moving within a world of exotic and naive paradises many of which were close to their own doorsteps, yet from which they were as distant and alienated as they were in many cases from the new and emerging industrial city.

That alienation took many forms. The turn away from this vulgar and materialist world of material progress and instability could lay hold of a concept of literature both aristocratic and elevated, a high culture towards which González Martínez might himself (ambiguously) have been pointing when he called for the strangling of the swan. That turn could find an imaginative site in a remembered or imaginary past, but that past was mediated through a European consciousness, and rendered exotic that which was immediate, or could have been immediate to the experience of Latin American artists. Those, like Martí and the Peruvian Manuel González Prada (1848–1918), who looked for roots in a popular culture, did have their followers. But in the world of 1914–18, it was a pervasive cultural despair that took hold of the leading intellectuals.

Thus, paradoxically perhaps, the Mexican Revolution (1910–17) did not produce poets, nor attract the Modernista generation. On the contrary,[58] most of them identified with the most reactionary currents; the revolution of Zapata and Villa did have its minstrels, of course, but they were the writers of *corridos*, ballads whose names were never preserved and whose devotion was to continuity rather than the sabotage of the prevailing culture.

Were the writers of the avant garde the bearers of a revolution in Latin America? By and large, the transformations they sought to bring about were in the sphere of form and language, disengaging language from social processes and form from tradition. If Lugones is generally taken to have presaged the avant garde, it is partly for reasons of form and partly in his elegy for a dying and irrecoverable world. The generation of writers who succeeded him came wide-eyed and lost to the burgeoning cities from a dying provincial world. Others, like Borges, lived its fervid growth ('Fervor de Buenos Aires'). They, for the most part, experienced the modern as alienation – as disintegration – and they responded with a cosmopolitanism learned in the post-war world of Europe. The revolution they made ran in parallel with significant social change; but it remained an alternative to it, though the analogies often drawn between the two can be deeply confusing. The term 'avant garde' in Spanish is 'vanguardia', which refers indistinctly to both artists and revolutionaries. Yet many of Latin America's avant-garde writers were very far from a revolutionary posture.

And yet they *were* resisters, opponents of the metropolitan order and its new manifestations. Some, like Borges or Huidobro, resisted for reasons of a Romantic, conservative kind; others, as a consequence of their hostility to exploitation and oppression. Yet within what is called the avant garde, the form that rebellion took was always one of rejection. There were of course others who resumed a national-popular current, who returned to the search for a democratic language and who found their sources in popular forms. We shall return to them. For the moment, however, it is the individual negation that concerns us. For while both were anti-bourgeois, anti-materialist in some sense, there is a paradox at the heart of most of the writing of the avant garde. While it is resolute in its critique of the metropolitan order, it is also of and within that order, having assimilated and accepted its unchallengable centrality in the field of culture. The paradox is expressed in the evolution of the metaphor of the city – standing for the metropolitan order as a whole – and in the innovative and experimental developments in artistic practice which are themselves critiques of the cultural confidence and universalism of the metropolitan world.

29

There is no date that marks the emergence of the avant garde out of Modernismo. Some forms persist, others disappear. But José Juan Tablada,[59] an acknowledged figure in the Mexican Modernista movement, is certainly among the most radical innovators in poetic form, and one who can claim to span the period of transition. Tablada first published his Symbolist poem 'ónix' in *Revista Azul*. Its powerful Baudelairean tone, its translation of spleen into tedium and disillusion, represented a very different direction from the Classical grace of the Parnassians.

> Porque la fe en mi pecho solitario
> se extinguió, como el turbio lampadario
> entre la roja luz de las auroras,
> y mi vida es un fúnebre rosario
> más triste que las lágrimas que lloras.
> . . .
> porque no me seduce la hermosura,
> ni el casto amor, ni la pasión impura;
> porque en mi corazón dormido y ciego
> ha caído un gran soplo de amargura . . .

(Because the faith in my solitary breast/has gone out, like the darkened lamp/amid the red dawn lights,/and my life is a funeral rosary/sadder than the tears you cry./. . ./I am not seduced by beauty,/nor chaste love, nor impure passion;/because in my sleeping, blinded heart/a great breath of bitterness has fallen . . .)

Later, his 'Misa Negra' (Black Mass) shocked the good burghers of the Porfiriato with its celebration of an overt sexual desire. Yet Tablada was a man of that society, and as the Revolution approached his comfortable lifestyle echoed through the lampoons he directed at all the forces for change in Mexico in the newspaper *El Imparcial*. He spent most of the period of the Mexican Revolution in Europe and the United States, since he was quite rightly identified with the counter-revolution whose leader Huerta he had praised to the skies in a commissioned panegyric. Tablada was an archetypal representative of Modernismo in its Symbolist phase, charging the word with an increasingly powerful sensual impact implicit in the semantic unit. Yet he was also in the vanguard of its ending and a leading writer in the post-Modernist epoch. Combining his fascination with Japan and his knowledge of the ideogrammatic poems of Appollinaire, Tablada introduced the haiku and the ideogram into Spanish poetry. Already in the poems of *Al sol y bajo la luna* (In the sun and under the moon) (1918) are prefigured the more radical experiments of his later work in

Li-Po. If his earlier work struck at the progressive historical thinking of the Positivists and the repressions of Catholicisim, Tablada still pursued his radical libertarianism into the realm of language. His 'Quinta Avenida' (Fifth Avenue), for example, is a poem of sound and form on the page, employing free conjunctions of word and sound, of different languages (from the Classical to the urban modern), of number and form for its precision, to evoke a different poetic word whose impact is visual and acoustic, evocative and imagistic – but increasingly distant from representation.

> Mujeres fire-proof a la pasión inertes
> hijas de la mecánica, venus made in America;
> de vuestra fortaleza, la de las cajas fuertes,
> es el secreto . . . ¡identica combinación numérica!

(Fireproof women immune to passion/daughters of the mechanical Venus made in America;/of your fortress, of safes,/it is the secret . . . the same combination of numbers!)

Here too is the bustle and crash, the constant but undirected movement of the city streets.

Tablada's haikus marked a dramatic contrast in theme and form; yet their precision and self-containment continue the direction of these words made form, pictures and sounds. The epigram, the single image encapsulating some sensual impression of the world, is the quality that Tablada found in the haiku:

El Sauz   La Luna

Tierno saúz   Es mar la noche negra
casi oro, casi ámbar   la nube es una concha
casi luz. . .   la luna es una perla

(Tender willow   (The dark night is sea
almost gold, almost amber   The cloud is a shell
almost light)   the moon is a pearl)

In describing his ideographic poems Tablada says this

Everything is synthetic, discontinuous and thus dynamic. The explanatory and the rhetorical are eliminated forever; it is a succession of substitute states; I believe it is pure poetry . . .

The ideograph has the strength of an expression at once lyrical and graphic . . . The graphic part successfully substitutes for the discursive or explanatory features of the old poetry, leaving the literary themes as pure poetry.[60]

The word, anticipating perhaps the 'pure poetry' (poesía pura) of Mariano Brull, becomes form only, elements of a closed self-referential system. Thus poetry escapes the external pressures and demands, the communicative requirements of social language. In his poem 'El loro' (The parrot) the poet himself reappears, a voice linking the provincial past of his grandmother's house, and the loud anarchic present of the early twenties. In this respect Tablada is both a precursor and a clear representative of the two aspects of the avant garde – innovation and experiment, the defiance of logic and reason, and an immersion in the speed and aimlessness of the modern world.

Out of the Prison of Language: The Avant Garde and the First Crisis of the New World

Turning into Poetry

There is no precise date and time when Modernismo becomes post-Modernismo or avant garde, nor any identifiable 'growing over' of one into the other as a result of any inertia within the movement. And it is difficult to define any external event, or set of events, which set that process in train.

The second decade of the twentieth century produced enormous transformations in the relations between Europe and Latin America. The First World War undermined the integrity of the world system into which Latin America found itself integrated. The United States, the new power in the region, became, albeit indirectly, a cultural power too. In Mexico, the beginnings of the Mexican Revolution in November 1910 exposed the roots of many of the Modernistas in the old order where their cosmopolitanism located them as the dissident intellectuals of the bourgeoisie of the new city. The Mexican Revolution did throw up its organic intellectuals, in the process of consolidation of the new Mexican state; they defined themselves by their nationalism, by their emphatic search for origins in the distinctive experience of Latin America. That 'return' to origins also entailed the rediscovery of long-neglected popular traditions, icons and histories in creating the symbolic universe of a nascent national state – a universe capable of forging a new public under a nationalist aegis and defined by its hostility to imperialism and to the cosmopolitanism that was its cultural face.[1]

Yet this was not the response that prevailed among the poets of Latin America. One characteristic voice of this poetry of transition struggled to make itself heard from within a double oppression. The work of Alfonsina Storni (1892–1938), for example, belongs in the Modernista epoch; her work is less adventurous that that of her contemporary Norah Lange (1906–), who won a right to speak within the avant garde; language remains for her a store of classical reference and timeless value. Yet among the fairly conventional expressions of unrequited love and private longing, there are explosions of barely contained rage and allusions to a passion capable of breaking every conventional bond.

> Quiero un amor feroz de garra y diente
> Que me asalte a traición en pleno día
> Y que sofoque esta soberbia mía
> Este orgullo de ser todo pudiente
> ('Animal cansado' – Tired animal)

(I want a love fierce in tooth and claw/that treacherously assaults me in full light of day/and chokes this pride of mine/this pride in all my modesty)

> Las mujeres solteras sueñan de varios modos.
> Unas sueñan con joyas, otras sueñan con flores.
> Otras sueñan con vagos y tímidos amores.
> ¡Son mis ardientes sueños tan distintos de todos!
>
> Porque son mis deseos rebeldes a la brida
> – Como potros – yo sueño con músculos de atleta
> Repujados en bronce . . .
> ('Sonar' – to dream)

(Single women dream in various ways./Some dream of jewels, others of flowers./Still others dream of vague and timid loves./How different are my passionate dreams from all of those!//For my dreams resist the bridle/ – Like wild horses – I dream of athlete's muscles/moulded in bronze . . .)

There is in these poems an unrestrained erotic charge, still incomplete and tentative, still hidden in some secret and allusive poetry. That repeated note among women poets of the period and beyond attests to the multiple resistances – social and literary – that women faced in seeking to become subjects of the world. They appeared frequently enough in the poetry of Modernismo, as statues, princesses, objects of passion. Yet even in those artificial landscapes women were limited to the realm of the private, to the role of inhabitants. This does not suggest passivity. Storni's own poems explode from time to time in protest and defiance,[2] and many of her contemporaries express no contentment with or fatalism towards the condition of women. The

Honduran Clementina Suárez (1903–85) asked questions of the future, and assaulted the rhythmic structure of the poem with her dissonant demands:

> Alba que tiras tu brisa mojada de estrellas
> que entregan su secreto
> en los agudos oídos de las aguas insomnes,
> ¿cuándo?
>
> Río que navegaste los ojos
> del misterio perpetuo.
> ¿Dónde?
>
> Realidad sin relojes de los hombres
> y la tierra que ando . . .
> ¿Qué día me dirás que comienzo a nacer?

(Dawn that throws its moist breeze of stars/that deliver its secret/to the sharp ears of the sleepless waters/when?//River that navigated the eyes/ of the perpetual mystery/Where?//Reality without clocks of the men/and the earth that I travel . . ./When will you tell me the day I begin to be born?)

The demand could hardly be clearer: to live a sensual immediacy that is subject to time and within history. For in the realms of a writing that undergoes no change through time, there can be no wider transformation. Language itself, it seems, reproduces and reinforces this universe – and only absence, marginality, non-existence can carry the force of protest and distress.

It is that absence and marginality, that persistent sense of exile, that marks the work of the best-known woman poet of the period, the Chilean Gabriela Mistral (1889–1957).[3] Yet this element is curiously set aside by critics for whom she has come to represent quite different values. On the one hand, the Nobel Prize for Literature which she received in 1945 acknowledged her gentle provincialism and her absorption in the Latin American landscape; others have placed her in a strange category of 'pure poetry', laying emphasis on the limpidity and simple rhythmic quality of her verse.

The sonnets and rhyming couplets of *Desolación* (1922) are rigorous and formal in their structure. Their tone, too, is measured and their theme often a traditional religiosity. Yet the Christ figure that appears in them is not gentle but more often bloody and bruised; and the tone is of protest, or rather complaint. Sometimes the underlying despair explodes through the surface and the contained anguish of so much of Mistral's poetry becomes uncontrollable. In her early work the

persistent theme is of loss, of a lover (in 'Los Sonetos de la muerte' –
Death sonnets) or a child ('Poema del hijo' – Poem for a child).

> ¡Un hijo, un hijo, un hijo! Yo quise un hijo tuyo
> y mío, allí en los días del éxtasis ardiente,
> en los que hasta mis huesos temblaron de tu arrullo
> y un ancho resplandor creció sobre mi frente.
>
> Decía: ¡un hijo! como el árbol conmovido
> de primavera larga sus yemas hasta el cielo.
> ¡Un hijo con los ojos de Cristo engrandecidos
> la frente de estupor y los labios de anhelo!
> . . .
> Y como si pagara la deuda de una raza,
> taladran los dolores mi pecho cual colmena.
> Vivo una vida entera en cada hora que pasa;
> como el río hacia el mar, van amargas mis venas.

(A child, a child, a child! I wanted a child that was yours/and mine, in
those days of burning ecstasy,/when my very bones trembled at your
whisper/and a broad glow spread across my brow.// I used to say: a
child!, like a tree moved/by spring stretches its palms towards the sky./A
child with the wide eyes of Christ/its brow of wonder and its lips of
desire!. . ./And as if I had to pay the debt of a people,/pain bores into my
heart as if it were a beehive./I live a whole life in every hour that passes;/
and as the river flows to the sea so my veins flow with bitterness.)

How does one reconcile this barely suppressed anger, this sense of
persecution, with the gentler and unprotesting nostalgia of the better
known and more often anthologized poems like 'La maestra rural'
(The country schoolteacher) and 'Todos íbamos a ser reinas' (We were
all going to be queens)?

> La maestra era alegre. ¡Pobre mujer herida!
> Su sonrisa fue un modo de llorar con bondad.
> Por sobre la sandalia rota y enrojecida
> tal sonrisa, la insigne flor de su santidad.
>
> ¡Dulce ser! En su río de mieles, caudaloso,
> largamente abrevaba sus tigres el dolor.
> Los hierros que le abrieron el pecho generoso
> ¡más anchas le dejaron las cuencas del amor!
>
> (La maestra rural)

(The teacher was cheerful. Poor wounded woman!/Her smile was a way
of weeping with kindness./Above her broken and reddened sandal/such
a smile, the noble flower of her saintliness.//Sweet being! In her full-
flowing river of honey/her tigers howled at length with pain./The irons

that opened up her generous breast/left wider still the gaping wounds of love!)

The rural teacher shares much of Gabriela Mistral's own biography, though she later became a widely travelled diplomat. What is clear from the poem is that the placidity and contentment of its subject is mere appearance, a forced surface saintliness. But the same exasperation and pain that underpins the earlier work remains just beneath that surface – a rage as fierce as a wounded tiger. The contrasting images are shocking. Yet here as so often in Mistral's writing the pain is only alluded to, and the foreground of the poem is occupied with an essentially passive acceptance of what is unchanging and stable in the outside world. Nonetheless, the stability of that world is a source of despair and not joy. Gabriela Mistral does not often express the rage and defiance that characterized the life and writing of Storni, for example. But to describe her, as one critic does, as the 'rural poet par excellence' is to misunderstand her completely. The landscape of Mistral's poetry contains some comforts, but it is also a mirror of her entrapment. As a woman and a Latin American that encompassing nature has a profoundly ambiguous impact; it reassures in its sheer power but it also isolates and overwhelms the individual.

> El viento hace a mi casa su ronda de sollozos
> y de alarido, y quiebra, como un cristal, mi grito.
> Y en la llanura blanca, de horizonte infinito,
> miro morir inmensos ocasos dolorosos.
> . . .
> Miro el llano extasiado y recojo su duelo,
> que vine para ver los paisajes mortales.
> La nieve es el semblante que asoma a mis cristales:
> ¡siempre será su albura bajando de los cielos!
>   ('Desolación' – Desolation)

(The wind on its rounds circles my house sobbing/and wailing, and breaks my cry like glass./And on the white plain, with its endless horizons,/I watch the death of vast and painful sunsets./. . ./I see the plain in ecstasy and I share its sorrow,/for I came to see the mortal landscapes./The snow is the face pressed against my windows:/it will always be its whiteness descending from the sky!)

There are moments of consolation. Mistral's children's rhymes have a genuine innocence that stems from a childhood world prior to the knowledge of loss and despair. The innocence of her later work is overlaid with irony. For that stable and largely domestic world in which she is enclosed is not a place of stability but a site of pain and enduring frustration. For the most part, she suppresses that sense of rage, seeks solace later in religion, contemplates nature as an instrument of fate. But, as in the work of Storni, there is a deep and enduring sense of loss, of privation – although here without the erotic challenge or the attitude of defiance. Yet Mistral's work, so often misread, is a testimony to a terrible emptiness at the centre of the self, whose source is in the double exile of the experience of a Latin American woman.

Both Mistral and her contemporary Pedro Prado (1886–1952)[4] in their intense inwardness spoke of the deeper isolation, the radical withdrawal into the self, that underlay the practices of the avant garde. Trapped in a culture whose central global concepts now lay wrecked in the aftermath of war, few of the poets seemed able to elaborate any alternative totality. The cultural spokespeople of the nationalist movements gradually found their voice through the decade of the twenties. But the dominant tone of the poetic movements that followed Modernismo was set by a group of writers for whom the collapse of a world of European values and perceptions entailed the collapse of *all* explanation, and the futility of *any* search for truth. The radicalism of the avant garde was, in the literal sense, a *return* to roots, a construction of new universals or a restatement of the old – but in the curious context of a class severed from its historical destiny and cast adrift without a future.

The new directions in poetry now developed the exploration of the potentialities of language, and refined and stripped the explorations of personal experience. One current moved towards a progressive denuding of the personal, leading towards the eventual loss of all social reference. The endless death of 'Muerte sin fin' (Death without end) by José Gorostiza (1901–80) for example, became not so much a culmination of physical decay as a metaphor for the emptying of the social self. The process was akin to the pursuit of Nirvana, the still centre at the heart of things.

> Mas nada ocurre, no, sólo este sueño
> desorbitado
> que se mira a sí mismo en plena marcha;
> presume, pues, su término inminente, . . .
> así, aún de su cansancio, extra
> ¡hop!

largas cintas de cintas de sorpresas,
que en un constante perecer enérgico,
en un morir absorto,
arrasan sin cesar su bella fábrica
hasta que – hijo de su misma muerte,
gestado en la aridez de sus escombros –
siente que su fatiga se fatiga . . .[5]

(But nothing happens, no, just this dream/wild/looking at itself in full flight;/for it presumes its imminent end,. . ./and so, from its very tired-ness it extracts/Hup!/long ribbons of ribbons of surprises,/that in a continuous energetic dying,/in a self-absorbed dying,/endlessly destroy their beautiful fabric/until – child of its own death,/born in the dryness of its own rubble – /it feels its very tiredness grow tired . . .)

Circling endlessly around its own demise, the central figure of the poem approaches the realm of non-being and the poem ends with a children's guessing game ('Knock, knock, who's there') which makes life and death the subject of a capricious and absurd ritual.

It is that withdrawal into a text made arbitrary by its severance from all social reference that characterizes much of what is called the poetry of the avant garde. Yet the so-called post-Modernist schools[6] embrace a range of ideas concerning the relationship between the poet and the world and the nature of poetic language, not all of them by any means the continuation of the post-Romantic rejection of the real. Their work does, however, contain an ever-strengthening current of poetic prac-tice which defines its object as the creation of an alternative reality, situated within a category of culture that is an alternative to history. Thus Vicente Huidobro's *Creacionismo* seeks to recreate the universe no less; from there to Paz and beyond is a single step. But it is by no means the case that this was the sole or even the dominant current of thought. It is not inherent in the act of poetic creation to seek the creation of alternative symbolic universes which address human experience as alien to history and affected only by the continuum of sense. Georg Lukács argued that the function of art 'is to express the integrity of human life, men's conscious mastery and development of their own nature through the purposive action of transforming the world'.[7]

'The coincidence of the changing of self and the changing of circumstances'[8] to which art may contribute is very far from the disengagement of self from circumstance that was characteristic of Modernismo and those that followed it. Their loss of that sense of 'the integrity of human life' was not objective reality but the ideological response of those embedded in a culture that had lost *its* integrity. The alternative totality as yet had not found its voice; in the interregnum the material of poetry was a language emptied of history,

If the writers of Modernismo called that culture into question, in the post 1914–18 world the historical direction of Latin America was no longer in question. The integration of even the most backward republics into the world system in a subordinate role was exemplified in the Dance of the Millions in Cuba, the establishment of the Mexican state in the wake of the 1917 constitution, the post-nitrate boom in Chile, etc.[9] The certainties of the old world, embedded both in the provincial world of Latin America and the civilizational monuments of Europe, were crumbling in the wake of 1918. And if many of the writers of the avant garde sought to abstract themselves from the historical process in an act of elitist refusal, others – like Vallejo – developed the technical means to confront that disintegration in all its horror and pain. And there were also those within the general movement who set themselves to speak with a voice echoing from the hitherto silent depths of the oppressed. Thus the avant-garde period in Latin America is not a simple linear succession of schools of thought, but a field of conflict and struggle whose central issue was the role and contribution that poetry itself might offer – as resistance, critique, consolation, or testimony to a deep cultural crisis.

The Chilean Vicente Huidobro (1893–1948)[10] is a central figure in the avant garde. His particular school of thought – *Creacionismo* – had a more coherent and consistent manifesto than most; it came some seven years before the magazine *Prisma*'s Declaration, published in Buenos Aires and signed by Borges and Guillermo de Torre among others.[11] Huidobro spent the First World War years in France and Spain, working with the groups of avant-garde artists that so influenced this whole generation of Latin American artists. Many of his early poems, for example, were written in French, an indication of how far Huidobro saw his poetic experience and practice in terms of developments in Europe. His 'Tour Eiffel' (from *Horizon Carré*), for example, experimented with new organizations of words on the page, with the unexpected conjunction of images and statement. The words climb or descend, verses stand side by side, capital letters shout from the page as lines of poetry become slogans or cries. His first major collection of avant-garde works was *Poemas árticos* (Arctic Poems) (1918), thirty brief and adventurous poems.

'Exprés' lists the passing of places, impressions isolated from one another on the page, and momentary contacts with times and places encountered on the endless journey – 'la vida ha de pasar' (life passes). 'Alerta' sees images of nature ironized in the exploding bombs in the sky. This is war. The injunction to 'Apaga tu pipa' (Put out your pipe) plunges the speaker back into the darkness that is silence and waiting. The house where he lives is open to the sky with its single star. But there is a sense of isolation, of solitude: 'había tantas cosas que no pude encontrar' (there were so many things I couldn't find). Watching the soldiers in the station the fleeting and insubstantial impressions are underlined – and again in the darkness there is the point of light 'en torno de mi cigarro' (around my cigarette). 'Sobre la niebla de todos los caminos/me encontraba a mí mismo' ('VII') (Above the fog of every road/I found myself). The poetry of the past, the seabirds, the mountains, the old pastoral world is lost in the terrible beauty of this lonely cityscape where the only presence of which we can be sure is the poet/speaker who is little more than a fleeting point of light in this desolate night.

'Hijo' (Son) is particularly poignant:

> Al fondo de los años
> Un ruiseñor cantaba en vano
> La luna viva
> Blanca de la nieve que caía
>
> Y sobre los recuerdos
>   Una luz que agoniza entre los dedos
>
>   MAÑANA PRIMAVERA
>
> . . .
> Una canción asciende sobre el humo
>
> Y tú
>   Hijo
>   hermoso como un diós desnudo
> . . .
>   Un día tendrás recuerdos.

(In the depths of the years/A nightingale sang in vain/The moon alive/ White of the falling snow//And above the memories/A light dying between the fingers//MORNING TOMORROW SPRING//. . . A song rises above the smoke//And you/my son/beautiful as a naked god/ . . . one day you will have memories)

The smoke is presumably that which rises over the rubble of a Europe where a nightingale used to sing, but its voice is now silenced. The son will have memories, but for the speaker in the poem there are only momentary and short-lived images that do not cohere into a continuity or a vision or a history. There is only a past that is irrecuperable, and a present full of loneliness in this unmistakably urban landscape.

41

> del sexto piso
>> desciende el ascensor mejor que un buzo

(from the sixth floor/the lift descends better than a diver)

And the isolated observer again appears:

> He visto mi cigarro
>> Que humea en las más tibias lejanías.

(I have seen my cigarette/smoking in the warmest distances)

This is *creacionismo*, where the word stands alone, close to the absolute, capturing essences and producing as nature does a universe distinct from any other. Denying vehemently that this is a capricious or arbitrary exercise, Huidobro speaks of a poetry as refuge and solace – closer to that of Baudelaire than Apollinaire.[12] His sardonic tone and refusal to expatiate on the dimensions of the heart are a reaction in some ways against that sentimental, indulgent emotionalism of much of Modernismo. And in the Chilean context, the sarcastic and superior response to emotion is in marked contrast to the intense subjectivism of his contemporaries, Prado and Mistral, whose practice was summed up by Mistral: 'Stylistic perfection . . . could be sacrificed, if necessary, for the sake of making poetry warm and human and of bringing it close to the spoken idiom, rather than the erudite.'[13]

Huidobro declares himself to be an *anti*-lyrical poet, who personifies in his public declarations and his theory of poetry a cold and intellectual separation from the complexity of feeling and experience. The poetic form denies the connectedness of experience, its roots in past and future, in history; it is defiantly in the present of the poem. Yet as 'Altazor' shows, the human eventually overwhelms the theoretical and recreates a fragmented and despairing universe.

Yet the Chilean poet Enrique Lihn sees in Huidobro,[14] despite what he says to the contrary, a sentimentalist and a poet still firmly attached to a Romantic tradition, as well as a Hispanic one to which he later returned with his 'Mío Cid Campeador'. Huidobro was a late but enthusiastic arrival at the European banquet, writing often in French, buried in a kind of uneasy provincialism which he partly mocked in himself but mostly in others. For Lihn there was a certain dandyism and infantilism in Huidobro's constant assertions of his own genius. His emergence from underdevelopment brought confusion and unresolved contradiction. And of Huidobro's enthusiasm for different areas of study, Lihn says,

It will be said that this is the normal expression of a great intellectual

42

curiosity . . . but I think that these separate compartments multiplying in every direction often strike us as superficiality, as the defects of a fragmented personality, as the weaknesses of an eccentric.[15]

Thus he is two things at once; the spiritual aristocrat opposed to bourgeois philistinism; and a bourgeois humanist, drawn sentimentally to the notion of a collective future. Huidobro, in this precise sense, is a poet of transition.

Things Fall Apart

Huidobro's 'Altazor'[16] is a marvellous Babel of a poem; it is undoubtedly a work of its time (despite its claim to universality), and thus today in some sense outmoded – yet it is also rich in possibilities. It is a poem made with ideas rather than things; yet the fearless exploration of the contradictions unresolved within those ideas leads, through a reductionist procedure, to an ending of pure sound. But after the confident and rather arrogant anti-bourgeois assertions of his earlier work – so obviously designed to 'épater le bourgeois' – the experiment appears to end here in fragmentation, alienation and despair. In the post-war world where the hopes invested in concepts of change and progress seemed now to have been only cruel deceit, there were available a range of responses. A revolutionary perspective, identified with the October Revolution of 1917, was one; another was to discover optimism in technology and development themselves; a third to seek utopian solutions enshrined in petty bourgeois myths of restoration and control; and a final one, a solution for an isolated aristocratic elite now curiously anachronistic in its belief in the old static universals, was withdrawal, rejection and refuge. Where the representations of ancient truths no longer offered any solace as the material and social base of such illusions lay in tatters on the battlefields of Ypres and the Somme, then other exotic or unreal utopias could replace them. (References to a Latin American past did not of themselves bespeak a new national self-consciousness; the evocations of Indians, Incas or Aztecs could as easily fit into the exotic and profoundly alien stereotypes of European escapist literature[17] as reflect a renewed awareness of the reality of the continent.)

Huidobro's scornful cosmopolitanism was clearly influential among his contemporaries; he helped to found one school – *ultraísmo* – which included Borges and a whole consequent current of thinking about poetry. He produced a theory of *creacionismo* which provided a vocabulary, or a partial one, for many of the avant-garde artists and writers. His 'Altazor', then, came as something of a surprise. Subtitled 'journey in a parachute', it was in every sense a descent.

The poem begins with a certainty of extinction – 'Altazor morirás' (Altazor, you will die) – undermining that perilous journey into an underground world that begins a few lines later. The historical optimism that is assumed in the notion of a progress towards self-knowledge and growth is sabotaged, and the purpose of this journey of enlightenment parodied in this way: 'Sin miedo al enigma de tí mismo/Acaso encuentres una luz sin noche' (Fear not the enigma of your own self/you may find a light without the night). The journey is an endless falling through phases and stages and experiences, each of which is powerless to halt the descent ('de muerte en muerte' (from death to death). The poet's voice wrenches away the veils from the truth of human mortality.

> Yo estoy aquí de pie ante vosotros
> En nombre de una idiota ley proclamadora
> De la conservación de las especies
> Inmunda ley
> . . . Por esa ley primera trampa de la inconciencia
> El hombre se desgarra
> Y se rompe en aullidos mortales por todos los poros de su tierra.

(I stand here before you/In the name of a stupid law that proclaims/The conservation of the species/A disgusting law/. . . Because of that law, the first trick of the unconscious/Man tears himself apart/And breaks into mortal wailing through all the pores of the earth)

There are no comforting images here, no niches of refuge. There is in this poem a total exposure to the one-dimensional mortality of men. Hence the cry '¿qué has hecho de mi Vicente Huidobro? . . . ¿Qué has hecho de mi voz cargada de pájaros en el atardecer? (What have you done with my Vicente Huidobro? . . . What have you done with my voice filled with birds in the evening?) At the end of Part V there is genuine pain, the fruit of loneliness and timelessness. In a yearning climax the poetic voice clamours for a past ('Dadme una certeza de raíces' – Give me some certainty of my roots), for certainties ('[Dadme] un descubrimiento que no huya a cada paso' – [Give me] a discovery that does not flee from me at every turn), for an end to solitude ('Liberado de este trágico silencio entonces' – And so free from this terrible silence). And there is no one to blame; there is a genuinely tragic capriciousness about the catastrophes that attend human experience.

44

> Soy todo el hombre
> El hombre herido por quién sabe quién
> Por una flecha perdida del caos . . .

(I am the whole of man/Man wounded by who knows whom/By a stray arrow out of chaos . . .)

It is this same protest at the arbitrary injustice of it all that informs poems like Vallejo's 'Los dados eternos' (The eternal dice) where all is debris in the wake of the great truths – Religion, Science, History – which provided comfort for a pre-war generation. Part V contains much that is reminiscent of the floating eyes of Cubism,[18] suggesting fragmentation and aimlessness. For the first time the factory multitudes appear in the poem, but they are the marching lines of underground dwellers of Fritz Lang's 'Metropolis', marching towards the 'párpado tumbal' (the eyelid of the tomb).[19] Briefly, there is love and passion, but it too comes apart in the imminent arrival of 'la golondrina monotémpora' (the momentary swallow), not the swallow announcing spring but perhaps the swan song of the poet's hope. Here all language is arbitrary too, changing, without stability, and the images of poetry become increasingly form and sound.

> Su piel de lágrima el rofañol
> su garganta nocturna el rosoñol
> El rolañol
> El rosiñol.

(tears on the skin of the nifingale/the night throat of notingule/The naitingole/The nightingore.)

And finally, everything culminates in the yawning tomb which has swallowed time, the seasons, mountain and sea, all life; now these things can only be glimpsed in the depths of the bottomless pit. Slowly all of it becomes fossilized and frozen in a timeless place where the abandoned imagery of earlier Romantic poetry, and indeed of Huidobro's own early *creacionismo*, are to be found. The rubble engulfs too the idea of poetry as an alternative to or enrichment of language and experience. 'Altazor' does represent a radical movement in the poetry of the avant garde – a despair emerging from the childish arrogance of the experimental artist of the war years. Despite his occasional references to the hordes of working people, Huidobro is essentially an aristocrat of the spirit, a true inheritor of the late Romanticism of the Modernistas, save that the artist-hero is, in 'Altazor', lost and afraid. Withdrawal has become solitude and pain, and the confident Formalist assertion that all language can be insulated as an internally coherent system gives way to the sudden stuttering loss of communicative power, wherein the verb replaces the image. 'Altazor' is often attributed to a later period in Huidobro's work – to the early thirties and the decline of the avant-garde movement. In fact it dates from 1919–20 and thus coincides with the searing despair of Vallejo's *Los heraldos negros*. 'There is no meaning outside the social communication of understanding, i.e. outside the united and mutually coordinated reactions of people to a given sign.'[20]

No poet addresses the consequences of the loss of that communicative relationship as powerfully as César Vallejo (1892–1938).[21] The material of his writing is not language as such but culture, the universe of meaning produced by and through social experience and given form in language. If it was a feature of the avant garde that the lessons of Formalism were mis-learned so that language, for example in the poetic world of Huidobro, was deemed to be the primary material, Vallejo's poetry seeks the causes and explanations of that original error.

Vallejo's world was, of course, a colonial society; he grew up in provincial Peru, set in an unquestioning collusion with metropolitan culture. In the second decade of the century, that centre was disintegrating under the impact of its own modernity, and the predominant experience of the peripheral and dependent recipients of that change was of collapse. The refuge of a poetic language and form was available to some. The Formalists identified the central procedure of poetry as a linguistic one – 'making strange' or defamiliarizing the conventional representations.[22] In Latin America, however, it was not designed to recover or reconstruct the external world in a new knowledge of its complex internal relations, but to construct an autonomous linguistic *alternative* to that world. The prior assumption was that culture, art and literature could derive their material from some other – non-social – experience, and that its material of expression was a neutral medium. The material was art itself, perhaps, or its history rendered separate from the social contradictions which gave all art is meaning. The alternative, ironically (for a group whose lifestyle and perceptions were so radical), was to withdraw again into timeless universals or to parody them (as Borges did) and to take refuge in a kind of artistic and linguistic nihilism.[23] Poetry itself, in such a conception, becomes an autonomous realm of withdrawal, an imaginary (illusory) alternative.

In a sense such a conception is itself ideology, a false representation of the world. Turning away from the world into art is an act of faith, but also an act of self-delusion. After all, only social life can generate or produce language.[24] Yet language is also ideology, a *representation* of social life and subject to the same critique and subversion as all ideologies, all falsifications. Vallejo, like Huidobro, did seek refuge in language, addressing the world through the structures and forms of culture – for it was culture that gave *meaning* to the world. Yet his poetry is a record of the collapse of meaning, and of the terrible isolation and abandonment which is the result. Poignant and lived though that experience is, it is not Vallejo the individual person whose world is set before us here, nor is the insistent nostalgia for family, past and certainty the exploration of personal experience alone. The source of his anguish is neither Vallejo's individual circumstances nor his psychological condition, but rather social. The collapse of meanings is the crisis of a 'structure of feeling'[25] which Vallejo records and in which he participates socially. It is that structure of explanation and socially available meanings that is the material of Vallejo's poetry – that is, ideology itself.

If Vallejo grew up amid the secure certainties of a peripheral provincial world, then he came to maturity as they began to come apart under the impact of modernization. But there is no sense in his world of the excitement of a burgeoning alternative – that the old world is bursting apart to yield a new and frightening yet exhilarating set of possibilities. The process appears only as disruption; and its impact is to *empty* experience, leaving an absence, a loss of meaning and of humanity. Unlike that of his avant-garde contemporaries Vallejo's poetry was not a place of refuge but a relentlessly honest geography of a process of disintegration and uncertainty. If he dreamt of childhood it was not in the sense of yearning for an epoch of primal innocence, a world of myth, but of looking back without full understanding to a time before consciousness, when the certainties functioned to cushion him from the world. His adulthood in an epoch of far-reaching change has brought only pain, an anguish of uncertainty. And his poetry traces that collapse with ruthless and often painful truthfulness.

José Carlos Mariátegui, the important and influential Marxist activist and cultural critic, called it 'la inquietud de la época' (the concern of the times)[26] which 'in some is despair, in others simple emptiness'. He accused the intellectuals of his own time of 'refusing, out of pride or out of fear, to see in their own insecurity and anguish the reflection of the crisis of capitalism.'[27] Certainly Vallejo at this early stage made no reference to the crisis of the capitalist system, but he expressed it unremittingly as a cultural and ideological crisis of catastrophic dimensions, in which he was equally a victim. And in the whole body

47

of Vallejo's work, the causes and the possible solutions, the potentiality unlocked by the cracking of the old stability were a central element. Certainly Mariátegui describes the search for a refuge from the preoccupations of the time as 'cowardice'[28] – but the accusation could not reasonably be levelled at Vallejo.

There were two central features of Vallejo's work: his despair, as the world of the past dissolved and left him in solitary abandon; and humanism, a deep and enduring sympathy for those, like himself, who suffer this mournful exile, and the belief in a spiritual and political potentiality expressed here in the constant search for understanding and meaning even in the darkest times. The first and most significant insight was the acknowledgement of the contingency of human affairs and of the institutions that embody them. Yet at this stage this was little more than a general pity amid his 'protesta sentimental o protesta metafísica. Nostalgia del exilio, nostalgia de ausencia' (sentimental or metaphysical protest. Nostalgia for exile and for absence).[29]

Los heraldos negros was published in 1919. It was here that the sense of betrayal was most powerfully addressed. The old certainties – the structures of social life, religion, culture itself – had begun to disintegrate as they entered history and the realm of contingency. Nothing was certain because nothing escaped the ravages of time. And the language available, though structured around the assertion of stable values, was no more than an arbitrary and accidental sign. Between Vallejo and his avant-garde contemporaries stood his despair and his lack of faith in the autonomy of culture. *Los heraldos negros* mapped that slow but disturbing realization, and traced a mounting confusion and uncertainty. The recurring images were signifiers of emptiness, hollowness and loss. The bed, the open mouth, the empty cup, the abandoned bed, the ditch and the yawning tomb[30] all stood for the absence that was the constant theme of *Los heraldos*:

> Hay un vacío
> En mi aire metafísico
> que nadie ha de palpar;
> el claustro de un silencio
> que habla a flor de fuego.
> Yo nací un día que
> Dios estuvo enfermo.

(There's an empty space/in my metaphysical air/that no one may touch;/ the cloister of a silence/a fire about to speak./I was born on a day when/ God was sick.)

Religion above all had cemented the conservative provincial order from which Vallejo came, but religion and the reassuring omnipotent deity on which it rests could no longer provide solace or reassurance. The last supper could no longer stand as the epiphany or the ritual reintegration of the community of its Christian symbolism; it had become a wretched meal of unassuaged hunger.

> Hasta cuándo estaremos esperando lo que
> no se nos debe . . .
>   . . . Ya nos hemos sentado
> mucho a las mesa, con la amargura de un niño
> que a media noche, llora de hambre, desvelado . . .
>
> ¿Y cuándo nos veremos con las demás, al borde
> de una mañana eterna, desayunados todos?

(How long must we sit here waiting/for what we are not owed . . ./We have sat at the table/often, with the bitterness of a child/that at midnight, cries with hunger, unable to sleep . . .//And when shall we be together with the rest, on the eve/of an endless morning, all of us well breakfasted?)

The act of communion becomes here an act of separation. The poem registers and enacts that experience as protest – like all the poems of the collection it moves between despair and rage, between hope and deep dissatisfaction. The promise of eternal life, of permanence and duration outside time is here replaced by a pressing and inescapable sense of decay. The persistent image of unity, wholeness – the number 1, the unified self – are mocked by time and history. The sense of purpose in human affairs is lost in the most poignant expression of the reduction of God to human dimensions, of the loss of a sense of overarching truth.

> Dios mío, si tu hubieras sido hombre,
> hoy supieras ser Dios;
> pero tú, que estuviste siempre bien,
> no sientes nada de tu creación.
> Y el hombre sí te sufre: el Dios es él.

(My God, if you had been a man,/today you would know how to be God;/but you, you were always all right/and you feel nothing for your creation./And man must suffer you; he is God.)

This is a fragile, limited God as subject to the arbitrary destiny of time as anyone else, an old dice player watching his luck.

Dios mío esta noche sorda, oscura
ya no podrás jugar, porque la Tierra
es un dado roído y ya redondo
a fuerza de rodar a la aventura
que no puede parar sino en un hueco,
en el hueco de inmensa sepultura.

(My God, and on this dark deaf night/you won't be able to play, because Earth/is a worn dice now round/from rolling around aimlessly/and it will only come to rest in a hole,/the empty hole of the great tomb.)

In the section 'Canciones del hogar' (Songs of home) Vallejo evoked the family as another metaphor of wholeness and completeness, of communion/community. This is one pole of his vision; the other of course is emptiness. The family represented, in Marx's terms, 'the heart of a heartless world',[31] a refuge and a consolation. But it too was lost now, and with it the comforts it could bring and the defences it could offer (for all its contradictions) against an arbitrary destiny and a merciless history. The comforts to which Vallejo referred were the material comforts of maternal protection and warmth, and the specific love of a brother expressed in the innocent games of childhood. Those childhood games now took on a far more sinister dimension as even the memory of the family was lost, and with it the sense of a personal history. God and family have left man alone and abandoned, orphaned in the world. This is expressed with the greatest emotive power in the poem 'A mi hermano Miguel' (To my brother Miguel). It begins by remembering the games of hide and seek in and around the family home – but then there occurs a slippage in time and through time, as the past becomes a dark present.

Miguel, tú te escondiste
una noche de agosto, al alborear;
pero, en vez de ocultarte riendo, estabas triste.
Y tu gemelo corazón de esas tardes
extintas se ha aburrido de no encontrarte. Y ya
cae sombra en el alma.

Oye, hermano, no tardes
en salir. ¿Bueno? Puede inquietarse mamá.

(Miguel, you hid/one August night as the dusk was setting in;/but instead of smiling when you went to hide, you were sad./And your twin heart of those lost/evenings has grown weary of not finding you. And the/darkness falls across the soul.//Brother, listen, come out/soon. OK? Mother might start to worry.)

The poem ends with a suspended question that is never finished because that would somehow be too definitive, too final. Instead everything hangs in the breathless, querulous half-articulated question mark towards the poem's end. This was the prevailing note of these early, disturbed poems of Vallejo, expressed most agonizingly in the volume's dedicatory eponymous poem 'Los heraldos negros', in which Vallejo began to use the typographical devices so central to his next volume *Trilce*, and which expressed on the printed page the break-up of truths, the fragmentation of certainty.

> Hay golpes en la vida . . . ¡Yo no sé!
> Golpes como el odio de Dios; como si ante ellos
> la resaca de todo lo sufrido
> se empozara en el alma . . . ¡Yo no sé!
> . . .
> Y el hombre . . . ¡Pobre . . . pobre! Vuelve los ojos, como
> cuando por sobre el hombro nos llama una palmada;
> vuelve los ojos locos, y todo lo vivido
> se empoza, como charco de culpa, en la mirada.
>
> Hay golpes en la vida, tan fuertes . . . ¡Yo no sé!

(There are some hard blows in life . . . I don't know!/Blows like God's hatred; as if in the face of them/the undertow of/everything we have suffered/became poison in the soul . . . I don't know!/. . ./And man . . . Poor thing . . . poor thing! He turns his eyes/like we do when a slap on the shoulder claims our attention;/he turns his crazy eyes and everything he has lived/is poisoned, like a pool of guilt, in that look.//There are blows in life that are so hard . . . I don't know!)

Vallejo's *Trilce*[32] represents a still more radical dimension of despair. If *Los heraldos negros* mapped an experience of breakdown, of crisis, it left at least one level of language intact. The poetic aspiration was the victim of the loss of *any* transcendental possibility – there remained only the realm of everyday experience and its corresponding vernacular. Prosaic, without peaks or emotional explosions of rhetoric or rhythm, this language transmitted above all hesitancy and self-absorption. In *Trilce* even that language cannot survive the loss of any and every coherence. Language itself is an elaborate subterfuge, a trick, an ideological instrument creating false truths and universals on the basis of a consensus of the blind – for the words themselves have neither solidity nor purpose. These grand explanations, the universal truths and the enduring and comforting certainties prove to be as fragile as the words that compose them. Language, meaning, sequence and grammatical coherence are metaphors for an underlying optimism, a

51

conviction of order – and Vallejo in his *Trilce* calls them all into question.

Poem III, for example, returns (if not explicitly so then clearly by internal reference) to Miguel and his family at the moment of 'A mi hermano Miguel'. But now the tone is more shrill, more insistent, more desperate.

> Las personas mayores
> ¿a qué hora volverán?
> Da las seis el ciego Santiago
> y ya está muy oscuro
>
> Madre dijo que no demoraría
> . . .
>
> Aguardemos así, obedientes y sin más
> remedio, la vuelta, el desagravio
> de los mayores siempre delanteros
> dejándonos en casa a los pequeños,
> como si también nosotros
>   no pudiésemos partir.
>
> ¿Aguedita, Nativa, Miguel?
> Llamo, busco al tanteo en la oscuridad.
> No me vayan a haber dejado solo,
> y el único recluso sea yo.

(The grown ups/when will they get back?/Blind Santiago says it's six o'clock/and it's dark already.//Mother said she wouldn't be long/. . .// Let's wait, like this, obedient, what else/can we do. Wait for them to get back, the excuses/of the grown-ups who have always got the upper hand/leaving us little ones at home/as if we/couldn't leave either.// Aguedita, Nativa, Miguel?/I call out, feel in the darkness./Don't leave me alone,/don't let me be the only one hiding here.)

Here, as in other poems of the volume, the voice of the central persona is alone and isolated, his world populated by ghosts, memories, chimeras. Hence the sudden panic that grips the speaker and interrupts the flow of thought. The book is a record of desperate and unfulfilled desire; the absence of any sense of development or growth makes the past the only possible area of fertility and exploration – yet here again the past is lost and all the people in it have become phantoms.

Esta noche desciendo del caballo,
ante la puerta de la casa, donde
me despedí con el cantar del gallo.
Está cerrada y nadie responde

. . .

Numerosa familia que dejamos
no ha mucho, hoy nadie en vela, y ni una cera
puso en el ara para que volviéramos.

. . .

Llamo de nuevo y nada.
Callamos y nos ponemos a sollozar, y el animal
relincha, relincha más todavía.

(On this night I get down from my horse,/at the door of the house that/I left at cockcrow./It's locked and no one answers./. . ./We left behind a big family/not long ago, today no one is waiting, not even a candle/in the ring so that we would come back.//I call again – nothing./We fall silent and begin to sob, and the animal/neighs and neighs again and more and more.)

If there is no refuge in the past, then the alternative is the construction of the self, the differentiation of the person from both environment and temporal process. This indeed is the very act of cultural creation,[33] the assimilation of nature and time to human purposes. Yet the whole of *Trilce* represents an ironic commentary on the fatuous illusion that is culture itself – and at its heart the belief in the possibility of creating in and through language a cultural sphere that escapes the processes of physical or moral decay. The hedonistic hope of sexual pleasure or ecstasy is also savagely parodied, in Poem LX, for example:

Es de madera mi paciencia
sorda, vegetal.

. . .

Y se apolilla mi paciencia,
y me vuelvo a exclamar: Cuándo vendrá
el domingo bocón y mudo del sepulcro;
cuándo vendrá a cargar este sábado
de harapos, esta horrible sutura
del placer que nos engendra sin querer
y el placer que nos DestieRRa

(My patience is made of wood/mute and vegetable./. . ./And my patience grows motheaten/and I exclaim to myself again, when will/that wide-mouthed and silent/Sunday of the tomb come;/when will that Saturday bear down/covered in rags, the horrible suture/of pleasure that

53

gives birth to us without meaning to/that pleasure that casts us into
eXiLE)

Exile here is a casting *into* the world, into a place where culture is
disrupted and mocked like the word 'DestieRRa'. The vagina is a
metaphor for emptiness and terror; sex a deep and enduring disap-
pointment. Time is a prison encasing with ironic persistence all our
words describing freedom. The systemic explanations we evolve – be
they religion or science – are light veils over an arbitrariness to which
even God is subject. The stable from which the Christ figure was born
this time yields up no satisfactory myth to give solace.

> Oh sangabriel, haz que conciba al alma
> el sin luz amor, el sin cielo,
> lo más piedra, lo más nada,
> > hasta la ilusión monarca.
>
> ¡Quemaremos todas las naves!
> ¡Quemaremos la última esencia!
>
> Mas si se ha de sufrir de mito a mito,
> y a hablar me llegas masticando hielo,
> mastiquemos brasas,
> ya no hay dónde bajar,
> ya no hay dónde subir.
>
> Se ha puesto el gallo incierto, hombre.

(St Gabriel make the soul conceive/the love without light, the non-
heaven/the rest stone, the rest nothing/until the final illusion.//We'll
burn all the boats!/We'll burn the final essence!//But if we have to suffer
from myth to myth,/and you come to speak to me chewing ice,/let's
chew hot coal,/there's nowhere to descend to,/there's nowhere to climb
up to.//The Cock has grown uncertain, man!)

In these desolate poems, then, César Vallejo offers the most radical
vision of the modernist despair of the Latin American poets. If the
central theme of this study is the search for the reappropriation of an
alien language and culture in Latin American poetry, then the early
Vallejo suggests its impossibility. Typically, his procedure is metony-
mic, seeking the whole through a partial referent – the poetic proce-
dure par excellence according to Roman Jakobson.[34] And Vallejo's
poetic method does not *deny* this process – it negates it. The assump-
tion that each reference will open access to a wholeness, an integrity
beyond, is continually undermined and ridiculed; the hand and

mouth do not guarantee the presence of the body, except insofar as it is an endless combination of separate functions – eating, defecation, walking, sex; it has no integrity as a combination of activities. There is a direct analogy between that loss of totality, of wholeness in physical function and the fragmentation of cultural cohesion, of understanding and consciousness itself.[35] Language combines levels and layers of meaning into a complex metaphorical understanding, establishing the relationship between areas of experience and social knowledge at the level of consciousness. That at least should be the metaphorical function. The angst of Vallejo's writing is that the procedures yield only more confusion and contradiction – orders of language which do not seem capable of integration. So the slippage from one order of reference to another yields only a growing perplexity and a deepening sense of *dis*integration. What function then can poetry have when the arbitrary juxtaposition of elements is all that it can possess, and where its communicative potential is thus lost? This in many ways is the *reductio ad absurdum* of the concept of an autonomous and analogous realm of poetic reality.[36]

Later, in the context of the rising struggles of the thirties, Vallejo rediscovered a sense of lost communion, though he never lost his doubt and fear of its fragility. At this stage, however, Vallejo represents the most radically pessimistic, and the most poetically powerful statement of the avant garde. It did not settle the argument that it implicitly addressed, because Vallejo did not, as a poet, acknowledge any alternative popular tradition. But he set out the most relentless challenge to the horizons and perceptions of his own middle class. Other poets came later to rescue the concept of communion for poetry, most notably Octavio Paz. Others, like Pablo Neruda, began some years later to seek a poetry of communion in a language of everyday life. What Vallejo challenged and called into question was the double alienation of the poet and the Latin American; his distance from the sources of the still dominant culture and his lack of sympathy, or disconnection from those projects of cultural emancipation which were forming in Latin America at that stage. The ambiguity of his relationship with the intellectual tradition of the West reproduced an ambiguity that was present in the work of many other poets of his time. At the highest level of expression this was the paradox that he most powerfully explored. For the solution to it lay not in any renewal of his own poetic method – he had taken the form of poetry to new and untravelled places already – but in a new and different relationship with language itself.

Craterizados los puntos más altos, los puntos
del amor de ser mayúsculo, bebo, ayuno, ab-
sorbo heroína para la pena, para el latído
lacío y contra toda corrección.

¿Puedo decir que nos han traicionado? No.
¿Que todos fueron buenos? Tampoco. Pero
allí esta una buena voluntad, sin duda,
y sobre todo, el ser así.

Y ¡que quién se ame mucho! Yo me busco
en mi propio designio que debió ser obra
mía, en vano: nada alcanzó a ser libre.

Y sin embargo, quien me empuja.
A que no me atrevo a cerrar la quinta ventana.
Y el papel de amarse y persistir, junto a las
horas y a lo indebido.

Y el éste y el aquél.

(Full of craters the highest points, the points/of the love of being upper case, I drink, I fast, I ab-/sorb heroin for sorrow, for the slow/heartbeat and against all correction.//Can I say they have betrayed us? No./That all were good? No. But/there is goodwill there, no doubt of it,/and above all, being this way.// And that there are people who love each other a great deal! I look for myself/in my own scheme which should have been my/own work, in vain; nothing succeeded in being free.//And nevertheless, let someone push me./I bet I won't dare to open the fifth window./And the role of loving oneself and persisting, side by side with/the hours and what should not be.//And the this and the that).

Neruda: Survival Amid Chaos

Born in Parral in 1904, Pablo Neruda grew up in Temuco where his father worked on the railways. At the time, Temuco could be described as frontier territory,[37] where an expanding capitalist economy and a hitherto unused or underused land met. In the epoch of expansion arising out of the nitrate boom and an emerging copper industry,[38] Neruda's father was one of that early working class that Luis Emilio Recabarren later organized into trade unions, and who provided the foundation of the Communist Party he also formed.[39] Neruda, however, went to Santiago, the capital, to develop his literary career. There, through his brother, he became part of the student literary circles still fascinated by a Modernismo which shaped his first book of poetry,

Crepusculario (Sunset song) (1923), with its refined and deeply European tastes. In 1924 he published his hugely popular *20 poemas de amor y una canción desesperada* (20 poems of love and a desperate song), which offered a succession of deeply personal, sensual explorations against a landscape of an abstract and classical kind. The land was inert, or at best a mirror and echo of his own desire and erotic need. Here, woman was not companion or responsive other, but inert matter to be given life by the lover's arrival. Nature and woman are indistinguishable in these early poems; both are landscapes to be travelled in an epic journey by a persona constantly seeing himself as a hunter, a primitive explorer armed only with bow and arrow. What is noticeable about the landscape is that it is *empty*, devoid of any other creative life except the speaker. The eroticism in this sense becomes a kind of auto-eroticism, an act not of communion but of solitude. Its exuberant sensuality does not alter the fact that it seems to require no living companion, no lasting response or resonance in another for its completion. It is, therefore, a sexuality without temporal or social reference, an act of self-affirmation in a world without others. But there is also a deep sense of the fragility and transitoriness of this physical reality. The landscape ceases to exist when it ceases to be evoked; it has neither permanence nor history. Thus this apparent poetry of nature is a poetry without a sense of an external world. And it was that feeling which was continued and developed in *Residencia en la tierra* (Residence on Earth).

> He ido marcando con cruces de fuego
> el atlas blanco de tu cuerpo.
> Mi boca era una araña que cruzaba escondiéndose.
> En, detrás de tí, temerosa, sedienta.
> . . .
> Entre los labios y la voz, algo se va muriendo.
> Algo con alas de pájaro, algo de angustia y de olvido.
> . . .
> Cantar, arder, huir, como un companario en las manos de un loco.
> Triste ternura mía,¿ qué te haces de repente?
> Cuando he llegado al vértice más atrevido y frío
> mi corazón se cierra como una flor nocturna.

(I have marked out with crosses of fire/the white atlas of your body./My mouth was a spider crossing it and hiding./In and behind you, fearful, thirsty/. . ./Between the lips and the voice, something is dying/Something with bird's wings, something full of anguish and forgetfulness./

. . ./to sing, to burn, to flee, like a bell in a madman's hands./Sad tenderness of mine, what are you doing to yourself suddenly?/When I reached the most adventurous and cold line/my heart closed like a nocturnal flower.)

The two bodies replace and stand for the physical world; the self is the whole universe in these poems and nature is analogous to the parts of the body and its functions. The integrity of the body, the unity of its functions, occur for Neruda at the moment of sex – unlike Vallejo, Neruda optimistically sees that possibility of unity. But there is neither unity nor disintegration beyond the self. There is a parallel too between the act of writing and the sexual encounter; both are affirmative but transitory. The very structure of these early poems, their short sentences and mounting desperation as the twenty poems progress, suggests a growing panic beneath the lush self-assertion. It is rendered explicit in the final desperate song:

> Puedo escribir los versos más tristes esta noche.
> Yo la quise, y a veces ella también me quiso.
>
> En las noches como ésta la tuve entre mis brazos.
> La besé tantas veces bajo el cielo infinito.
>
> Puedo escribir los versos más tristes esta noche.
> Pensar que no la tengo. Sentir que la he perdido.
>
> Oir la noche inmensa, más inmensa sin ella.
> Y el verso cae en el alma como al pasto el rocío.
> . . .
> Yo no la quiero, es cierto, pero tal vez la quiero.
> Es tan corto el amor, y es tan largo el olvido.

(I can write the saddest verses tonight./I loved her and at times she loved me too.//On nights like these I had her in my arms./I kissed her so many times under the infinite sky.//I can write the saddest verses tonight./To think I do not have her. To feel that I have lost her.//To hear the endless night, more endless without her./And the verses fall in the soul like dew on the grass./. . ./I don't love her, it's true, but perhaps I love her now./ Love is so short and forgetting is so long.)

The brevity of pleasure and the endless night of regret and memory is a theme familiar in the poetry of Spain particularly – Quevedo appears here for the first but not the last time as Neruda's mentor. And despite the temptation to ascribe some Latin American impulse to Neruda, the landscapes of these early poems are projections of personal and global despair, locked into a European philosophical tradition. As love poems, their intensity and passion has made them enormously popular; the deep sense of the transience of all human relationships that underpins them has perhaps been less readily acknowledged. Yet that is the continuity between these poems and the more substantial and sustained pessimism of *Residencia en la tierra*.

These collections (Books 1 and 2 of *Residencia*[40]) are closer to the Vallejo of *Trilce* than to the Neruda of *Canto General*[41]. What Neruda and Vallejo share is their individual testimony to the collapse of culture. Shared structures are disintegrating – structures of thought and feeling, shared philosophical frameworks, institutional certainties. And as they collapse the alternative permanence of nature is available. Nature, however, proves to be immune to human imprint, as the last of Neruda's *20 poemas* had shown. Whereas the map, the atlas, might serve as an analogy for the human body, nature is fundamentally inert and unable to provide forces or energy to transform the body into a consciousness again. Nature, in other words, cannot regenerate culture; it can only serve as the reflection of culture's collapse. Culture, in this sense, indicates a nature humanized, transformed in the light of human purposes; this is the process of history itself, and of human progress. But all concepts of progress had died on the fields of the Somme, and for those Latin American intellectuals who had assimilated a concept of universal culture, there was no credible alternative. Thus the demise of Western Classical culture was the demise of culture itself. In such circumstances, only the self remained, the individual personality was the only certain truth in the endlessly shifting pattern of arbitrary relations that characterized the world outside the self. This was the lyrical radicalism of Neruda. To suggest that at this stage Neruda was a social poet *malgré soi* and to see in the central relationship around which *Residencia* is built (the relationship between a single isolated self and an impermanent and shifting external world) any parallel with a vision of man as socially formed is absurd. And it makes Neruda's eventual transformation in Spain inexplicable or meaningless.

In 'Galope Muerto' (Death gallop) the transience of life and nature is the central theme, and the constant use of the present participle suggests the forming and unforming of the world in endless process. It begins 'como cenizas, como mares poblándose . . .' (like ashes, like seas filling with life . . .) and continues:

Aquello todo tan rápido, tan viviente,
inmóvil sin embargo, como la polea loca en sí misma,
esas ruedas de los motores, en fin.
Existiendo como las puntadas secas en las costuras del árbol,
callado, por alrededor, de tal modo
mezclando todos los limbos sus colas.
¿Es que dónde, por dónde, en qué orilla?
El rodeo constante, incierto, tan mudo,
como las lilas alrededor del convento
. . .
Por eso, en lo inmóvil, deteniéndose, percibir,
entonces, como aleteo inmenso, encima,
como abejas muertas o números,
ay, lo que mi corazón pálido no puede abarcar
en multitudes, en lágrimas saliendo apenas,
y esfuerzos humanos, tormentas,. . .
para mí que entro cantando,
como con una espada entre indefensos.

(All of that so fast, so alive,/yet immobile, like the pulley set alone,/those wheels of motors, let's say./Existing like the dry stitches in the seams of the tree,/silent, all around, in such a way/that all the limbos mingle their tails./So from where, where to, on what shore?/The constant walking around, uncertain, so silent,/like the lilacs round the convent/. . ./That is why in the midst of motionlessness, waiting, to see,/then, like an immense flapping of wings, above,/like dead bees or numbers,/oh, what my pale heart cannot cope with/in multitudes, in tears scarcely emerging,/and human efforts and torment,. . ./for me who enters singing,/as with a sword among the defenceless).

What sense of wholeness, of integrity, there is is sensed or imagined only: 'Hay algo denso, unido, sentado en el fondo,/repitiendo su número, su señal idéntica' (There is something dense, united, sitting on the bottom, repeating its number, its identical signal). This is the number one that Vallejo yearned for too. And since that is now unattainable in this disintegrating space, where there is neither a sense of place nor of history, the integrity of the isolated self is the only fullness that can be attained.

> Trabajo sordamente, girando sobre mí mismo,
> como el cuervo sobre la muerte, el cuervo de luto.
> Pienso, aislado en lo extremo de las estaciones,
> central, rodeado de geografía silenciosa:
> una temperatura parcial cae del cielo,
> un extremo imperio de confusas unidades
> se reúne rodeándome.

(I work without hearing, turning on myself,/like the crow works on death, the crow in mourning./I think, isolated at the extreme of the seasons,/central, surrounded by silent geography:/a partial temperature falls from heaven,/an extreme empire of confused unities/gathers surrounding me.)

The poet here is the sole focus of meaning, yet he is defined by his isolation, his permanence at the core of a transient reality: '. . .y un golpe de objetos que llaman sin ser respondidos/hay, y un movimiento sin tregua, y un nombre confuso' (and the clash of objects knocking but there is no answer/there, and a ceaseless movement, and an obscure name). Only the poet's body offers certainty. In 'Ritual de mis piernas' (Ritual of my legs) he examines each part of that body, individually and separately, and derives from it the certainty of his own physical existence: 'nada, sino la forma y el volumen existiendo,/ guardando la vida, sin embargo, de una manera completa (nothing, only the form and the volume existing/holding on to life, nevertheless, in a complete way).

Two poems from the collection summarize the radicalism of Neruda's poetic despair, and confirm his place among those of the avant garde for whom life exists only in the refuge of poetry – 'Significa sombras' (Meaning shadows) and 'Walking around'. Neruda's subsequent assumption of the central place of honour among the poets of social awareness does not alter the reality of his earlier scepticism. That he should have shared the distress and anguish of his contemporary intellectuals in the twenties bears testimony to the framework from which he viewed the world. That he was transformed by the external world and its unexpected and shattering changes perhaps subverts Neruda's (and his hagiographers') claims to be above society, superhuman and hypersensitive. But it can do little discredit to a poet who described himself as

> ardiente testigo
> cuidadosamente destruyéndose y preservándose incesantemente
> evidentemente empeñado en su deber original

> (burning witness/carefully destroying himself and preserving himself incessantly/obviously devoted to his original duty).

The shadows of the poem 'Significa sombras' refer to the darkness, the void that awaits just beyond the word. There is no substance beyond the word, only silence and emptiness.[42] This of course is not an observation of an existential reality but an ideology. The loss of certainty is not general, not universal (though the poets seek to make it

61

so); but it is a crisis of that metropolitan bourgeoisie with whose culture the Latin American intellectuals were imbued, and reflects the collapse of their capacity for self-universalization. Neruda reproduces that sense of terminal crisis, offering only a self-referential language as a defence against chaos. That self-enclosure is the autonomy of poetry and poet which Neruda sought out; that is the organizing principle of the early work. It is the apotheosis of the late Romantic ideal, a logical continuation of the Modernista legacy. And despite everything it is conservative in impulse – albeit, as Neruda insists, extreme in expression. Not because there is a world to be recovered, but because nostalgia for what was is set against a contemporary reality covered in rubble and debris, the dissociated parts of a once coherent reality. What is lacking is any sense of continuity (i.e. history), of tradition, of cumulative understanding; and thus there can be no sense of otherness, material or human. The world is as it is, a given, outside human agency except in a completely arbitrary way. The disaggregation of the parts of the body resonates in a world composed of capriciously conjoined parts, where there is no cohesion or purpose.

> Sucede que me canso de ser hombre.
> Sucede que entro en las sastrerías y en los cines
> marchito, impenetrable, como un cisne de fieltro
> navegando en un agua de origen y ceniza.
>
> El olor de las peluquerías me hace llorar a gritos.
> Sólo quiero un descanso de piedras o de lana,
> Sólo quiero no ver establecimientos ni jardines,
> ni mercaderías, ni anteojos, ni ascensores.
>
> Sucede que me canso de mis pies y mis uñas
> y mi pelo y mi sombra.
> Sucede que me canso de ser hombre.

(It so happens I am tired of being a man./It so happens, going into tailorshops and movies/I am withered, impervious, like a felt swan/ navigating waters or beginnings and ashes.//The smell of barbers' shops makes me weep aloud./All I want is a rest from stones or wool,/all I want is to see no establishments or gardens,/no merchandise or glasses or elevators.//It so happens I am tired of my feet and my nails/and my hair and my shadow./It so happens I am tired of being a man.)

In a curious way, this fatigue with his humanity is not part of a process of withdrawal from the world; he is travelling in the opposite direction – *towards* his own humanity, though it is a humanity described as 'marchito' (withered) and 'impenetrable' (impervious). He remains an actor in a scenario which contains only objects and commodities, of which his body is one, all subject to erosion and decay. Yet his poem 'Entrada en la madera', written at the same time, prophesied or promised his return to the world. Like many of his contemporaries, Neruda found that journey to be longer, more beset with accident and disaster, and more dependent on the external world than he might have anticipated.

====================================== 3 ======================================

The Peanut-eating Poet:
Brazilian Modernism

Revolution and Tradition

In Brazil, perhaps more than anywhere else in Latin America, poetry lies at the heart of the debates and practices that have shaped the country's cultural history this century. From Oswald de Andrade's *Brazil-wood Poetry Manifesto* of 1924 to the formalist avant-garde movements of the 1950s and '60s, and from the anguished writing of Vargas's 'New State' to the Tropicalist and Marginal compositions of the post-1964 dictatorship, the theoretical and creative efforts of poets to explore the dialectic of language and form have played a pivotal role in articulating the shared 'structures of feeling', the patterns of social experience generated by the last seventy years of life in Brazil. Feeding into and deriving fresh impulse from those other forms of expression on which it impinges – the performance and visual arts, but above all song – poetry has been central to the search for solutions to the major cultural problems of the century: the crisis of the artistic subject and the relationship between author, text and reader; the possibility of a politically committed art, and the function of art in an industrializing, mass society more and more dominated at every level by the dynamics of production and commodity exchange; finally, the crisis of identity, as Brazil's increasingly prominent but always subordinate status within the world economy has repeatedly brought to a focus the conflict between traditional, indigenous and popular sources of cultural identity and the dominant civilization of the metropolitan powers.

What is most remarkable about this history is its self-reflective, dialogical character and, above all, the authority and legacy of its first,

65

revolutionary decade, the decade of the Modernist movement, as the initiator of that dialogue. Later generations have repudiated it, identified with it and often sought in it their own legitimation, but first and foremost they have found it necessary to define themselves in relation to the Modernist movement. The reasons for this pre-eminent status and the strength of the Modernist tradition as an ever-present point of reference for the subsequent history of Brazilian culture are not difficult to understand, as the following account will make clear. The Modernists of the 1920s were the first to engage imaginatively, critically and consciously with the processes of economic and social change which brought the initial phase of capitalist modernization in Brazil to its climax in 1930. The country has since undergone much more profound, intensive and wide-reaching cycles of capitalist development, specifically those of the 1950s and 1964–73, and on each occasion their cultural implications have been posed afresh against a shifting background of changing technologies, ideologies, institutions, and political and social forces. But, as the generation first exposed to this experience, and informed moreover by the wealth of artistic responses which in Europe and North America greeted the global crisis of the turn of the century, the Modernist movement was forced to lay the foundations for the new culture in Brazil, to establish the parameters for the expression of the experience of modernity and its recurrent themes: the disintegration and loss of traditional ways of life, the social dislocation and alienation of the individual in the city, but the liberation of new forces, too, and the discovery of infinite possibilities of human development and collective self-realization.

The authority of the Modernist tradition also derived from its crucial historical triumph over what had gone before. If Spanish American Modernismo registered a paradoxically negative response to modernity, a withdrawal into a timeless, mythical past or into the solitude of the self, while the periodization of the much broader cultural phenomenon of Europe and North America known as Modernism tends to be a moveable feast reflecting particular ideological intentions,[1] Brazilian Modernismo is by comparison much more clearly located as a moment of rupture with the existing cultural language and institutions, and as a moment of self-declared commitment to the aesthetic and ideological modernization of the arts. Brazilian Modernismo was not the transitional product of fin-de-siècle decadentism, but a consciously revolutionary challenge to the conservative cultural establishment as led by Rio de Janeiro's Academy of Letters and the Parnassian school of poets. At this great watershed, as on so many subsequent occasions, the decisive struggle was that between rival conceptions of poetry, in which the victorious Modernists identified themselves aggressively with the spirit of the Western avant garde.

Symbolism never really took root in Brazil as a coherent and organized movement, and its impact was negligible within a culture dominated by Positivist, pseudo-scientific rationalism and naturalism. Significantly, though, some of those poets who only later joined the Modernist movement or remained at its fringes, such as Manuel Bandeira (1886–1968) and Cecília Meireles (1901–64), were heavily influenced by the Symbolist style, whose one enduring legacy was the innovation of free verse.[2] This was highly provocative to the Parnassians, whose supreme goals were the perfection of formal construction, and a rigid adherence to rules of metre and rhyme, principles analogous to those governing the work of the skilled artisans, such as the goldsmith, who were their models. This extreme formalism was matched by a thematic repertoire emptied of any trace of lived experience, subjective emotion or social reality, and which instead recycled sanitized versions of Romantic Indianist tableaux and topics drawn from Classical history and mythology.[3] Unlike the Spanish American Modernistas, whose enthusiasm for contemporary French poetry was symptomatic of a progressive, incipient anti-bourgeois dissatisfaction, the Brazilian Parnassians identified with French and Classical civilization as a way of legitimizing, with aristocratic credentials, the reactionary, élitist rule of the old planter oligarchy which, in the shadow of financial collapse and economic stagnation, had temporarily dislodged the progressive, Jacobin wing of the Republic.[4] Nothing better conveys the anti-populism of the belle époque culture, its fear and hatred of the new social forces waiting to be unleashed by the delayed tide of modernization, than Olavo Bilac's 'Profissão de fé' (Profession of faith) in the Goddess of Form:

> Deusa! A onda vil, que se avoluma
>   De um torvo mar,
> Deixa-a crescer; e o lodo e a espuma
>   Deixa-a rolar!
>
> Blasfemo, em grita surda e horrendo
>   Ímpeto, o bando
> Venha dos bárbaros crescendo
>   Vociferando . . .
>
> Deixa-o: que venha e uivando passe
>   – Bando feroz!
> Não se te mude a cor da face
>   E o tom da voz!

Olha-os somente, armada e pronta
Radiante e bela:
E ao braço o escudo, a raiva afronta
Dessa procela![5]

(Goddess! Let the wretched wave, mounting on/an awful sea,/let it swell; and let the mire and foam/swirl on!//Let the swelling horde of barbarians/come surging hideously forward,/blaspheming, clamouring/ with dull shrieks . . .//Let it be: let it come howling past/ – Savage horde!/ Alter not the colour in your cheek/nor the accent of your voice!//Merely gaze at them, armed and ready,/radiant and beautiful:/and, your shield upon your arm, defy the rage/of that storm!)

Bilac (1865–1918) was one of five 'Masters of the Past' who were the subject of a polite but devastating critique published by the young poet Mário de Andrade (1893–1945) (often referred to simply as Mário, to distinguish him from his namesake Oswald) in the pages of a major national newspaper, the *Jornal do Comércio*, between August and September 1921, paving the way for the official launch of the Modernist movement the following year. Mário's own highly theorized conception of poetry appeared that year in the 'Prefácio Interessantíssimo' (Extremely Interesting Preface) to *Paulicéia Desvairada* (Hallucinated City), the work which prompted Oswald de Andrade (1890–1954) to pronounce him 'My Futurist poet' and to declare him the leader of the new movement.

It may appear perplexing, then, perverse even, that a less familiar text of 1924, the ironically titled 'O poeta come amendoim' (The poet eats peanuts), is to serve here as an introduction to the poetry of Mário de Andrade and of Brazilian Modernism as a whole. Why choose to discuss a poem of such modest, downbeat intimacy, a poem from which the bustle and excitement of the city, the grinding and clanking of industrial machinery, and the delirious outpourings of the subconscious are conspicuously absent?

The poetry considered here as representative of the 1920s contradicts a widely-held assumption about the historical significance of the period: that the first Modernist generation played a chiefly preparatory role, that its characteristic irony, childlike vision and revolutionary language, while necessary to effect the aesthetic break with the past, were nevertheless symptoms of artistic and ideological immaturity, compared with the more 'serious' writing of the 1930s. In fact, the irony of Mário de Andrade, Carlos Drummond de Andrade (1902–87) or Manual Bandeira was a most serious response to the inadequacies of the kind of elegant, 'objective' writing which had ignored the social and cultural contradictions and realities of life in Republican Brazil. The ingenuous, infantile perspective of Oswald de Andrade, Bandeira or Murilo Mendes (1901–75) arose out of the need for a fresh, unprejudiced means of apprehending and expressing the strange new experience of modernity in the undeveloped world. The utopian vision of Manuel Bandeira, Mário and Oswald, meanwhile, expressed not only a profound sense of the alienated social existence which capitalist modernization had produced in Brazil, but also a belief in the possibility of constructing an independent, liberated cultural identity out of the contradictions of the present. It is a mark of maturity that in 1924 Mário de Andrade should write 'The poet eats peanuts', a composition which critically addressed all of those social, cultural and artistic issues, yet did so with an individual, human voice.

Indeed, it was not until 1924 that the ambiguity of modernization, its promise of expansion, liberation, and self-development, and its already evident capacity for disintegration, marginalization and alienation, began to be seriously confronted by Brazilian Modernism. For all the mythical aura that still surrounds it, the 1922 Week of Modern Art, with its poetry recitals, concerts and exhibitions, was essentially a moment of formal self-assertion. Deliberately timed to coincide with the centenary of Independence, in a year which also saw the founding of the Brazilian Communist Party and an important rebellion of junior army officers in Rio de Janeiro, as well as a major exhibition of Russian art in Berlin, the Week represented an official, rhetorical statement of the movement's commitment to change, to experimentation, to the struggle against the aesthetic conservatism of the Parnassian poets and the Academy of Letters.

This was a battle which began as early as 1917, when the first major exhibition by a native modern artist, Anita Malfatti, met a storm of criticism, congregating a number of intellectuals around it in her defence, Mário and Oswald among them. The battle for ideas, though, still remained to be fought in 1921, when Mário himself complained, on the eve of the Week of Modern Art:

> It is, moreover, a pity to discover how the poets of Brazil – all Brazilians – not only lack philosophical and religious principles but also make no effort to have any. They are generally speaking weather-vanes of the principles of the moment. They are blown in a particular direction by the aesthetics of the latest poet whom they have memorized, the philosophy of the latest Bergson whom they have not digested.[6]

It took another two years before the ideological vacuum began to be filled, and before the movement seriously began to consider the question of national identity. If 1922 was the year of symbolic public declarations of disaffection, of the inauguration of new political institutions and of the rehearsal of a new artistic language, it was not until 1924 that those statements were put to the test. Then the contradictions within the Modernist movement and in Brazilian society as a whole began to find more organized expression; in that year the São Paulo Republican Party (PRP) underwent a fundamental split from which it never recovered, establishing a new, more progressive opposition centred around the Mesquita family and the newspaper *O Estado de São Paulo*. The split also exposed the fragile, superficial unity of the Modernist movement itself, for while the PRP had remained under the control of its traditional masters, the big landowners of the state of São Paulo, it had also provided a common home for the chief *paulista* Modernists,[7] almost all of whom had collaborated on the Party's mouthpiece, the *Correio Paulistano*. The temporary unity of interests represented by the PRP disintegrated under the tensions produced by the rise of industrial capitalism which eventually led to the crisis of 1930, and new realignments found the same writers at different points on the political spectrum, with Oswald de Andrade and Plínio Salgado facing each other at its extreme ends of Communism and Fascism, respectively.[8]

In 1924, too, Luís Carlos Prestes, the future General Secretary of the Brazilian Communist Party, led a 'long march' of radical junior army officers through the Brazilian interior in an attempt to mobilize a popular armed rebellion demanding measures such as electoral reform and state assistance for impoverished rural workers.[9] The march, which lasted until 1927, was the first of a number of attempts to bridge the gulf between the experiences and aspirations of the rural masses and those of the burgeoning urban society, a gulf which provided the Modernist movement with one of its richest sources of cultural theory and practice.[10] In the same year Oswald formulated his *Manifesto da Poesia Pau-Brasil* (Brazil-wood Poetry Manifesto), a cultural project which offered a critical examination of Brazilian national identity and a dynamic synthesis of its contradictions.

The Modernist movement's first manifesto, in 1922, had confidently expressed its commitment to the future: 'KLAXON sabe que o progresso existe. Por isso, sem renegar o passado, caminha para diante, sempre' (KLAXON knows that progress exists. Therefore, without renouncing the past, it marches onward, ever onward).[11] By 1924, however, there was a growing awareness that Brazil's actuality embraced both tradition and modernity, a languishing provincialism and a dynamic cosmopolitanism, and that a simple break with the post-colonial past might prove more difficult and problematic than had seemed the case at first. Already in *Hallucinated City* Mário had made plain the reasons for his repudiation of the title 'Futurist poet'; São Paulo, the heart of the industrial and cultural revolution, emerges as a gloomy landscape of grey drizzle, economic booms and busts, foreign-owned railways and disillusioned farmers, watched over by the indifferent gaze of an uncaring motherland. When, in the best known line of the poem, he declared: 'Sou um tupi tangendo um alaúde!' (I am a Tupi Indian strumming a lute!), he was not celebrating a fertile synthesis of civilizations; the peculiar clash of traditions and cultures, out of whose originality Oswald de Andrade made a virtue, constituted for Mário an absurd, painful and perhaps insoluble contradiction: 'Galicismo a berrar nos desertos da América!' (Gallicism bellowing in the deserts of America!).

In 'The poet eats peanuts', Mário withdrew from the nervous, apprehensive excitement of the Hallucinated City and its cultural revolution to contemplate the huge world of backwardness that lay beyond. For in reality, the Week of Modern Art was little more than an island in the midst of a sea of conservatism, a predominantly rural, coffee-exporting society for which the name Republic seemed singularly inappropriate. Weighed down by the burden of a colonial past and aware at the same time of the grotesque caricature of modernization in the Third World, Mário could only long for disaster, for some explosion which might compensate for the revolution Brazil had never had. In a poem of 1929, when the contradiction was near breaking point, he would write 'Eu sou trezentos, sou trezentos-e-cinqüenta,/Mas um dia afinal eu toparei comigo . . .' (I am three hundred, I am three three hundred and fifty,/But one day at last I will find myself).[12] Like the characterless hero of his prose 'rhapsody' *Macunaíma* (1929), Indian, black, white, primitive, civilized, European, American, all of these yet none of them, Mário was struggling to find himself in the midst of a world of alienation and change, whose fragmentation is suggested by the very structure of 'The poet eats peanuts'. This was by no means a unique experience; it was shared by a whole generation of intellectuals and artists who were disinherited by the shift of wealth from country to city and who, obliged to find some niche in the new urban environment, recognized in their own displacement the mood of the nation as a whole. Yet, as Mário himself acknowledged twenty years later, the early movement, revolving around the sophisticated high-society gatherings of the *salons*, retained its elitist links with the order it was pretending to challenge. Its ties with the latifundist aristocracies of São Paulo and Minas Gerais were very real; one of the chief sponsors of the Week of Modern Art was Paulo Prado, heir to one of the most prestigious *paulista* landowning families. As the poet of provincial Minas Gerais, Carlos Drummond de Andrade, put it in his 'Explicação' (Explanation):

> Ah, ser filho de fazendeiro!
> À beira do São Francisco, do Paraíba ou de qualquer córrego vagabundo,
> é sempre a mesma sen-si-bi-li-da-de.
> E a gente viajando na pátria sente saudades da pátria.
> Aquela casa de nove andares comerciais
> é muito interessante.
> A casa colonial da fazenda também era . . .
> No elevador penso na roça,
> na roça penso no elevador.[13]

(Oh, to be the son of a rancher!/On the banks of the São Francisco, the Paraíba or any meandering stream,/it's always the same sen-si-bi-li-ty./ And travelling in your homeland you start to miss your homeland./That building of nine commercial floors/is very interesting./So was the colonial house on the plantation . . ./In the lift I think of the country,/in the country I think of the lift.)

With which world or class were they to identify themselves, then: the planters and ranchers of the colonial and imperial era, the new industrial bourgeoisie, the urban working class or the rural masses? For Drummond there were no simple answers, not even artistic ones. The only possible alternative, as his 'Poema de sete faces' (Seven-sided poem) suggests, was to keep a discreetly gauche, ironic distance, retreating behind his moustache and spectacles into his own subjective world:

> Mundo mundo vasto mundo
> se eu me chamasse Raimundo
> seria uma rima, não seria uma solução.
> Mundo mundo vasto mundo,
> mais vasto é meu coração.

(World world world so vast/if my name were Henry the Last/it would be a rhyme, not a solution./World world world so vast/much vaster is my heart.)

Mário, meanwhile, offered in 'The poet eats peanuts' a route towards the discovery of identity which neither divorced itself from a sense of collective, social experience nor abstracted itself falsely into some national-historical destiny. Penetrating beyond the triumphalist rhetoric of the typical avant-garde manifestos of the time, the poem sought to locate the individual artist within the process of change and conflict and at the same time to identify in him/her a genuinely creative, expressive function. Between the title and the closing line there is a search for the meaningful ordinariness of lived experience which, though it is informed and moulded by the grand themes of national life, is nonetheless never reducible to them. The historical traumas and burdens, the geographical rifts, the political projects, the ethnic clashes are invoked, but with an ironic distance that betrays their inadequacy to express the full reality of national experience. That detachment gives way in the second half of the poem to a personal, emotional voice which looks beneath the 'facts' of national life, for a more intimate sense of Brazilian identity,[14] and discovers it above all in the creation of an individual language, out of the act of 'chewing' the substance of day-to-day human experience.

O Poeta Come Amendoim

Noites pesadas de cheiros e calores amontoados . . .
Foi o Sol que por todo o sítio imenso do Brasil
Andou marcando de moreno os brasileiros.

Estou pensando nos tempos de antes de eu nascer . . .

A noite era pra descansar. As gargalhadas brancas dos mulatos . . .
Silêncio! O Imperador medita os seus versinhos.
Os Caramurús conspiram na sombra das mangueiras ovais.
Só o murmurejo dos cre'm-deus-padres irmanava os homens de meu
    país . . .
Duma feita os canhamboras perceberam que não tinha mais escravos,
Por causa disso muita virgem-do-rosario se perdeu . . .

Porém o desastre verdadeiro foi embonecar esta República temporã.
A gente inda não sabia se governar . . .
Progredir, progredimos um tiquinho
Que o progresso também é uma fatalidade . . .
Será o que Nosso Senhor quiser! . . .

Estou com desejos de desastres . . .
Com desejos do Amazonas e dos ventos muriçocas
Se encostando na cangerana dos batentes . . .
Tenho desejos de violas e solidões sem sentido
Tenho desejos de gemer e de morrer.

Brasil . . .
Mastigado na gostosura quente do amendoim . . .
Falado numa língua curumim
De palavras incertas num remeleixo melado melancólico . . .
Saem lentas frescas trituradas pelos meus dentes bons . . .
Molham meus beiços que dão beijos alastrados
E depois semitoam sem malícia as rezas bem nascidas . . .

Brasil amado não porque seja minha pátria,
Pátria é acaso de migrações e do pão-nosso onde Deus der . . .
O gosto dos meus descansos,
O balanço das minhas cantigas amores e dansas.
Brasil que eu sou porque é a minha expressão muito engraçada,
Porque é o meu sentimento pachorrento,
Porque é o meu jeito de ganhar dinheiro, de comer e de dormir.

(The poet eats peanuts//Nights heavy with heaped up smells and heat
. . ./It was the Sun which throughout the huge smallholding that is
Brazil/Gradually left its brown mark on the Brazilians//I am thinking of
the time before I was born . . .//The night was a time to rest. The
mulattos' pale peals of laughter . . ./Silence! The Emperor is pondering
his little verses./The Caramurus[15] conspire in the shade of the oval
mango-trees./Only the murmur of the credo joined in brotherhood the
men of my country . . ./All of a sudden the runaway blacks realized
there were no slaves any more,/That was the ruin of many a virgin-of-
the-rosary . . .//The real disaster, though, was dolling up this precocious
Republic./We didn't yet know how to govern ourselves . . ./Progress,
we've progressed an inch/For progress too is an inevitability . . ./God
knows what it must be!. . .//I have a longing for disasters . . ./A longing
for the Amazon and for the mosquito winds/Resting against the timber
of the doorways . . ./I long for guitars and solitudes without meaning/I
long to moan and to die.//Brazil . . ./Chewed in the warm deliciousness
of the peanut . . ./Spoken in a kiddish tongue/Of uncertain words in a
honeyed melancholic swaying drawl . . ./They emerge slow cool
mashed by my good teeth . . ./They moisten my lips which scatter
kisses/And then they innocently mouth the prayers of good descent. . ./
/Brazil beloved not because it is my fatherland,/Fatherlands are an
accident of migrations and of where God chooses to give us our daily
bread . . ./The pleasure of my hours of rest,/The swaying of my songs
loves and dances./Brazil that is me because it is my funny expression,/
Because it is my unhurried feeling,/Because it is the way I earn my
money, the way I eat and sleep.)

74

Shifting Identities

Mário opened 'The poet eats peanuts' with an ambiguous evocation of a collective historical memory (slavery was abolished in Brazil in 1888, just five years 'before I was born'), ambiguous because of the relationship between light and dark, and the 'brown mark' which it has left on Brazilian society. Again, we are reminded that Brazil is no more than one huge plantation. The accumulation of nocturnal heat and smells calls up at once both the atmosphere of the *senzala*, or slave-quarters, and a whole oppressive history of coercive labour under the cruel sun of Colony and Empire. Yet in what sense had all Brazilians been 'marked' by that experience, and given a uniformly brown skin?

The mulatto poet, Jorge de Lima (1895–1953), evoked the continuity of the legacy of slavery for Republican society in 'Essa nega Fulô' (That nigger girl Fulô) (1930), which took the form of a short ballad recalling the fate of an anonymous young black girl on an archetypal plantation, 'isso já faz muito tempo' (a long time ago). The endless litany of demands imposed on her by her master and mistress culminates in an accusation of theft and her punishment – rape – at the hands of the master. Predictably, Fulô is found guilty twice over, bearing the responsibility for the social and sexual transgression of which she is merely the victim:

> Ó Fulô? Ó Fulô?
> Cadê meu lenço de rendas
> cadê meu cinto, meu broche,
> cadê meu terço de ouro
> que teu Sinhô me mandou?
> Ah! foi você que roubou.
> Ah! foi você que roubou.
>
> Essa negra Fulô!
> Essa negra Fulô!
>
> O Sinhô foi açoitar
> sozinho a negra Fulô.
> A negra tirou a saia
> e tirou o cabeção,
> de dentro dele pulou
> nuinha a negra Fulô.
>
> Essa negra Fulô!
> Essa negra Fulô!

Ó Fulô? Ó Fulô?
Cadê, cadê teu Sinhô
que nosso Senhor me mandou?
Ah! foi você que roubou,
foi você, negra Fulô?

Essa negra Fulô![16]

(Hey Fulô? Hey Fulô?/Where is my lace handkerchief/Where is my belt, my brooch,/where is my piece of gold/that your Massa sent me?/Ah! it was you who stole it./Ah! it was you who stole it.//That nigger girl Fulô!/ That nigger girl Fulô!//Massa went alone/to whip the nigger girl Fulô./ The nigger girl took off her skirt/And took off her collar,/stark naked she leapt out/the nigger girl Fulô.//That nigger girl Fulô!/That nigger girl Fulô!//Hey Fulô? Hey Fulô?/ Where, where is your Massa/whom our Lord sent to me?/Ah! was it you who stole him from me,/was it you, nigger girl Fulô?//That nigger girl Fulô!)

Thirty years of fierce debate around the issue of race, precipitated by Abolition and by a massive wave of European immigration, had bequeathed to the Modernists a deeply embedded pessimism rooted in the Positivists' theories of *mestiço* degeneracy. The fusion of the advanced white, European with the primitive Indian and African races had, it was claimed, produced a series of biologically and culturally unstable 'mongrel' types which served to explain Brazil's social and economic backwardness, its inability to assimilate modern, Western political institutions and models of development.[17] With time this pathological atavism would be overcome, in deterministic Darwinian terms, through a process of 'whitening', but for the moment Brazilian society was languishing under the burden of a national malaise of decadence and listlessness, the notorious 'tristeza brasileira' (Brazilian melancholy), inherited from the lascivious African and the slothful Indian. The Parnassian poet Olavo Bilac had sentimentalized and popularized this myth of the 'three sad races' in his 'Música brasileira' (Brazilian music), and as late as 1928 the patron of the Modernist movement, Paulo Prado, gave it renewed academic respectability in his *Retrato do Brasil: ensaio sobre a tristeza brasileira* (Portrait of Brazil: essay on the Brazilian melancholy).

The Modernists never refuted the existence of this 'malaise' as such. What they did challenge, as Lima's 'That nigger girl Fulô' indicates, was the biological determinism which had blamed the 'primitive' races themselves for the pernicious social consequences of a history of brutal colonialism and slavery. Mário and Oswald de Andrade, amongst others, explored the utopian and revolutionary possibilities of Brazil's 'primitive cultures' and their potential to subvert the oppressive structures of capitalism and imperialism. However, the positive re-evaluation of *mestiço* identity involved problems of its own. The sociologist Gilberto Freyre, for instance, constructed on the basis of his analysis of plantation society[18] a theory of nationality which eliminated all internal contradictions and instituted the myth of a Brazilian 'racial democracy'. He argued that a collective history of cordial, intimate social and sexual relations between master and slave had laid the basis of a harmonious *mestiço* national community transcending any potential class or racial antagonisms.

But had slavery, miscegenation and a tropical climate really engendered a common, 'brown' identity of Brazilian nationhood? Drummond, healthily sceptical as ever, exposed the superficiality of such ready-made, stereotypical notions of identity in 'Também já fui brasileiro' (I was a Brazilian once, too). Moreover, he extended that scepticism to all the spheres of public, private and artistic life, and the reassuring but fragile categories which are imposed on them. As the past tense of the title suggests, something had changed; if, once upon a time, the poet's innocent bar-room nationalism could ignore the irony of an imported American automobile, now he was forced to confront the bewildering reality of the street outside, under a global, international sky. His confidence in the certainty of personal and social identity had disintegrated: the 'rhythm' which, for a culture so strongly attached to music and dance, represents a vital point of stability, had been lost:

> Eu também já fui brasileiro
> moreno como vocês.
> Ponteei viola, guiei forde
> e aprendi na mesa dos bares
> que o nacionalismo é uma virtude.
>
> Mas há uma hora em que os bares se fecham
> e todas as virtudes se negam.
>
> Eu também já fui poeta.
> Bastava olhar para mulher,
> pensava logo nas estrelas
> e outros substantivos celestes.
> Mas eram tantas, o céu tamanho,
> minha poesia perturbou-se.

Eu também já tive meu ritmo.
Fazia isto, dizia aquilo.
E meus amigos me queriam,
meus inimigos me odiavam.
Eu irônico deslizava
satisfeito de ter meu ritmo.
Mas acabei confundindo tudo.
Hoje não deslizo mais não,
não sou irônico mais não,
não tenho ritmo mais não.

(I was a Brazilian once, too/brown like the rest of you./I strummed my guitar, I drove my Ford/and learnt at bar-room tables/that nationalism is a virtue.//But there comes a time when bars close up/and virtues are all denied.//I was a poet once, too./I just had to look at a woman,/and I'd think of stars/and other heavenly nouns./But there were so many, the sky so big,/my poetry got the shakes.//I had rhythm once, too./I'd do this, say that./And my friends would love me,/my enemies would hate me./I'd glide about ironically/happy that I had my rhythm./But I ended up confusing everything./Today I don't glide about no more,/I ain't ironic no more,/I ain't got rhythm no more.)

Whether one should read some of the same irony and scepticism in Mário's image of his fellow countrymen being tanned a uniform brown in the great Brazilian plantation is arguable. It is interesting that, although a mulatto himself, Mário did not at this stage identify himself personally within, or with, that process, and seemed unwilling to explore its contradictions.

The situation had changed dramatically, though, by the time 'Improviso do mal da América' (Impromptu on the American malady) revealed the poet's struggle, in 1928, to find his direction in the midst of a storm of conflicting tides and currents. The poem opens with the extraordinary utterance: 'Grito imperioso de brancura em mim' (Imperious cry of whiteness in me), and ends with a startling paradox: 'Me sinto só branco, só branco em minha alma crivada de raças!' (I feel only white, I feel only white in my soul riddled with races!) Here Mário confronted the other dimension of the problem, the impact of the growing cosmopolitanism of Brazilian society on the sense of national identity. As in 'The poet eats peanuts', the 'facts' of national life, 'coisas de minha terra, passados e formas de agora' (things of my land, pasts and forms of presentness), had lost their meaning. It was no longer simply that they were incapable of expressing the totality of his experience, but that they had become as estranged from him as the manifestations of any foreign culture. Even the most intimate, sensual expressions of national identity, 'ritmos de síncopa e cheiros lentos de sertão' (syncopated rhythms and slow smells of the backlands), were as much distant echoes as the prayer of an Indian in a stone temple or the feats of Communist soldiers fighting for the liberation of China. Alienated, travelling, like Drummond, in a land which he does not recognize, 'um ser de mundos que nunca vi' (a being of worlds I have never seen), Mário looks in vain for an oar to guide his canoe as he is swept upstream by the tide of change. Immigration has flooded his being with an exciting new wealth of cultures, but his instinctive internationalism is tinged with a sense of loss:

> Vão chegando italianos didáticos e nobres;
> Vai chegando a falação barbuda de Unamuno
> Emigrada pro quarto-de-hóspedes acolhedor da Sulamérica;
> Bateladas de húngaros, búlgaros, russos se despejam na cidade . . .
> Trazem vodka no sapiquá de veludo,
> Detestam caninha, detestam mandioca e pimenta,
> Não dançam maxixe, nem dançam catira, nem sabem amar suspirando.

> (Didactic, noble Italians are arriving;/The hirsute chatter of Unamuno/ Emigrating to the welcoming guest-room of South America;/Boatloads of Hungarians, Bulgarians, Russians spill out into the city . . ./They bring vodka in their velvet *sapiquá*,/They detest sugarcane rum, they detest manioc and pepper,/They don't dance the *maxixe*, they don't dance the *catira*, and they don't know how to sigh when they make love.)

He greets them and wishes them well, but is aware that his very cosmopolitanism, his rebellion against national chauvinism, colonialism and sectarianism, his willingness to bathe in the tide of Brazil's internationalization, has also washed away the colour which had once identified him with the history and society of the continent, leaving behind only a rootlessness and a void. Thus the multiplicity of races and cultures enriched his harlequin's costume, but concealed beneath its fabric a dual 'whiteness': the guilt of betrayal, the sense of a whole people, Brazil's coloured communities, the blacks, Indians, mulattos and *caboclos*, left behind by the process of modernization; and the subjective void of 'blankness', the loss of all identity. This was exactly the tragedy of *Macunaíma* (published in the same year), whose magical powers of metamorphosis offered infinite freedom, but in transforming him stripped away all that bound him to the world of his birth:

> Mas eu não posso não me sentir negro nem vermelho!
> De certo que essas cores também tecem minha roupa arlequinal,
> Mas eu não me sinto negro, mas eu não me sinto vermelho,

Me sinto só branco, relumeando caridade e acolhimento,
Purificado na revolta contra os brancos, as pátrias, as guerras, as posses,
    as preguiças e ignorâncias!
Me sinto só branco agora, sem ar neste ar-livre da América!
Me sinto só branco, só branco em minha alma crivada de raças!

(But I just can't feel black or red!/Sure, these colours too are woven into
my harlequin clothes,/But I don't feel black, but I don't feel red,/I feel
only white, gleaming with charity and welcome,/Purified in my revolt
against white men, fatherlands, wars, possessions, indolences and
ignorances!/I feel only white now, airless in the open air of America!/I
feel only white, only white in my soul riddled with races!)

To those two meanings a third, perhaps so obvious it is easily over-
looked, can be added: the desperate realization that the artist-intellec-
tual's very consciousness of his rootless non-identity, his alienation
from the life of 'the people', forces him to assume the colour of those
who pretend to stand above the conflicts of race and class, who gleam
with moral righteousness, but who by declaring themselves colour-
less, ultimately betray their membership of the white ruling elite. The
latter would be a harsh and unfair description of Mário himself, but it
anticipates the much more tormented self-interrogation of the 1930s,
when racial, cultural or national loyalties were forced to give way to
the struggle between the classes.

True and False Modernity

The dilemma of racial identity is but one dimension of a problem
running right through the poetry of the 1920s: the consciousness of a
kind of absurd falseness about the notion of Brazil's modernity. Such
is the sense of 'false modernity' in the third and fourth stanzas of 'The
poet eats peanuts', as Mário continues his recollections. At first sight a
profound historical rupture appears to take place: the stifling, repres-
sively stagnant and grotesquely conspiratorial atmosphere of the
Empire is shattered by the trauma of Abolition and the collapse of the
monarchy. No sooner has it been announced, however, than the
event's significance is comically belittled, reduced to a banal episode
in the sexual life of the nation: 'All of a sudden the runaway blacks
realized that there were no slaves any more,/That was the ruin of many
a virgin-of-the-rosary . . .' The momentous change which the break
between stanzas should represent is no such thing at all; the Republic
is a sham caricature, a doll or dummy dressed up in the precocious
clothes of the twentieth century, but yet to attain political adulthood

and to fulfil the Positivist promise of progress. Indeed, this was true: Modernism represented a struggle not only with the cultural conservatism of Brazil's francophile belle époque élite, but also with the political reaction which had made the belle époque possible.[19]

Some things had changed, but much had not. Mário expressed the disorientation of a generation which was born and grew up in the city. For other poets who had lived the transition between the two worlds, the old, rural Brazil was more than a historical memory, it was a living reality, stubbornly imposing itself on the present. Manuel Bandeira, for instance, had moved to Rio from Recife, in the country's backward northeast, and had long been writing poetry in the mould of the Symbolists and Parnassianists before the publication in 1930 of *Libertinagem* (Libertinage), marking his late adherence to the Modernist movement. 'O cacto' (The cactus), written in 1925, conveys, with a combination of epic grandeur and comic irony, the grotesque permanence of a pre-industrial society and culture within the fragile technological order of the New Age. The cactus, a being of mythical proportions and primitive defiance, is torn from the ground by the storm of change, but demonstrates its continuing power by devastating buildings, disrupting traffic and breaking power cables, so bringing a modern town to a complete halt:

Aquele cacto lembrava os gestos desesperados da estatuária:
Laocoonte constrangido pelas serpentes,
Agolino e os filhos esfaimados.
Evocava também o seco nordeste, carnaubais, caatingas . . .
Era enorme, mesmo para esta terra de ferocidades excepcionais.

Um dia um tufão furibundo abateu-o pela raiz.
O cacto tombou atravessado na rua,
Quebrou os beirais do casario fronteiro,
Impediu o trânsito de bondes, automóveis, carroças,
Arrebentou os cabos elétricos e durante vinte e quatro horas privou a
 cidade de iluminação e energia:

– Era belo, áspero, intratável.[20]

(That cactus recalled the desperate gestures of the sculpture:/Laocoontes held fast by the serpents,/Agolinus and his starving children./It also evoked the dry northeast, carnauba palms, scrub . . ./It was huge, even for this land of exceptional savageries.//One day a furious typhoon toppled it at the roots./The cactus crashed sideways across the street,/Broke the overhanging roofs of the row of houses opposite,/Blocked the

81

passage of trams, cars and carts,/Smashed through the electric cables and for twenty-four hours deprived the town of light and power://It was beautiful, harsh, intractable.)

The dialectic of continuity and change was also expressed in the poets' re-encounter with the provincial towns and cities they left behind. Drummond, revisiting the colonial monuments of his native Minas Gerais in 'Lanterna Mágica' (Magic Lantern), found that the legendary heroes of the past had disappeared beneath a proudly crumbling, ragged landscape, or had been shunted into oblivion by the loco-motives of progress:

> Nem Siderúrgica nem Central nem roda manhosa de forde
> sacode a modorra de Sabará-buçu.
>
> Pernas morenas de lavadeiras,
> tão musculosas que parece foi o Aleijadinho que es esculpiu,
> palpitam na água cansada.
>
> O presente vem de mansinho
> de repente dá um salto:
> cartaz de cinema com fita americana.
>
> E o trem bufando na ponte preta
> é um bicho comendo as casas velhas.

(Neither the National Iron and Steel Works nor the Central Railway nor the mischievous wheel of the Ford/shakes the drowsiness of Sabará-buçu.//Brown legs of washerwomen,/so muscular they look as though Aleijadinho had sculpted them,/tremble in the tired water.//The present creeps softly along/suddenly it takes a leap:/cinema poster with an American film.//And the train puffing over the black bridge/is an animal eating up the old houses.)

Bandeira's 'Evocação do Recife' (Evocation of Recife), meanwhile, attempted to recapture, not the historical face of the city, which had irrevocably gone, but the intimate, lived childhood experience of the place, whose moments of human communion gave it immortality in the memory and being of the poet:

> [. . .] o Recife sem história nem literatura
> Recife sem mais nada
> Recife da minha infância

A rua da União onde eu brincava de chicote-queimado e partia as
  vidraças da casa de dona Aninha Viegas
Totônio Rodrigues era muito velho e botava o pincenê na ponta do nariz
Depois do jantar as famílias tomavam a calçada com cadeiras mexericos
  namoros risadas
A gente brincava no meio da rua
Os meninos gritavam:

> Coelho sai
> Não sai!

([. . .] Recife without any history or literature/Just Recife, that's all/Recife
of my childhood//Union Street where I would play treasure-hunt and
break the window-panes of Dona Aninha Viegas's house/Totônio Rodri-
gues was very old and perched his pince-nez on the tip of his nose/After
dinner the families would take to the pavement with chairs/gossip
courting laughter/We'd play in the middle of the street/The children
would shout://Rabbit's out/No he's not!)

Childhood recollections attest to a world that has been lost, but
simultaneously construct an intact poetic space which both restores
the individual's ties to the past and allows that past to flow continu-
ously into the present. Hence Drummond's insistence, against the
advice of his editors, on the unending present tense of his life's story
in 'Infância' (Childhood):

> Meu pai montava a cavalo, ia para o campo.
> Minha mãe ficava sentada cosendo.
> Meu irmão pequeno dormia.
> Eu sozinho menino entre mangueiras
> lia a história de Robinson Crusoé,
> comprida história que não acaba mais.

(My father would ride out into the countryside./My mother would be left
sitting with her sewing./My little brother would be sleeping./I a child
alone amongst mango-trees/would read the story of Robinson Crusoe,/a
long story that never ends.)

The childlike imagination that pervades so much of this poetry repre-
sents, too, an attempt to come to terms with the bewildering spectacle
of modernization in a tropical Latin American country, and to con-
struct a vision of the future. If the poet is, as Mário says, 'a being of
worlds I have never seen' or, like Drummond, he is travelling like a
foreigner in his own land, then his only option is to apprehend that
world as if for the first time, with the eyes of a child unprejudiced by
inherited traditions and instruments of perception. In his poem 'O
menino sem passado' (The child without a past), Murilo Mendes,

better known for his surrealist and mystical writing of the 1930s and 1940s, conveys this sense of the child-poet stripped of all cultural baggage and ready to face the world with a kind of naive internationalism:

> [. . .]
> A mãe-d'água só se preocupava
> em tomar banhos asseadíssima
> na piscina do sítio que não tinha chuveiro.
> De noite eu ia no fundo do quintal
> pra ver se aparecia um gigante com trezentos anos
> que ia me levar dentro dum surrão,
> mas não acreditava nada.
>
> Fiquei sem tradição sem costumes nem lendas
> estou diante do mundo
> deitado na rede mole
> que todos os países embalançam.[21]

(The water-fairy was only bothered/about having nice clean baths/in the swimming-pool of the farm which had no shower./At night I would go to the end of the garden/to see whether a three-hundred-year-old giant would appear/and carry me off in a haversack,/but I didn't believe in it at all.//I was left without tradition without customs or legends/I lie before the world/in the soft hammock/which swings in every country.)

It was Oswald de Andrade who embodied most completely the perennial innocence of the child-poet seeing his country for the first time. In the little-known *Primeiro Caderno do Alumno de Poesia Oswald de Andrade* (Poetry Pupil Oswald de Andrade's First Exercise Book) (1927) he deliberately adopted the form of a schoolchild's exercise book illustrated with naïve pencil drawings. The poem 'brinquedo' (game), for instance, reduces to its barest visual essentials the child's surrealistic perception of a burgeoning metropolis:

> Roda roda São Paulo
> Mando tiro tiro lá
>
> Da minha janela eu avistava
> Uma cidade pequena
> Pouca gente passava
> Nas ruas. Era uma pena
>
> Depois entrou no brinquedo
> Um menino grandão
> Foi o primeiro arranha-céu
> Que rodou no meu céu

Do quintal eu avistei
Casas torres e pontes
Rodaram como gigantes
Até que enfim parei

Roda roda São Paulo

Mando tiro tiro lá

Hoje a roda cresceu
Até que bateu no céu
É gente grande que roda
Mando tiro tiro lá[22]

(Round and round São Paulo goes/Bang bang let me shoot it down/From my window I could see/A little town/Not many people were going by/In the streets. It was a shame//Later a big lad/Came into the game/He was the first skyscraper/To go round in my sky//From the garden I saw/ Houses towers and bridges/They went round like giants/Until at last I stopped//Round and round São Paulo goes//Bang bang let me shoot it down//Today the wheel has grown/So that it hits the sky/It's grown-ups going round/Bang bang let me shoot them down.)

For Mário, who never set foot outside his native country, the contradiction between Brazil's underdevelopment and the struggle for modernization was cause for personal anguish and bewilderment. By contrast, Oswald, while just as acutely aware of the contradictions, simply turned the problem on its head, transforming dilemma into originality, the crisis of identity into the point of departure for a project of cultural liberation. No mere posturing rhetoric, Oswald's eternal optimism was rooted in an innocent idealism which can be seen in his abstract, Hegelian rather than Marxist, conception of dialectics, and which is both the strength and the weakness of his utopian vision. Like many of his fellow intellectuals, he made a number of journeys to Paris, the first in 1912, coming into direct contact with the leaders of the European avant-garde movements; these visits, and in particular his association with the French-Swiss poet Blaise Cendrars, were the key formative experience in developing his unique perspective on Brazilian culture.

Visions of Utopia: Oswald's Brazil-wood Poetry

Oswald's manifestos and philosophical writings made liberal use of the language of psychoanalysis, and the liberation of the subconscious was an important element of his utopian vision of Brazilian culture.

85

Benedito Nunes is right to draw attention to Oswald's notion of a 'pensamento selvagem' (savage thinking), a primitive mentality that could free the artist and the individual from the repressive limitations of 'o pensar cultivado, utilitário e domesticado' (cultivated, utilitarian, domesticated thinking).[23] However, the primitivist perspective of the *Brazil-wood Poetry* and *Cannibalist* manifestos differed from that of the Surrealists and Dadaists in an important respect. Indeed, Oswald was obliged to explain the point when the critic Tristão de Athaíde later accused the Brazil-wood poetry, 'o modernismo destruidor' (destructive Modernism), of seeking to 'abolish all poetic effort in the way of logic, beauty, construction, and to swim about in the instinctive, in foolery, in mediocrity'.[24] For if Oswald had inherited an instinctive anarchism from his bohemian days, it was allied to a critical, objective rationalism which saw the artistic fragmentation of the world as a necessary prerequisite for the construction of a new, coherent conception of Brazilian culture. Speaking of the Europeans' modern 'discovery' of African culture, in a lecture at the Sorbonne in 1923, Oswald had pointed to the revelatory potential of this primitive perspective as a means of returning to artistic essentials, to the 'concrete and metaphysical origins of art'.[25] It was this perspective, deconstructing the prevailing ideological interpretation of Brazilian culture, which formed the core of the Brazil-wood poetry, and which prepared the way for the revolutionary analysis of Oswald's *Cannibalist Manifesto*.

In 1924 Blaise Cendrars made a visit to Brazil whose importance for Oswald's cultural theory is now generally acknowledged. Exchanging poems and accompanying each other's creative activity, Oswald and Cendrars enjoyed a relationship of artistic symbiosis; later Oswald said of Cendrars that 'he too consciously wrote Pau-Brasil poetry'.[26] Discovering Brazil for the first time with the help of Oswald and his future wife, the artist and sculptress Tarsila do Amaral, Cendrars provided his hosts with a fresh perspective on their native landscape, the 'camera-eye' of his *Kodak* and *Feuilles de Route*.

The *Manifesto da Poesia Pau-Brasil* (Brazil-wood Poetry Manifesto) (1924) took Cendrars's objective, fragmented photo-perspective and added to it Oswald's 'savage thinking' which later became so central to his theory of Anthropophagy. Within this 'naïve' vision, images which, according to conventional notions of artistic perspective, might be ordered into separate categories – the physical landscape, cultural data or historical experience – are instead scattered uniformly across a flat, one-dimensional canvas, without any obvious logical organization:

Poetry exists in facts. The saffron and ochre shacks in the greens of the shanty-town, beneath the Cabraline blue, are aesthetic facts.

Carnival in Rio is the religious happening of the race. Brazil-wood. Wagner sinks beneath the samba parades of Botafogo. Barbarous and ours. Rich ethnic background. Vegetable wealth. Minerals. Cooking. The vatapá stew gold and dance.[27]

However, as the Manifesto progresses, this confused montage of apparently unrelated fragments making up the reality of contemporary Brazilian life begins to reveal a different order, whose key is the reiterated phrase 'Brazil-wood'. A culture of contradictions emerges, more complex than the simple struggle between modernity and underdevelopment. A whole series of polarities can be glimpsed beneath the random juxtaposition of 'facts', setting the natural, the popular, the primitive, the indigenous and the American against the technological, the élitist, the civilized, the cosmopolitan and the European. Yet even as the contradiction becomes apparent, its constituent elements do not remain distinct but interact, giving rise to a richly original, often grotesque syncretism, the peculiar product of a Western civilization in the tropics:

> The whole pioneering history and the trading history of Brazil. The doctor part, the quotations part, the well-known authors part. Moving. Rui Barbosa: a top-hat in Senegambia. Everything turning to wealth. The wealth of balls and set-phrases. Black women dressed as jockeys. Odalisques in Catumbi. Difficult talk.

The history of this dialectical relationship has been one of unequal struggle; four centuries of colonialism and imperialism have meant that the indigenous identity has been dominated, suppressed, negated by the 'lado doutor' (educated side):

> The fatal moment of the first white man landing and politically conquering the savage jungles. The graduate. We cannot help being learned. Doctors. A country of anonymous pains, of anonymous doctors. The Empire was like that. We made everything erudite. We forgot the plumed falcon.

The following section ends with the image of a latent, authentic Brazilian identity waiting to emerge from the parasitic tangles of the 'school' that are choking the 'forest': 'Poetry wanders hidden in the mischievous creepers of wisdom. In the lianas of university nostalgia'.

The dialectic progresses towards its synthesis, the negation of the negation, the totality which integrates both terms of the contradiction in a dynamic form. The symbol of that totality is Brazil-wood, the colony's earliest commercial export, the product of the first encounter between technology and nature, Europe and America, and the commodity which gave a name to the country's singular identity. The culture of the future will be a necessary fusion of elements, but one in which the instinctive, ingenuous vitality of the 'forest' will act as a corrective to the dominating, repressive tendencies of the 'school', distilling the best of modern Western civilization and liberating a new, authentic national consciousness:

> We have the dual basis in our midst – the forest and the school. The credulous, dualist race and geometry, algebra and chemistry straight after the feeding-bottle and mint tea. A mixture of 'go to sleep baby or the bogey-man will get you' and equations. . . .

> The counterbalance of native originality to defuse academic consensus.

> The reaction against all the indigestions of wisdom. The best of our lyric tradition. The best of what we have to offer today.

In the *Poesia Pau-Brasil* (Brazil-wood Poetry), Oswald attempted to apply the principles of this dialectical theory of the reconstruction of Brazilian culture, both at a thematic and formal level. As in the *Manifesto*, the new cultural synthesis emerges out of fragments of reality in the form of short phrases or lines of poetry. The group entitled 'História do Brasil' (History of Brazil), for example, is a reformulation of the classic tests of Discovery and of the geography, ethnography and early history of Brazil, the chronicles of Pero Vaz de Caminha, Pero de Magalhães Gandavo, Claude D'Abbeville, Frei Vicente do Salvador and others. They are in one sense literally a rediscovery, adopting the naïve, enthusiastic voice of those who first recorded the marvels of the New World, and giving them a new significance by the addition of incongruous or anachronistic headings.

The first section is based on Vaz de Caminha's letter of 1500 to King Manuel of Portugal, 'on the discovery of Brazil'. Caminha's long and detailed description of the behaviour and appearance of the first Indians met by the Portuguese is reduced to the two observations which most effectively suggest the contrasting mentalities of the 'forest' and the 'school'. First, the Indians' reaction to the sight of a chicken:

> Quase haviam medo dela
> E não queriam pôr a mão
> E depois a tomaram como espantados;

(They were almost afeared of it/And would not lay a hand upon it/And then they took it as though in fright);

and then the Portuguese sailors' first sight of the naked Indian girls, and Caminha's contorted attempt to rationalize the hypocrisy of his society's sexual attitudes – the title invites the reader to compare Caminha's sailor with his modern counterpart, sizing up the local prostitutes as his ship enters port:

> as meninas da gare
>
> Eram três ou quatro moças bem moças
> Com cabelos mui pretos pelas espáduas
> E suas vergonhas tão altas e tão saradinhas
> Que de nós as muito bem olharmos
> Não tínhamos nenhuma vergonha

(the station girls//There were three or four maids of maiden years/With hair right dark down their backs/And their shames so upstanding and so well-kempt/That we took no shame/From looking well upon them)

Similarly, in 'São Martinho', the title 'prosperidade' (prosperity) parodies the reader's assumptions about the nature of progress, by confronting images of the colony's early economic development with those of the modern, industrial culture to which its history of exploitation has given birth – ironically, that development is still breeding 'colonies':

> Plantaram fazendas como sementes
> E fizeram filhos nas senhoras e nas escravas
> Eis-nos diante dos campos atávicos
> Cheios de galos e de reses
> Com porteiras e trilhos
> Usinas e igrejas
> Caçadas e frigoríficos
> Eleições tribunais e colônias

(They planted farms like seeds/And made children in their ladies and in their slave-women/Here we stand before the ancestral fields/Full of cockerels and cattle/With gates and drives/Mills and churches/Hunts and refrigerators/Elections courts and colonies)

The chroniclers' descriptions of the indigenous communities are defamiliarized by the choice of observations which, removed from their original context, are able to communicate the sense of surprise experienced by the early traveller. On the other hand, the peculiar disparity between the headings of the poems (for example, 'primeiro chá' (first tea-party), 'corografia' (chorography), 'sistema hidrográfico' (hydro-graphic system), 'prosperidade de são paulo' (prosperity of são paulo)) and the landscape and environment to which they refer, draws special attention to the central dialectic in the *Manifesto*. The source texts for 'History of Brazil' are all prime examples of 'academic' perceptions of the Brazilian colony; and this is underlined by retaining their archaic orthography. Emphasizing these qualities in his reconstruction of those texts, Oswald shows how they reflect that synthesis of cultures, indigenous and European, primitive and academic, which he calls Brazil-wood:

> Brazil-wood is the first chroniclers, the sculptors of saints of Minas Gerais and Bahia, the politicians of Empire, the overcoated Romanticism of the Republic and all the guitarists in general. Brazil-wood was the painter Benedito Calixto before he unlearnt it all in Europe. Brazil-wood is Sr Catulo [*da Paixão Cearense* – popular singer], when he remembers Ceará and my friend Menotti when he writes poetry about Brás.
>
> It was Columbus who discovered America and Vespuccio who gave it its name. Brazil-wood Poetry, emerging from the sea-salty hands of the scribe Caminha, was always there but shied away like some flower by the wayside. The time was right to identify it and save it.
>
> Just as happened with our country in the sixteenth century, which to obvious geographical, political and commercial advantage, ceased to be called Vera Cruz, Santa Cruz and Land of the Parrots. And became the Land of Brazil-wood.[28]

As the theory of a 'poetry for export', Brazil-wood suggests by its choice of metaphors that in 1924 Oswald identified with a specific economic, as well as cultural, project for the new Brazil. The notion of a shared community of interests over and above class differences, a feature of bourgeois nationalist conceptions of development, is reflected in the rather abstract, even deterministic character of the *Manifesto*. Markedly absent from the dialectic is the sense of an active human subject making the process happen or suffering its contradictions. The attempt to remedy this deficiency in the second version of his theory of Brazilian culture, the *Manifesto Antropófago* (Cannibalist Manifesto) (1928), was part and parcel of Oswald's continuing political radicalization during this period; he joined the Communist Party in the following year. Although still limited by his rather mechanical use of the dialectical method, the *Cannibalist Manifesto* is a more fully developed theory, one which unites the liberation of the individual with that of the national culture in a truly revolutionary project. However, in order to reach this point, Oswald had to bring to the centre of his thinking a theme which until now he had considered only in the most abstract of terms – the symbolism of Amazônia and the Indian.

Amazonian Utopias

It was Mário, though, who first turned to Amazônia as an alternative to the illusory progress of the Brazilian Republic when, in the second half of 'The poet eats peanuts', he uttered the poem's first statement of individual longing and anguish: 'I have a longing for disasters . . ./A longing for the Amazon and for the mosquito winds/Resting against the timber of the doorways . . ./I long for guitars and solitudes without meaning/I long to moan and to die.' The political and economic revolutions which supposedly confirmed the country's entry into the twentieth century had proved a bitter disappointment, for they had left Brazil's social and cultural contradictions intact. All that was left to Mário was a visceral destructive impulse, the desire for an apocalyptic explosion which might open up another world, where the impossible dilemmas of self and society would be melted into the solitude of unconscious being. As early as 1918, in an article entitled 'A divina preguiça' (Divine indolence), Mário had associated this vision of a liberated state of pure, uncomplicated being with the world of Amazônia. All his life he had cherished a frustrated desire to 'go and live far from civilization, on the bank of some little river in Amazônia, or on some seashore of the Brazilian North, amongst simple folk'.[29]

The 'Two Acrean poems' of *Clã do Jaboti* (Clan of the Tortoise) (1927) attempted an imaginary realization of that dream, bridging the chasm of geographical and social alienation in a meditative act of communion with his fellow Brazilian, the Amazonian rubbertapper. Sitting late at night at his desk in the city Mário makes the emotional discovery of his other self, asleep in the rainforest of Acre:

Não vê que me lembrei que lá no norte, meu Deus! muito longe de mim
Na escuridão ativa da noite que caiu
Um homem pálido magro de cabelo escorrendo nos olhos,
Depois de fazer uma pele com a borracha do dia,
Faz pouco se deitou, está dormindo

Êsse homem é brasileiro que nem eu.

(Don't you see, it just occurred to me that up north, my God! far far away from me/In the active darkness of the night which has fallen/A pale thin man with hair hanging down over his eyes,/After making a bale out of

91

the day's rubber,/Has not long gone to bed, and is sleeping.//That man is Brazilian just like me.)

In 'Acalanto do seringueiro' (Lullaby of the rubbertapper), he imagined himself watching over the sleeping rubbertapper, looking for the words of the lullaby which would protect his unconscious being. Yet, as the poem rocks itself towards its sleepy conclusion, it becomes clear that the lullaby is as much for Mário himself, the labouring intellectual oppressed by the 'despotismo de livros' (tyranny of books). He might search in the pages of those books for the smell, the feel, the sound of that forest which should belong to him, but it remained always hidden and inaccessible. Only through an imaginative leap could he lie down in friendship and communion with this stranger, his Amazonian self, and rediscover the freedom of absolute, uncomplicated being, the 'immense indifference' which would be his liberation:

> Essas coisas pra você
> Devem ser indiferentes,
> Duma indiferença enorme . . .
> Porém eu sou seu amigo
> E quero ver si consigo
> Não passar na sua vida
> Numa indiferença enorme.
> Meu desejo e pensamento
>   (. . . numa indiferença enorme . . .)
> Ronda sob as seringueiras
>   (. . . numa indiferença enorme . . .)
> Num amor-de-amigo enorme . . .

(To you these things/Must be indifferent,/Immensely indifferent. . ./Yet I am your friend/And I want to see whether I can't/Enter your life, that life/Of immense indifference./My desire and mind/(. . . immensely indifferent . . .)/Wanders beneath the rubber-trees/(. . . Immensely indifferent . . .)/In the immense love of a friend . . .)

Mário explores a similar idea in the 'Rito do irmão pequeno' (Little brother's ritual) (1931), except that, here, the self with which he attempts to commune is not a distant stranger, but a purely imaginary being born from within him, the explicit projection of his aspiration to wholeness. He imagines a life with his brother, spent hunting in the forest, or in silent contemplation of the harmonious unfolding of a natural world of which pain is no less an integral and necessary moment than happiness:

Chora, irmão pequeno, chora,
Cumpre a tua dôr, exerce o rito da agonia.
Porque cumprir a dôr é também cumprir o seu próprio destino:
É chegar àquela coincidência vegetal
Em que as árvores fazem a tempestade berrar,
Como elementos da criação, exatamente.

(Weep, little brother, weep,/Realize your pain, exercise the rite of agony./
Because to realize pain is also to realize your own destiny:/It is to reach
that vegetable coincidence/In which the trees make the storm cry out,/
Like elements of creation, exactly.)

The invitation to 'Exercer a preguiça, com vagar' (Exercise indolence,
leisurely), in the context of the corporativist dictatorship of Vargas,
with its ideology of the Family, Nation and Work, assumed a particular
significance: the repudiation of a social order in which all human
activity had been reduced to alienated labour. There is a clear link
between this theme, the figure of the work-shy *malandro* or 'spiv' of
samba mythology that was evolving during the same period,[30] and
Mário's best-known fictional creation, 'the characterless hero' Macu-
naíma; Macunaíma brings with him into the city a tribal culture to
which the notion of routine wage-labour is quite alien; his repudiation
of that social order is expressed in his familiar refrain: 'Macunaíma
ficou muito contrariado. Ter de trabucar, ele, herói . . . Murmurou
desolado:/ – Ai! que preguiça!. . .'[31] (Macunaíma was very put out. To
have to toil and sweat, him, the hero . . . He mumbled inconsolately:/ –
Aah! how lazy I feel!. . .) But if Macunaíma's magical capacity for self-
transformation, like the *malandro's* agile manoeuvres in the urban
underworld of gambling and crime, might provide a momentary
escape from the alienating routine of capitalist labour, it was ultimately
incapable of reconstructing the lost harmony, 'that vegetable coinci-
dence', which Mário was seeking in the 'Little brother's ritual'. Macu-
naíma is corrupted and eventually destroyed, both physically and
morally, by his encounter with modern civilization, only to be spurned
when he takes up his place as a constellation in the night's sky. In the
samba compositions of the 1930s, meanwhile, the *malandro* is brought
to order and appears as an increasingly reformed character seeking
respectable employment.[32] Whereas the reactionary 'Modernists' of
Verdeamarelismo (Greenyellowism) and the Anta (Tapir) movement
were attempting to turn the clock back with their mystical revival of
Romantic Indianist nationalism and its nostalgia for the pre-industrial
age, Mário remained honestly aware of how fragile and perhaps
unattainable his 'culture of indolence' was.

The most sustained, ambitious composition dedicated to the quest for an Amazonian utopia was Raúl Bopp's *Cobra Norato* (Honorato the Snake) (1931), whose thirty-three sections begin and end with an appeal to a kind of never-never land, the 'terra do Sem-fim'. The poem is a fertile, if ultimately unsatisfactory attempt to take over a traditional, semi-indigenous legend – the epic journey of the good snake, Norato, to recover the 'filha da rainha Luzia' (Queen Luzia's daughter) from the clutches of the evil Cobra Grande – and to weld it to another narrative structure, the course of the Amazon river from its upper reaches in the densest region of the forest to its Atlantic estuary, where it meets the tidal wave of the *pororoca*.

Bopp believed in the industrial potential of Amazônia and in the need for its rational exploitation; yet *Honorato the Snake* suggests that the radically different nature of that world, its very freedom from the artificial structures of civilization, will make such a task difficult, if not impossible. Much of the poem reveals a rebellious, chaotically animate order, one which, like Macunaíma's 'primitive' mentality, permanently frustrates any rational effort to create organized forms. Although the two narratives appear to move in the same direction, everywhere the hero's quest is obstructed by the consciously conspiratorial action of the forest. Having entered the snake Honorato's skin, the human protagonist is initiated into a new, intuitive perception of the forest, into whose seductive, liquid oblivion he is in danger of being swallowed up. In a mocking parody of the language of organization and construction, the young trees receive lessons in geometry and geography; yet they learn nothing, and the classroom scene serves rather to enforce the river's tyranny of chaos over the forest and to obscure the hero's path:

> Vocês estão condenadas a trabalhar sempre sempre
> Têm a obrigação de fazer folhas para cobrir a floresta
> Ai ai! Nós somos escravas do rio
>
> – Vocês têm que afogar o homem na sombra
> A floresta é inimiga do homem
> – Ai ai! Nós somos escravas do rio[33]

(You are condemned to work for ever and ever/Your duty is to make leaves to cover the forest/Oh Oh! We are slaves of the river//You must drown man in shadow//The forest is man's enemy/ – Oh oh! We are slaves of the river)

Further on, the sounds of hammering and sawing are heard, but this illusory echo of construction in the forest is belied as its percussive plosives are dissolved by nasal vowels and liquid consonants, and everything sinks back into the formless swamp. The prohibitive shout 'Não pode!' (You can't!) seems not only directed against Norato's journey but also against the attempt to establish order from the chaos:

> Ouvem-se apitos um bate-que-bate
> Estão soldando serrando serrando
> Parece que fabricam terra . . .
> Ué! Estão mesmo fabricando terra
>
> Chiam longos tanques de lodo-pacoema
> Os velhos andaimes podres se derretem
> Lameiros se emendam
> Mato amontoado derrame-se no chão
>
> Correm vozes em desordem
> Berram: *Não pode!*
> – Será comigo?

(There's a sound of whistling a knock-knocking/They're soldering sawing sawing/They seem to be making earth . . ./Wow! They *are* making earth//Long pools of pacoema-mud squeal/The rotten old scaffolding melts/Sludge-pools come together/Piles of forest pour on to the ground// Voices run wildly about/They shriek: *You can't!!* – Do they mean me?)

As the river approaches its own destination, meanwhile, there is an atmosphere of bloated satiety and suffocated, agonized pregnancy, as if its desire to unburden itself or to produce something were being blocked. Only the apocalyptic force of the *pororoca* can bring relief, not by easing the river's exit into the sea, but by thrusting it back upon itself in a violent embrace, restoring to its origins the land that has been swept away, and beginning a different order of reconstruction:

> Voltam lentamente rio acima
> comboios de matupás pra construção de novas ilhas
> numa engenharia silenciosa

(Convoys of natural rafts float/Slowly back upstream to build new islands/with the silent work of engineers)

Honorato the Snake was one of the few substantial texts that can be said truly to have emerged out of the Movimento Antropofágico (Cannibalist Movement), which was launched with the publication of the *Cannibalist Manifesto* in the movement's journal in May 1928. Interestingly, Mário de Andrade distanced himself from the movement and was even denounced in the pages of the *Revista* for his academicism and Catholic beliefs. Yet the Cannibalists hailed his book *Macunaíma* as a masterpiece, as the total realization of the objectives set out in the *Cannibalist Manifesto*. Since it was the *Manifesto* that offered the most coherent and explicitly theoretical interpretation of an Amazonian, Indian utopia, it is worth briefly considering how it compares with Mário de Andrade and Raúl Bopp's own treatment of the subject.

Anthropophagy

For all the anecdotal explanations of the movement's birth (such as Tarsila do Amaral's painting 'Aba-poru' – 'The Cannibal'),[34] it seems most likely that Anthropophagy was a conscious attempt by Oswald to develop and radicalize the ideas of the *Brazil-wood Poetry Manifesto*. These had been under attack since at least 1926 from the Greenyellow-ism group, which defended an extreme right-wing brand of Indianist nationalism, taking its name from the colours of the Brazilian flag. During the five years since the Week of Modern Art, and in the three since the *Brazil-wood Poetry Manifesto*, a number of other magazines had appeared (for example, *Klaxon*, *Revista do Brasil* and *Terra Roxa e Outras Terras*), but no new movement or theory of ideological clarity or originality. Greenyellowism (later Anta – 'Tapir') was able temporarily to appropriate the nativist rhetoric of Brazil-wood, proposing an alternative form of radical nationalism which repudiated altogether the influence of the European avant gardes, and based itself on a horribly distorted rewriting of colonial history, celebrating the physical annihilation and assimilation of the *tupi* tribes as the necessary foundation of the Brazilian people's subjective, mystical sense of integral racial and national identity. Central to this mythology were the *bandeiras*, the seventeenth-century pioneering and slaving expeditions led by hardened *mamelucos* or *mestiços* of Portuguese and Indian origin. Pursuing the atavistic call of their ancestral Indian blood to push back the country's frontiers in the legendary Far West, these *bandeirantes* symbolized, like the pathbreaking Tapir, the spirit of a *paulista* neocolonialism uniting the Brazilian people in the realization of its cosmic destiny. Cassiano Ricardo (1895–1974), the most success-ful poet of the movement, first applied these ideas in his *Borrões de Verde e Amarelo* (Sketches in Green and Yellow) (1926), but he is better known for *Martim Cererê* (1928), excerpts of which were broadcast on local radio stations during the 1932 Constitutional Revolution, an unsuccessful challenge on the part of the São Paulo landowning and middle classes to the new forces represented by Vargas. In this 'myth of the Brazil-child', the exploits of the 'race of Giants' serve to legiti-mize retrospectively the oppressive history of Conquest and slavery, which is incorporated into an account of the *paulista* ruling class's rise to power:

> todos três
> e todos de uma só vez,
> calçaram Botas Sete-Léguas
> e entre a voz que chamava (a magia)
> e outra voz que mandava (a ambição)
> e uma outra que não discutia (a obediência)
>
> todos três,
> de mãos dadas
> . . .
> bateram à porta do Sertão antropófago num tropel formidável:
> 'Nós queremos entrar!'
> Era uma vez . . .[35]

(all three of them/and all at once/put on Seven-League Boots/and between the voice that called (magic)/and another that commanded (ambition)/and another that did not argue (obedience)//all three/hand in hand/. . ./knocked at the gate of the man-eating Hinterland in a formidable throng:/'We want to come in!'/Once upon a time . . .)

In 1936 Ricardo entered the political sphere, founding an anti-communist movement under the name *Bandeira*, only to find it dissolved by Vargas's Estado Novo. Plínio Salgado (1895–1975), meanwhile, the leading ideologue of the Greenyellowist group, went on to organize Brazil's fascist organization, Ação Integralista Brasileira. Brazilian Modernism had thus by now become clearly polarized along ideological lines, and it was now up to Oswald, as leader of the cultural left wing, to re-establish its hegemony within the nationalist debate by challenging the crudely irrational chauvinism of the right.

The *Brazil-wood Poetry Manifesto* had taken as its symbol of the dialectical relationship between European civilization and the indigenous American world a commercial commodity. The central metaphor of the new *Manifesto* was a ritual commonly attributed to tribal cultures: cannibalism. However, Oswald's interpretation of the phenomenon broke completely with traditional assumptions, which saw it most often as evidence of barbarism, or exceptionally as an expression of social integration. What made the *Manifesto* genuinely subversive and revolutionary was its suggestion that, far from deriving exclusively from an alien culture light-years distant from the cultural codes of modern Western society, cannibalism was in fact the fundamental motor of human behaviour in Brazilian and Western civilization as a whole. The *Manifesto* begins:

Only anthropophagy unites us. Socially. Economically. Philosophically.

The only law of the world. The masked expression of all individua-
lisms, of all collectivisms. Of all religions. Of all peace treaties.

The central principle of this universal law is that 'Só me interessa o que
não é meu' (I am only interested in what is not mine), which is later
explained in the following terms:

Anthropophagy. The permanent transformation of the Taboo into a
totem . . . The struggle between what might be called the Uncreated and
the Creature . . . Absorption of the sacred enemy. To transform him into
a totem.

As the terminology suggests, there was some dependence on the
conceptual framework provided by Freud's *Totem and Taboo*; the primal
violation of the taboo, a prohibition invested with irrational magical
power, was the act of murder and cannibalism committed against a
violent, jealous father by his horde of sons, whom he had driven away
from the females of the tribe. The totem meal was thus both a
commemoration of this deed, and the act through which the sons
identified with their feared model and incorporated a portion of his
strength. On a more philosophical level, the act of cannibalism symbo-
lized an urge to dissolve the barriers between the self and the world,
between subject and object, a proposition which appears in a number
of forms throughout the *Manifesto*:

What got in the way of the truth was clothes, the impermeable layer
between the internal world and the external world . . .

The spirit refuses to conceive of the spirit without the body. . . . From
the equation *self* part of the *Cosmos* to the axiom Cosmos *part of the self*.

The theory of Anthropophagy then invested this metaphor with a
more specific cultural and political substance. Alongside the universal,
psychological prohibitions and repressions which could be collecti-
vely described as the 'reality principle' or the *id* were the cultural
taboos, the sacred institutions and texts of the European and Brazilian
heritage, the hallowed figures of a colonial and imperial history
written by its victors – 'Father Vieira; the Law; the Conservatoires;
Goethe; the mother of the Gracchi, and the Court of King John VI;
histories of mankind which begin in Cape Finisterre; Anchieta singing
the praises of the eleven thousand virgins of heaven, in the land of
Iracema – the patriarch João Ramalho, founder of São Paulo'.

If these taboos were repudiated in the *Manifesto* by the word
'Contra', a different set of values deriving from Brazil's indigenous

98

culture and its instinctive unity of individual and world, were celebrated:

> It was because we have never had grammars, nor collections of old plants. And we've never known what was urban, suburban, frontier, and continental. Lazy in the mapa-mundi of Brazil.
>
> A participating consciousness, religious rhythmics. . . . The Caraiba instinct. . . .
>
> . . . In communication with the soil.
>
> . . . the reality without complexes, without madness, without prostitutions and without penitenciaries of the matriarchy of Pindorama.

This last phrase, the 'matriarchy of Pindorama' embodies the cultural ideal towards which the dialectical process of Anthropophagy was leading. Pindorama was a Tupi-Guarani name for Brazil, while the notion of an indigenous matriarchy, explored at greater length in Oswald's later philosophical works, was taken from J.J. Bachofen's *Myth, Religion and Mother Right*. At this stage, it represented essentially the idea of a society free from the repressive features of the male-dominated regime which provoked Freud's primal crime of patricide. As well as the ideal of harmony between individual and nature, it assumes a dynamic world of action, participation and experience, as opposed to the reigning order of stasis, routine, abstraction and conservatism:

> Down with the reversible world and objectified ideas. Cadaverized. The *stop* of thought which is dynamic. . . .
>
> The undated world. Unlabelled. . . .
>
> Migrations. Flight from tedious states. Down with urban scleroses.
> . . .
> We are concretists. Ideas take charge, react, burn people in the public squares. Let us suppress ideas and other paralyses. In favour of itineraries. Believe in signs, believe in instruments and in the stars.

Matriarchy signified for Oswald a culture of ideal psychological, social and economic liberation: 'without complexes, without madness, without prostitutions and without penitentiaries. We already had communism. We already had the surrealist language. We had the relations and distribution of physical wealth, moral wealth, dignitary wealth.'

The conflict between the existing reality of taboos and the matriarchy of Pindorama, or between the academic, European, ruling-class culture of the colonizer, and the primitive, indigenous, popular culture of the *mestiço* masses, forms the central dialectical struggle of the *Cannibalist Manifesto*, a combination of class, ethnic, cultural and imperialist struggles. The synthesis which must ultimately emerge could only be achieved by 'a Revolução Caraíba', a revolution at all levels, comparable to the other great political and cultural upheavals of history: 'From the French Revolution to Romanticism, to the Bolshevik Revolution, to the Surrealist Revolution and to Keyserling's technicized barbarian'. It was also a nationalist revolution, articulating an as yet undeclared independent consciousness: 'We need to expel the Bragantine spirit, the ordinations and Maria da Fonte snuff.' But the 'Revolução Caraíba' was not a simple assertion of indigenous, primitive values and a total repudiation of European culture. Instead, Anthropophagy called for a genuine synthesis, whose key was a concept already foreshadowed in the *Brazil-wood Manifesto*: 'Only Brazilians of our time. What is necessary from chemistry, mechanics and ballistics. All digested.' The assimilation of the oppressive alien culture and its recreation in an autonomous form was to be achieved by a critical act of 'devouring', consuming and totemizing the taboo.

The 'anthropophagous' instinct had manifested itself repeatedly throughout Brazil's history by inverting or subverting the surface relationship between colony and colonizer, digesting imported values and reconstructing, or regurgitating them in a more idiosyncratic form. One example was *macumba* or *candomblé*, the syncretic Afro-Brazilian religions fusing the tribal *orixás* with the Catholic saints – 'We were never catechized. . . . We gave birth to Christ in Bahia.' Similarly, the heroes of Romantic Indianism – 'The Indian son of Mary, adopted son of Catherine of Medici and son-in-law of Dom Antonio de Mariz' – were unmistakably the creations of an academic, ruling-class civilization, yet they had not escaped the subversive influence of popular culture, as the samba parades and lyrics of Carnival frequently bear out. In this revision of traditional colonial history, then, the European was no longer a conqueror, but the unwitting victim of a process of cultural cannibalism: 'But it wasn't crusades that came. They were fugitives from a civilization that we are eating, because we are strong and vengeful like the Jabuti tortoise.'

A further 'victim' of this process was the very phenomenon which, for someone like Mário de Andrade, was so alien to Brazilian culture and so difficult to come to terms with – capitalist technology. Yet for Oswald, the technological age actually represented a return to the instinctive relationship between individual and world which had been lost during the generations of erudite, academic culture: 'The fixing of progress by means of catalogues and television sets. Only machinery.

And blood transfusions.' Through its fusion of man and machine, Anthropophagy would be able to participate in the last of the great revolutions, that of the 'bárbaro tecnizado' (primitive man made technical), by rediscovering humanity's primitive urge for power and freedom within the dynamic potential of inventions such as the motorcar.

After fifteen years of militant activism in the Communist Party following the collapse of the Cannibalist movement in 1929, Oswald returned to his theory and continued until the end of his life to revise the terms of the cultural dialectic in the light of the disillusioning political experiences of the period: the Stalinist distortion of Marxism, the Brazilian Communist Party's support for Vargas at the end of the war, and the aftermath of the war itself. That he could do so, substituting for his 'Revolução Caraíba' the capitalist technocracy of Burnham's *Managerial Revolution*, is revealing of the difference separating him from Mário de Andrade.[36] Oswald's utopian conception of the dialectical process is just that, the manipulation of an abstract analytical framework without any rigorous reference to a social and historical practice which might give it living validity. Ironically, this descent into pure abstraction led him eventually to announce the imminent arrival of the very 'culture of indolence' which Mário had constructed in the imaginary space of the 'Little brother's ritual'. Few would now consider Oswald's optimism to have been vindicated by the development of post-war capitalism, either in Brazil or outside, and Mário would hardly have been surprised. His own *Macunaíma* dared to confront the potentially destructive threat which modernization posed to the survival of Brazil's fragile, 'primitive' cultures. The transformation of the world, whether in the historic revolutionary upheavals of mass movements, or in the daily individual struggle with words and matter, is the work of a conscious human agency which may be inspired by a common dream, but is neither infallible nor certain of success.

From the Mouths of the People

It must be significant that the best-loved poetic version of utopia from the 1920s is Manuel Bandeira's 'Vou-me embora pra Pasárgada' (I'm going away to Pasárgada); for Bandeira's 'other civilization', while it has an exotic name and playfully promises the poet royal connections, makes no outrageously extravagant claims. Its 'inconsequential adventure', by which Juana La Loca of Spain comes to be the distant relative of a non-existent daughter-in-law, seems to mock any serious excursion into the fantastic. Rather, his utopian dream asks for little more (but how much that is!) than to enjoy the simple pleasures of the normal, healthy child that he never was, to have the certainty that the technology and commodities of this alienated, commercialized society will actually work, and to continue believing in the dream itself, so that life can at least remain bearable:

> Em Pasárgada tem tudo
> É outra civilização
> Tem um processo seguro
> De impedir a concepção
> Tem telefone automático
> Tem alcalóide à vontade
> Tem prostitutas bonitas
> Para a gente namorar
>
> E quando eu estiver mais triste
> Mas triste de não ter jeito
> Quando de noite me der
> Vontade de me matar
>
> – Lá sou amigo do rei –
> Terei a mulher que eu quero
> Na cama que escolherei
> Vou-me embora pra Pasárgada.

(There's everything in Pasárgada/It's a different civilization/There's a sure way of avoiding conception/There's an automatic telephone/All the alkaloid you want/There are pretty prostitutes/For you to make love to// And when I am sadder still/So sad there's nothing for it/When at night I feel/Like killing myself// – There I am friends with the king –/I'll have the woman of my desires/In the bed of my choosing/I'm going away to Pasárgada.)

Bandeira has been described as 'o poeta do humilde cotidiano' (the poet of the humble day-to-day),[37] and the description nicely defines the quality in his poetry which distinguishes it from that of Oswald de Andrade. A genuine physical and material poverty (Bandeira suffered all his life from tuberculosis and, with the death of his father in 1920, saw the disintegration of his family and his own exile from his native Northeast) brought him into direct contact with the poor of the Rio backstreets. Drawing on this experience, the modest, unpretentious fantasy of 'I'm going away to Pasárgada' offers a human warmth and subjective intimacy that are missing from the ironic detachment of the Brazil-wood poetry and its defence of Brazil's previously despised popular cultures.

In some of the earlier poems of *O ritmo dissoluto* (The dissolute rhythm) (1925), marking Bandeira's transition from the decadent Symbolism of *Carnaval* to the fully Modernist *Libertinagem* (Libertinage), this identification with the people verges on the sentimental: 'Meninos carvoeiros' (Coal-boys), for instance, with its pathetically picturesque impression of child-labour and poverty. 'Na Rua do Sabão' (In Soap Street) is more convincing, uniting as it does the irony of a humble paper balloon with an image of transcendence and liberation. Painfully assembled by the laundrywoman's tubercular son (recalling a young Bandeira), the balloon rises into the air as if inflated with his sickly breath and, in quiet dignity, defies the shouts, missiles and municipal regulations which try to forbid its flight into freedom. In *Libertinage* itself, the charge of irony is heavier and the emotional impact therefore often more acute. 'Pneumotórax' (Pneumothorax) is one of many poems which deal directly with the problem of illness; in this instance, the insoluble case of the patient's perforated lung represents a whole life of unfulfilment, for which the doctor's apparently facetious remedy offers the only possible consolation:

Febre, hemoptise, dispnéia e suores noturnos.
A vida inteira que podia ter sido e não foi.
Tosse, tosse, tosse.

Mandou chamar o médico:
– Diga trinta e três.
– Trinta e três . . . trinta e três . . . trinta e três . . .
– Respire.
. . . .

– O senhor tem uma escavação no pulmão esquerdo e o pulmão direito
  infiltrado.
– Então, doutor, não é possível tentar o pneumotórax?
– Não. A única coisa a fazer é tocar um tango argentino.

(Fever, haemoptysis, dyspnea and nocturnal sweating./A whole life that could have been and was not./Cough, cough, cough.//He called for the doctor:/ – Say thirty-three/ – Thirty three . . . thirty-three . . . thirty-three . . ./Breathe in.// – You have a cavity in your left lung and your right lung is perforated./ – So, doctor, isn't it possible to try the pneumothorax?/ – No. The only thing to do is play an Argentinian tango.)

Bandeira's poetry illustrates how the Modernists' preoccupation with popular, everyday experience led them to break with the rigid linguistic and formal conventions of traditional poetry in order to accommodate the rhythms and idiosyncrasies of colloquial speech. As Bandeira put it in his 'Evocation of Recife', 'Life didn't reach me via newspapers or books/It came in the mouths of the people, in the

incorrect language of the people/The right language of the people/
Because they are the ones who speak the delicious Portuguese of
Brazil.' This intimate relationship between language and experience is
vividly captured in the image which opens the last two stanzas of
Mário de Andrade's 'The poet eats peanuts' – a Brazilian language
emerging from between the poet's teeth and on to his lips like the
moist, crushed fragments of peanut. Form and expression, language
and experience are not divorced from each other, nor is poetry a battle
on the part of the first to impose its order on the second. In Mário's
conception of poetry, the function of art is to facilitate the articulation
of the unformed subconscious inspiration:

> I believe that lyricism, born in the subconscious, . . . creates phrases
> which are complete lines of poetry, free from the damage caused by
> measuring so many syllables, with a given stress. . . .
>   Inspiration is fleeting, violent. Any impediment will disturb and even
> silence it. Art, which, added to Lyricism, produces poetry, does not
> consist of prejudicing the mad dash of the lyrical state in order to warn it
> of the stones and barbed-wire fences along the way.[38]

There is no better declaration of such principles in verse-form than
Manuel Bandeira's 'Poética' (Poetics). The poem's uninhibited metri-
cal freedom constitutes in its own right a repudiation of the formal and
thematic conventions which the Parnassianists had worked with.
After denouncing the well-behaved, pedantic, 'civil-servant' brand of
lyricism, Bandeira opens up his poetry to the wealth of real linguistic
practice which has until now been excluded from literary language
because of its 'incorrectness':

> Todas as palavras sobretudo os barbarismos universais
>
> Todas as construções sobretudo as sintaxes de exceção
>
> Todos os ritmos sobretudo os inumeráveis
>
> Estou farto do lirismo namorador
> Político
> Raquítico
> Sifilítico
> De todo lirismo que capitula ao que quer que seja fora de si mesmo
>
> (All words especially universal barbarisms//All constructions especially
> syntaxes that are the exception to the rule//All rhythms especially
> uncountable ones//I'm sick of lovemaking/Political/Rickety/Syphilitic
> lyricism/Of all lyricism that surrenders to whatever is outside itself.)

But as Drummond was not afraid to show, that task is by no means easy or unproblematic for the poet. In his 'Seven-sided poem' he despaired of coming to a coherent, meaningful understanding of himself; instead, he left the reader with seven disjointed perspectives, whose only common denominator was a sense of ironic withdrawal from the world.

Similarly, in 'Explicação' (Explanation) the poet defiantly challenged the notion of a public poetry, obliged to be communicative and comprehensible to the reader; his verse is rather a form of consolation, like his glass of rum, and its occasioal somersaults are for private view only: 'Se meu verso não deu certo, foi seu ouvido que entortou./Eu não disse ao senhor que não sou senão poeta?' (If my poem didn't turn out right, it was your ears that screwed it up./Didn't I tell you I'm just a poet?) The most controversial challenge to conventional public expectations of the function of poetry was, however, 'No meio do caminho' (In the middle of the road), which was labelled the representative Modernist poem after its publication in 1928 and as such became the target of academic and media ridicule. The text's obsessive statement – the stone which refuses to be anything but a stone – suggests several possible readings, all of which point in the direction of an artistic and philosophical scepticism. The artist's commitment to realism threatens to transform him into a mere empty reflection of reality, to reduce his subjective perception of the world to a mechanical, physiological process, and the poem itself to a purely objective and therefore meaningless statement. Whatever our interpretation, we should be clear that the aggressive irony with which Drummond confronts his readers is not the facetious smile of some puerile 'joke-poem' intended merely to 'épater le bourgeois'. Far more seriously than that, it cuts to the heart of the fundamental problems in culture and art that Brazilian Modernism had raised:

No meio do caminho tinha uma pedra
tinha uma pedra no meio do caminho
tinha uma pedra
no meio do caminho tinha uma pedra

Nunca me esquecerei desse acontecimento
na vida de minhas retinas tão fatigadas.
Nunca me esquecerei que no meio do caminho
tinha uma pedra
tinha uma pedra no meio do caminho
no meio do caminho tinha uma pedra.

(In the middle of the road there was a stone/there was a stone in the middle of the road/there was a stone/in the middle of the road there was

105

a stone.//I shall never forget that event/in the life of my tired, tired retinas./I shall never forget that in the middle of the road/there was a stone/there was a stone in the middle of the road/in the middle of the road there was a stone.)

Drummond voiced the uncertainty of someone who, in the words of 'I was a Brazilian once, too', had 'lost his rhythm' and his confidence in the expressive power of language. The closing lines of Mário's 'The poet eats peanuts' offered an alternative to that despair: a poetry which, by identifying in one's subjective experience something of the complex life of the community, would create a calm space of understanding and communication within the maelstrom of modernization. Mário's Brazil is the 'rhythm of my adventurous arm', 'the swaying of my songs loves and dances', 'the way I earn my living, the way I eat and sleep'. Meaning and identity could be forged through the recognition of a common set of experiences, a 'way of life' whose rhythm was simultaneously that of popular music, dance and speech.

Mário's peanut-eating poet thus spoke of the struggle of a whole intellectual generation to come to terms with the complex experience of capitalist modernization in a still predominantly pre-industrial society. Even Oswald de Andrade's highly intellectualized theoretical constructions were informed with the same sense of spontaneous bewilderment with which that generation responded to the novelty of a Brazil whose racial, social and cultural identity was torn between tradition and change. Modernism did indeed seek consciously to break the stifling formal and linguistic chains in which the belle époque had enslaved the expression of both subjective and objective experience. That struggle was only intelligible in the context of the poets' visceral identification, as a dislocated, marginalized group, with the rural and urban masses who were now being forced to engage in a struggle of their own, and whose experience had until now remained largely invisible in the country's literature. However, if this decade of flux and uncertainty gave room for a variety of responses, from sceptical disillusionment to optimistic, even revolutionary expectation, the political and economic crisis of the late 1920s demanded a clearer, more urgent understanding of the particularly oppressive form which modernity looked set to take in Brazil, and of the role which the artist should and could assume.

4

Awakenings:
The Slow Return to the Real

The Poet and Politics

If the rejection of the world, the creation of an autonomous alternative in art, is the hallmark of Modernismo, it is a feature of the avant garde too. Perhaps a redefinition of avant garde is required, so that the artificial line drawn under Modernismo can be replaced by a less formalistic distinction between poetic movements. Withdrawal and rejection, the absolute priority of the text as defined by Formalism, are certainly characteristic of sections of an avant garde defined by the radicalism of its formal and linguistic experimentation. Confusingly, that experimentation is sometimes described as revolutionary, insofar as it overturned existing formal precepts and practices in art. Yet such revolutionary practices could have their origin in deeply conservative visions of the world, in nostalgia for a lost order (however reactionary that order may have been), in a defence of ageing universals against their detractors. If there is a definition of Modernism that can be sustained, it will rest on the disengagement of language from its social origin, the pursuit of the autonomy of the sign, the word. All art would thus be self-referential, enclosed within its own sign-system; and poetry would be 'the self-consciousness of language' in Jakobson's classic formulation.[1] In a sense his formula is also the most radical expression of what distinguishes the Modernist rejection of any relationship between art and social experience from the radical avant garde that followed it. Just as the Formalists were obliged to respond to the revolutionary demands of the Futurists, so the 'vanguardia' was divided in Latin America between those whose response to the post-war ideological crisis was the *conservation* at the level of ideas of the

107

universal truths that lay in the ideological rubble of the post-war world, and those who saw their work as a contribution to the transformation of the world. Raymond Williams defined it thus:

> The avant garde, aggressive from the beginning, saw itself as the breakthrough to the future: its members were not the bearers of a progress already repetitiously defined, but the militants of a creativity which would revive and liberate humanity.[2]

The limitations of the real were the starting point for all the artistic radicals; and they shared a vision of the alternative – creativity (in the Romantic sense of an activity outside production, outside the market), enshrined at that stage in a very few, singular writers.[3] Equally, as Williams underlined, there was a general hostility to tradition, to the continuity of values and structures which had inhibited that creativity, to the tyranny of a unilinear vision of history which had veiled the multiple and contradictory nature of reality – the very optimism so brutally exposed in the 1914–18 war. In Latin America, there was an additional dimension, insofar as that continuity of values and structures was one in which Latin America appeared as the *object* of a history whose subject was the metropolis. Yet the implications were not always radical or emancipatory in content. We have seen how Modernismo turned *back* towards an aristocracy of the spirit, claiming a place at the European banquet and access to metropolitan culture. In a curious atavism, it was Latin American intellectuals who became the stoutest defenders of a cultural and symbolic universe whose organic functionaries had themselves grown disillusioned and become disenfranchised from it.

This atavistic conservatism was entirely compatible with a radical form, insofar as it expressed a rejection, a defamiliarization of the then prevailing bourgeois culture of the kind denounced by Darío in the preface to his *Prosas Profanas*. The hostility to the narrow materialism of a burgeoning bourgeoisie gained a particularly contemptuous edge in Latin America, whose middle class was weak and vacillating, subservient to a scornful metropolitan bourgeoisie. Culturally that subservience was confirmed in the prevailing tastes and preferences of the early twenties. Yet they were now contested by powerful nationalist movements inspired by the Mexican Revolution of 1910–17, by the October Revolution in Russia, and by the crisis in Europe. The old imperialisms were struggling and the new power in the region, the United States, was still seeking to establish its dominion. As the decade ended, and the bubble burst in the Great Crash of 1929, the implications of colonial dominance became brutally clear. The Latin

American economies, tied to the northern power by their integration into the latter's economy – producing raw materials for the factories of the industrialized countries and purchasing in return consumer goods for luxury consumption – were now unceremoniously abandoned. The severance of the arteries of supply left them with no other markets for their products and no alternative economic activity into which to direct them. Crisis was rapid and dramatic. The protest and rage at colonial exploitation fuelled and reinforced the nationalist response, and a new vocabulary of nationalist reference emerged from the movements. In much of Latin America the symbolic universe of this thrust towards the creation of independent nation-states crystallized around the figure of the Indian.[4]

Further, the beginnings of industrialization and the integration of the Latin American economies into the world market set in motion a process of proletarianization on the land and in the city equally. The October Revolution provided a focus of identity for the emerging proletariat, as the Latin American Communist parties were progress-ively established through the twenty republics in association with a growing trade-union movement.[5]

The range of Modernist expression mounted a challenge to the dominant colonial culture; yet it took profoundly different forms. Several began with an ostensible anti-bourgeois position, scornful of the subaltern bourgeoisie of Latin America so abjectly dependent on its European masters and so incapable of evolving its own self-expression in the face of the cultural crisis of the twenties. Bitterly critical of the cultural conservatives, they also turned their fire against an alienating tradition. Yet even within this common response there were alternative directions. Against the overpowering determinations of Western history they counterposed the spontaneity of the evanes-cent moment, spurning continuity, tradition, progress for the celeb-ration of the here and now. In this sense the hedonism of Gutiérrez Nájera[6] was more truly in tune with the imitators of Dada and the celebrants of Carnival in Latin America than many of his more imme-diate contemporaries.

For some poets of the avant garde, the rejection of rationality in language did not indicate cultural catastrophe, but led them to a poetry of form and sound – a 'pure poetry' as one of them, the Cuban Mariano Brull (1891–1956), described it. While his earliest poetry was perhaps closest to the personal and intimate writing of Mistral or Prado, Brull took his place among Latin American poets with his soundscapes and poems whose logic was that of visual or acoustic association progressively dissociated from meaning. In this sense his affinities may have been with the early poets of *negritud*.[7]

> Por el verde, verde
> verdería de mar verde
> Rr con Rr

(Through the green, the green/greenness of green sea/Gg and Gg)

The explanation for the poem's title, 'Verde halago' (Green solace), is in its final couplet: 'Vengo del Mundodolido/y en verdehalago estoy.' (I come from Hurtworld/Now I'm in Greensolace). What is this 'halago'? The solace of language itself, or the search for its perfection as form?

> En hora rosa se detiene el cielo
> para vivir su eternidad más lenta,
> y una orilla de frescores defiende
> el hueco, sin contornos, de la rosa.

(The sky pauses at a pink time/to live out its slowest eternity,/and a bank of freshness is defended/by the emptiness, without shape, of the rose)

The rejection of the bourgeois order took many forms. Each new manifestation gave itself name and title with arbitrary ease, and formed its own short-lived literary magazines; each of them offered a global redefinition of the role of culture and as often as not disappeared, with all their world-historical assertions, before the ink was dry. Indeed the plethora of little magazines was a concrete manifestation of the multiplicity of world-views and the absence of any authoritative centre which the avant garde might generally assert to be the core of their assault upon bourgeois truth.

Buenos Aires and the Avant Garde

The first twenty years of the century produced a rich crop of avant-garde writers, declarations, programmes and manifestos in Buenos Aires in particular. This was, at its heart, a paradoxical development. The enormous expansion of the Argentine economy after 1880 was experienced and manifest in Buenos Aires above all. Since economic growth was fundamentally externally led – it took place primarily in agriculture and produced for an external market – Buenos Aires was both the point of export and the seat of the financial and administrative centres of the new burgeoning meat and agricultural industries. The growth of the bourgeoisie that resulted did not produce a class increasingly in opposition to the old landed oligarchy whose victories in the period of the Independence wars had ensured its power through most of the nineteenth century. On the contrary, the economic boom took place in the context of a fundamentally unaltered distribution of land ownership. Nonetheless, manufacturing grew from 22,000 establishments in 1895 to nearly 49,000 in 1914, employing over 400,000 workers. More than half of them worked in Buenos Aires, and more than 35 per cent of industry was located within the city. Further, more than a third of the national population were of recent European origin, and the bulk of them – despite the intention to create a rural middle class through immigration – had remained in the city of Buenos Aires.[8]

This expanding and prosperous economy had not undergone any major social upheavals in the course of its rapid thirty-year growth. There had been no revolution because there had been no fundamental social transformation; but there were major changes and these provoked conflicts and tensions. The growth of the working class produced an increasing trade-union membership, many of whom brought with them political traditions from Europe, fundamentally of a syndicalist kind. The result was a growing number of strikes, particularly after 1914. The working class thus made a definitive entry into the political sphere, though its political leadership came still from a patrician Socialist Party under Justo. The chief political influence within the trade unions – the anarchists – spurned political organization. Thus the burgeoning demands for social reform coming from the growing middle class found expression in the Radical Party, which was able to extend its influence among workers as the electoral voice of reform. The Saenz Peña Law of 1908, extending the franchise, was a significant recognition of the demands of the immigrant populations and of the workers; but it was insufficient to stem an approaching social crisis. When the Radicals did come to power under Yrigoyen in 1916, the pressure from below for reform, and the expectations invested in Yrigoyen himself, go far to explain the limited nature of his reforms as he faced that rising movement with trepidation.

The Russian Revolution of 1917 provided a political focus for the radicalization of working-class politics, and a clearer enemy for the increasingly nervous Radical Party. For this new force was urban and organized, and increasingly literate. The Cordoba University Reform Movement generated a new layer of radical intellectuals, nationalist and communist, who contested the leadership of this working-class movement through the twenties.[9]

The election of Yrigoyen served not to solve but to highlight a

111

central contradiction of Argentine development – that it took place in collaboration with both the old landed oligarchy and colonial capital. There was no independent project for a growing middle class; but neither was there a refuge from modernization. Among the patrician intellectuals modernity was destructive of the cosmopolitan intellectual heritage of which they were the defenders; the newly literate urban population required different cultural aliment, and it was provided by a wholly new diet of radical journalism, radical literature, a nascent cinema, and above all by a tango which embodied both music and a vehicle for poetry. Although the poetry often reflected a nostalgia for a world more akin in its certainties to the oligarchic past, it was also urban and sentimental in a way that echoed the domestic and personal horizons of a class without aspirations to bearing the greater certainties.

It was as if the past had been colonized by masses emerging from a Europe very different from the one dreamed of in the patrician philosophy. Thus the modern was retrospectively disruptive and, above all in its best-known representative Borges, only a present imbued with scepticism and distanced by irony could provide a refuge. This was the invisible world where the protagonists of the novels of Eduardo Mallea sought escape from the irruptions of the mindless masses. But Borges clearly did not share Mallea's curious atavistic optimism, nor his idealism. Here the assertion by each of the schools and declarations that the poet must in one guise or another be emperor in his own domain or an endless and deeply sceptical traveller in the realms of others reflected directly a cultural loss experienced by these intellectuals.[10] The economic and political compromise had, it was true, diverted a social conflict for the moment; but it involved an immersion in a project of modernity for which they had little sympathy.

On the other hand, the organic intellectuals of the new class began to distinguish themselves in language and method. The radical writers of the decade identified with the Russian Revolution, but shared predominantly not the joyful creativity of its early years[11] but the gloomy tendentiousness of the 'proletarian realist' phase which brought the Russian revolution in art to an end. But in the early years the exhilaration in the face of modernity, and its contradictory underpinnings, could still provide the colour of an avant garde for whom experiment and change were an act of *engagement* with change rather than a sceptical resistance to it.

This was the background to the Prisma Declaration, published in Buenos Aires in 1922, which began with an attack on the followers of

Rubén Darío, with their obsession with swans and roses and Greek gods. They were accused of suffering from 'miedo altanero de adentrarse en las cosas' (an arrogant fear of going into things)[12] whose source was what the manifesto called 'la superstición del yo' (superstition of the self) – an obsession with personal development and the complexities of experience. The *ultraísta* group around the magazine *Prisma* reserved their scorn for the 'mercachifles' (traffickers). The anti-bourgeois thrust of the declaration was unmistakable, with the greatest scorn reserved for those who allowed their words to become objects to be bought and sold. For this turned art into a commodity and produced an art in which the creative freedom of the artists was compromised by market needs. Art, therefore (and creativity itself), was *defined* by its exclusion from social relations.[13] The *ultraístas* set out to 'descubirir facetas insospechadas al mundo' (uncover unsuspected facets of the world); the metaphor was the central element of the poem – each one novel and standing alone. The emphasis then was on originality, uniqueness, the absolutely new and unrepeatable quality of the metaphor.

The Prisma Declaration was signed by Jorge Luis Borges, Guillermo de Torre and two others. Two years later a slightly wider group supported a manifesto appearing in the first issue of a new magazine called *Martín Fierro*;[14] its central influence was the poet Oliverio Girondo, whose authority stamped itself on this and several subsequent groups of writers. Girondo was in many ways a more genuinely representative figure of this group, even though his international reputation has been overshadowed by that of Borges, a much more shortlived adherent of the principles of the magazine.

In its opening editorial in 1924 *Martín Fierro* immediately established its anti-bourgeois credentials – 'Frente a la impermeabilidad hipopotámica del honorable público' (Faced with the thick, hippopotamus-like skin of the honourable public), it began, and went on to denounce the empty obsession with the past and the mimeticism so characteristic of that reading public. The other major sins were its pusillanimity and above all its literary nationalism, its provincialism. The magazine's response was to emphasize the new, placing the word in defiant capitals. *Martín Fierro* 'sabe que "todo es nuevo bajo el sol"' (knows that 'everything is new under the sun'); its exponents are happier in a 'transatlantic liner' than in a 'Renaissance palace', and see the past only as a place to find some more absurd examples of the provincialism of their grandparents. The magazine's cosmopolitanism was fierce and crushing, and insisted on the value of sources of culture elsewhere in the world. Constant renewal and rebirth were the theme of

113

this literary current. No comparisons, no weighing of things against one another – only an immersion in what is.

Despite his role as a purveyor and defender of the ideas of the European avant garde, Borges practised what he preached only briefly. His first collection, *Fervor de Buenos Aires*[15] already marked a shift from *ultraísmo* towards a very different set of preoccupations which became consistently central to his subsequent work. The self-conscious metaphors, familiar in Eliot, of moons in windows and empty streets, denoted a perception of the poet in an isolated landscape. But Borges filled that landscape with a pastoral, or at least a nostalgic vision of his city which turned its back on the real history of his time and began to reconstruct the past through a series of myths which were to become a persistent component of all his work. The poem 'Fundación mítica de Buenos Aires' (Mythical foundation of Buenos Aires), for example, was a reconstruction of the origins of the city:

> Lo cierto es que mil hombres y otros mil arribaron
> por un mar que tenía cinco lunas de anchura
> y aún estaba poblado de sirenas y endriagos
> y de piedras imanes que enloquecen la brújula

(What is certain is that one thousand men and then another thousand arrived/across a sea that was five moons wide/and it was still populated by sirens and monsters/and hid magnetic stones that drove the compasses wild)

Out of myth and magic emerged this curious timeless city, whose city walls bore pro-Yrigoyen graffiti and whose milieu was the sentimental soundscape of the timeless tango.

> . . . La tarde se había ahondado en ayeres,
> los hombres compartieron un pasado ilusorio.
> Sólo faltó una cosa: la vereda de enfrente.
>
> A mí se me hace cuento que empezó Buenos Aires
> La juzgo tan eterna como el agua y al aire.

(. . . The evening had grown deep in yesterdays,/men shared an illustrious past./Only one thing was lacking: the pavement opposite.//It sounds to me like a story to say that Buenos Aires began/I judge it to be as eternal as the water and the air.)

Thus was born the Buenos Aires of patrician myth; yet its central figures, paradoxically, are the urban and rural poor like Martín Fierro himself. There was clearly a conscious irony in the writers' choice of

114

that name for their journal. José Hernández's marvellous poem *Martín Fierro*, written in 1872 (Part 1, 'La Ida' – Leaving) and 1879 (Part 2, 'La Vuelta' – the Return),[16] certainly did not share Borges's perspective on either Argentine history or Buenos Aires. Martín Fierro's voice was that of a disappearing class, the herdsmen and artisans whose social death was the inescapable consequence of economic modernisation and the expansion of the economy. As the material foundation of that world disappeared, so Martín Fierro was first driven to the margins of social life and then faced with a choice between two kinds of extinction – collective (as a class) or individual (in the struggle for life on the margins of society). Martín's choice of the latter course has about it a noble quality – heroic even – despite its futility. For there was no world to return to. And the future world, represented in the poem by a figure called Vizcacha, offered Martín an alienation so absolute that he elected to retain his humanity despite its material cost. What convinces him is what he discovers in Vizcacha's drawers after his death: the detritus of an urban life in which the broken and useless mementoes of rural life, and their symbolic representation of an autonomy and freedom now lost, say clearly that the future here is one of a loss of self.[17]

So why should the avant-garde writers of Buenos Aires select Martín's name for the review? The choice could only work once a key sleight of hand had been made. Fierro, instead of being the noble and tragic victim of progress, here became a symbolic crystallization of a desocialized rural experience. It functioned at two levels – as pastoral, and as an embodiment of an abstract concept of national character embedded in a continuity from prehistory until the sudden and disruptive birth of the modern world. Hence the mythic founding of Buenos Aires or of Martín Fierro are acts in the same process of literary reappropriation of a past lost in reality. The empty landscape of Borges's 'Calle con almacén rosado' (Street with pink shop) was now recaptured as a past rendered as dream.[18] From now on Borges was to be a key figure in the evocation of a national past removed from the modern, longed for and celebrated. Yet it was undoubtedly the past of a landowning class whose harmonious relationship with its rural world was a function of its dominion over it.[19] Borges mourned the passing of a world tranquil in its inequality and secure in its umbilical connection with the Europe which gave it culture and lifeblood.[20]

Oliverio Girondo remained more faithful to the original precepts of the group. His first book of poetry *veinte poemas para ser leídos en un tranvía* (twenty poems to read on the tram)[21] was representative in its prosaic quality, in its rejection of rhythm or musicality and in the absence of the marks of poetry. Each unit is a prose tableau, unrelated to the next, faithful to the short-lived experiences that mark urban life; each is the length of a tram stop, the arbitrary duration of a breath, as transitory and ephemeral as an encounter in a crowd.

> Una corriente de brazos y de espaldas
> nos encauza
> y nos hace desembocar
> bajo los abanicos,
> las pipas, los anteojos enormes
> colgados en medio de la calle;
> únicos testimonios de una raza
> desaparecida de gigantes.
>
> Sentados al borde de las sillas,
> cual si fueran a dar un brinco
> y ponerse a bailar,
> los parroquianos de los cafés
> aplauden la actividad del camarero,
> mientras los limpiabotas les lustran los zapatos
> hasta que pueda leerse
> el anuncio de la corrida del domingo.

(A current of arms and backs/sweeps us along/and brings us to rest/ under the fans/the pipes, the huge spectacles/hanging in the middle of the street;/only witnesses to a race/of giants, now disappeared.//Sitting on the edge of their seats,/as if about to jump/and start to dance/the clients of the café/applaud the activity of the waiter,/while the shoeshine boy shines their shoes/until you can read in them/the adverts for the bullfight on the following Sunday)

The characteristic note here comes from the succession of disconnected images in the urban milieu, the fleeting experiences that are signs of a world adrift. The title of 'Otro nocturno' (Another nocturne) must be a reference to the dream landscapes of the Romantic nocturne, but here is made ironic as the night is hostile and without promise, full of unanswered questions and objects humanized. The natural world is supplanted by the manmade: 'La luna, como la esfera luminosa del reloj de un edificio público' (The moon, like the luminous dial of the clock on a public building). The image is a familiar one, as the transfer of qualities from one dimension to another makes the known unfamiliar, and the habitual suddenly insecure. It is closer of course to the practice of surrealism. In *Calcomanías* (Transfers), the surrealist tone is more playful and more emphatic – and resolutely urban and novel; visual in a succession of images without an imposed continuity or rationality and acoustic in the association of sound. As they later became more radical, they became also perhaps more despairing:

> Es la baba
> Su baba
> La efervescente baba
> La baba hedionda
> caustica

(It's the dribble/Its dribble/Bubbling dribble/Stinking caustic/dribble)

and in 'Lo que esperamos' (What we are waiting for) Girondo generalizes that despair in a rare direct comment on social experience:

> Ya sé que todavía
> los émbolos,
> la usura,
> el sudor,
> las bobinas
> seguirán produciendo,
> al por mayor,
> en serie,
> iniquidad,
> ayuno,
> rencor . . .
>
> Y entonces . . .
> . . . usaremos palabras sustanciosas
> auténticas;
> no como esos vocablos erizados de inquina
> que babean las hienas
> al instarnos al odio
> . . . sino palabras simples
> de arroyo,
> de raíces
> que en vez de separarnos
> nos acerquen un poco . . .

(I know that still/embolisms,/usury,/sweat,/bobbins/will go on producing,/wholesale,/in bulk,/iniquity,/want,/rage . . .//And then . . ./. . .we shall use substantial words/authentic words,/not like those words stiff with bitterness/that hyenas' dribble in provoking us to hatred/. . . but simple words/of streams,/of roots/which instead of separating us/will bring us a little closer together. . .)

In his 'En la masmédula' (At the innercore) the sense of disintegration

THE GATHERING OF VOICES

and self-loathing is expressed as lists of half-formulated half-voiced questions without answers, as breathless successions of incomplete words: 'por mucho que se apoye en las coyunturas de lo fortuito/a mí a mí la plena íntegra bella a mi hórrida vida . . .' (however much it leans on the conjunctures of chance/to me to me the full integral beautiful to my awful life).

Despite their common origins, there is in Girondo a deeper humanism than in Borges, a sort of pity for those figures hurrying through the city streets. In that sense he moved from the cool, self-consciously literary pursuits of Borges towards the tense encounter of dream and reality more characteristic of surrealism.[22] That note is more emphatic still in the work of his wife Norah Lange (b. 1906), where irony serves to distance the writer from the intense but suppressed personal feelings. Here the emptiness of language becames a defence, full of allusions yet without a material presence beyond the word.

> Y lo hecho ya, sin deshacer,
> como un grito que ya nunca
> volverá a la boca que lo ha dado
> por más que la intención, callada,
> hacia dentro lo repita y lo detenga
> de golpe sobre labios afanosos.

(And what's done, not to be undone,/like a scream that never again/will return to the mouth it came from/however much the intention, silently,/ is to repeat it and hold it back/suddenly on hardworking lips.)

This nightmare urban landscape, with its fragmented images and its dismembered experience, produces the urgent and sometimes despairing tone of the small group of Peruvian surrealists. Martin Adan (b. 1908) and José Maria Eguren (1882–1942) sustained a fragile hold on a collapsing and alienated culture.[23]

> El oscuro andarín de la noche,
> detiene el paso junto a la torre,
> y al centinela
> le anuncia roja, cercana guerra.
>
> Le dice al viejo de la cabaña
> que hay batidores en la sábana;
> sordas linternas
> en los juncales y oscuras sendas . . .

En la batalla cayó la torre;
siguieron ruinas, desolaciones;
canes sombríos
buscan los muertos en los caminos.

Suenan los bombos y las trompetas
y las picotas y las cadenas;
y nadie ha visto, por el confín;
nadie recuerda
al andarín.[24]

(The dark wanderer through the night/stopped walking near the tower/ and informed the sentinel/that a red war was approaching.//He told the old man in the hut/that there were scouts on the plain;/muted lanterns/ in the shrubs and dark paths . . .//In the battle the tower fell;/then there was ruin, desolation;/grim dogs/seeking out the dead on the roads.// Drums and trumpets sound/and pikes and chains;/and nobody around has seen;/nobody remembers/the wanderer.)

The wanderer, like the poet, is marginal and rejected; whether his words are prophetic, visionary or critical, they find no echo in the surrounding reality. The line of inheritance from late Romanticism and Modernismo remains clearly visible.

Future Shock

The Futurists, too, wandered the streets of the expanding cities;[25] the movement had its echo in Latin America, particularly in Mexico where the Estridentistas celebrated the excitement of the modern and the new. The obsessive impact of the city and the machine bred among the Expressionists a kind of mesmerized horror as the self was broken down and converted into a drab mass conformity overpowered by this manmade environment. The Futurists, however, addressed the same phenomenon from an exactly opposite perspective, celebrating the enormous power unleashed in the new urban landscape and appropriating the dissolution of individual personality into the birth of a new 'mass man'. But the Futurists and their followers elsewhere shared the anti-bourgeois feeling and the distrust of tradition generally associated with the avant garde. Their celebration of the future enshrined in the machine age was coupled with a dismissal of the past, a rejection of a history that was deemed bourgeois.

Manuel Maples Arce (1898–1972), the most accomplished of the Mexican Estridentistas, celebrated the city in overtly revolutionary terms:[26]

119

Entre los matorrales del silencio
la oscuridad lame la sangre del crepúsculo.
Las estrellas caídas
son pájaros muertos
en el agua sin sueño
del espejo.
. . .
Los ríos de blusas azules
desbordan las esclusas de las fábricas
y los árboles agitadores
manotean sus discursos en la acera.
Los huelguistas se arrojan
pedradas y denuestos,
y la vida es una tumultuosa
conversión hacia la izquierda.
. . .
¿De quién son esas voces
que sobrenadan en la sombra?
        ¿Y estos trenes que aúllan
        hacia los horizontes devastados?

(Among the shrubs of silence/darkness licks up the blood of dusk./The fallen stars/are dead birds/in the sleepless water/of the mirror./. . ./The rivers of blue blouses/spill over the factory sluices/and the agitator trees/ handle their speeches on the pavement./The strikers throw/stones and insults,/and life is a tumultuous/turn to the left./. . ./Whose voices are those/swimming through the dark?/And those trains that howl/at the devastated horizons?)

Nature and the artificial manmade landscape are now indistinguishable, or rather nature is absorbed into the city streets occupied by a collective subject and shrouded in the mists and sounds of urban living. There is of course an irony here, in this celebration of a twentieth-century modernization which Mexico had barely begun to undergo when *Urbe* was published in 1924. In no sense can the Estridentista milieu be read as document[27] – there was little comparison between industrial heartlands of Turin (where Marinetti wrote) or St Petersburg and Moscow (the setting for Mayakovsky's urban satires) and the nascent manufacturing industries of Mexico, where this celebration of capitalist growth could stand only as metaphor and prophecy (though the Mexico of 1990 has amply demonstrated its accuracy!).[28] The city was a vision of a collective future, and one that anticipated the overt political writing of the 1930s. It was in that sense a model of a future society, an image of the fundamental social character of this envisaged future world, a kind of positive response to

120

the thoroughly disintegrative vision of Vallejo or the Neruda of *Residencia*.

The first urban poets, like Maples Arce and Girondo but also López Velarde, identified the urban mass as the protagonist of their work. But the crowd in the street had no class character, and the poet stood as the aloof observer, watching the movements of the masses as part of a symphony of sound and movement. Words reproduced sounds – of marching feet or crashing machinery – and the visual panorama of modern life – trams, aeroplanes, flashing neon advertising signs, imposing buildings. Although the city streets were also proletarian spaces, the poet did not speak for them but with the equanimity of a detached spectator. Like Baudelaire's *flaneur* 'he found his asylum in the crowd'.[29] For in a sense, although the crowd was human, it had no social character, no location in the world of classes and social forces. This city was concerned only with consumption, an activity with neither a history nor a future development, but only endless reproduction. In that sense, it was a place where 'the laws of the dialectic were at a standstill'[30] – even though at first sight it may have seemed to represent a step back towards the social. In that sense, for all its subversive intent, the metaphor it presented still corresponded to the Modernista vision.

There were other voices, however, now beginning to be heard in the city. In a sense, the Futurist vision brought the poets back into the living environment, whose contours were recognizably historical. The impulse to re-enter history, however, to assume the 'creative militancy' of which Williams speaks, arose from another tradition of poetry whose sources lay in popular culture.

In Raúl González Tuñón (b. 1905)[31] the *flaneur* awakes from his reverie and comes in from the cold. The city is palpable and located in time and space; the people in it are no longer shadowy passengers but living beings in struggle with this new urban monster. The rush and rhythm of the place no longer simply sweep along the crowd but are symptoms of a living social conflict. And the poet is within those conflicts, not now merely an observer but a participant in change. It is still not identifiably a proletarian environment, still not the site for a collective definition. But objectively the fragmented individuals perceptibly share a common social experience and in the sharp commentary on their lives and battles there is a sense of active engagement between poet and subject, who now cease to be distinct. The *flaneur* has disappeared and in his place the excited and committed companion to the crowd has emerged.

121

Discurro la Dialéctica, mas sin fruncir el ceño.
Me gusta lo concreto, pero también el sueño
Huyo a la gente Babbit[32] y a la supuesta rara.

Aún hay que gritar: ¡Abajo los salones!
Hay espacio en el mundo para la poesía.
Estaciones, mercados, puertos y corralones.
Los palacios vacíos de nuestra geografía.

Siempre digo lo clásico y digo lo moderno
– moderno, léase continuidad, eterno –
Detesto al erudito minucioso y oscuro
increador y frío. ¡De sangre es la cultura!
Idolatro ese fresco, humano, impuro y puro
realismo – romántico de la 'literatura'

(I make speeches about the Dialectic,but without knitting my brows./I like the concrete, but dreams too/I flee people like Babbit and those that seem bizarre.//We still have to shout out Down with salons!/There is space in the world for poetry./Stations, markets, ports and slums./The empty palaces of our geography.//I always say classical and modern/– for modern read continuity, eternal –/I hate the scholars, nitpicking and obscure/uncreative and cold.Culture is made in blood!/I adore that fresh, human, impure, pure/romantic-realism of 'literature')

This particular poem begins, ironically, with the opening line of a famous Darío poem 'Yo soy aquél que ayer no más decía' (I am the one who was saying only yesterday), the most far-reaching statement of the otherness of poetry, of its location in another, cultural realm. This is González Tuñón's reply. The locus of poetry is social life itself (streets, stations, slums), the material of culture is lived and felt and not the product of a process of distancing and rationalization. The framework is the modern city, but one without the residual provincial nostalgia that is there in some of the tango lyrics or their poetic exponents. It is a landscape where the cosmopolitan dreams of the patrician wanderers, like Borges, have also foundered on the resolute historicity of this place and time. For Tuñón, the excitement and exhilaration are in modernity itself, as his breathless testimony extends to other cities (like 'Ese Bul'Mich de quien nunca dirán: Una calle, ya olvidada. . .!'– That old Boulevard Saint Michel of whom they'll never say: A street, now forgotten . . .!). These are streets full of poor and brutalized people, but ones which will also produce change and transformation.

External events helped to make the city the locus of social *conflict*, the arena of struggle. The impact of the Crash of 1929 drove forward the organization of social resistance and the debate around political alternatives; and the role of culture and ideas in that process was everywhere accepted as central. The artists were now under pressure to respond with new forms and a new language appropriate to collective experience in an era of social tension. The implication was that they must renounce that most precious of philosophical legacies from the Romantic tradition – the creative freedom of the individual artist. From the absolute absorption of the poet in his autonomous linguistic universe, some of the avant-garde poets responded by moving their attention back towards the world and its functioning dynamics.

Rubén Martínez Villena (1899–1933) was a leading member of the Cuban Communist Party. His 'Mensaje lírico-civil' (Civic-lyrical message) of 1923 was an early assumption of social commitment.

> hace falta una carga para matar bribones
> para acabar la obra de las revoluciones;
>
> para vengar los muertos, que padecen ultraje,
> para limpiar la costra tenaz del coloniaje;
>
> para poder un día, con prestigio y razón
> extirpar el Apéndice de la Constitución . . .[33]

(We need a charge to kill scoundrels/and to bring to completion the work of revolutions;//to avenge the dead who still suffer violation,/to scratch away the scab of colonialism;//to be able one day, with honour and reason/to extirpate the Appendix to the Constitution . . .)

This sonorous doggerel is far less interesting than the daring experiments of his contemporaries; yet it is not so much *bad* poetry as poetry of a different kind (albeit not the best example of that either). Villena used poetry to address immediate and explicitly political questions, albeit in the tone of the civic anthems of the nineteenth century.

Theodor Adorno argued that 'Art's social character is its immanent movement against society, not any manifest pronouncement on that society'.[34] Reflecting the unspoken assumptions underpinning the avant garde, Adorno asserts the subversive character of art, the creative act as subversion in itself. But as Walter Benjamin had said,

Commitment is more than just a matter of presenting correct political opinions in one's art; it reveals itself in how far the artist reconstructs the artistic forms at his disposal, turning authors, readers and spectators into collaborators.[35]

while Brecht was clear that art should 'discover social laws and developments and unmask prevailing ideologies by adopting the standpoint of the class which offers the broadest solution to social problems'.[36]

Clearly a social poetry must in some way address the material world and actual social relations. Beyond that Brecht's advocacy of a poetry of direct intervention prescribes no form, but it does assume a 'creative militancy'. And Benjamin's position would seem to enjoin the poet of social commitment to seek the voice of the collective protagonists of the poetry – the language of lived experience. It was the poets of the black experience in Cuba who provided the earliest response to the demand to address social experience in language and form as well as explicit content.

Negritud

The Cuban poet Nicolás Guillén (1904–1990) soon abandoned his youthful formulaic Modernista poems to assume a very different voice. That voice and accent were his own; he assumed the *speech* of black Cuba (he himself was mulatto) and in his early publications in the pages called 'Ideales de una raza' in Havana's *Diario de la Marina*, developed the form of Cuban popular music called the *son*.[37]

From the early part of the decade of the twenties writers adapted the percussive and rhythmic shape of music to poetic form. But there was an ambiguity within it. The early impulse for that sonorous percussive poetry came from the new irrationalist philosophies which took root in Europe in the wake of the First World War. Western intellectuals rejected the rational historicism that had produced the barbarity of the fields of France and whose progressive optimism was mocked by the millions of dead buried there. They turned instead towards a world of instinct and sensuality, of anti- or pre-rational response, and celebrated it in the hedonistic ambience of the 'lost generation' of post-war youth. This sprint was reflected in the new dances, like the Black Bottom and the Charleston, with their open and provocative sensuality and their curious pastiche of the ceremonial dances of Africa; in the enthusiasm for the adapted folk rhythms of Cuba (renamed rumba, with its plosive onomatopoeic impact) or the sensual celebration of the Argentine tango. But there was a fundamental ambiguity in these new fashions, an ambiguity that derived precisely from the underpinning of ritual primitivism that all this implied. If it liberated sexuality and challenged puritanism and materialism, it reduced those cultures whose forms it borrowed to a primitive, pre-social status. What was celebrated was their *lack* of development, their *naturalness* or, to put it another way, their very backwardness. This was not an assimilation of or discovery of the complex hidden cultures of Africa or Latin America by the new metropolitan consciousness, nor an expiation of colonial guilt. Rather it was a new folklore, a new exoticism.[38]

The Puerto Rican Luis Palés Matos (1898–1959) is usually regarded as the earliest of the Latin American poets of *negritud* (blackness); yet his approach to black America is through the glass of Spengler's irrationalist theories, rather than arising from any investigation of its historical or social reality. It was that instinctual quality he celebrated in his 'Danza Negra' (Black Dance):

> El Gran Cucurucu dice tu-cu-tú.
> La Gran Cocoroca dice to-co-tó.
> Es el sol de hierro que arde en Tombuctú
> Es la danza negra de Fernando Poó

(The Great Cucurucu says tucutu./The Great Cocoroca says tocoto./The iron sun that burns in Timbuktoo/It's the black dance of Fernando Po)

and its ambivalence in his 'ñam ñam':

> America baila el jazz
> Europa juega y teoriza
> Africa gruñe: ñam-ñam.

(America dances to jazz/Europe plays and theorizes/Africa grunts: nyamnyam)

For black America or black Latin America this rediscovery of their culture carried no critique of their enslavement, no promise of emancipation from their colonial status – quite the contrary, it celebrated and dehistoricized it. Yet that articulation of black voices, however idealized they may have been, did acknowledge the existence and the vitality of these previously hidden cultures. Their silence had been broken for the white world, and their legitimacy had been recognized by the central institutions of cultural dissemination – whatever the ambivalence that infused their recognition. In the aftermath of war, the sounds of jazz and blues emerged from the ghetto: the Original Dixieland Jazz Band brought together a group of Harvard graduates to play the forbidden music of the black ghetto – and in the Waldorf Astoria to boot! And the brothel piano players of yesteryear with their suggestive soubriquets, like Jelly Roll Morton, became the official musicians of black America. In New York the Harlem Renaissance gave proud utterance to black experience – but it did so at the Cotton

125

Club and the Apollo, where white New Yorkers came in convoy to hear the black artists of their city perform in their district.

The ambiguities and contradictions of the movement are summed up in the work of two of its finest poets – Langston Hughes, himself an interracial, and Claude McKay, a black Jamaican resident in New York.[39] In *The Weary Blues* Hughes parodied savagely the safe simplicity of Stephen Foster's southern anthem:

> Way down south in Dixie
> (break the heart of me)
> they hung my young black lover
> to a crossroads tree.

And Claude McKay, in a statement of militancy and struggle, satirized the safe rural refuge of Rupert Brooke's foreign field: 'If I should die, let it not be like a hog . . .' The lynchmob reality of black experience here penetrated the joyful celebrations of the natural life; the aesthetic and sensual experience was punctured by the social.

It is not clear what mutual influence was at work between the black poets of North America and Guillén and the 'Afrocubans'. Guillén and Hughes certainly met shortly before the publication of Guillén's *Motivos de son* (*Son* themes) in 1930. The dominant register of that first collection reflects the Afrocuban poetry of Ramón Guirao and José Zacarías Tallet;[40] yet there was already a note of parody, of reversal, which became more emphatic in the following year in Guillén's second book of poems, *Sóngoro Cosongo*.

From the outset there was a distinction between the work of Guillén and the more exoticist elements of the Afro-Cuban school. It was a difference at two levels. First, there was in Guillén a sense of a cultural history, a sense of origin in an Africa which was something more than simply the site of primal innocence. Langston Hughes had said:

> I am a Negro
> Black as the night is black
> black as the depths of my Africa

Guillén re-evoked the curiosity of those arriving in the New World, into slavery:

> ¡Aquí estamos!
> La palabra nos viene húmeda de los bosques,
> y un sol enérgico nos amanece entre las venas.
> El puño es fuerte
> y tiene el remo.

126

Traemos el humo en la mañana
y el fuego sobre la noche,
y el cuchillo, como un duro pedazo de luna . . .
Traemos
nuestro rasgo al perfil definitivo de América.

(We're here!/The word reaches us, still wet, from the forest,/and a lively
sun is born in our veins./Our fist is strong/and grips the oar.//We bring
the morning smoke/fire over the night,/and a knife like a sharp piece of
the moon . . ./We bring/our features to the definitive profile of America.)

The second movement in Guillén's poetry is his search for a vernacu-
lar idiom, a reflection of the speech of black Cuba – a genuinely
democratic voice. In this sense, it was Guillén's work that most clearly
prefigured the drive towards a poetry of public utterance which this
study traces. For the early poetry of black experience turned instinct
against reason; the dominant voice remained that of the Western
intellectual 'lowering' the tone of his work, mimicking the 'barbarous'
tone of his mute protagonist. In *Motivos de son* Guillén sought to give
the *object* of this poetry a recognizable voice.

¿Po qué te pone tan brabo
cuando te disen negro bembón
si tiene la boca santa
negro bembón?

Bembón así como ere
tiene de tó
Caridá te mantiene
te lo da tó

(Why do you get so mad/when they call you fatlipped black man/is your
mouth sacred/black man? //Fatlips you may have/but you've got it all/
You live on handouts/you got it all)

Here Guillén poked gentle fun at the wiseguys of the red-light districts
and the flyboys of the docks who lived on their wits and by exploiting
this new Western obsession with things black and natural. Yet it was a
humour from within, a self-parody that he offered. If Guillén aban-
doned this method of representing street speech, it was because on the
printed page it appeared inescapably patronizing and ridiculous,
losing its element of sympathy and solidarity. From then on, it was
form and rhythm that Guillén used to reproduce the patterns of
speech and to echo the shape of popular culture. 'Talking Negro' in
Sóngoro Cosongo meant discovering a language of pride and solidarity,

and appropriating the language of the exotic to the project of self-expression and liberation.

> Y ahora que Europa se desnuda
> para tostar su carne al sol
> y busca en Harlem y en La Habana
> jazz y son,
> lucirse negro mientras aplaude el bulevar
> y frente a la envidia de los blancos
> hablar en negro de verdad.

(And now Europe strips off/to tan its skin in the sun/and it goes to Harlem and Havana/in search of jazz and the *son,*/to be proudly black while the boulevard applauds/and faced with the envy of the whites/to speak real Negro)

Africa is there in these early poems:

> Signo de selva el tuyo,
> con tus collares rojos,
> tus brazaletes de oro curvo
> y ese caimán oscuro
> nadando en el Zambesí de tus ojos

(Yours is the sign of the jungle,/you with your red necklaces,/your curved golden armbands/and that dark alligator/swimming in the Zambezi of your eyes)

But so too are the descendants of the African slaves in the urban reality of 1920s Havana – Papa Montero, for example, the old singer and the forerunner of the enraged troubadour José Ramón Cantaliso.

> En el solar te esperaban,
> pero te trajeron muerto;
> fue bronca de jaladera,
> pero te trajeron muerto;
> dicen que el era tu ecobio,
> pero te trajeron muerto;
> el hierro no apareció,
> pero te trajeron muerto.
>
> Ya se acabó Baldomero
> ¡Zumba, canalla y rumbero!

(They were waiting for you in the shanty,/but they brought you back dead;/it was a brawl over a woman,/but they brought you back dead;/ they say he was your sidekick,/but you came back dead;/they never found the knife,/but they brought you back dead.//That's the end of Baldomero/Flyboy, rat and rumba dancer!)

Nicolás Guillén began writing within an exoticist framework which saw black culture as a simple negation of Western culture – sensuous as against cerebral, instinctual as against rational, natural as against conventional. By the time he published *West Indies Ltd* in 1934, while he retained the idiom and the form of his earlier work, the implied subject had changed, as well as the central set of relationships that the poetry addressed. As Keith Ellis points out,[41] there was a curious absence of any reference here to the reality of racial discrimination and oppression. Blackness became coterminous with nationhood, and the *son* and the black voice that sang it became representative of *national* pride. It was Cuban rather than black culture that Guillén ultimately celebrated, a culture that, like the poetry, was the product of a combination of elements, currents and histories. So *Sóngoro Cosongo* contained decimas in the Spanish popular tradition; and the *son* stood in a tense relationship with a more formal poetry.[42] Nonetheless the voice that spoke the poetry, the persona at its core, was black, rooted in popular culture and speech, and the bearer of a collective experience of oppression:

El son no es del negro bembón, chulo . . . sino del trabajador que muere en una faena en los cañaverales cuya dureza bárbara no resiste su cuerpo mal pagado . . .[43]

(The *son* doesn't belong to the black wise guy or the pimp . . . but to the worker dying on the sugar plantation because his poorly paid body can't withstand the brutal hardship of his work there)

With Guillén there emerged a vernacular poetry of self-expression, a representative voice eschewing the autonomy of poetry in favour of a concept of shared and common experience. The collective voice was Cuban (and not an ancestral African voice); it had a history and was informed by a social experience and a collective response enshrined in popular culture.[44] Culture was now seen in relation to socio-economic relations; thus the black idiom expressed a general experience of exploitation and oppression.

The source of the relationship of inequality was located by Guillén in the international arena, and the protagonists of those relations were defined as the oppressed nation versus imperialism. Clearly this reflected a major change in Guillén's perception of the central dynamics of his own society. He had disengaged from any racial explanation of that dynamic at an early stage; but he seems also to have moved away fairly quickly from a class definition of that central conflict. The title poem of the volume *West Indies Ltd* alternates, through its eight sections, explicitly political verse with joyful interludes of *son* poetry.

¡West Indies! ¡West Indies! ¡West Indies!
Este es el pueblo hirsuto,
de cobre, multicéfalo, donde la vida repta
con el lodo seco cuarteado en la piel.
Este es el presidio
donde cada hombre tiene atados los pies.
Esta es al grotesca sede de companies y trusts.
Aquí está el lago de asfalto, las minas de hierro,
las plantaciones de café,
los ports docks, los ferry boats, los ten cents.
Esta es el pueblo de all right,
donde todo se encuentra muy mal;
este es el pueblo del very well,
donde nadie está bien.

(West Indies! West Indies! West Indies!/This is the hairy people,/copper-coloured, multicephalous,/where life crawls along/with dry mud stuck to its skin./This is the prison/where the feet of every man are tied./This is the grotesque headquarters of companies and trusts./Here are the lake of pitch, the iron mines,/the coffee plantations,/the ports, docks, ferry-boats, ten cent stores./This is the country of all right,/where everything is all wrong;/this is the country of very well,/where nobody is well.)

In this extract Guillén parodied the exoticist image of Latin America, and the Caribbean in particular ('life crawls along', a 'hairy copper-coloured people', etc.). Further, the alienation of language itself – the invisibility of black or Cuban experience in the dominant language, a cosmopolitan tongue – is ironized in the final four lines. The reappropriation of language is conducted elsewhere in the poem through the *son*:

Me matan si no trabajo,
y si trabajo me matan.
Siempre me matan me matan
siempre me matan.

(They kill me if I don't work,/and if I work they kill me./They always kill me, kill me/they always kill me)

The *son* here becomes a vehicle for the expression of a more general experience of exploitation; by analogy black oppression was transformed into national oppression.

Regino Pedroso (b. 1896), from Cuba, addressed the black population with a call to political consciousness in 'Hermano negro' (Black brother):

130

Negro, hermano negro,
enluta un poco tu bongo.

¿No somos más que negros?
¿No somos más que jácara?
¿No somos más que rumba, lujurias negras y comparsas?
¿No somos más que mueca y dolor,
mueca y dolor?[45]

(Brother, black brother,/wrap your bongo in mourning for a while.//
Aren't we more than just black?/Aren't we more than just joy?/Aren't we
more than just rumbas, black sensuality, and dances?/Aren't we more
than just grimaces and pain/grimaces and pain?)

There is here a powerful and direct resonance of speech, of argument,
that is absent still in the abstractions of poems like 'Mañana' (Tomor-
row) a prophetic poem without any sense of place or time.

Spain: The Long March

In the early thirties, those who defined themselves as proletarian poets
were largely associated with the Communist parties. As the crash had
its devastating effect on Latin America, the Communist International
was locked in its 'third period'. This proclaimed the imminent final
collapse of capitalism, and drew the conclusion that communists
should differentiate themselves clearly from social democrats and
reformist movements in general. Stalin argued that this was a time for
a sharp polarization between the communists and the rest.[46]

The effects of the policy were disastrous throughout the world
communist movement. In Latin America its consequence was that the
vanguard of a newly established workers' movement deliberately
withdrew from it on the basis of a theoretical abstraction that bore no
relation to the material reality of Latin America, effectively delivering
leadership into the hands of petty bourgeois anti-imperialist currents
represented by APRA[47] and its associated organizations. The procla-
mations of an imminent new dawn of communism were fantasies,
however prophetically they were articulated in the rhetorical trans-
ports of some of the 'proletarian poets';[48] they abjured the long haul of
united organization and struggle over partial or economic issues. And
when, in 1934, Stalin proclaimed a new international policy of 'popular
frontism', arguing for the necessity of the broadest possible front of
political forces in defence of democracy, the communists were in a

131

position of weakness and marginality in relation to the working-class organizations. The imperative need for a broad front, therefore, led to a complete reversal of earlier policies and the acceptance of a politics of consensus which consigned the business of revolutionary change (recently so imminent) to an undefined later stage. The primary task, on which general agreement with other social classes could be achieved, was economic development and national independence – to which any independent organization of workers must subordinate itself.[49]

The economic and political orthodoxies had their corresponding orthodoxy in the field of culture – the 'socialist realism' proclaimed by Stalin's Commissariat for Culture under Zhdanov.[50] Socialist realism laid down formulae for writers: proletarian heroes marching to victory and an unproblematical representation of dogma as reality – the glistening well-fed peasant reproduced so often in Stalinist painting of the thirties, who had little in common with the actual starving and persecuted peasantry of Russia in the 1930s. By proclaiming the prophecy fulfilled, these works of art removed contradiction from art and with it all sense of tension and struggle. Stalinist ideology replaced bourgeois optimism as the material of literature. It is because it is essentially falsification that the endless hymns of praise to heroes and successful plans are so profoundly unsatisfactory as poems, for they have no sense of time or place, no sense of lived experience. The finest political poetry trembles with anger, or doubt, or rage – with a human response; public issues are lived as individual or collective experience, and in a language resonant with that lived reality. Thus Guillén's marvellous 'José Ramón Cantaliso' is a vindication of Bowra's characterization of his work.

> Guillén's art is not a reversion to popular methods, not even a survival of them; it is an authentic extension of them to meet needs which have long been met in this way but not with this degree of attention and skill . . . He makes the *son* work hard and gets many new effects from it, but they are such as his countrymen will understand at once, and through this complete unity of outlook he succeeds in being a truly proletarian poet who does not allow social theories to interfere with his political methods.[51]

> Duro espinazo insumiso:
> Por eso es que canta liso
> José Ramón Cantaliso,
> José Ramón.

132

En bares, bachas, bachatas,
a los turistas a gatas,
y a los nativos también,
a todos, el son preciso
José Ramón Cantaliso
les canta liso, muy liso,
para que entiendan bien.
. . .
El sabe que no hay trabajo,
que el pobre se pudre abajo,
y que tras tanto luchar,
el que no perdió el resuello,
o tiene en la frente un sello,
o está con el agua al cuello,
sin poderlo remediar.

Por eso de fiesta en fiesta,
con su guitarra protesta,
que es su corazón también,
y a todos el son preciso,
José Ramón Cantaliso
les canta liso, muy liso,
para que lo entiendan bien.
                ('José Ramón Cantaliso')

(Hard unbending backbone:/that's why he sings softly/José Ramón Softsinger/José Ramón.//In bars, dives, pocheens,/to the tourists on all fours,/and to the natives too,/for all of them, the exact *son*/José Ramón Softsinger/sings to them all, softly,/so that they understand him well./. . ./He knows there is no work,/that the poor man is rotting down below,/and that after so much struggle,/the one that didn't run out of breath,/either has a mark on his forehead,/or is up to his neck in water,/and can't do a thing about it.//That's why from one party to the next,/with his protest guitar,/which is also his heart,/he sings his precise *son* to everyone,/José Ramón Softsinger/sings softly, softly to them,/so they understand it clearly.)

The idiom of the *son* is now not only a celebration of an alternative culture but the voice of an *oppositional* culture, and the poetry is a poetry of protest. José Ramón Cantaliso mocks and defies those who dominate him ('the tourists on all fours'), but in a language and form that mobilizes that protest from within the community of the oppressed. That is perhaps the key distinction between the high rhetoric of much socialist realism and this art which does connect with popular culture, with the *self*-expression of the exploited classes. In that respect, as Bowra suggests, Guillén extends the range and register

133

of the language of popular culture beyond its actuality into the realm of potentiality and possibility. That extension of the frontiers of knowledge and self-awareness is, I believe, the valid task of a political poetry, whose imaginative elision of real and potential is its major power. A political poetry that merely enunciates moral or political positions in some mnemonic or musical structure is not poetry in this sense. It is the active component that is definitive – which is what Walter Benjamin intended when he said,

> political commitment, however revolutionary it may seem, functions in a counter-revolutionary way as long as the writer experiences his solidarity with the proletariat only *in the mind* and not as a producer.[52]

The Spanish Civil War had an enormous impact on writers and artists throughout the world; some commentators have described it as 'the poets' war', though the facts do not quite fit the soubriquet.[53] Nonetheless, the Cultural Congress held at first in Madrid in July 1937 did bring together a group of intellectuals whose names are a catalogue of the best-known left artists and intellectuals of the period.[54] The reasons for its significance are complex and in some sense contradictory. Spain produced two myths, in the sense of symbolic statements crystallizing a set of aspirations and perceptions. For some, notably George Orwell and Felix Morrow,[55] Spain placed on the agenda of history a genuine possibility of revolutionary change. In Barcelona, between July 1936 and May 1937, the workers not only assumed direct power, but new relationships and new perceptions of human potential were forged in a real social experience. Orwell's most famous passage from *Homage to Catalonia* rests his initial optimism and commitment on the transformations of everyday life.[56] Following the troops to the front Orwell and others were inspired by their passionate commitment, their self-motivation, the sense of the exploited shaping their own life and future. This was revolutionary Spain.

May 1937 brought that to an end, as the central government based in Valencia sent its (largely Communist Party) Assault Guard to bring an end to the Spanish Revolution, to persecute and repress those forces grouped around the POUM and the CNT, the revolutionary organizations who saw Spain as a testing ground for the creation of a workers' state.[57] The issue was control and power; the workers' organizations who held effective power in Barcelona after Franco's declaration of his armed rebellion in July 1936 were now seen to represent a direct challenge to government. The refusal of the workers to yield control of the telephone system to government appointees provided the battlefield where the struggle for power was enacted. The assault on the

Barcelona Telephone Exchange on 5 May 1937 was the manifestation of a struggle within the Republican camp and between forces who at the level of rhetoric supported the same causes. Yet they confronted one another in Barcelona in armed conflict,[58] and after the reimposition of control by the Republican government the POUM and the anarchists suffered grievous suppression. The POUM's leader, Andres Nin, died at the hands of jailers who laid claim to the same revolutionary tradition as that which Nin had defended and sought to enact in practice, the tradition whose objective is the self-emancipation of the working class.[59]

Yet those contradictions are rarely the subject of the poetry of the war. Between 1937 and 1939 the vision of the Spanish Civil War that prevailed described it as a confrontation between a consensual anti-fascism and a Nazi machine. Certainly the forces of Franco were sustained by Nazi Germany and its Italian allies with men and matériel. Equally, the Republic found itself bereft of allies who had agreed to non-intervention on the grounds that the Republic was merely a protective veneer for Bolshevik intentions. The one ally that the Republic did have, Stalin's Russia, viewed the Spanish Civil War from the perspective of its own foreign policy needs, and above all the desire to establish alliances with France and Britain in order to hold back Nazi expansionism. Germany's eyes were firmly set on the East, as Hitler had explicitly declared through his 'lebensraum' policies.

The test of Stalin's credibility as an international ally of Western imperialism, of course, was his readiness to use Soviet Russia's considerable influence over communists throughout the world to demonstrate the moderation of communist objectives. This demonstration of bourgeois discipline and reformist intent was given specific form in the Popular Front policy adopted in the mid-thirties after the monstrous lurch into ultra-left isolationism in the immediately prior period. The concept of a consensus of democratic forces enshrined in the Popular Front underpinned the definition of the central issues at work in the Spanish War. For revolutionary socialists like Orwell, Spain was an enactment of the self-emancipation of workers, the reshaping of all human relationships in pursuit of workers' power.[60] The success of the Spanish Revolution in these terms rested on its ability to represent in practice the interests of the exploited classes, and to set in motion a movement for change both behind Franco's line and beyond Spain's frontiers. In that sense, it expressed a first manifestation of resistance to the burgeoning fascist axis, a workers' response to totalitarianism.[61]

135

For the exponents of the Popular Front, Spain was an exemplary battlefield in the defence of democracy, a concept which provided the central ideological motif of that consensus of social forces. Its contradiction was fascism, opposition to which was the binding feature of the front or alliance. The thrust behind the Popular Front was the need for Russia to create a broad anti-German alliance in defence of its own territorial existence. In the context of Spain that meant finding common ground with the very imperialist interests, Britain in particular, which had actively withdrawn support from the Spanish Republic through the non-intervention policy and effectively cut off the republican side from access to arms or supplies. The Soviet policy towards Spain was to use its influence (and its weapons) to induce the Spanish Republic to demonstrate its willingness to fight only for those values acceptable to the bourgeois democracies of the West. There can be little doubt that the test of their integrity in this respect would be their readiness to repress the revolutionary response to the nationalist coup, to locate the conflict on the terrain of the defence of (bourgeois) democracy. The revolutionaries, on the other hand, argued that the key step to winning the war was to win the direct support of workers on both sides by demonstrating to them that the Republic was carrying forward the kind of social changes that would benefit them and represent their aspirations. And on an international scale, the future of the Spanish Revolution depended on its ability to achieve the same resonance among workers. By attacking the Barcelona Telefónica on 5 May the Spanish Republican government set itself firmly against revolutionary change, and claimed its right to coexistence with bourgeois democracy on a world scale. It was a particular irony that one of the most powerful advocates of this policy was the Spanish Communist Party.

There can be little doubt that the general expectation among both the Nationalists under Franco and most governments outside Spain was that a Spanish Republic starved of funds and weapons could not last more than a matter of days or weeks at most. In fact the struggle lasted for three years – and the key defence came in the first year, precisely when a mass voluntary mobilization of armed workers mounted a spirited and courageous resistance to Franco without waiting for guidance from a vacillating government. When that government abandoned Madrid, for example, to take refuge in the safer climate of Valencia, it effectively abandoned the capital; yet it was another two years before the capital finally fell. And the extraordinary defence of the city was testimony to the creativity and obdurate resistance of the population of Madrid under the clear leadership of the working-class organizations.[62]

The struggle for Madrid took on enormous symbolic significance in the movement to break the blockade of non-intervention by pressure on the governments of Western Europe and the United States. Yet it is curious that the battle in Barcelona's streets in May 1937 – an event of equal significance – seems to have merited no poetic commentary. When the intellectuals giving their support to the Spanish cause gathered in Madrid in July 1937, and moved from there to Valencia and later to Barcelona, they did not comment on the social and political contradictions that were racking the Republic. They presented instead an image of consensus around central and key themes, a unity of purpose in the campaign to defend an embattled bourgeois democracy. In this sense, Spain could be seen in two very different lights. Either it illustrated the intensity of the class struggle, and the enormous possibilities that were available to those who were prepared to overthrow the crippling bourgeois order in pursuit of a very different, socialist world. Or it was evidence of the assault on democracy by barbaric forces so devastating that all differences of class interest should be set aside in the primary defence of a threatened *bourgeois* order.

For those Latin Americans who went to Spain, it illustrated many different aspects of the global struggle. But it had a further effect. In a curious way it again placed Europe at the centre of the argument about cultural advance; once again, the universal categories – this time democracy and fascism – were the product of European experience, and represented unquestionable moral imperatives. It shifted the argument from politics to morality, and from questions of class to questions of humanity. That at least was the course of development of public debate about Spain as the war progressed; and the future of the war was couched in these terms by intellectuals and public figures whose political allegiance was to the Communist Party, which had now identified itself completely with the Republic and had moved the war from the terrain of class struggle to the terrain of national defence. There were few dissident voices in this debate, and the few that there were were harried by Stalinism everywhere.[63] But in the Latin American context there was a different political analysis, which addressed the central contradictions in Latin American society through a different set of categories which were social and economic. The paradox is that these were associated with the specificities of Latin American history – the exploitation of Indians and blacks – and thus with a radical nationalist perspective. The moral power of the Spanish cause

137

was ultimately associated with global moral categories which set out far less radical perspectives for the process of social change.[64]

The orthodoxies about the Spanish Civil War, however, were not immediately imposed. Pablo Neruda's 'Explico algunas cosas' (I explain a few things) is one of his most convincing poems in its depiction of the encounter between the individual and great historical events, in its perplexity, its lack of simple categorical explanations, its sense of genuine emotional outrage. It has the same feeling of personal pain as Picasso's 'Guernica'. Neither work is in any direct sense an explanation of events;[65] it is rather a cry of disbelief, of solidarity and of impotent anguish. It is that same quality of a suffering testimony that makes Vallejo's response to the war so immensely powerful – and his overtly political poems so contingent and so much less convincing as responses.

Explico algunas cosas

Preguntareis: ¿Y dónde están las lilas?
¿Y la metafísica cubierta de amapolas?
¿Y la lluvia que a menudo golpeaba
sus palabras llenándolas
de agujeros y pájaros?

Os voy a contar todo lo que me pasa.

Yo vivía en un barrio
de Madrid, con campanas,
con relojes, con árboles.

Desde allí se veía
el rostro seco de Castilla
como un océano de cuero.
        Mi casa era llamada
la casa de las flores, porque por todas partes
estallaban geranios: era
una bella casa
con perros y chiquillos.
        ¿Raul te acuerdas?
¿Te acuerdas Rafael?
        ¿Federico te acuerdas
debajo de la tierra,
te acuerdas de mi casa con balcones en donde
la luz de junio ahogaba flores en tu boca?
        ¡Hermano, hermano!

Todo
eran grandes voces, sal de mercaderías,
aglomeraciones de pan palpitante,
mercados de mi barrio de Arguelles con su estatua
como un tintero pálido entre las merluzas;
el aceite llegaba a las cucharas,
un profundo latido
de pies y manos llenaba las calles,
metros, litros, esencia
aguda de la vida,
              pescados hacinados,
contextura de techos con sol frío en el cual
la flecha se fatiga,
delirante marfil fino de las patatas
tomates repetidos hasta el mar.

Y una mañana todo estaba ardiendo
y una mañana las hogueras
salían de la tierra

devorando seres,
y desde entonces fuego,
pólvora desde entonces
y desde entonces sangre.
Bandidos con aviones y con moros,
bandidos con sortijas y duquesas,
bandidos con frailes negros bendiciendo
venían por el cielo a matar niños,
y por las calles la sangre de los niños
corría simplemente, como sangre de niños.

¡Chacales que el chacal rechazaría,
piedras que el cardo seco mordería escupiendo,
víboras que las víboras odiarían!

¡Frente a vosotros he visto la sangre
de España levantarse
para ahogaros en una sola ola
de orgullo y cuchillos!

Generales
traidores:
mirad mi casa muerta,
mirad Espana rota:
pero de cada casa muerta sale metal ardiendo

139

en vez de flores,
pero de cada hueco de España
sale España,
pero de cada niño muerto sale un fusil con ojos,
pero de cada crimen nacen balas
que os hallarán un día el sitio
del corazón.

Preguntareis porqué su poesía
no nos habla del sueño, de las hojas
de los grandes volcanes de su país natal.

Venid a ver la sangre por las calles,
venid a ver
la sangre por las calles,
venid a ver la sangre
por las calles.

(I explain a few things//You will ask where are the lilacs?/And the metaphysics covered in poppies?/And the rain which often hammered/his words filling them/with birds and spaces?//Let me tell you everything that has happened to me.//I lived in a district/of Madrid, with bells/with clocks, with trees.//From there you could look out on/the dry face of Castille/like an ocean of leather./My house was called/the house of the flowers, because everywhere/geraniums blossomed; it was/a beautiful house/with dogs and children./Remember, Raul?/Remember, Rafael?/Federico, can you remember/under the earth,/do you remember my house with the balconies where/the June light drowned flowers in your mouth?/Brother, brother!//It was all/loud voices, the salt of market places,/piles of throbbing bread,/markets in my district of Arguelles with its statue/with a pale inkwell in among the hake,/the oil reached the spoons,/a deep beating/of feet and hands filled the streets,/metres, litres, sharp essence/of life/fish in mounds/a context of roofs and a cold sun where/the arrow grows tired,/the wild fine ivory of the potatoes/tomatoes in a line to the sea.//And one morning everything was burning/and one morning the fires/grew out of the earth//devouring human beings,/and since then fire,/powder since then/and since then blood./Bandits with aeroplanes and Moors,/bandits with jewels and duchesses,/bandits with black friars' blessing/came from the sky to kill children,/and in the streets the blood of children/it simply flowed, as the blood of children does.//Jackals that even the jackals would reject,/stones that the dry scrub would spit out as it chewed,/vipers that the vipers would detest!//Before you I have seen the/blood of Spain rise up/to drown you in a single wave/of pride and knives!//Generals/traitors:/look at my broken house,/look at broken Spain;/but from every broken house burning metal emerges/instead of flowers;/but from every hole in Spain/Spain bursts forth,/but from every dead child there grows a rifle with eyes,/but every crime brings forth bullets/that one day will find the place where/ your heart is.//You will ask why his poetry/does not speak to us of dreams, of leaves/of the great volcanoes of his native land.//Come and see the blood in the streets,/come and see/the blood in the streets,/come and see the blood/in the streets.)

This is a poem written at a crossroads in Neruda's life and career. His mounting unease about the validity of his poetry as a refuge from the real grew as the sense of impending chaos and collapse seemed immune to the permanence of poetic language. The purity of poetry seemed now unreal and treacherous. In his important essay 'Sobre una poesía sin pureza' (On an impure poetry), written in October 1935, Neruda offered a tentative approach to the world of producers, but he was still very loath to surrender his autonomy, his otherness as a poet. Nonetheless, he argued for the inclusion of everything in poetry, every element of lived experience, of thought and culture – a kind of riotous simultaneity that would break the rigid ordering of experience. This would be a 'poetry like a suit, like a body, stained by food and shameful gestures, with creases, insights, dreams, wakeful nights, prophesies, declarations of love and hate . . .'. And it would embrace sentimentality, melancholy, outmoded images. 'Quien huye del mal gusto cae en el hielo' (He who flees bad taste will fall on the ice).

While this declaration spoke of renouncing the isolation of the poet, and welcomed into the stock of poetic material all manner and levels of experience, it still addressed the poet as the central consciousness of the poem. It was an argument about the openness of creative artists and their sympathy with the life of others; but it was still all offered up for lyrical transformation. There were absences too in this quasi manifesto – an absence of any idea of *change*; experience was accumulation, just as the imagery of the piece itself and its associated poem 'Walking around' embraced without distinction all objects and sensations. It enumerated, naming parts, but it could not yet describe the structure of their relationship, their shifting value through time; for there was only the present.

'Explico algunas cosas' together with 'Canto a unas ruinas' (Song to some ruins) written in October 1936, record the genuine shock and disruption that occurred when the conflictive reality of those relationships invaded Neruda's lyric world: 'Let me tell you what has happened to *me*.' The hurt is personal, the insult direct. The world of flowers, children and dogs, marketplaces piled high with fresh fruit and shining fish, offer a kind of pastoral vision to which Neruda would often return,[66] but it scarcely corresponded to the tense and dramatic experience of the brief peacetime Republic between February and July 1936, and less still to the repressive period of the preceding 'black two years' (el bienio negro). It was a utopia, an insulated paradise that Neruda invoked, but his pain was no less for that. Curiously, his pain was emphasized by understatement, by the simplicity of the utterance, by the refusal to dramatize the past or remove it from its timeless innocent tranquillity. For the central topic of the work was not the explosion of unresolved social struggles, nor was there any cause for the arrival of the jackals – it was violence for its own sake. The poet was a witness to violence and, despite himself, a witness to history. The timeless world of lyrical pursuits has been destroyed, and thus dragged into time and its depredations.

Here, for a brief moment, Neruda combined his shock and outrage with the resentment that he felt at having been bodily dragged into the world of history. He had been forced to see – there was no warning, no preparation for this moment. There were 'tomatoes in a line to the sea', then suddenly there was fire, violence, violation. He railed at the 'bandits' who had perpetrated this horror. 'Bandido' is rather a naïve, ineffectual word but it carries a moral charge which saves it from banality, because here the bandits were blessed by the sinister black friars and accompanied by the landed aristocracy – and they killed children. For once, you have a sense that Neruda is lost for words, too overwhelmed by despair to say anything except shake his head and repeat incredulously that the streets are full of blood, there is blood in *the streets* which were our avenues for walking and talking. Shock had exploded into the lyric world – yet that shock was ordered, contained and disciplined by the rhetorical structures of the poetic testimony. And perhaps that is the source of its power as a poem – that rage and sorrow are held within the discipline of rhetoric, the parts allowed to stand for the whole, the greater truths forcibly kept to the human scale.

That discipline often deserted Neruda, and when it did he generated the sonorous rhetoric of the grand abstraction for which sadly he has become a model. But when it is present, and the containment of a communicative language and a shared experience holds emotion and outrage in thrall, Neruda's is the most powerful of moral statements. A question still remains, however. Was this a political poetry?

César Vallejo always regarded overtly political poetry as a contradiction in terms: 'si el artista se reduce al rol secundario y esporádico de la propaganda . . . ¿a quien le tocaría aquella gran traumaturgia del espíritu?'[67] But the Vallejo of the late twenties was beginning to refine and develop that view.[68] Visiting Russia, and reporting on it for the

Peruvian press, Vallejo came to a sophisticated understanding of what he saw there. Unlike the many international visitors of the late twenties who were impressed by Russian industrialization and efficiency, Vallejo developed increasing doubts about the Soviet Union. The influence of the American Trotskyist Max Eastman,[69] whose disillusionment with Russia paralleled his admiration for Trotsky, was undoubtedly one factor. So too was Vallejo's rapprochement with José Carlos Mariátegui, whose extension and refinement of Marxism was producing a new and creative Latin American addition to Marxist theory.[70] But Mariátegui's contribution to politics was matched by his patronage of an important and rich debate on the cultural activity of socialists conducted through the pages of his fine magazine *Amauta*. There Vallejo both wrote and read articles and testimonials that reflected the concept of the political responsibility of artists – and in his own work he was beginning, at least in prose, to experiment with forms of socialist or proletarian realism. Yet it is clear that Vallejo remained uneasy about the practices and forms of political art, and that his political allegiances were equally ambiguous. Drawn by the Communist party and especially its cultural front organizations, he nonetheless maintained a studied silence after publishing his account of a visit to Russia in 1931.[71] Living in Spain, he appears to have had little artistic contact with the poets of the period, few of whom in any case were addressing political issues in their poetry. Undoubtedly, however, Vallejo was writing the poems that were to be published in his last books *España aparta de mí este cáliz* (Spain take this cup from me) and *Poemas humanos* (Human poems) (published posthumously).

Vallejo's visits to Soviet Russia convinced him that the future would be built by a 'new man' called into being by a mass movement[72] and born and forged in struggle. Despite his distrust of the vanguard concept, Vallejo undoubtedly saw the necessity of transforming the world. But the processes whereby that transformation of consciousness could come about were much less clear to him. The poetry contained in *Poemas humanos* renders the title ironic; yet it is built upon a deeply felt yearning for a world without alienation. That alienation, the distancing from the self, the sense of being without power in one's own individuality, is central to the volume. That it can be overcome is beyond question; these poems are set in a human world, one made and transformed by human agency. Yet there is a profound pessimism here too, for it seems that while human beings continue to engage in that transforming, life-enhancing activity called labour, it has as yet no resonance in consciousness. As an increasingly convinced Marxist, Vallejo acknowledged the 'coincidence of the changing of the self and the changing of circumstances'[73] which is the central dynamic of dialectics. Yet he did not see that unity of theory and practice in Russia or in the Spanish Republic of 1931, nor indeed in those around him. That the transformation was possible remained as a hope in him. How it occurred and through whom was a different and much more problematic question.

The speaker at the core of the *Poemas humanos* is not the heroic forger of new universes, nor yet a worker, but a petty bourgeois intellectual racked by doubt and indecision. The disintegration of the great universals has led not to a heroic isolation but to a parallel disintegration of the self, of personality. The search continues for integrity, the '1', for a means of overcoming; but in the real world the utopian dream is locked into an apparently inescapable biological necessity – 'El alma que sufrió de ser cuerpo' (The soul that suffered by being a body). The dream of redemption can be foreseen, but there is no material instrument available for its attainment. What is curiously lacking in Vallejo is any sense of the collective, of social forces which can construct new certainties out of their own collective interests and needs. It is that element of Marxist revolutionary theory which remains absent in Vallejo despite his personal convictions.

Yet what remains is a powerful moral charge, a raging faith in the *necessity* of change and human fulfilment. He is frustrated and distressed by that gulf, that material absence of an overcoming of present alienation that is *present in consciousness*. That is the meaning of his mutilation.

> Existe un mutilado, no de un combate sino de un abrazo, no de la guerra sino de la paz. Perdió el rostro en el amor y no en el odio. Lo perdió en el curso normal de la vida y no en un accidente . . . Este mutilado que conozco, lleva el rostro comido por el aire inmortal e inmemorial.

> (There is a mutilated man, mutilated not in combat but in an embrace, not in war but in peace. He lost his face in love and not in hate. He lost it in the course of living and not in an accident . . . This mutilated man I know has his face eaten away by the immortal and immemorial air.)

He himself is mutilated, his physical and his mental self irreparably severed from one another.

> Como el rostro está yerto y difunto, toda la vida psíquica, toda la expresión animal de este hombre, se refugia, para traducirse al exterior, en el peludo cráneo, en el tórax y en las extremidades.

144

(Like his face he is stiff and dead, all the psychic life, all the animal expression of this man, takes refuge and translates itself in the external world into the hairy cranium, the thorax and the extremities.)

In 'La rueda del hambriento' (The circle of the hungry man), the physical man disappears into his separate physical functions; the process of metonymy is cruelly reversed as the whole becomes the parts.

> Por entre mis propios dientes salgo humeando,
> dando voces, pujando,
> bajándome los pantalones . . .
> Vaca mi estómago, vaca mi yeyuno,
> la miseria me saca por entre mis propios dientes
> cogido con un palito por el puño de la camisa.

(I emerge smoking from between my own teeth,/shouting, pushing,/ pulling my trousers down . . ./Empty my stomach, empty my jejune,/ misery pulls me through my own teeth/holding me by a toothpick by the cuff of my shirt.)

In the end the poetic project is a failure because the aspiration to insight, wholeness and ultimately understanding is made impossible by the materiality of men, by the erosion of their functions and their unrealizable needs. And language is proved, in this continuation and extension of Vallejo's opaque and paradoxical poetry, to be inter-woven with experience, time and materiality and *not* capable of autonomy. Though the demonstration of the susceptibility of language brings with it too the impossibility of constructing the self, Vallejo pursues his demonstration of the falsehood of the assertion of art's autonomy. Yet his lesson is thoroughly negative,[74] and can offer no apotheosis, no utopia to replace the communion lost in the loss of childhood.

In Spain, however, Vallejo found at last an intimation of the future.

> España aparta de mí este caliz
>
> ¡Niños del mundo, está
> la madre España con su vientre a cuestas;
> está nuestra madre con sus férulas,
> está madre y maestra,
> cruz y madera, porque os dio la altura,
> vértigo y división y suma, niños;
> está con ella, padres procesales!
>
> Si cae – digo, es un decir – si cae
> España de la tierra para abajo,
> niños, ¿como vais a cesar de crecer?

145

¡cómo va a castigar el año al mes!
¡cómo van a quedarse en diez los dientes,
en palote el diptongo, la medalla en llanto!

Niños,
hijos de los guerreros, entretanto,
bajad la voz, que España está ahora mismo repartiendo
la energía entre el reino animal,
las florecillas, los cometas y los hombres.
. . .
Bajad el aliento, y si
el antebrazo baja,
si las férulas suenan, si es la noche,
si el cielo cabe en dos limbos terrestres,
si hay ruido en el sonido de las puertas,
si tardo,
si no veis a nadie, si os asustan
los lápices sin punta, si la madre
España cae – digo, es un decir –
salid,
niños del mundo; id a buscarla . . .

(Spain take this cup from me//Children of the world, Mother Spain sweats with weariness;/our teacher with her ferules,/our mother and mistress,/our cross and our wood, for she gave you height,/dizziness and division and addition, children;/she is hard-pressed, fathers of tomorrow!//If she falls – if it should happen – if/Spain falls, from earth downward,/children don't stop growing!/The year must not punish the month!/The teeth in your mouth will not stop at ten,/the diphthong must not end on a downstroke, nor the medal in tears!//Children,/sons and daughters of the warriors, for now,/lower your voice, for Spain is even now giving out/energy through the animal world/flowers, comets and men./. . . Hush your breath, and if/her forearm falls,/if the ferules rap, if night comes,/if the sky is contained in two terrestrial limbs,/if there is a creaking in the sound of doors,/if I am late,/if you see no one, if you are frightened/by pencils without points, if Mother/Spain falls – I say, if it should happen – /go forth,/children of the world; go and seek her . . .)

There are two registers in Vallejo's response to Spain. Active in the organizations of intellectuals for the defence of the Republic he contributed speeches and manifestoes to the cause.His speech to the Madrid Cultural Congress, 'Contra el secreto profesional',[75] was a call for a committed art, clearly at the service of a great cause. His own 'Himno a los voluntarios de España' (Hymn to the volunteers in Spain) acknowledges in the proletarian volunteer a unity of theory and practice, a great purpose married to the courage to struggle, which he has found himself incapable of achieving:

> Voluntario de España, miliciano
> de hueses fidedignos, cuando marcha a morir tu corazón,
> cuando marcha a matar con su agonía
> mundial, no sé verdaderamente
> qué hacer, dónde ponerme: corro, escribo, aplaudo . . .
> ¡Voluntarios
> por la vida, por los buenos, matad
> a la muerte matad a los malos!
> Hacedlo por la libertad de todos . . .

(Volunteer in Spain, militiaman/faithful in your bones, when your heart marches into death,/when it goes to kill with its anguish/for the world, I really don't know/what to do, where to put myself: I run, I write, I applaud . . ./Volunteers/for life, for the good people, kill/death, kill the evil ones!/Do it for the liberty of all . . .)

Yet even here there is a density of language, an ambiguity of expression, which belies the certainties that shape the poem. According to his widow, Vallejo experienced serious doubts about the course of the war at an early stage[76] but when he expressed those doubts, in 'España aparta de mí este caliz' it was with the customary allusive indirectness. The Bolsheviks, the volunteers, who appear in these anthems to the conduct of the war are redeemers, saviours, superhuman in their courage and selflessness. While the workers' poems of *Poemas humanos*, like 'Gleba' (The mob) and 'A los mineros' (To the miners) bore witness to the process of production itself as analogous to the transformation of the world, there was no sense of the self-transformation which had to accompany the process if it was to be the effective revolution that Vallejo foresaw and prophesied in his poetry. The movement from the present to the fulfilled future was fraught and obscure; and the new categorical imperatives of Spain seemed powerful yet far from realization – the more so as Vallejo began to experience personal disillusion with the progress of the war. It was those doubts that imbued 'España . . .' together with the utopian conviction that the resonance of the struggle and its heroic proportion would nonetheless live on in the residual memory of future generations. Yet that memory must be fought for, dragged from the anguish of abandonment ('if you see no one, if you are frightened by pencils without points') and orphandom ('our mother and mistress, she is hard pressed.') And culture, the accumulated insights of the past, is threatened by this loss, as indeed is the very possibility of developing in consciousness a vision of a better and integrated world. It is a prospect too terrible to confront, too awful to mention above a whisper, ('I say, if it happens') – and indeed there were very few who dared to speak of defeat.

There are then two conflicting perspectives in Vallejo's poetry in Spain. Sharing the collective conviction, he wrote with visionary confidence of the imminent victory of democracy, yet he harboured too a doubt too profound and too deeply embedded to be shed. Perhaps Vallejo was a cultural product of his age and class; his relentless honesty and his obvious revolutionary conviction could give him no refuge in ideological utopias or nostalgia, nor allow him the solace of a refuge in an autonomous realm of art. Vallejo acknowledged the material source of culture and its renewal in the transforming practice of human beings in the world – in that sense his poetry is human and humanistic. Yet when the revolution began, he found himself watching, a helpless witness without a role to play. Did this suggest that he felt himself imprisoned by his own class horizons, that he saw himself as incapable of breaking out of that trap and assuming a different world view? Or was he unable to overcome his uneasiness about the renunciation of individuality, fractured and crisis-ridden though it was, for a collective purpose – the selflessness he so admired in the 'voluntario'?

5

The Feeling of the World:
The Poet and Society under
Vargas

'I Have Just Two Hands'

Sentimento do Mundo

Tenho apenas duas mãos
e o sentimento do mundo,
mas estou cheio de escravos,
minhas lembranças escorrem
e o corpo transige
na confluência do amor.

Quando me levantar, o céu
estará morto e saqueado,
eu mesmo estarei morto,
morto meu desejo morto
o pântano sem acordes.

Os camaradas não disseram
que havia uma guerra
e era necessário
trazer fogo e alimento.
Sinto-me disperso,
anterior a fronteiras,
humildemente vos peço
que me perdoeis.

Quando os corpos passarem,
eu ficarei sozinho
desfiando a recordação

149

do sineiro, da viúva e do microscopista
que habitavam a barraca
e não foram encontrados
ao amanhecer

esse amanhecer
mais noite que a noite.[1]

(The feeling of the world//I have just two hands/and the feeling of the
world, but I am full of slaves,/my memories are a flowing stream/and my
body yields/in the confluence of love.//When I get up, the sky/will be
dead and pillaged,/I myself shall be dead,/dead my desire, dead/the
chordless swamp.//The comrades didn't say/that there was a war on/and
that we had/to bring fire and food./I feel dispersed, prior to frontiers,/I
humbly beg you/to forgive me.//When the bodies have passed on,/I shall
be left alone/telling the thread of memories/of the bellringer, the widow
and the microscopist/who lived in the shack/and were not found/at
dawn//that dawn/which is darker than the night.)

'I have just two hands/and the feeling of the world': after the complex
and multifarious writing of the 1920s, this is the single overriding
problem which was to occupy the fifteen years of poetry written in
Brazil under the regime of Getúlio Vargas. The opening statement of
Drummond's 'Feeling of the world', taken on its own, expresses a
familiar, perhaps banal response to the dilemma of social conscious-
ness; the individual's sense of inadequacy in the face of the collective
suffering of humanity. The poet recognizes himself as a social being,
but passively so; the knowledge weighs heavily like the inescapable
guilt of belonging to a history of slavery. His relationship to the world
is involuntary, instinctive, the melting together of bodies in the flux of
sexual intercourse.

What follows is the realization that his posture of impotent despair,
his failure to assume his social being in an active, conscious way will
be revisited upon him, as he is left amidst the rubble and corpses to
face the darkness of defeat alone. The poem is more than a simple
confession of guilt, for there is a certain inevitability in the future
tenses of the second and fourth stanzas, suggesting that he is con-
demned to this dilemma of unrealized social consciousness, of integ-
ration into the world yet alienation from it. The death of self and of all
desire which he contemplates in the second stanza is the proof of his
humanity, of his rootedness in the world, coming as it does as a kind of
post-coital anticlimax after the sexual flux of stanza 1. But his absorp-
tion in that world, paradoxically, has rendered him incapable of acting
consciously upon it, of taking a stand in the struggles of society, and

defending one part of it against another – 'I feel dispersed,/prior to frontiers.'

While this contradiction seems to condemn him to solitude, a role still remains for the poet in the aftermath of battle. A creative purpose inhabits the closing image of the poet unravelling the memory of the anonymous 'little' people destroyed by the conflict, telling their memories like beads on a rosary. The 'dawn/darker than the night' after the bodies have disappeared, while most obviously suggesting death and despair, also looks towards some kind of time or space in which the material conditions separating individuals will be broken down, and where understanding and communion between people can be recovered. While the poem suggests that the intellectual's relationship to the world remains highly problematic, artistic activity – the 'telling' of the rosary of human experience – perhaps continues to offer a focus of communication in the darkness.

'Feeling of the world' was first published in May 1935, before the major international conflicts of the decade – the Spanish Civil War and the outbreak of the Second World War – which might obviously be identified with the drama of the poem. Yet much had already happened within Brazil to give an immediate historical meaning to the poem's sense of dilemma and urgency. In October 1930, a number of junior army officers and the Liberal Alliance, a coalition of forces politically opposed to the ruling oligarchy, brought Getúlio Vargas to power in a coup. The new regime made room for a rising industrial bourgeoisie seeking protectionist measures to create an independent manufacturing base. At the same time it established the institutional structures which would be fully implemented with the Estado Novo ('New State') of 1937, introducing corporate, fascist-inspired labour legislation to suppress independent working-class organization.

The rise to power of Hitler and Mussolini had other repercussions, too; Brazil's fascist party, Ação Integralista Brasileira, founded in 1932, organized its first march in April 1933 and was able to mobilize 42,000 activists at a national congress in October 1935. In the previous year the *integralistas* had clashed with an anti-fascist Popular Front organization led by the Communist Party but including Troskyists, anarchists and socialists. In November 1935, the Aliança Nacional Libertadora, as it was now called, mounted a premature insurrection against the regime in Natal, Recife and Rio de Janeiro. It was easily crushed; 20,000 activists and sympathizers were imprisoned, and many tortured, ushering in the dark period of repression of the Estado Novo.[2]

151

The social and political contradictions that had crystallized during the 1920s, far from being resolved by the 'Revolution' of 1930, now entered into open, organized conflict. The ironic, objective distance assumed by the poets of that decade, the utopian, abstract idealism of some and the visceral, populist sympathies of others, were no longer adequate responses to the totalitarian structures of ideological and political power which were now being violently imposed on Brazilian society. If the dissidence of bourgeois intellectuals and artists could, in the 1920s, be expressed simultaneously as aristocratic detachment and avant-garde radicalism, the 1930s demanded a clearer examination and definition of their relation to the class forces now engaged in struggle.

A Critique of Self

For those closest to the organized left, in particular the Communist Party, that self-examination was ruthlessly imposed from above, with the 'proletarianization' of the Party in 1931 and the criticism of member intellectuals as petty bourgeois. Oswald de Andrade, who joined the Party in 1929, gave an evaluation of his own role in the Modernist movement in a 1933 preface to the novel *Serafim Ponte Grande* (Seraphim Grosse Pointe):

> The 'revolutionary' situation of this South American mental dung-heap appeared in the following terms: the antithesis of the bourgeois was not the proletarian – it was the bohemian! The masses, ignored within the country and then as now, under the economic debauchery of politicians and of the rich. The intellectuals playing ring-a-ring-a-roses. . . . Without much money, but outside the revolutionary axis of the world, knowing nothing of the Communist Manifesto and not wanting to be bourgeois, I naturally became a bohemian. . . .
>
> From my basic anarchism there always gushed a healthy spring, sarcasm. I served the bourgeoisie without believing in it. Like the exploited courtier I tailored the ridiculous clothes of the Regent.[3]

Regarding his dialectical theory of Brazilian culture, Brazil-wood, he drew the following economic analogy:

> The coffee valorization was an imperialist operation. So was Brazil-wood Poetry. It was bound to collapse with the fanfares of the crisis. Just like almost all the 'avant-garde' literature, it was provincial and suspect, if not extremely worn out and reactionary.[4]

152

Indeed, if the Vargas regime expressed something of the spirit of the Brazil-wood Manifesto, beginning the construction of a national industrial economy, the new 'independent' identity was falsely compromised, dependent upon heavy North American and European investment, and was achieved through the ruthless suppression of the libertarian social revolution envisaged in Oswald's *Cannibalist Manifesto*.

The best-known, and most influential appraisal of the experience of the 1920s was the conference paper given by Mário de Andrade in April 1942 under the title 'The Modernist Movement''. Although the failure of the movement, as Mário saw it, was linked to its 'destructive spirit', the problem lay not in the destructive spirit itself, which was both historically necessary and expressive of the social and political crisis that culminated in 1930. Rather it was that the generation's anti-bourgeois stance took the form of a festive, aristocratic individualism that, for all its doctrinaire radicalism, was more destructive of itself than of the order it pretended to challenge. There was no better illustration of this than the Modernists' nationalism:

> For in fact, what characterizes this numerous group of Modernists of startling political adaptability, prattling on about national definitions, these optimistic sociologists, what characterizes them is a legitimate, disguised conformism, ill disguised in the best of them, but in reality full of a cynical satisfaction. The rootedness in the land, shouted out in doctrines and manifestos, was nothing more than accommodating conformism. Less than rootedness, it was a deafening, rather academic sing-song, which not infrequently turned into an awful jingoistic chauvinism.[5]

What Mário missed from the writing of his generation was a sense of reality, 'a more worldly passion, a more vigorously living pain'. Instead of breaking windows and discussing passing fashions, 'we should have flooded the utilitarian decrepitude of our discourse with a greater anguish of our time, with a greater revolt against life as it is.' In the closing pages of this severely honest assessment of his own work and that of his generation, Mário arrived at a view of the kind of commitment which they lacked, not necessarily a party-political commitment, but a preparedness to intervene in the world and change it:

> I can't imagine myself as an active politician. But we are living a political age of man, and that is what I was bound to serve. But in short, I can only

153

see myself, like some Amador Bueno, saying 'I won't' and absenting myself from actuality behind the contemplative doors of a monastery. Neither would I want myself to be writing explosive pages, fighting tooth and nail for ideologies and winning the easy laurels of jail. All that's not me and not for me. But I am convinced that we should have turned from speculatists into speculators. There is always a way of slipping into a point of view, a choice of values, a misty tear which will swell even more the unbearableness of the present conditions of the world. No. We became abstemious and transcendent abstentionists. . . .[6]

It might be argued that Mário's direct experience of the Estado Novo and its devastating effect on his career must have coloured his disillusioned post mortem of the Modernist movement. As early as 1931, however, in the wake of the movement's dissolution and the politicization of many of its members, Drummond, too, was acutely aware of a sense of crisis and of the new challenges confronting the cultural community. In an interview whose title denounced the failure of a whole generation of intellectuals, Drummond remained pessimistic about the likelihood of that generation achieving anything concrete in the future. Faced with the grand ideological choices of the age and the difficulty (for the moment, at least) of commitment to any of them, the only alternative option might be to retreat into the subjective, into the interpretation of dreams and the Freudian paradise of Bandeira's Pasárgada:

> Spiritually, my generation stands before three paths, or three solutions –
> God, Freud and communism. To be precise, there are only two directions: a Catholic, fascist action organized in 'Defence of the West', on the one hand. And on the other hand the Muscovite paradise, with its terrible and therefore alluring seduction. Which is an appeal to all that persists within us that is romantic and uncontrolled.[7]

The poetry of Drummond's *Brejo das Almas* (Morass of Souls) (1934), which marks this moment of crisis, typically fights shy of the grand truths and solutions; death and especially suicide are constantly mocked as impossible options for an impossible existence. Where it differs from *Alguma Poesia* (Some Poetry) (1930), covering the previous decade, is in the meaning of its irony, which no longer permits the poet to view life from a safe distance; this impossible world is also an inescapable world. If there is no way out, yet no truth either, then the only response might seem to be a stoic silence, as proposed in 'Coisa miserável' (Miserable thing):

154

Mas de nada vale
gemer ou chorar,
de nada vale
erguer mãos e olhos
para um céu tão longe,
para um deus tão longe
ou, quem sabe? para um céu vazio

É melhor sorrir
(sorrir gravemente)
e ficar calado
e ficar fechado
entre duas paredes,
sem a mais leve cólera
ou humilhação.

(But there's no point/in moaning or weeping,/there's no point/in raising
hands and eyes/to such a distant heaven,/to such a distant god/or, who
knows? to an empty heaven.//It's better to smile/(to smile gravely)/and
remain silent/and remain shut in/between two walls,/without the sligh-
test anger/or humiliation.)

Silence is seemingly all that is offered in 'Segredo' (Secret), too, one of
the few poems in the volume to deal directly with the question of
poetry itself. That silence, though, is not now the ironically resigned
futility of 'Miserable thing', but a stubborn defiance, a dignified refusal
to be overwhelmed and subjugated by a universe of infinite possibili-
ties which the self cannot grasp:

A poesia é incomunicável.
Fique torto no seu canto.
Não ame.

Ouço dizer que há tiroteio
ao alcance de nosso corpo.
É a revolução? o amor?
Não diga nada.

Tudo é possível, só eu impossível.
O mar transborda de peixes.
Há homens que andam no mar
como se andassem na rua.
Não conte.

Suponha que um anjo de fogo
varresse a face da terra
e os homens sacrificados
pedissem perdão.
Não peça.

155

THE GATHERING OF VOICES

(Poetry is incommunicable./Sit wryly in your corner [song]./Don't love.//
I hear there is shooting/within reach of our bodies./Is it revolution?
love?/Don't say anything.//Everything is possible, only I'm impossible./
The sea is brimming over with fish./There are men walking on the sea/as
if they were walking in the street./Don't tell.//Suppose that an angel of
fire/swept the face of the earth/and the sacrificed men/asked forgive-
ness./Don't ask.)

Yet, paradoxically, Drummond continued writing. The key to the
paradox is contained in the ambiguity of the poem's second line and
the word 'canto': the poet is driven into his impossible corner of
incommunicability, but is forced nevertheless to express the very
distortedness of his position, to make poetry out of his contradiction.
This modest statement of the necessity of expression, even in a world
which seems to deny it meaning, reveals the same search for a genuine
artistic role which we saw in 'Feeling of the world', and which
Drummond was to pursue with increasing confidence and success
over the next decade.

In 1932 Mário de Andrade, a supporter of the liberal São Paulo
Democratic Party since 1927, wrote to Drummond of the moral conflict
which the middle-class constitutionalist rebellion of the same year
placed before him. On the one hand, his instinctive anti-militarism
and ideological agnosticism; on the other, the dedication of family and
friends to the cause, his brother's imprisonment and the proximity of
death, which eventually forced him to 'sell his objectivity' in a reluc-
tant self-surrender to the unanimity of social feeling. This brief
moment of unqualified commitment, his self-declared visceral com-
munism, he described elsewhere as a desperate 'mentira-verdade'
(lie-truth),

> to this very 'felt', very 'lived' awareness of the moment, that not only is
> a, my God!, communistic socialism bound to be the next social form for
> man, but that I must, without any bragging or 'hope' of personal benefit,
> fight for it. Even if I were wrong, even if I were to go crazy, even . . .
> middle-aged and clumsy, even with my impoverished possibilities, fight
> for it.[8]

The permanent torment of dilemmas such as this, which on at least
one occasion brought Mário to the brink of suicide, appears in its most
extreme form in 'O Carro da Miséria' (The Wagon of Misery), begun in
1930, continued in 1932 and completed in 1943. This is Mário at his
most anguished and surreal, where the grotesque, funereal carnival of
a distorted civilization drunkenly parades its heroes and plays its
devastating games of betrayal with the people:

V

Plaff! chegou o Carro da Miséria
Do carnaval intaliano!
Tia Miséria vem vestida de honour (honra)
Côr de cobre do tempo
Atrás dela recolhendo guspe.
O caronel, o ginaral o gafetão
O puro o heróico o bem-intencionado
Fio da usina brasilera
Requebra o povo de Colombo.

Tia Miséria vai se ajeita
E tira o peido da miséria

Mámores estralam rebentados
Vento sulão barrendo as chamas
Contorce os pinheiros machados
Zine o espaço carpideira
Arrancando os cabelos
Dos luminosos magistrais
E à luz dos raios que te partam
Colhida pelos vendavais
Faz bilboquê com a bolinha do mundo
A cibalização cristã.

(Bump! the Wagon of Misery's here/From the Eyetalian carnival!/Old Ma Misery is dressed in *honour*/The colour of the brass of our age/Gathering spittle behind her./The colonil the generul the kaptin/The pure the heroic the well-meaning/Childrin of the Brazilyun factory/Columbus's people are swinging.//Old Ma Misery gets herself settled/And lets out the fart of misery.//Marble statues crack and explode/Southern wind sweeping the flames/Twisting the pine-trees, axes,/The air whines in mourning/Tearing out the hair/Of the resplendent high-priests/And strike you, by the light of the thunderbolts/Seized by the gales/Christian civilarzation/Plays cup-and-ball with the world.)

Forced to pull the wagon like an ox, the poet sings, ironically, 'with conviction' and utters a delirious cry of disgust, rage and love, mutilating his language – 'Chorar é bom, rir bim, raivar é bão, pão pão' – in a desperate effort to shake himself free of the nightmare:

157

Tôrpe é a cidade. Um desejo sombrio de estupro
Um desejo de destruir tudo num grito
Num grito não num gruto
E dar um beijo em cada mão de quem trabalha . . .

(The city is foul. A sombre desire to rape/A desire to destroy it all in a shout/In a shout not a shart/And kiss every worker on the hand . . .)

As dawn approaches, in a parody of Bandeira's Pasárgada he promises to 'go away to Belém', to 'reentrar no meu povo/Reprincipiar minha ciência' (go back to my people/To begin again my science) and come back next week, when 'my land will belong to her or to no one'. With the cock-crow, however, no revolutionary saviour is born, only the sober expectation that Misery will give birth to vassals, decorative ribbons, crimes, gods of war and dances – in other words, to the stuff of a culture which is 'nossa exatidão', true to us, the sum of ourselves and perhaps the basis of a longer struggle to create a world which will truly belong to no one and everyone.

For all the despairing impotence of Mário's vision in 'The Wagon of Misery', it represents a significant advance from the poetry of the 1920s, in that the poet has now entered the world of which he is speaking; his language expresses a violent battle to recover a sense of sanity and integrity from the nightmarish chaos, but it is one that can only be waged from within.

The surrealist images of Drummond's 'Secret' and Mário's 'The Wagon of Misery' were symptomatic of the crisis of a petty bourgeois, intellectual consciousness forced by the spectacle of a savage social and political struggle to confront and question its own agnostic isolation. The surrealist tradition in Brazil is more commonly associated, however, with two other poets of the decade – Murilo Mendes and Jorge de Lima – whose Christian mysticism offered a reassuring alternative to the disturbing scepticism of the Andrades, one which still finds a wide audience today. Both were deeply influenced by the 'Catholic Renaissance' led by Jackson de Figueiredo and Tasso da Silveira and promoted via the review A Ordem (1921) and its successor Festa (1927). Despite their close association and even partnership as poetic visionaries, Mendes and Lima were products of different artistic backgrounds (the avant-garde experiments of the 1920s, and the Northeastern Regionalist movement, respectively), which perhaps explains the distinctive qualities of their work.

The poet of Murilo Mendes's O Visionário (The Visionary) (1930–33) is still a powerless spectator, despite his identification with the people ('the vendor on the corner, the priest, the beggar . . ., constructed in my image and likeness').[9] Mendes views the spectacle of tyranny and war as an archetypal conflict between the forces of innocence and evil in a world which, for the moment, God has abandoned or turned against. The figure of the Dictator, which appears more than once in this book, therefore has a dual identity, as the master of a metaphysical order and of a political-economic system against which the poet rebels in impotent isolation. In 'Novíssimo Prometeu' (The Last Prometheus), for instance, this rebellion is compared to that of the tragic creator figure of Greek mythology, punished by Zeus for bringing knowledge to mankind:

> Então o ditador do mundo
> Mandou me prender no Pão de Açúcar:
> Vêm esquadrilhas de aviões
> Bicar o meu pobre fígado.
> Vomito bílis em quantidade,
> Contemplo lá em baixo as filhas do mar
> Vestidas de maiô, cantando sambas,
> Vejo madrugadas e tardes nascerem
> – Pureza e simplicidade da vida! –
> Mas não posso pedir perdão.

(Then the dictator of the world/Had me imprisoned on the Sugar Loaf:/ Squadrons of aeroplanes come/And peck at my poor liver./I vomit bile copiously,/I contemplate below the daughters of the sea/Dressed in swimsuits, singing sambas,/I see dawns and evenings being born/ – Life's purity and simplicity! – /But I cannot ask forgiveness.)

As the last quotation suggests, the state of innocence, the possibility of communication and of a transcendent integration safe from the conflicts of time and space, all tend to be associated with the figure of woman, to which Mendes returned repeatedly throughout his work. The women of 'Mulher em todos os tempos' (Woman in all times), 'Dilatação da poesia' (Expansion of poetry) and 'Jandira' are mythical creatures protected by angels, untouched by the material vicissitudes of history and embodying a timeless spirituality that is manifested eternally through the generations of daughter, mother and wife:

> E as filhas de Jandira
> Inda parecem mais velhas do que ela.
> E Jandira não morre,
> Espera que os clarins do juízo final

159

Venham chamar seu corpo,
Mas eles não vêm.
E mesmo que venham, o corpo de Jandira
Ressuscitará inda mais belo, mais ágil e transparente.

(And Jandira's daughters/Seem even older than her./And Jandira does not die,/She waits for the clarions of the final judgement/To come and call for her body,/But they do not come./And even if they do, Jandira's body/Will be restored to life even more beautiful, agile and transparent.)

Insulated from the historical and social dramas taking place around her, Jandira preserves her own purity but by the same token leaves the world and its contradictions unaltered, unresolved. The poet may state, in 'Mulher vista do alto de uma pirâmide' (Woman seen from the top of a pyramid): 'Mulher, tu és a convergência de dois mundos' (Woman, you are the convergence of two worlds), but the real sense of a meeting between the spiritual and material spheres only occurs at moments of doubt. Ideal and reality instead occupy different, irreconcilable realms.

It is worth, in this respect, comparing Mendes's image of woman with that found in the work of Manuel Bandeira during the same period. Bandeira's women, although usually unattainable, are nevertheless the objects of an ordinary, plebeian love that reflects the poet's earthy, human conception of Catholicism, and which makes possible a sort of communion with his fellow beings. The title poem of *Estrela da manhã* (Morning star) (1936) makes the following plea:

> Pecai por todos pecai com todos
> Pecai com os malandros
> Pecai com os sargentos
> Pecai com os fuzileiros navais
> Pecai de todas as maneiras
> Com os gregos e com os troianos
> Com o padre e com o sacristão
> Com o leproso de Pouso Alto
>
> Depois comigo[10]

(Sin for everyone sin with everyone/Sin with scoundrels/Sin with sergeants/Sin with naval fusiliers/Sin in every way/With Greeks and with Trojans/With the priest and the sacristan/With the leper from Pouso Alto//Then with me.)

This objectification of woman as the focus of both spiritual redemption and sensual desire, alternately symbolic of transcendence and immanence, occupies a central place in the work of Mendes and Bandeira, in their attempts to come to terms with the problem of 'being in the world'. It may seem ironic, then, that the female figure who stands virtually alone (in more ways than one) in a tradition overwhelmingly dominated by male poets, yet who has been described as 'the most important female poet of the Portuguese language',[11] should have also apparently chosen to write squarely within a framework of literary conventions shaped by men. Cecília Meireles, like Lima and Mendes, began her career under the aegis of the philosophical and spiritualist tendencies of the Catholic renaissance, as well as absorbing much from the earlier work of the Symbolists. She first gained real recognition with *Viagem* (Journey) (1939), which seemed to have little in common with the experimentalism of the avant-garde Modernists, opting instead for 'universal' themes, a Baroque contemplation of the transitory nature of experience, the theme of *tempus fugit*, and exploiting the musicality of forms drawn from the medieval Portuguese tradition of the *Cancioneiro* (Songbook).

But, as Marta Peixoto argues in an important recent study of the poet,[12] Meireles's subtle and peculiar manipulation of these forms, and her exploration of a fragmented, alienated personal identity, suggest important parallels with the more radical concerns of the Modernists. In 'Rimance', from *Vaga Música* (Vague Music) (1942), for instance, a female voice protests against her imprisonment within a frail and vulnerable body, and its paradoxical denial of her living being:

> Por que me destes um corpo,
> se estava tão descansada,
> nisso que é talvez o Todo,
> mas parece tanto o Nada?
>
> Desde então andei perdida,
> pois meu corpo não bastava,
> – meu corpo não me servia
> senão para ser escrava . . .
>
> De longe vinham guerreiros,
> de longe vinham soldados.
> Eu, com muitos ferimentos
> e os meus dois braços atados . . .
>
> Uma lágrima floria
> no meio da sanha brava.
> Era a voz da minha vida
> que de longe vos chamava.[13]

161

(Why didst thou give me a body,/when I was so at rest,/in that place which perhaps is All,/but does so seem to be Nothing?//Since then I have wandered lost,/For my body was not enough/ – my body was of no use to me/except to be a slave . . . //Warriors came from afar,/soldiers came from afar./I, with many wounds/and my hands both tied . . .//A flower bloomed/in the midst of that savage fury./It was the voice of my life/ calling you from afar.)

'Auto-retrato' (Self-portrait), meanwhile, from *Mar Absoluto* (Absolute Sea) (1945), addresses more directly the multiplicity and elusiveness of a self which, like that of Drummond's poetry during this period, (see 'Secret' and 'I carry with me', *The Rose of the People*, below) knows itself to be invaded and fragmented by the world and struggles to restore its sense of continuity and integration:

> Se me contemplo,
> tantas me vejo,
> que não entendo
> quem sou, no tempo
> do pensamento.
>
> Vou desprendendo
> elos que tenho,
> alças, enredos . . .
> E é tudo imenso . . .
> . . .
>
> Múltipla, venço
> este tormento
> do mundo eterno
> que em mim carrego:
> e, una, contemplo
> o jogo inquieto
> em que padeço.
>
> E recupero
> o meu alento
> e assim vou sendo.

(If I contemplate myself,/I see so many selves,/that I cannot understand/ who I am, in the time/of thought.//I begin to loosen/the ties, loops, tangles/that are mine . . ./And it is all immense . . ./. . ./Multiple, I overcome/this torment/of the eternal world/I carry within me:/and, at one, I contemplate/the restless game/in which I suffer.//And I catch my breath again/and so I go on being.)

If, as Meireles acknowledged in a letter of 1946, 'Temos que falar segundo as suas convenções' (We have to speak in accordance with their conventions), this did not prevent her from ingeniously subverting those conventions in order to install the female self as the subject of a traditionally male discourse. One such example is her rewriting of the medieval Portuguese *cantiga de amor*, originally addressed by a male *trovador* to a remote and inaccessible lady. By adopting this viewpoint herself in 'Amor em Leonoreta', Meireles 'echoes the cross-gendered performance of the *cantiga de amigo*' (in which the male poet assumed a female voice), so that Leonoreta's lack of carnality, her material absence, is transformed into a space of emotional dialogue between two feminine personae, the focus of tension between desire for the other's presence and celebration of that absence and therefore of the permanence of desire. In Marta Peixoto's words, 'Meireles alters the convention with a masculine bias of the *cantiga de amor*, an apparently inhospitable one for woman as a speaker. She replaces the masculine voice with a generically unmarked first person, feminine with reference to the poem's signature, and foregrounds the narcissistic implications of that convention'.[14]

As in so many other compositions depicting solitary women – the Diana of *Absolute Sea*, the figure contemplating her shadow in 'Minha sombra', or the abandoned lover of 'A amiga deixada' – the female subject achieves a kind of celibate freedom in her dialogue with self or other, but a necessarily lonely freedom, perhaps the only kind available to a woman poet in Brazil in the first half of the twentieth century:

> Leonoreta
> fin'roseta,
> longe vai teu vulto amado.
> Porém resiste ao meu lado
> o espaço que ocuparias.
>
> . . .
>
> Leonoreta
> fin'roseta,
> não mais penso por onde andas . . .
> Guardo por altas varandas
> tua fala em meus ouvidos.
>
> . . .
>
> Leonoreta
> fin'roseta,
> não me vês, mas eu te vejo.
> Não te quero nem desejo:
> morrerei, se suspirares.

(Leonoreta/rosebud fair,/the shadow of your love roams far./Yet the space that you would occupy/remains beside me still.//. . .//Leonoreta/rosebud fair,/I no more think of where you wander . . ./In my ears I keep/ the words you spoke over lofty balconies.//. . .//Leonoreta/rosebud fair,/ you see me not, but I see you./I neither want nor desire you:/I shall die, if you breathe a sigh.)

Vinicius de Moraes (1913–80), whose work reached maturity during the same period, represents the antithesis of Meireles's detached, contemplative mood, although in his early work he, too, wrote in the mystical, symbolist vein of the Catholic revivalists. He shared with Meireles a growing preference for synthetic, musical forms, in particular the sonnet and ballad, but these were vehicles for the celebration of a sensual, erotically charged world of which he was a participant rather than an observer, 'a poet of biographies more than of ideas'.[15] Like Mendes's Jandira, the elusive figure of 'Ariana, a Mulher' (The Woman, Ariana) (1936) is 'mother, daughter, wife, bride, beloved!', but rather than an ideal being, she is the object of a passionate desire, investing with its energy the whole of the natural world through which the poet pursues her:

E perguntei: Pescadores, onde está Ariana? – e eles me mostravam o
peixe
Ferreiros, onde está Ariana? – e eles me mostravam o fogo
Mulheres, onde está Ariana? – e elas me mostravam o sexo.[16]

(And I asked: Fishermen, where is Ariana? – and they showed me the fish/Blacksmiths, where is Ariana? – and they showed me the fire/ Women, where is Ariana? – and they showed me their sex.)

The rhythmic and melodic qualities of the shorter verse forms tend to intensify this emotional flux, indeed, when combined with the colloquial register inherited from the 1920s Modernists and Moraes's own familiarity with guitar-accompanied song, they would find their most natural expression in the samba compositions of the 1950s and '60s. During the war years, though, this directly participative, social engagement with the world led him to address political themes, as in the 'Balada dos mortos dos campos de concentração' (Ballad of the dead of the concentration-camps) and 'A bomba atômica' (The atomic bomb). Here, his customary celebration of female sexuality is turned to a different emotional effect, as he longs to cradle the bomb in his arms, to console and lay to rest the pent-up, explosive force that has, ironically, already been unleashed:

164

Para te defender, levanto o braço
Paro as radiações espaciais
Uno-me aos líderes e aos bardos, uno-me
Ao povo, ao mar e ao céu brado o teu nome
Para te defender, matéria dura
Que és mais linda, mais límpida e mais pura
Que a estrela matutina! Oh bomba atômica
Que emoção não me dá ver-te suspensa
Sobre a massa que vive e se condensa
Sob a luz! Anjo meu, fora preciso
Matar, com tua graça e teu sorriso
Para vencer?

(I raise my arm to defend you/I block the radiation-waves from space/I unite with leaders and with bards, I unite/With the people, I cry out your name to the sea and sky/To defend you, harsh matter/Who are more lovely, more crystalline and pure/Than the morning star! Oh atomic bomb/How moved I am to see you suspended/Over that living mass gathering close/Beneath the light! My angel, did you,/With your grace and smile, need to kill/In order to conquer?)

Listening for the Clash of Time

The spectacle of social conflict had rocked the old certainties, then, but did not necessarily put anything in their place. Not everyone who identified with the oppressed saw any hope of emancipation in their own independent struggle, as Murilo Mendes's *The Visionary* demonstrated. In the 'Third Book' of the collection, Mendes's crisis of faith reaches its culmination, as he stands powerless at the margins of the struggle, unable 'to breathe the spirit of life into anyone, . . . or to change the direction of the world' (Alta tensão – High tension), casting the image of the Virgin into the fire as the 'hour of general protest' seems to announce its apocalyptic consummation:

Fomes desejos ânsias sonhos perdidos
Misérias de todos os países uni-vos
Fogem a galope os anjos-aviões
Carregando o cálice da esperança
Tempo espaço firmes porque me abandonastes.
('O filho do século' – Child of the century)

165

(Hungers desires longings lost dreams/Miseries of all countries unite/
The angel-planes gallop in flight/Carrying off the cup of hope/Steady
time and space why have you abandoned me.)

This contradiction was not confined to the poetry of the period, but
was central to the entire cultural movement generally referred to as
regionalism. Brazilian literature in the 1930s is known above all for the
large body of 'committed' neo-realist fiction devoted to the socio-
economic problems and changes experienced by the people of the
underdeveloped and drought-ridden Northeast. Yet, just as the anti-
fascist Popular Front of the same period could bring together commu-
nists, anarchists, socialists and liberals, the ideological expressions
taken by Brazilian regionalism ranged from the revolutionary Marxism
of Jorge Amado to the nostalgic conservatism of José Lins do Rego and
Gilberto Freyre, for whom industrialization brought the disintegration
of the social and spiritual cohesion of the traditional plantation
economy.

The same ambivalence is present in the work of the mulatto Jorge de
Lima, whose *Poemas negros* (Black poems) (1947) have been seen as a
poetry of social revindication comparable to the Afro-Cubanism of
Nicolás Guillén. Certainly a poem such as 'Rei é Oxalá, Rainha é
Iemanjá' (Oxalá is king, Yemanjá is queen) unequivocally situates the
exploitation of black Brazilians within a general framework of class
exploitation, and calls on the divinities of Afro-Brazilian religion to
avenge them:

> Rei é Oxalá que nasceu sem se criar.
> Rainha é Iemanjá que pariu Oxalá sem se manchar.
> Grande santo é Ogum em seu cavalo encantado.
> Eu cumba vos dou curau. Dai-me licença angana.
> Porque a vós respeito,
> e a vós peço vingança
> contra os demais aleguás e capiangos brancos, Agô!
> que nos escravizam, que nos exploram,
> a nós operários africanos,
> servos do mundo,
> servos dos outros servos.
> Oxalá! Iemanjá! Ogum!
> Há mais de dois mil anos o meu grito nasceu![17]

(Oxalá is king and was born without being conceived./Yemanjá is queen,
who bore Oxalá without being dishonoured./Ogum is a great saint on
his enchanted horse./I, brave one, give you *curau*. Excuse me *angana*./
Because I respect you,/I ask you for vengeance/on the white thieves and

other scum, Agô!/who enslave us and exploit us/African workers,/ servants of the world/servants of other servants./Oxalá! Yemanjá! Ogum!/My cry was born two thousand years ago!)

Elsewhere, however, Lima's defence of black identity rests upon the kind of 'positive' racial stereotyping which, as so often in the fiction of Jorge Amado, celebrates the African's inherent spontaneity, musicality and good humour. 'Olá negro' (Hello black man), for instance:

A raça que te enforca, enforca-se de tédio, negro!
És tu que a alegras ainda com os teus jazzes,
com os teus songs, com os teus lundus!
Os poetas, os libertadores, os que derramaram
babosas torrentes de falsa piedade
não compreendiam que tu ias rir!
E o teu riso, e a tua virgindade e os teus medos e tua bondade
mudariam a alma branca cansada de todas as ferocidades.

(The race that is hanging you, is hanging itself with boredom, black man!/And it is you who makes it merry with your jazz,/your songs, your *lundus*!/The poets, liberators, those who have spouted/drivelling torrents of false pity/did not understand that you would laugh!/And that your laughter and your virginity and your fears and your goodness/ would change the white soul, weary of all its brutality.)

The defence of the black is essentially a defence of moral values, of spirituality, innocence, 'poetry' against the prosaic materialism represented by the 'whitening' of Brazilian society. The religious poetry which occupies the bulk of Lima's output during the rest of his career does not therefore mark a break with his Africanism but rather a continuation and development of it.

In 1935 Lima published *Tempo e eternidade* (Time and eternity) in collaboration with Murilo Mendes. At a moment when the class antagonisms generated by Brazil's modernization were reaching their most violent political expression, Lima and Mendes discovered a visionary, evangelical role for themselves as poets, announcing the resolution of those conflicts in another realm. Thus Mendes could write, in 'Vocação do poeta' (Vocation of the poet):

Vim para anunciar que a voz dos homens
Abafará a voz da sirene e da máquina,
E que a palavra essencial de Jesus Cristo
Dominará as palavras do patrão e do operário.

(I have come to announce that the voice of men/Will hush the voice of the siren and the machine,/And that the essential word of Jesus Christ/ Will subdue the words of the boss and the worker.)

THE GATHERING OF VOICES

or, in 'Filiação' (Lineage), that

> Sinto-me acima das bandeiras,
> Tropeçando em cabeças de chefes.
> Caminho no mar, na terra e no ar.
> Eu sou da raça do Eterno,
> Do amor que unirá todos os homens:
> Vinde a mim, órfãos da poesia,
> Choremos sobre o mundo mutilado.

(I feel I am above flags,/Stumbling over the heads of leaders./I walk on the sea, on the earth and in the air./I am of the race of the Eternal one,/Of the love which will unite all men: Come to me, orphans of poetry,/Let us weep over the mutilated world.)

Jorge de Lima's *A Túnica Inconsútil* (The Seamless Tunic) (1938), meanwhile, promised the hungry, the desperate, the afflicted and abandoned, an eternal sleep which would put to rest the drama and pain of the archetypal conflict, the Creation, Fall and Christ's crucifixion. The essential human struggle was not therefore about the contradictions of the world as it is lived, but about transcending those material conditions. In *Anunciação e encontro de Mira-Celi* (Annunciation and discovery of Mira-Celi) (1943), Lima dramatized this struggle through the relationship with his spiritual alter ego, the mythical Mira-Celi, who is symbolic of a childlike innocence profaned by the history of human activity, but capable of being recovered in the upward striving for spirituality:

> Subimos em espiral, e em cada volta descrita
> nos encontramos de novo, frente a frente, mais puros.
> As leis da gravidade foram quebradas sobre as pedras das tumbas.
> Superamos o homem e o jugo do horizontal:
> o sentido da Trindade Perfeita é para cima, para cima, para cima.

(We climb in a spiral, and at each turn that we make/we meet again, face to face, ever purer./The laws of gravity have been broken on the stones of the tombs./We have surpassed man and the yoke of the horizontal:/the direction of the Perfect Trinity is upward, upward, upward.)

Whereas Lima's religious poetry described a more or less uninterrupted, unproblematic course of development out of his identification with the spirituality of black culture, Mendes's work continued to be punctuated by moments of human doubt. In 'O Exilado' (The Exile), from *A Poesia em Pânico* (Poetry in Panic) (1936–37), for instance, he was once again alone in a universe where the Devil is stronger than God, where children deny divine grace and where the crowd denounces him as a false prophet. 'Weary of bearing the machine of the world', he awaits 'the tempest of fire/rather than a sign of life.' He may be able to fly freely with his mythical friend above 'the kingdom of barbarous men/Who machine-gun children with dolls in their arms' ('Poema Lírico' – Lyrical poem, *As Metamorfoses*), but he is continually reminded that the contradictions of the world, and the gulf between the material and the ideal, are not altered by such flights of transcendence, as in 'Choques' (Clashes) (*Poesia Liberdade*):

> Um ouvido resistente poderia perceber
> O choque do tempo contra o altar da eternidade.
> Choca-se a enorme multidão sacrificada
> Com o ditador sentado na metralhadora.
> Choca-se a guilhotina erguida pelo erro dos séculos
> Com a pomba mirando a liberdade do horizonte.

(A determined ear might hear/The clash of time against the altar of eternity./The enormous sacrificed multitude clashes/With the dictator seated at his machine-gun./The guillotine erected by the error of the centuries clashes/With the dove gazing at liberty on the horizon.)

The poetry of Murilo Mendes, then, more than that of Jorge de Lima, spoke honestly of the failure of the neo-Catholic revival of the 1930s to get to grips constructively with the dilemma of Drummond's 'Feeling of the world'. Interestingly, the same images of individual inadequacy in the face of a world 'machine' recur throughout Mendes's work, and in the poetry of Drummond and Mário de Andrade. Where Drummond and Mário differ from Mendes is in their discovery that this 'machine', the system of political, economic, cultural and linguistic structures which moulds both individual and social life, is all-embracing and cannot be simply circumvented by some act of religious or revolutionary voluntarism. In 'Elegia 1938' (Elegy 1938), from the volume entitled *Feeling of the World* (1940), Drummond addressed the frustration of the intellectual faced with such a system, but refused to content himself, either with the refuge offered by the unconsciousness of sleep, or with the passive isolation that is engendered by an attitude of impotent despair:

> Amas a noite pelo poder de aniquilamento que encerra
> e sabes que, dormindo, os problemas te dispensam de morrer.
> Mas o terrível despertar prova a existência da Grande Máquina
> e te repõe, pequenino, em face de indecifráveis palmeiras.
>
> Caminhas entre mortos e com eles conversas
> sobre coisas do tempo futuro e negócios do espírito.
> A literatura estragou tuas melhores horas de amor.
> Ao telefone perdeste muito, muitíssimo tempo de semear.

Coração orgulhoso, tens pressa de confessar tua derrota
e adiar para outro século a felicidade coletiva.
Aceitas a chuva, a guerra, o desemprego e a injusta distribuição
porque não podes, sozinho, dinamitar a ilha de Manhattan.

(You love the night for the power of annihilation which it enfolds/and
you know that, by sleeping, problems will exempt you from dying./But
the terrible awakening proves the existence of the Great Machine/and
reinstalls you, tiny thing, before undecipherable palm-trees.//You walk
amongst the dead and converse with them/about things of the future
tense and matters of the spirit./Literature has ruined your best hours of
love./On the telephone you have wasted much, oh so much time for
sowing.//Proud heart, you hurry to confess your defeat/and to put off for
another century the collective happiness./You accept rain, war, unem-
ployment and unjust distribution/because you cannot, by yourself, blow
up Manhattan Island.)

As early as 1933, Mário too had understood that, if the world itself
was impossible, then so too was a transcendent detachment from it.
Grã-Cão do Outubro (Great Hell-hound of October) was written in
October of that year, soon after Hitler had become Chancellor of
Germany, and is a courageous and disturbing examination of the
ambiguous relationship between the isolated individual and the crea-
ture of fascism. Rather than mounting a moralistic denunciation of
fascism as ideology or political practice, the poem takes up the
imagery of a sado-masochistic sexuality in order to explore the way in
which its irrational appeal seductively insinuates itself into the
psychological being of a mass society, distorting the individual's
struggle for a sense of collective identity. In the first section, 'Vinte e
nove bichos' (Twenty-nine beasts), a deceptive calm conceals the
growth of a teeming bestial spirit, threatening to invade the vacuum of
passivity and alienation into which the poet's social and sexual life has
degenerated:

> No meu enorme corpo fatigado
> Todo mole com as almofadas,
> Você se aninha sem beijar.
>
> Estou sem forças feito um cáos.
> Você é uma via-látea errante
> Que não desejo mais valorizar.
>
> Paz. A falsa paz vascila disponível
> Enquanto à sombra da cheia fruteira
> Os bichos se alimentam sem cessar.

Um desespero me arde, eu te repilo.
É a arraiada que vem, é o sol imundo
Que vai mostrar a bicharada
Aos emboléus, vinda do cáos.

(Into my huge weary body/All soft with the pillows,/You nestle without a kiss.//I am devoid of strength, like a chaos./You are a wandering milky way/Which I have lost the will to value.//Peace. The false peace hovers in readiness/While in the shade of the full fruit-tree/The beasts feed incessantly.//I burn with despair, I spurn you./It is the dawn that is coming, it is the foul sun/Which will reveal the wanton herd of beasts out of the chaos.)

The threat assumes a more tangible form in the second section, 'Os gatos' (The cats), whose two halves convey the ambivalent attraction of a feline sexuality that is at once dangerous and vulnerable. In the first part, the poet's kisses encounter a cat-like 'Hitlerite' mouth, torn and striped in black and white, imitating a tiger. Thousands of cats line the walls and streets with erect tails and threatening claws like a disguised army waiting to explode. Yet, in his desire for communication and love, the poet fears that a deluge will sweep away and drown this instinctive gathering of animal beings, and leave him alone in the deserted street. The decision to surrender to the tide of irrational destruction is therefore explained, if not defended, as a desperate fear of exclusion from the community in a hostile world:

Vamos enrolados pelas enxurradas
Em que boiam corpos, em que boiam os mortos,
Em que vão putrefatos milhares de gatos . . .
Das casas cai mentira,
Nós vamos com as enxurradas,
Com a perfeita inocência dos fenômenos da terra,
Voluptuosamente mortos,
Os sem ciência mais nenhuma de que a vida
Está horrenda, querendo ser, erguendo os rabos
Por trás da noite, em companhia dos milhões de gatos verdes.

(We roll over and over in the torrents/In which float bodies, in which float the dead,/In which flow thousands of rotting cats . . ./Lies fall from the houses,/We flow with the torrents,/With the perfect innocence of the phenomena of the earth,/Voluptuously dead,/Those whose only wisdom is that life/Is horrendous, wanting, by raising our tails/Behind the night, to stand in the company of the millions of green cats.)

After attempting in this way to account for the power of fascism, in offering the isolated individual a sense of mass, corporate identity,

171

Mário turns in the second part of the poem to a different image of the cat – that of intimate domesticity, affection and recognition, not the 'gatos tedescos' (Teutonic cats) of war, but 'minha rosa sincera . . ., brasileira à vontade,/Feito um prazer que chega todo dia' (my sincere rose . . ., comfortably Brazilian,/Like a pleasure which comes every day). Identified by the name 'China', this feline pet constitutes a fragile refuge of consolation, an object of love rescued from the street and nurtured 'through centuries of possession and uses'. Given that the Japanese conquest of Manchuria was completed in 1932, the imminent tragedy which Mário's 'Chinese cat' seems to evoke may also be associated with the rise of fascist imperialism in the East. The poet fearfully murmurs, 'Oh China! oh minha China!' in her ear as he lives 'devastated by the news' and hides his tears in her fur, as if unable to protect her or himself from some inevitable disaster.

Until now, the only choice has been between a blind self-surrender to an irrational collective will or a retreat into domestic intimacy. In its later stages, however, the poem attempts a more critical examination of the forces at work in the world, and moves towards the discovery of a voice which, even if it cannot detach itself from the social maelstrom, may nevertheless give some expression and meaning to the experience of those about him. What is remarkable about the poem is the uncertainty of Mário's place within the conflict; he seems both to be struggling with the Great Hell-hound, yet also to have been subsumed into it, as if to suggest that a phenomenon such as fascism is not merely a political force to be fought on the streets, but also fights for its existence within the consciousness of individuals. Thus in the 'Trident poem' he is locked in a cataclysmic battle with an 'accursed wild animal', whose ravenous arm, ending in the flash of a sword, cuts blindly through the people, leaving orphans, lepers, exiled Jews and Cuban students in its wake. The embrace is both violent and passionate, as if he were struggling with himself:

> Eu te amo de um amor educado no inferno!
> Te mordo no peito até o sangue escorrer
> Me dando socos, chorando, chamando de bruto, de cão,
> O Grão Cão é o Mildiabo educado sozinho no inferno!

(I love you with a love educated in hell!/I bite your breast until the blood flows/Punching me, weeping, calling me a beast, a dog,/The Great Hound is the Thousand-devils educated alone in hell!)

His antagonist, if that is the right word, is 'the Law', refined, infallible and measured, and appears to represent the cold institutional structures of the State, which fascism needs to give itself a semblance of legitimacy, but which barely conceal or keep in check the bloody barbarism that lies at its heart:

Você é lindíssima! É polida e cadencial feito uma lei!
Mas eu sou o Grão Cão que te marquei um bocado com o crime dos
  mundos!
E agora nem de perdão carecemos
No mesmo abraço desaparecidos.

(You are so, so beautiful! You are refined and measured like a law!/But I am the Great Hound who has marked you a little with the crime of the worlds!/And now we do not even need forgiveness/As we are lost in the same embrace.)

In the final section, 'Dor' (Pain), the poet still maintains that his steps have been guided by the firebrand of the Great Hound, but the mark of those origins, the descent into the hell of battle with the devil of fascism, now enables him to articulate the experience of a whole community and contribute to the reconstruction of a genuine sense of solidarity. The citizens arrange their meetings on his lips, while his mouth is a male fish scattering its seed of love through the streets in the hope of 'fertilizing the ovaries of life one day'. After confessing that he has been forced to conceal his true self and voice in order to survive in the city, he returns at the end of the poem to the idea of speech and poetry as a necessary means of communication and comprehension between individuals overwhelmed by suffering and pain:

Mas eu venho das altas torres trazido ao facho do Grã Cão,
Lábios, lábios para o encontro em que cantareis fatalmente,
Ameaçados pela fome que espia detrás da cochilha,
A dor, a caprichosa dor desocupada que desde milhões de existências
Busca a razão de ser.

(But I have been brought from the high towers by the torchlight of the Great Hell-hound,/Lips, lips for the meeting in which you are bound to sing,/Threatened by the hunger which watches from behind the rolling hills,/The pain, the wayward, idle pain which for millions of existences/ Has been seeking its reason for being.)

The Rose of the People

Mário recovered a role for himself as a poet, then, not by abstracting himself from the conflicts of society or seeking individual spiritual

173

solutions, but by recognizing his common involvement with those around him in the reality of contemporary life, whether through the experience of fascism or of the Brazilian Estado Novo. As he put it in 'A Meditação sobre o Tietê' (Meditation on the river Tietê), the other highpoint of this period of his writing, composed in late 1944 and early 1945, shortly before his death:

> Já nada me amarga mais a recusa da vitória
> Do indivíduo, e de me sentir feliz em mim.
> Eu mesmo desisti dessa felicidade deslumbrante,
> E fui por tuas águas levado,
> A me reconciliar com a dor humana pertinaz,
> E a me purificar no barro dos sofrimentos dos homens.

(I am no longer embittered by the rejection/Of individual victory, and of feeling happy in myself./I, I have renounced that dazzling happiness,/ And have been carried away by your waters,/To be reconciled with the persistence of human pain,/And to be purified in the mud of mankind's sufferings.)

As a metaphor for society, and in particular that of São Paulo, Mário's depiction of the river deliberately contradicts the traditional notion of a teleological journey towards the destiny of the open sea. Instead, the Tietê stubbornly shies away from the coast, denying the poet 'the lovely verses which talk of leaving and ever returning', and fertilizing the humus of the earth, 'Impelling me with your obstinate *paulista* insistence/Towards the human storms of life'. The goal of the river's course is not his 'final point', but the point 'between the waters and the night, . . . that point loyal to the earthly question of mankind,/ Out of which man must be born'. The journey is thus a continual questioning, a permanent dialectic between water and land, between the flux of human activity and the material substance in which he moves.

For the moment, though, the social river is a corrupted, oozing sludge of demagoguery, its swollen sharks and whales, the presidents and ministers, feeding on the worm-eaten small fry who must push the water onwards as they are dissolved into its anonymous liquid mass. The voice of protest and the urge for human contact seem to be drowned in the oily darkness. But the proximity of the city invites the poet to seek out a glancing reflection of light on the surface, the fleeting shape of something living born out of, and in spite of, the river's corruption and oppression:

174

São formas . . . Formas que fogem, formas
Indivisas, se atropelando, um tilintar de formas fugidias
Que mal se abrem, flor, se fecham, flor, flor, informes, inacessíveis,
Na noite. . . .

(They are shapes . . . Shapes which slip away, undivided/Shapes, jostling one another, a jingling of fleeting shapes/Which no sooner opened, flower, close again, flower, flower, shapeless, inaccessible,/In the night. . . .)

This glimpse of a barely formed flower is the belief that 'another, better life must exist beyond the mountains', and that man, however small, humiliated and defeated, is nevertheless greater than the worms, plants and oceans through which he moves, and is capable, through his consciousness and vision, of liberating himself. The poem ends, not with a triumphalist cry of emancipation or hope, but with a quiet determination not to lose sight of that knowledge:

Eu recuso a paciência, o boi morreu, eu recuso a esperança.
Eu me acho tão cansado em meu furor.
As águas apenas murmuram hostis, água vil mas turrona paulista
Que sobe e se espráia, levando as auroras represadas
Para o peito dos sofrimentos dos homens.
. . . e tudo é noite. Sob o arco admirável
Da Ponte das Bandeiras, morta, dissoluta, fraca,
Uma lágrima apenas, uma lágrima,
Eu sigo alga escusa nas águas do meu Tietê.

(I reject patience, the ox has died, I reject hope./I am so weary in my fury./The waters only murmur with hostility, filthy but stubborn *paulista* water/Which rises and washes ashore, carrying the pent-up sunrises/To the breast of mankind's sufferings./. . . and all is dark. Beneath the wonderful arch/Of the Bridge of the Bandeiras, dead, dissolute, weak,/Just one tear, a tear,/I follow something, the algae hidden in the waters of my Tietê.)

The idea of a plant or flower as a fragile expression of the possibility of liberation and communion, born out of and in spite of a soil of corruption and oppression, is one of the central themes of Drummond's *A Rosa do Povo* (The Rose of the People) (1945). The climax of Drummond's work under the Vargas regime, and without doubt the highpoint of Brazilian verse writing during this period, *The Rose of the People* was published when he was co-editor of the *Tribuna Popular*, a pro-Communist Party newspaper. Drummond never actually joined the Party, and this hesitancy finds an echo in a continuing thread of scepticism which gives the poetry its human tension and vitality. Yet beside this scepticism is a growing confidence in the power of language to express and communicate a common social experience, and therefore in the possibility for the artist of playing the role of an actor, rather than of a spectator, in the struggles around him. Like Mário, Drummond reaches this confidence, not through some effort of transcendence, withdrawing from or abstracting himself from the horror of a world distorted by dictatorship, but through a sober recognition of his part in that world and of the difficulty of living in it.

The Rose of the People includes some of his longest and most powerfully sustained poems, whose structures acknowledge the power of the 'system' to invade all levels of experience, yet also offer a space of dialogue with the past and present, in which alternative structures of communication can crystallize and flower. 'A flor e a náusea' (The flower and the nausea) finds the poet wandering the streets 'Preso à minha classe e a algumas roupas' (Tied to my class and to some clothes). The sensation of being trapped within these social and material conditions is intensified by his questions: 'Devo seguir até o enjôo?/Posso, sem armas, revoltar-me?' (Must I carry on until I am sick?/Can I rebel without weapons?). By contrast with the poetry of the 1920s, it is not his ironic detachment from the world, but his inevitable integration into it, which seems to prevent him acting upon it or rebelling against it:

> O tempo é ainda de fezes, maus poemas, alucinações e espera.
> O tempo pobre, o poeta pobre
> fundem-se no mesmo impasse.

> (The time is still one of faeces, bad poems, hallucinations and waiting./
> The poor time, the poor poet/are fused in the same impasse.)

Language, which should make possible some critical reflection on and protest against these conditions, is itself also moulded and constrained by the same oppressive system, and therefore offers only incomprehension, riddles and false consolations:

> Em vão me tento explicar, os muros são surdos.
> Sob a pele das palavras há cifras e códigos.
> O sol consola os doentes e não os renova.

> (In vain I try to explain myself, the walls are deaf./Beneath the skin of words there are ciphers and codes./The sun consoles the sick and does not renew them.)

This regime of incomprehension has not simply been imposed upon a passive society, though, for if he is to survive, the individual must participate in it and assume its deceptions. Here, like Mário in his poem on fascism, Drummond makes a chilling admission of his necessary complicity in the conspiracy:

> Crimes da terra, como perdoá-los?
> Tomei parte em muitos, outros escondi.
> Alguns achei belos, foram publicados.
> Crimes suaves, que ajudam a viver.
> Ração diária de erro, distribuída em casa.
> Os ferozes padeiros do mal.
> Os ferozes leiteiros do mal.

(Crimes of the earth, how can one forgive them?/I've taken part in many, I've concealed others./Some I thought beautiful, they've been published./Soothing crimes, that help you to live./Daily ration of error, delivered to your doorstep./The savage bakers of evil./The savage milkmen of evil.)

Suddenly, though, the poet makes an unexplained announcement, puncturing the veil of nausea and silence which this guilty realization has cast over him: 'Uma flor nasceu na rua!' (A flower has been born in the street!) The significance of the birth of the flower appears to be related, although still only implicitly, to an irrepressible instinct for revolt which redeems him and some of those around him:

> Pôr fogo em tudo, inclusive em mim.
> Ao menino de 1918 chamavam anarquista.
> Porém meu ódio é o melhor de mim.
> Com ele me salvo
> e dou a poucos uma esperança mínima.

(Set fire to everything, including myself./They called the boy of 1918 an anarchist./Yet my hatred is the best of me./With it I save myself/and I give to a few a barest measure of hope.)

In the closing stanzas of the poem this inchoate impulse to rebellion and hatred is transformed on contact with the flower into a fragile but defiantly living form, which breaks through the alienation and seems to presage a storm:

> Passem de longe, bondes, ônibus, rio de aço do tráfego.
> Uma flor ainda desbotada
> ilude a polícia, rompe o asfalto.
> Façam completo silêncio, paralisem os negócios,
> garanto que uma flor nasceu.
>
> Sua cor não se percebe.
> Suas pétalas não se abrem.

177

Seu nome não está nos livros.
É feia. Mas é realmente uma flor.

Sento-me no chão da capital do país às cinco horas da tarde
e lentamente passo a mão nessa forma insegura.
Do lado das montanhas, nuvens maciças avolumam-se.
Pequenos pontos brancos movem-se no mar, galinhas em pânico.
É feia. Mas é uma flor. Furou o asfalto, o tédio, o nojo e o ódio.

(Trams, buses, steel river of traffic can keep their distance./A flower, pale
as yet,/eluding the police, is breaking through the tarmac./Be absolutely
quiet, shut down your businesses,/I swear a flower has been born.//You
can't make out its colour./Its petals do not open./Its name isn't in the
books./It's ugly. But it really is a flower.//I sit down on the ground in the
capital of the country at five in the afternoon/and slowly run my hand
over this uncertain form./From the direction of the mountains, massive
clouds swell./Little white points stir on the sea, panicking hens./It's
ugly. But it is a flower. It has pierced the tarmac, the tedium, the disgust
and the hatred.)

The germination of the flower is the culmination of a long process
sustained through this and the two previous books, *Feeling of the World*
and *José* (1942), by which Drummond sought to overcome the aliena-
tion which political repression and a brutal modernization had engen-
dered. The form this takes most typically is the struggle to recover a
sense of communication with his family and with a past from which he
had become separated by his own experience and by the economic
changes suffered by his home town, Itabira. A quiet, provincial town
in the state of Minas Gerais, Itabira was transformed during the 1930s
into a centre of iron mining, and became the subject of a fierce debate
about national control over the exploitation of its mineral resources.
Drummond expressed this dual alienation, the transformation of his
home and the expropriation of its wealth, in 'Confidência do itabirano'
(Confession of the man from Itabira):

Alguns anos vivi em Itabira.
Principalmente nasci em Itabira.
Por isso sou triste, orgulhoso: de ferro.
Noventa por cento de ferro nas calçadas.
Oitenta por cento de ferro nas almas.
E esse alheamento do que na vida é porosidade e comunicação.
. . .
Tive ouro, tive gado, tive fazendas.

178

Hoje sou funcionário público.
Itabira é apenas uma fotografia na parede.
Mas como doi!

(I lived a few years in Itabira./Above all I was born in Itabira./That's why I
am sad, proud: of iron./Our pavements: ninety per cent iron./Our souls:
eighty per cent iron./And that estrangement from what in life is porous-
ness and communication/. . ./I had gold, I had cattle, I had ranches./
Today I am a civil servant./Itabira is just a photograph on the wall./But
how it hurts!)

However, by 'Retrato de família' (Family photograph) (from *The Rose
of the People*), the photograph is no longer a symbol of estrangement
but, like the poem itself, has become a vehicle, a framework through
which a fluid sense of community, the 'idea of family', is able to flow,
abolishing the barriers between past and present and the divisions
between individuals and generations, between subject and object. The
dusty, ageing yellow of the photograph has blurred the features, the
personalities and experiences of the people represented, but by the
same token, as if to suggest the ghostlike movement of figures often
seen in long-exposure photographs, it allows the children to change
places noiselessly, and one smiling face to present itself as another
fades. As Drummond says:

A moldura deste retrato
em vão prende suas personagens.
Estão ali voluntariamente,
saberiam – se preciso – voar.

(The frame of this photograph/holds its characters in vain./They are
there voluntarily,/they could – if need be – fly away.)

This elision of the boundaries between self and other extends to the
poet and his own relationship to the family; if the characters compose
an irreducible whole which defies the limits of the photographic
frame, they can also subvert the relationship between observer and
observed, reflecting the poet's own experience in his eyes:

O retrato não me responde,
ele me fita e se contempla
nos meus olhos empoeirados.
E no cristal se multiplicam

os parentes mortos e vivos.
Já não distingo os que se foram

179

dos que restaram. Percebo apenas
a estranha idéia de família

viajando através da carne.

(The photograph does not answer me,/it stares at me and contemplates
itself/in my dusty eyes./And in the glass there multiply//the dead and
living relatives./I can no longer distinguish those who have left/from
those who have remained.I can only make out/the strange idea of family/
/travelling through the flesh.)

Paradoxically, while the structure of the poem allows that 'idea of
family' to be intuited by the poet and reader, a silence remains, the
picture of life which Drummond continually interrogates remains
irreducible, stubbornly refusing to answer. Similarly, in 'Onde há
pouco falávamos' (Where we were just talking), an old piano occupies
a room in the abandoned family house, and concentrates in itself the
experiences and memories that it has witnessed. But, as Drummond
makes clear, the piano is not simply a metaphor for the family as such;
it is awkward, clumsy, obstinately refusing to be confined within the
bounds of walls and ceiling, defying all threats to chop it up or bury it.
It will play, weep and sing on its own but 'angrily refuses to let a
single/chord slip out, if a young girl's hand/wounds it here and now'.
The piano therefore insistently imposes itself on the present as the
spirit of a collective past, but cannot be made to yield up that spirit
through the literal expression of language. In 'Viagem na família'
(Journey in the family), too, where Drummond revisits the ghost of his
father amidst the decaying desert of Itabira, he repeatedly shouts at
the figure whom childhood resentments and pride had alienated from
him, begging him to speak; but he refuses, and the sleeve of his jacket
crumbles to dust. Nevertheless, a meeting does eventually take place,
Drummond is pressed close to him in a 'diaphanous embrace', and a
watery river of blood submerges both them and the world which they
inhabited and which divided them, in a flood of forgiveness and
reconciliation:

Senti que me perdoava
porém nada dizia.

As águas cobrem o bigode,
a família, Itabira, tudo.

(I felt that he forgave me/yet he said nothing.//The waters cover his
moustache,/the family, Itabira, everything.)

180

In compositions such as this, Drummond approaches a complex and difficult conception of the communicative possibilities of poetry. He implicitly acknowledges the Modernist problematic, that art can no longer be expected to offer a transparent image or reflection of the world. As we have seen, for the individual artist that world ultimately remains irreducible and indefinable because he can no longer divorce himself from it; it invades and surrounds the totality of his subjective life. But if it cannot hope to hold the mirror up to nature, the poem can nevertheless provide a dynamic medium in which the objective structures of the world are 'carried', revealed indirectly through the analogous structures of the imagination which revolve around them. A whole number of compositions attempt in this way to explore and convey the forms which reality assumes without naming or defining them: 'O mito' (The myth), for example, in which Fulana – 'so-and-so' or 'Miss X' embodies a succession of identities which contribute to the male myth of woman, but whose totality remains always elusive; or 'Carrego comigo' (I carry with me), in which the poet tries to discover the identity of the unnameable parcel that he has carried with him for centuries – the acceptance of its impenetrable silence is the discovery of his own integration into the objective world of society, and of the penetration of that world into his subjective self:

> Perder-te seria
> perder-me a mim próprio.
> Sou um homen livre
> mas levo uma coisa.
>
> Não sei o que seja.
> Eu não a escolhi.
> Jamais a fitei.
> Mas levo uma coisa.
>
> Não estou vazio,
> não estou sozinho,
> pois anda comigo
> algo indescritível.

(To lose you would be/to lose myself./I am a free man/but I carry something.//I don't know what it can be./I did not choose it./I have never set eyes on it./But I carry something.//I am not empty,/I am not alone,/for with me walks/something indescribable.)

181

It is this approach to the relationship between art and the world it seeks to communicate, that seems to be expressed in Drummond's 'Consideração do poema' (Consideration of the poem):

Dar tudo pela presença dos longínquos,
sentir que há ecos, poucos, mas cristal,
não rocha apenas, peixes circulando
sob o navio que leva esta mensagem,
e aves de bico longo conferindo
sua derrota, e dois ou três faróis,
últimos! esperança do mar negro.
Essa viagem é mortal, e começá-la.
Saber que há tudo. E mover-se em meio
a milhões de formas raras,
secretas, duras. Eis aí meu canto.

Ele é tão baixo que sequer o escuta
ouvido rente ao chão. Mas é tão alto
que as pedras o absorvem. Está na mesa
aberta em livros, cartas e remédios.
Na parede infiltrou-se. O bonde, a rua,
o uniforme de colégio se transformam,
são ondas de carinho te envolvendo.

(To give everything for the presence of distant things,/to feel that there are echoes, not many, but crystal,/not just rock, fish moving about/ beneath the ship which carries this message,/and long-beaked birds discussing/their defeat, and two or three lighthouses,/the last ones! hope of the black sea./This voyage is mortal, and to begin it./To know that there is everything. And to move in the midst/of millions of rare, secret, hard/forms. That is my song.//It is so low that not even an ear close to the ground/will hear it. But it is so high/that the stones absorb it. It is on the table/open in books, letters and medicines./It has permeated the wall. The tram, the street,/the school uniform are transformed,/they are waves of tenderness enveloping you.)

Drummond's struggle with language and the world, which he began in *Feeling of the World*, has thus converged in a difficult, but movingly optimistic conception of the expressive potential offered by poetry, and by art in general. The poet of 'Miserable thing' or 'Secret' was immobilized in his corner of silence by an overwhelming world of opaque, impenetrable structures and was forced to make his verse out of that imprisonment. Drummond now moves within that world, like Mário in his river, and through that movement illuminates the forms of collective being and experience which saturate our lives but which are normally hidden and obscured by the darkness of alienation. The poem does not capture these forms – the family, community, solidarity – for they are dynamic and fluid, but rather allows them to flow through its structures and so reveal their shape in moments of sublime human recognition – the birth of the rose.

Drummond reserved his most confident affirmation of this redemptive power of art, and the climax of the book as a whole, for the last poem of *The Rose of the People*. His subject, though, was not his own poetry, but the work of a fellow artist, one whose ability to articulate and communicate the experience of an entire class across international boundaries makes him the supreme representative of Drummond's idea of a unity of social consciousness recovered from the fragments of individual lives. 'Canto ao homem do povo Charlie Chaplin' (Song to the man of the people Charlie Chaplin) is, to take up once again the paradox of Drummond's poetics, a tribute to an artist who rarely spoke but nevertheless expressed 'the feeling of the world' through the unified multiplicity of his cinematic roles. In the relationship he established with his audience, Chaplin constructed an identity of feeling on a mass scale, assuming a succession of familiar, anonymous characters drawn from contemporary society, but always recognizable as the clown-like, bowler-hatted Jew, innocently subverting even the most brutalizing forms of capitalist life, including fascism.

Significantly, though, this act of continual subversion, the counterposing of Chaplin's unified identity as the 'man of the people' against the social fragmentation and alienation imposed by the machine of capitalism, emerges out of that very alienation, out of his belonging to the world and its contradictions. This notion of a commonality of alienation inhabited by both the artist and society, and out of which they realize their collective being, is suggested masterfully in the second section of the poem. Here Drummond evokes the atmosphere of the cinema itself, in particular the darkness in which the audience has taken refuge, 'com a aflição de ratos fugindo da vida' (distressed like rats fleeing from life). As in so many poems from this period, night or darkness represent a space in which individuals are obscured from one another but which simultaneously gathers them together and offers a potential medium of communication. At first fused with this darkness in his black costume and with the audience in their common experience, Chaplin emerges from it on the screen, the whiteness of his face ambiguously deathly and inspiring, and takes the viewers with him into an alternative world of light, of rebellion and liberation:

> E a lua pousa
> em teu rosto. Branco, de morte caiado,
> que sepulcros evoca mas que hastes

submarinas e álgidas e espelhos
e lírios que o tirano decepou, e faces
amortalhadas em farinha. O bigode
negro cresce em ti como um aviso
e logo se interrompe. É negro, curto,
espesso. Ó rosto branco, de lunar matéria,
face cortada em lençol, risco na parede,
caderno de infância, apenas imagem
entretanto os olhos são profundos e a boca vem de longe,
sozinha, experiente, calada vem a boca
sorrir, aurora, para todos.

E já não sentimos a noite,
e a morte nos evita, e diminuímos
como se ao contato de tua bengala mágica voltássemos
ao país secreto onde dormem meninos.
Já não é o escritório de mil fichas,
nem a garagem, a universidade, o alarme,
é realmente a rua abolida, lojas repletas,
e vamos contigo arrebentar vidraças,
e vamos jogar o guarda no chão,
e na pessoa humana vamos redescobrir
aquele lugar – cuidado! que atrai os pontapés: sentenças
de uma justiça não oficial.

(And the moon rests/on your face. White, whitewashed with death,/ which evokes graves but underwater,/icy stems too and mirrors/and lilies that the tyrant beheaded, and cheeks/shrouded in flour. Your black/moustache grows on you like an announcement/and is then cut short. It is black, short,/thick. Oh white face, made of moon matter,/a face cut out of a sheet, a sketch on the wall,/a children's exercise book, an image and no more/meanwhile your eyes are deep and your mouth comes from afar,/alone, experienced, silent comes your mouth/to smile, dawn, at us all.//And we no longer feel the night,/and death avoids us, and we shrink/as if at the contact of your magic cane we were returning/ to the secret country where children sleep./It is no longer the office with a thousand files,/nor the garage, the university, the alarm-bell,/it is really the street, now abolished, shops full to the brim,/and we are going with you to break windowpanes,/and we are going to push the security guard over,/and in the human person we are going to rediscover/that place – watch out! – which invites your kicks: the sentences/of an unofficial justice.)

It is worth emphasizing the extent to which the poem relies on a visual evocation of Chaplin's work, rather than on a discursive analysis of its significance. One of the more remarkable aspects of Chaplin's cinema was his insistent use of the silent genre, long after the 'talkie' had become the norm for commercial film-making. Drummond finds reflected in Chaplin his own mistrust of language, with its capacity to obscure rather than illuminate, to invent reassuring solutions to impossible contradictions:

> Bem sei que o discurso, acalanto burguês, não te envaidece,
> e costumas dormir enquanto os veementes inauguram estátua,
> e entre tantas palavras que como carros percorrem as ruas,
> só as mais humildes, de xingamento ou beijo, te penetram.

(Well I know that speech, that bourgeois lullaby, does not turn your head,/and you are used to sleeping while the exuberant are unveiling statues,/and amongst so many words that run through the streets like cars,/only the humblest, words of abuse or kisses, reach through to you.)

Communication takes place instead through Chaplin's magical manipulation of the objects of his alienated world, as he makes them speak to his audience, transforming them from the inert, mute agents of his oppression and poverty into fertile, expressive creatures that give meaning and sustenance to their individual lives:

> E falam as flores que tanto amas quando pisadas,
> falam os tocos de vela, que comes na extrema penúria, falam a mesa, os
>   botões,
> os instrumentos do ofício e as mil coisas aparentemente fechadas,
> cada troço, cada objeto do sótão, quanto mais obscuros mais falam.

(And the flowers that you love so when they are trampled, they speak,/ the pieces of candle that you eat in extreme penury, they speak, the table, the buttons,/the tools of your trade and the thousand apparently closed things, speak,/each bit and piece, each object from the attic, the more obscure the more they speak.)

Chaplin's creative activity, and that of Drummond in interpreting his work, is the revelation of a common identity reassembled from the fragments of his fictional lives and the lives of his audience. Rather than a systematic process of reconstruction, it is the underlying consistency of the Chaplin persona, which runs through the succession of detailed roles and situations drawn from *Modern Times*, *The Gold Rush*, *The Great Dictator* and other films, and which remains always recognizable and faithful. The halting, broken lines which end the following extract remind us, though, that this persona, the bond of solidarity and recognition, is also elusive and fragile, and may not survive long after the cinema lights have gone up and the audience have returned to their individual, isolated existences:

Colo teus pedaços. Unidade
estranha é a tua, em mundo assim pulverizado.
E nós, que a cada passo nos cobrimos
e nos despimos e nos mascaremos,
mal retemos em ti o mesmo homem,
  aprendiz
  bombeiro
  caixeiro
  doceiro
  emigrante
  forçado
  maquinista
  noivo
  patinador
  soldado
  músico
  peregrino
  artista de circo
  marquês
  marinheiro
  carregador de piano
apenas sempre entretanto tu mesmo,
o que não está de acordo e é meigo,
o incapaz de propriedade, o pé
errante, a estrada
fugindo, o amigo
que desejaríamos reter
na chuva, no espelho, na memória
e todavia perdemos.

(I stick your pieces together. Strange/unity is yours, in a world pulverized like this./And we, who at every step clothe ourselves/and undress ourselves and mask ourselves,/barely hold on to the same man in you,/apprentice/fireman/sales assistant/confectioner/emigrant/convict/machine-operator/fiancé/skater/soldier/musician/wayfarer/circus artist/ marquis/sailor/piano remover/always though just yourself,/the one who is at odds and is tender,/the one incapable of property, the wandering/foot, the disappearing/road, the friend/whom we would like to hold on to/in the rain, in the mirror, in our memory/and whom we nevertheless lose.)

However, in the final section of the poem Drummond goes beyond this cinematic persona to discover the deeper, more durable unity which Chaplin inspires: 'Já não penso em ti. Penso no ofício/a que te entregas.' (I am no longer thinking of you. I am thinking of the trade/to

which you devote yourself.) It is the common identity derived from
the human activity of labour, the creative magic of Chaplin the worker
revealing 'artes não burguesas' (non-bourgeois skills) which are cap-
able of bringing books and pictures to life, and of producing trains and
ships which transport their passengers through time. Significantly, it
is precisely at this point that Drummond introduces Chaplin's first
talking movie, *The Great Dictator*. It is as if he has until now been
gathering all of the unspoken words of his accumulated oppression
and that of his class which, fragmented and atomized, could not yet be
articulated. Now, having finally revealed that real underlying unity of
class, the common experience of labour, they are able to burst into
flower, as the Jewish barber takes the place of the dictator Hynkel and
makes his speech of democracy and human solidarity. Published just
ten years before a generation which was to question radically the
ability of art and language to communicate the experience of the
world, *The Rose of the People* is the testament, not only of Drummond's
personal optimism, but that of millions who, glimpsing the end of the
Estado Novo and of the war, came to believe in the possibility of
creating, with their own words and hands, a new society free from
exploitation.

O ofício, é o ofício
que assim te põe no meio de nós todos,
vagabundo entre dois horários; mão sabida
no bater, no cortar, no fiar, no rebocar,
o pé insiste em levar-te pelo mundo,
a mão pega a ferramenta: é uma navalha,
e ao compasso de Brahms fazes a barba
neste salão desmemoriado no centro do mundo oprimido
onde ao fim de tanto silêncio e oco te recobramos.

Foi bom que te calasses.
Meditavas na sombra das chaves,
das correntes, das roupas riscadas, das cercas de arame,
juntavas palavras duras, pedras, cimento, bombas, invectivas,
anotavas com lápis secreto a morte de mil, a boca sangrenta
de mil, os braços cruzados de mil.
E nada dizias. E um bolo, um engulho
formando-se. E as palavras subindo.
Ó palavras desmoralizadas, entretanto salvas, ditas de novo.
Poder da voz humana inventando novos vocábulos e dando sopro aos
    exaustos.

187

Dignidade da boca, aberta em ira justa e amor profundo,
crispação do ser humano, árvore irritada, contra a miséria e a fúria dos
   ditadores,
ó Carlito, meu e nosso amigo, teus sapatos e teu bigode caminham numa
   estrada de pó e esperança.

(The trade, it is the trade/which sets you thus in the midst of us all,/a
vagrant between two shifts; a hand skilled/at beating, cutting, spinning,
plastering,/your foot insists on taking you through the world,/your hand
takes up the tool: it is a razor,/and to the beat of Brahms you shave/in this
all-forgotten room at the centre of the oppressed world/where at the end
of so much silence and hollowness we recover you.//It was good that
you kept silent. You were thinking in the shadow of keys,/chains,
striped clothes, barbed-wire fences,/you were gathering hard words,
stones, cement, bombs, invectives,/you were noting down with a secret
pencil the deaths of a thousand, the bloody mouths/of a thousand, the
folded arms of a thousand./And you said nothing. And a lump, a nausea/
forming. And the words rising./Oh corrupted words, yet rescued,
spoken afresh./Power of the human voice inventing new terms and
giving breath to the exhausted./Dignity of the mouth, open in righteous
anger and profound love,/convulsion of the human being, angry tree,
against the misery and fury of dictators,/oh Charlie, my and our friend,
your shoes and your moustache walk along a road of dust and hope.)

   The events of the 1930s and '40s, then, gave a real social and political
content to the ideological divisions which had begun to emerge within
the cultural movement of the previous decade. The realization that
there was not one, but many modernisms, many different responses,
both within and beyond art, to the contradictory experience of moder-
nization, became not merely a theoretical but a practical matter. The
poet was now forced out into the world, to assume a conscious
position within, and in relation to a reality that had previously only
been observed from the vantage-point of irony, utopian imagination
or reaction. Such a realization could, on the one hand, lead to a sense
of social identity born out of the collective suffering and oppression of
humanity; if it went no further that this, however, that social con-
sciousness might be silenced by the barriers of impotence, frustration
and passivity. On the other hand, such despair in the face of the chaos
and conflict of the real world might lead to a search for some transcen-
dent unity, as in the religious mysticism of Mendes and Lima, resolv-
ing its contradictions in the realm of language or spirituality, but
leaving the individual as a powerless victim, the object of a universal
history, whose only refuge was an unconscious absorption into the
divine.

Alternatively, as Mário de Andrade and Drummond showed, the facts could be confronted and the hard battle undertaken to discover meaning within and beneath the confusing, corrupt material of daily existence, to search for the flower of creative consciousness born out of the mud. This was the struggle pursued by Drummond from *Feeling of the World* to *The Rose of the People*; from the poet's self-conscious isolation as a marginal, impotent witness of a collective history, to the discovery of an identity between himself and the other workers of the world – an identity founded on the creative force of labour. Like any other worker under Vargas's Estado Novo, the poet was obliged to work for, and within, the oppressive structures imposed by a world capitalist system, but was at the same time capable of articulating an alternative voice of rebellion and self-emancipation, crystallized out of that common experience of labour.

The tone of this poetry is thus markedly different from that of the 1920s and from what was to follow. At its height it affirmed a belief in the possibility of language as critical and conscious, necessarily rooted in reality yet capable of challenging it and intuiting other, human structures of fellowship and struggle. However, as the poetry of the late 1940s and '50s proved, the confidence in that belief remained fragile, deprived as it was of the real victories which might have given the vision of revolutionary social transformation some substance. Paradoxically, the defeats of the 1930s could actually reinforce the loyalty of a small minority to the idea of a beacon of socialism in Stalinist Russia, at least until other events brutally shattered those illusions. But for most people, the virtual destruction of independent working-class organization in Brazil, the international defeat of fascism, the removal of Vargas and the ability of world capitalism to reassert itself in preparation for a new era of expansion after the pre-war crisis – all these things seemed to make an irrelevance of the utopian vision of the 1920s and '30s. The poetry of the early post-war years reflected the abandonment of that vision of a collective voice pursuing its own independent project of liberation, as all, the organized left included, were swept into the drive for capitalist development and into the anonymity of a 'universal', 'classless' spirit of construction. Mário de Andrade and Drummond's realization of an integration between individual and society, between subjective consciousness and a collective language was soon abandoned in favour of a false dichotomy between subjectivism and abstraction, between a poetry expressive of social and individual experience, and one dedicated to the construction of pure, self-reflecting objective forms. A sterile, destructive dichotomy, it has left an almost indelible mark on the verse writing of the last twenty years, and has left contemporary poets with the difficult task of rediscovering the dialectic of self and community – 'the feeling of the world'.

6

Retreats and Rediscoveries: Public and Private Voices of the Forties and Fifties

Acts of Withdrawal

The decade of the forties, so often represented in critical approaches as an era of the formalization of poetry, the return to the grand manner and the resumption of the search for universals, was a time of artistic debate as bitter as that of the twenties. The period's criticism, of course, was more tendentious in its allegiances. By defining poetry as an exercise in the liberation of language,[1] the analysis excluded a priori a wholly different definition of literary practice; yet that alternative was as legitimate and rooted a tradition as the Formalist explanation. The point is not crudely to suggest a conspiracy to exclude from the frame of poetry all writing that rejected the Formalist conception; but it is true that poets and critics have often been one and the same, and that a description of a particular method has somehow elided into a theoretical prescription for the practice of poetry itself.

Literary histories of Latin America repeat predictably that the poetry of the forties and fifties represented a reaction against the social poetry of the previous decade.[2] Those elected to represent the period range from the Cuban José Lezama Lima (1910–76) to the Mexican poet and critic Octavio Paz, and their journals *Orígenes* and *Taller* figure among those whose influence was most pervasive. It is absurd to suggest that at a given signal all social poets ceased to commit their political preoccupations to paper, or that the beginning of a decade marked a general resurgence of literary Formalism. Two things *can* be said. First, that certain ideas about poetry and poetic practice came to prevail at certain times, and that this occurred with the collaboration of critics

191

and literary historians who projected that dominion back into a literary tradition. Second, that the authority gained by certain literary theories and ideas can only be explained by reference to a broader cultural and ideological panorama which resonates with a struggle between contesting values and truths.

Many poets in the period did see poetry as an intellectual exercise, an elevation of thought towards universal categories – a deeply Platonic vision of poetry.[3] The language of poetry aspired therefore to a purity of purpose and expression which implied its loss of historical reference, of contingency. Octavio Paz developed the theory of poetry as a field of conflict between contingency and universality, and in his practice explored the transition from one to the other as a linguistic and a cultural act.[4] Yet in no sense was this the only type of poetry produced in this period. While Paz sought the means to escape the prison of history, others – Neruda in particular – embarked on a journey of rediscovery and recuperation of the historical sources of Latin American experience. These two, then, clearly represented opposed methods and practices; yet they were contemporaries whose different views mirrored a wider philosophical debate. And even these very influential perspectives did not represent the totality of available poetic practices.

While the Second World War occupied the horizons of Western intellectuals, its impact on Latin America was very different. The dramatic increase in prices for Latin American raw materials and agricultural goods set in motion new processes of economic growth – and new aspirations to development and change.[5] Roosevelt's adoption of the Defence of the Four Freedoms produced some unexpected democratic openings into which those aspirations could be channelled.[6] In many countries legal oppositional activity became possible (albeit briefly). Economic growth brought with it some manufacturing investment, generating a growing urban population and a rising trade-union membership. Social conflict took on recognizably urban forms, as Efrain Huerta for example recorded in many of his poems about Mexican politics.[7] This is not to say, of course, that the social problems of the countryside were somehow solved or simply disappeared from current writings; nor is it to suggest that artists suddenly lost their awareness of the indigenous populations.[8] Nonetheless, the urban nightmare – the sense of alienation that John Dos Passos had earlier captured in his portrait of a fragmented and individualized community[9] – became a central preoccupation of novelists like Juan Carlos Onetti of Uruguay and Salvador Garmendia from Venezuela, and of poets like C. German Belli (Peru, b. 1927), Nicanor Parra (b. 1914) and Enrique Lihn (b. 1929) from Chile, Pedro Geoffroy Rivas (El Salvador 1908–79), and to an extent the eccentric Chilean poet Pablo de Rokha (b. 1894)

For all of them, the experience of the modern metropolis was centrally one of loss – loss of a community that is an implicit but silent interlocutor in much of what comes to be called *antipoesía*. And that sense is shared, paradoxically, by both the poets of solitude and the poets of communion (as Paz called them). Some artists sought out the substitute community of an aesthetic elect, others the community of myth. Neruda and others disinterred it from the buried social history of Latin America, like the Guatemalan novelist Miguel Angel Asturías who rediscovered the collective in the preserved traditions of the Mayas.[10] The radical poets of anti-poetry, of the urban nightmare, assessed modernity to be synonymous with the definitive loss of that collective possibility, and made of themselves the protagonists of desperate solitary journeys through urban landscapes. But the impression of the global village with its endless immediacy and transitory experience seemed to herald a post-modernist despair. What preserved the poets' humanity was their anger and sense of injustice.

Each of these very distinct currents shared the environment of Latin America in the post-1945 period. If the preoccupation with the urban produced a tragic or an absurd sense of human inadequacy, its expression in *antipoetry* elicited a language and a form without rhetoric or epiphany, prosaic and undramatic for the most part, and formed out of an undifferentiated mosaic of impressions and fragmentary experiences. This fragmentary 'found' quality of the poem, its sense of an arbitrary juxtaposition of elements, made experience something distinct from consciousness. Things happen to you, but there can be no assumption that those incidents or moments will be assimilated into consciousness. The protagonist is capable of sensation, and registers occurrence – but there is no human response. In that sense, *antipoesía* was the diametrical opposite of the poetry of Octavio Paz, where the memory of community provided a locus of resolution. He shared with Parra and the others a profound suspicion of the modern world and its destructive effect; both were in that explicit sense conservatives. The community that Paz sought, however, was one that lay outside history, or which was to be found in an indigenous world which was treated as prehistory, as a world of myth without time. It involved a *rejection* of the modern, and a conscious turning back. For the *antipoetas* no such option was available – but the absence of the past was also a void in the future. The heroic survival of the individual, the artist as shipwrecked mariner, was what remained.

In that sense, this was a plausible response to the realities of Latin America in the fifties. It was a period of growth and economic change, pervaded by a technocratic optimism – development and growth must equal progress.[11] The reintegration of Latin America into the world market, coupled with the manifest determination of the United States to brook no opposition to that absorption (as exhibited in Guatemala and Iran[12]), produced a climate of cold war hysteria. Nicolás Guillén spent much of the fifties outside Cuba and Neruda rarely re-entered Chile during the period. The visions of socialism enshrined in the communist tradition had long since become compromised and tainted by the opportunism of the Communist parties, and it was Peronism in Argentina, APRA in Peru and similar populist movements elsewhere that absorbed the frustrations and discontents of the rebellious young.[13]

There can be no doubt that the theories of literary practice that became pervasive during this period corresponded to and reflected a positivistic historicism which also reduced the conscious role of the masses in history. Consciousness was increasingly located outside the victims/objects of history, and civilization lay as an atavistic culture embedded among what Eduardo Mallea called 'the invisible world' of the intellectuals.[14]

For Neruda and Guillén as well as the Nicaraguan Ernesto Cardenal (1925–), the artist could still stand in defence of a humanism lost in the economic determinism of the period. In a different sense, the Nicaraguan poets José Coronel Urtecho (b. 1906) and Pablo Antonio Cuadra (b. 1912) suggested that the act of withdrawal could ensure the role of art as a repository of a human potentiality that, although presently incapable of realization, was nevertheless a possible alternative history, a force in reality. Both perceptions led in a sense to a substitution of the poet's consciousness for the collective consciousness; both saw the art work as a repository of hidden values. Yet they drew from that perception very different conclusions about human emancipation and potential. Where Paz's conclusion was deeply negative, interweaving an idea of progress with the loss of solidarity and communion, others, Ernesto Cardenal for example, saw in the shadowy people in down-town late-night Managua the community of equals that would one day overturn the world.[15]

Thus the redemptive possibility enshrined in much of Latin America's poetry was not simply lost in the wake of major defeats like the Spanish Civil War or the overthrow of Arbenz in Guatemala. There was a continuity of vision and of a corresponding (but changing) poetic practice; the search to make the vision real, to move from the idea to the act was the defining procedure of what we may call social poetry, whose role was to demonstrate the actuality, the irrepressible necessity of that transformation. The poets, it might be argued, interpreted the world; the point remained, however, to change it. In poetry that procedure functioned by analogy: poetry itself enacted the passage from the literary to the social, from the ahistorical to the historical, from a language without social reference to a language contingent in its sociality.

This is not to say that poetry could move only through the language of political statement. Sometimes what appeared to be a political poetry proved to be little more than resounding rhetoric and verbal gesture. What differentiated political writing from mere rattle was the quality of lived experience, so that a poetry of public utterance could provide the locus of an encounter between private and public, individual and social. The encounter could enact an alternative public language, overcome the separation of public and private, creative and determined, in a reappropriation of the terrain of collective communication.

Thus the period witnessed two distinct and conflicting responses to the question of the responsibility of poetry. One direction led towards the recreation of a poetic elite and a practice of separation, the other towards the reintegration of poetry and the poet into the public realm. This public accession involved the celebration of collective culture, the absorption into poetry of all areas of shared experience. It meant that nothing was alien to poetry, and that typicality supplanted the quality of originality and uniqueness so central to the Romantic idea. All this was implied in the adventurous conception of a *conversational poetry*, which represented a creative intervention in the world reappropriated as utopia, as vision, as shared language. But in the end, the implication is always the recovery of the collective voice, the resumption of community. If for Paz that is a historical impossibility, and a utopia realized only in imaginative *retreat* from the world, the finest poets of contemporary Latin America have *entered* the world to discover community and a solidarity found not outside it, but veiled and hidden, yet always present in the world of loving human beings in their material relations.

For Cardenal, that hope is coterminous with God and with the realization of the Kingdom of God on earth.

195

A tu pueblo lo han borrado del mapa
y ya no está en la Geografía
Andamos sin pasaporte de país en país
sin papeles de identificación
Y tú eres ahora un Dios clandestino . . .[16]

(They have rubbed your people off the map/it is no longer in Geography/
passportless we move from country to country/with no identity papers/
And you now are an underground God . . .)

But soon

El pueblo se divertirá en los clubs exclusivos
tomará posesión de las empresas privadas
el justo se alegrará con los Tribunales Populares
Celebraremos en grandes plazas el aniversario de la Revolución
El Dios que existe es el de los proletarios

(The people will enjoy themselves in the exclusive clubs/they will take
possession of the private enterprises/the just man shall be joyful before
the Popular Tribunals/We shall celebrate in the great squares the anni-
versary of the Revolution/The God that does exist is the god of the
workers)

Cardenal's vision of a community restored to itself, of a just resolu-
tion to human suffering, was profoundly religious, and arose from a
vision of a purifying apocalypse. The power of transformation, how-
ever, lay not outside human beings but *within* their powers. For Pablo
Neruda, the equally certain transformation lay embedded in the
progressive force of history, of which human beings were the bearers
and instruments. Later he would more clearly see history as the
product of conscious human intervention, rather than as a power
working *through* human beings. In any event, the poetry of Cardenal
and Neruda was not given a central place in the literary canon through
the forties and fifties, perhaps because it anticipated its own public, or
spoke with the voice of a protagonist still unable to articulate its own
demands or its own aspirations to liberty. Hence the fundamentally
prophetic character of this writing. For until that subject took the
historical stage, the voice would echo in the darkness.

For Cardenal, the psalms are prophecies and instruments for forg-
ing community through the common language of redemption.[17]

Es la hora de las tinieblas.
Y la iglesia está helada, como llena de demonios,
mientras seguimos en la noche recitando los salmos.

(It is the hour of darkness./The church is freezing cold, as if it were full of demons,/while we go on through the night intoning our psalms.)

After Spain

Spain, as we have seen, was a crossroads for many poets and artists. For Neruda it was the turning-point in his life as a poet, calling him into the public arena where he was to remain for the bulk of his subsequent career. For Guillén it was a confirmation of his identification of the central issues in human affairs. For Octavio Paz, however, Spain had another and different impact. In one of his best-known poems 'Piedra del Sol' (Sunstone),[18] the experience of the defence of Madrid is the poem's central dividing point. The sunstone is the complex circular 'calendar' encapsulating the Aztec cosmogony;[19] and the poem's theme arises out of that circularity. For Paz, as he has repeatedly expressed it, poetry is the negation (or the opposite) of history. 'Poetry is our only course against rectilinear time, against progress.'[20] The milieu of the poem is 'paradisiacal', a return to the kind of communion, of oneness with the self and the environment, which religion once provided: 'Religion and poetry tend towards communion; both start from solitude and try, through the nourishment of the sacred, to break down that solitude and return to man his nature.'[21] This nature is expressed in a language whose source is prior to and outside history, in a realm of myth or 'culture'[22] which is also a perennial moral order.

It is interesting to approach Paz's poetic work as a response to the questions raised by the avant garde of the 1920s, a response which returned to the Formalist view of poetry and to an assertion of the autonomy of poetic practice. Out of Spain and Paz's disillusionment with it came an explicit counterposition of politics and art. As a critic and a theorist of poetic practice, Paz's generalization of that disillusionment has provided the framework for the debate about poetry in Latin America for several decades,[23] and has excluded from consideration one of the most exciting and creative developments of recent times.[24]

Paz's poetry is a considerable oeuvre in its own right; and his stimulating essays provide a perhaps unique insight into his own evolving ideas about his own practice. The first and formative experience of Paz's poetry is twofold. In 'La piedra y la flor' ('The stone and the flower') – its title a binary set of assertion/negation so often encountered in his work – Paz's journeys through Yucatán in southern Mexico reveal a barren landscape where the struggle for survival is unrelenting; this desert is an external and an inner landscape, whose flowers are memories, potentialities lost in time. They can be reappropriated in language, in a reconciliation of opposites which for Paz is the very ritual power of poetry. But first the desert must be confronted in its rural and its urban dimensions. Yucatan has its equivalent in Spain where Paz (like Stephen Spender[25]) drew deeply conservative conclusions from his experience of the Civil War. The bitter conflict he saw there found its cause in progress, change, the pursuit of material fulfilment as he saw it: 'Porque el dinero es infinito y/crea desiertos infinitos' (Because money is infinite and/creates infinite deserts).

'Himno entre ruinas' (Hymn amongst the ruins)[26] develops that dialectical structure, a structure that recurs in many of Paz's individual poems and in the body of his work as a whole. The binary set is the form, the resolution or reconciliation is the apotheosis, but one that can only be achieved in the realm of culture and in the medium of language. The metaphor of reconciliation is expressed through sex as a means of overcoming and fusion. Thus in 'Piedra del sol' (Sunstone) the response to the anguish of bombing is in a sexual encounter between a man and a woman amid the ruins:

> los dos se desnudaron y se amaron
> por defender nuestra porción eterna,
> nuestra ración de tiempo y paraíso,
> tocar nuestra raíz y recobrarnos
> recobrar nuestra herencia arrebatada
> por ladrones de vida hace mil siglos;
> los dos se desnudaron y besaron
> porque las desnudeces enlazadas
> saltan el tiempo y son invulnerables . . .

(they undressed and made love/to defend our eternal portion/our portion of time and paradise/to touch our roots and rediscover ourselves/ rediscover the inheritance taken from us/by robbers of life a thousand centuries ago;/they undressed and kissed/for nakedness interwoven/ jumps across time and is invulnerable . . .)

In the set 'hymn' (ritual celebration) and 'ruin' (destruction and collapse) sex again provides synthesis and resolution – 'Los ojos ven, las manos tocan' (Eyes see, hands touch); the woman looks 'desde lo alto de su morenía' (from the height of her brownness) and 'la luz crea templos en el mar' (light builds temples in the sea). This awakening of sensuality which precedes the entry into paradise is contrasted with those who live among the ruins:

Cae la noche sobre Teotihuacán.
En lo alto de la pirámide los muchachos fuman marihuana,
suenan guitarras roncas.
¿Qué yerba, qué agua de vida ha de darnos la vida,
dónde desenterrar la palabra,
la proporción que ridge al himno y al discurso,
al baile, a la ciudad y a la balanza?
El canto mexicano estalla en un carajo . . .

(Night falls on Teotihuacán./At the top of the pyramid the young men smoke marihuana,/harsh guitars sound./What weed, what living waters will give us life/where shall we unearth the word,/the sense of proportion governing hymns and speeches,/the dance the city and the measuring scale?/Mexican song bursts out in a curse . . .)

In his essay *El laberinto de la soledad*[27] (The labyrinth of solitude), (1949), written at the same time as 'Himno entre ruinas', Paz explored the impotence and the self-depreciation inherent in the 'carajo' and the multiple curses that speak of violation in the Mexican vocabulary. In all of them he identified the separation from a source of life and truth, demeaning those who have been orphaned by the process in the modern deserts, the great cities.

Nueva York, Londres, Moscú
La sombra cubre al llano con su yedra fantasma,
con su vacilante vegetación de escalofrío,
su vello ralo, su tropel de ratas.
A trechos tirita un sol anémico.
Acodado en montes que ayer fueron ciudades,
    Polifemo bosteza.
Abajo, entre los hoyos, se arrastra un rebaño de hombres.
Hasta hace poco el vulgo los consideraba animales impuros

(New York, London, Moscow/Shadows cover the plain with their ghostly ivy,/with their swaying, feverish vegetation,/with their scant fur and their swarm of rats./Here and there an anaemic sun shivers./Propping himself up on mounds that yesterday were cities,/Polyphemus yawns./Below, among the holes in the ground, a herd of men drags itself along./Until a short time ago people thought of them as impure animals.)

The poetic voice asks '¿Y todo ha de parar en este chapoteo de aguas muertas?' (And must everything end in splashing about in stagnant waters?). And the response is that through the epiphany, the reconciliation with nature outside time, the self-completion of language, the 'two hostile halves can become one' and man rediscover 'palabras que son flores que son actos' (words that are flowers that are acts). As he wrote in an earlier prose-poem 'Puntos de partida hacia el poema' (Starting points for a poem), 'Damos vueltas y vueltas en el vientre animal, en el vientre mineral, en el vientre temporal. Encontrar la salida: el poema' (We twist and turn in the animal belly, in the mineral belly, in the belly of time. To find a way out: the poem).

Paz has repeatedly returned in his essays and criticisms to the central formula governing his work – that the poem is a form of ritual accession to a second and different realm of understanding and of culture, escaping the prison of language and history in a synthetic reconciliation. That reconciliation takes place in a space which Lévi-Strauss has called Culture and which corresponds too to Frye's conception of myth as a repository of universal humanist values.[28] It is hard to avoid the feeling that this is in new terms a concept of 'human essence', a return to idealism. What is curious and specific about Paz is that he locates the 'otra orilla' (the other shore), the survival of myth, as Lévi-Strauss did, in the world outside Europe.[29]

Paz sets out to resurrect or generate new universals, new general and global truths about human experience in a world that has seen their collapse. The idiom he elects, that of poetry, has been in Latin America particularly a locus where the disintegration of the universal truths of Western civilization has been confronted and exposed. In the twenties and thirties, the alternative to that echo of fragmentation and alienation was found credibly only in a popular vernacular tradition or in a poetry of forceful critical explorations of the collapse of the dominant culture.

Paz in his essays and his activity as a poet has erected another tradition, a tradition continuous with the universals of the past, but preserving them in the face of the disappearance of their source. Or, to put it another way, he has disengaged those universals from their specific historical origins and relocated them in a place outside history and outside time which is perhaps more accessible at the margins of world civilization, be it in Latin America or the East. For in the heartlands of contemporary civilization there is only a devastated wasteland, a mirror on the inner devastation that pervades the general consciousness. The city appears repeatedly as an equivalent of the open desert. In 'El río', the river's flow back to origins is contrasted to the city, full of stones and shadows and incoherent noises, while the poet sits at its outer edges, seeking contact with the river beyond and outside time.

That view is delivered with great power in 'El cántaro roto', a vision of Mexico written in 1955 (the year that Juan Rulfo published his novel *Pedro Páramo*, a rich metaphorical presentation of the decline and death of a Mexican rural community[30]) which describes a place whose people are stricken with the exhaustion of hope and love. Waking from the dream (nostalgia) of rich landscapes,

> La mirada interior se despliega y un mundo de vértigo y llama nace bajo
>   la frente del que sueña;
> soles azules, verdes remolinos, picos de luz que abren astros como
>   granadas,
> tornasol solitario, ojo de oro girando en el centro de una explanada
>   calcinada,
> bosques de cristal de sonido, bosques de ecos y respuesta y ondas,
>   diálogo de transparencias . . .

> (The inward look unfolds and a world of vertigo and flame is born in the dreamer's brow;/blue suns, green whirlwinds, birdbeaks of light pecking open the pomegranate stars,/and the solitary sunflower, a golden eye revolving at the centre of a burnt slope,/and forests of ringing crystal, forests of echoes and answers and waves, a dialogue of transparencies . . .)

The vision ends with a chorus of harps. But on waking to the real world,

> Sólo el llano; cactus, huizaches, piedras enormes que estallan bajo el sol.
> No cantaba el grillo,
> había un vago olor a cal y semillas quemadas,
> las calles del poblado eran arroyos secos
> y el aire se habría roto en mil pedazos si alguien hubiese
> gritado: ¿quién?, ¿quién vive?

> (There was only the open plain: cactus, thorns, great rocks cracking in the sun./The crickets were silent,/there was a stray odour of quicklime and burnt seeds,/the village streets were dry gullies/and the air would have shattered into a thousand pieces if someone had/shouted: is there anyone there?)

The two landscapes are obviously irreconcilable; the process of overcoming their separation is akin to dreaming backwards ('soñar hacia atrás'), to the point of reunification that is like an erotic encounter. And indeed that erotic encounter, that immersion in a sensuality which both emphasizes the transitory quality of human experience and gives access to an enduring range of meanings in the mythic realm became the central topic of Paz's later poetry in *Ladera este* (Eastern shore) and *Viento entero* (Full wind).[31]

201

Antipoetry

The aspirations to religious truth that are embedded in the poetry and criticism of Octavio Paz have not completely dominated the debate or the activity of poetry. In many ways the counter-current to the elevation of poetry has expressed itself in a growing body of work called *antipoesía*. It is not, of course, non-poetry; but it is writing that is defined by its clear differentiation from the philosophical idealism of Paz and especially from the grandiose rhetoric of Neruda. It is signifi-cant in this sense that the outstanding exponents of antipoetry should be Nicanor Parra and Enrique Lihn, both of them Chilean. It is thus a poetry without aspiration to grand truth, to elevation, to a penetration beyond the real to realms and understandings that shelter unrealized imaginative potentials. Though Parra learned his poetry in the ambit of surrealism[32] and employs some of its techniques of montage and juxtaposition, he is in many ways an anti-surrealist too. Describing his own work, Parra acknowledged, 'the adjective I most willingly accept is existential. I work with permanent problems, rather than with what is transitory.'[33]

The consequences of his immersion in the real are far-reaching at every level. The sublime language and transcendental impact of poetry are specifically rejected – this is a poetry that demystifies and undermines the lyrical promise, the refuge of the 'world of poetry'. It also specifically rejects the aristocratic perception of the poet, embodi-ment of the highest individual aspirations. In some ways Parra could be seen as the poetic representative of those very ordinary, mediocre petty bourgeois to whom Darío referred so savagely in his Preface to *Prosas Profanas*; his is the voice of the *homme bourgeois moyen*. He is also the product of a continuing ideological crisis, however, and his deci-sion, to write from an immersion in the reality of everyday experience implies an acceptance of the horizons of the possible, the limited frontiers of the consciousness of the actual. In Lukács's terms, there is no dimension of the 'ought', only what 'is'.[34] There are no transcen-dent values in Parra, no metaphysics, no god; by extension there can be no vision of change brought about by human agency, by purposive human action. The dynamics of the world are the product of chance and arbitrary conjunction. The techniques and suppositions beneath much surrealist method, therefore, are here reversed, negated or parodied. For the montage effect does not produce a vision of new and unexpected relations, a sudden and unexpected insight into the hid-den relations at work in the world as the radical surrealists may have hoped.[35] Instead the conjunctions are accidental, disconnected and thus purposeless; they yield no conclusion and produce only an attitude of fatalism (but without any concept of fate) in the face of the random associations and encounters out of which the course of actual history is seen to be formed. And human relations at all levels, collective and individual, social and sexual, are shaped by the same random movements and juxtapositions.

> Plaga de motonetas en Santiago.
> la Sagan se da vuelta en automóvil.
> Terremoto en Iran: 600 víctimas.
> El gobierno detiene la inflación.
> Los candidatos a la presidencia
> Tratan de congraciarse con el clero.
> Huelga de profesores y estudiantes.
> Romería a la tumba de Oscar Castro.
> Enrique Bello invitado a italia
> Rosselini declara que las suecas
> Son más frías que témpanos de hielo.
> Se especula con astros y planetas.
>
> Su Santidad el Papa Pío XII
> Da la nota simpática del año:
> Se le aparece Cristo varias veces.
>
> El autor se retrata con su perro.

(Plague of motor scooters in Santiago./Sagan overturns her car./Earthquake in Iran: 600 victims./The government controls inflation./The presidential candidates/Try to win the sympathy of the clergy./Strike of teachers and students./Pilgrimage to Oscar Castro's grave./Enrique Bello invited to Italy./Rossellini declares that Swedish women/are colder than blocks of ice./There is speculation about stars and planets.//His Holiness Pope Pius XII/Provides the year's amusing note://Christ appears to him several times.//The author has his picture taken with his dog.)

Events are presented in matter-of-fact tones appropriate for a 'Noticiario 1957' (1957 News Bulletin); they have no moral charge, and evoke no response of sympathy, horror or shock. Neither are the events given any order of importance – they are merely signs, undifferentiated data. And the observer, the poet him or herself, is no more than an additional sign, a spectator without critical capacity. Thus the laws that operate outside social control are also invasions of the person of the poet, who is as powerless as any other spectator. There is an unmistakably anti-heroic and thus anti-Nerudian tone in his 'Soliloquio del Individuo' (Soliloquy of the Individual), whose allusions to Neruda's *Canto General* are obvious.

> Di a luz libros de miles de páginas
> se me hinchó la cara
> construí un fonógrafo,
> la máquina de coser.
> empezaron a aparecer los primeros automóviles,
> yo soy el Individuo.
> . . .
> Se construyeron también ciudades,
> rutas,
> instituciones religiosas pasaron de moda,
> buscaban dicha, buscaban felicidad,
> yo soy el Individuo.
> Después me dediqué mejor a viajar,
> a practicar, a practicar idiomas,
> idiomas.
> Yo soy el individuo.
> Miré por una cerradura,
> sí, miré, qué digo, miré,
> para salir de la duda miré,
> detrás de unas cortinas
> yo soy el Individuo.
> Bien.
> Mejor es tal vez que vuelva a ese valle,
> a esa roca que me sirvió de hogar,
> y empiece a grabar de nuevo,
> de atrás para adelante grabar
> el mundo al revés.
> Pero no: la vida no tiene sentido.

(I brought forth books thousands of pages long,/my face swelled up,/I built a phonograph,/the sewing machine,/the first cars began to appear,/ I am the Individual . . ./Cities were also built,/roads,/religious institutions went out of fashion,/people looked for joy, for happiness,/I am the Individual./Then I thought it better to travel,/to practice, practising languages/languages./I am the individual./I looked through the keyhole,/yes, I looked, I mean to say, I looked,/to resolve my doubts I looked,/behind some curtains./I am the individual./Okay./It would be best perhaps if I went back to that valley,/to that rock that gave me shelter,/and started to carve again/carve from the back to the front,/the world turned upside down./But no; life is senseless.)

The echo of Vallejo is strong; the ironic response to the world is self-directed too, as the speaker is of the world and subject to its arbitrary laws and movements and to its cruel and unpredictable twists. In *Poemas y antipoemas* (Poems and antipoems)[36] there is a pervasive horror and despair at the futility of human affairs. His *Versos de salon* (Drawing-room verses) from which 'Noticiario' came are more playful, closer to burlesque, playthings. Yet beneath is a deadly serious purpose, as each system of meaning is caricatured and ridiculed by the central persona of the book – a kind of malicious Rumpelstiltskin, the 'energúmeno'. Sex and love are rendered futile in 'Se me ocurren ideas luminosas' (Bright ideas come to me); death made insignificant in 'Discurso fúnebre' (Funeral oration). 'Versos sueltos' (Free verses) are free-association games which mock the aspiration to discover embedded meanings in arbitrary associations of words and deride the arrogance of philosophy.

> Un ojo blanco no me dice nada
> ¡Hasta cuándo posar de inteligente
> Para qué contemplar un pensamiento
> Hay que lanzar al aire las ideas!
> El desorden también tiene su encanto
> Un murciélago lucha con el sol:
> La poesía no molesta a nadie
> Y la fucsia parece bailarina.

(A white eye tells me nothing/How much longer should I pretend to be intelligent/Why contemplate a thought/Ideas should be thrown into the air!/Disorder also has its charm/A bat struggles with the sun:/Poetry doesn't bother anyone/and the fuchsia is like a ballerina.)

The disintegration of the Romantic self continues, and in the chaos of the world, personality and identity are shifting truths. The individual cannot rise above this constant movement, nor evade it in some transcendental realm; the poet is defined by his likeness to all others, his closeness to the average experience – as his 'Epitafio' makes clear. He is 'El pequeño burgués' (the petty bourgeois)

> Si desea brillar en los salones
> El pequeño burgués
> Debe saber andar en cuatro pies
> Estornudar y sonreir a un tiempo
> Bailar un vals al borde del abismo
> Endiosar a los organos sexuales
> Desnudarse delante del espejo
> Deshojar una rosa con un lapiz
> Y tragar toneladas de saliva.
> . . .

205

¡Con razón el artista verdadero
Se entretiene matando matapiojos!

(If he wishes to shine in the salons/the petty bourgeois/He must know
how to walk on all fours/Sneeze and smile at the same time/Dance a
waltz at the edge of the abyss/Deify the sexual organs/Strip in front of
the mirror/Strip the petals from a rose with a pencil/And swallow tons of
saliva./. . ./No wonder the true artist/Spends his time killing fleakillers!)

Language descends through Parra's poetry from the self-con-
sciously poetic to the absolutely prosaic, from the artifact to the found
object – slogans, graffiti, disparate phrases. They can express frust-
ration, rage, despair – and that is their residual humanity. But they
cannot contest the shape of experience. It is in that sense that Parra
shares the nihilism and desperation of the avant-garde. Despite the
extraordinary contribution made by other members of his family, his
sister Violeta in particular,[37] to the knowledge and recuperation of
popular culture, Parra himself has sustained a deeply sceptical view of
human action.

Enrique Lihn, while sharing much of Parra's despair, as well as his
scepticism about social movements and change, retains a vision of the
redemptive powers of language.[38] The parallels with the poetry of
Parra (and another contemporary Chilean poet Gonzalo Rojas (b.
1917)[39]) are in the trajectory of the poet's disillusionment as well as in
more direct similarities of language and style. Lihn's *Poesía de paso*
(Poetry passing through) is a record of a journey through Europe. As a
Latin American, Lihn made that journey as so many other Latin
American intellectuals have done, in search of a cultural heritage, of a
continuity to make sense of the present. But the grandeur he found in
Italy, for example, proved elusive and illusory. The images he brought
with him were not guides to the real but an incomplete memento of
childhood dreams, signs of an aspiration to knowledge (and with it a
sense of place in the world) of which he is now cheated:

> El extranjero trae a las ciudades
> el cansado recuerdo de sus libros de estampas
>   ese mundo inconcluso que veía girar,
> mitad en sueños, por el ojo mismo
> de la prohibición – y en la pieza vacía
> parpadeaba el recuerdo de otra infancia
> trágicamente desaparecida . . .

(The outsider brings to cities/the tired memory of his picture books/that incomplete world that he used to see turning,/half in a dream through the very eye/of prohibition – and in the empty room/the memory of another childhood/tragically now gone, blinked . . .)

Europe and its culture then proved inaccessible ('inabordable' – the poem's final word). His subsequent 'Homenaje a Freud' (Homage to Freud) turns on all those explanatory systems that have colonized the deepest recesses of the human heart:

> El árbol de la ciencia
> es una gran patraña abominable:
> ha florecido a expensas del espíritu;
> es natural que todo lo envenene . . .

(The tree of science/is a great abominable hoax/it has flowered at the expense of the spirit/so naturally it has poisoned everything . . .)

But the poem also has close to its surface a rage and a feeling of deep offence. The poetic voice rails at those ideologies that have stolen from man his freedom and authenticity – even if that freedom has brought human beings face to face with suffering and the awareness of their own limitations. It is the right of everyone to confront their own personal pain and to seek out its causes. And the measure of humanity is not the discovery of new truths, new icons to adore in the name of science or religion. It is the search itself, the struggle for understanding that renders material existence truly human. To retrieve the past and recuperate the future, and to construct it in concrete or imaginative practice is what defines the human. The need and energy to strive for that comes from a buried power that can be disinterred only through an imaginative leap; Freud named it and in the final analysis it will overcome all those who try to imprison the human spirit.

> En el brasero de los acusados,
> aunque brillen cien años por su ausencia,
> terminarán asándose los jueces.

(On the fire of the accused,/though they shine by their absence for a hundred years,/the judges will themselves burn in the end.)

The poet's effort, isolated and individual though it is, asserts the vitality of the human spirit – that at least is the import of Lihn's wonderful 'Porque escribí' (Because I wrote).

207

Ahora que quizás, en un año de calma,
piense: la poesía me sirvío para esto:
no pude ser feliz, ello me fue negado,
pero escribí.

. . .

Escribí, mi escritura fue como la maleza
de flores ácimas pero flores en fin,
el pan de cada día de las tierras eriazas:
un caparazón de espinas y raíces.
De la vida tomé todas estas palabras
como un niño oropel, guijarros junto al río:
las cosas de una magia, perfectamente inútiles
pero que siempre vuelven a renovar su encanto.

. . .

Porque escribí no estuve en casa del verdugo
ni me dejé llevar por el amor a Dios
ni acepté que los hombres fueran dioses
ni me hice desear como escribiente
ni la pobreza me pareció atroz
ni el poder una cosa deseable
ni me lavé ni me ensucié las manos
ni fueron vírgenes mis mejores amigas
ni tuve como amigo a un fariseo
ni a pesar de la cólera
quise desbaratar a mi amigo.
Pero escribí y me muero por mi cuenta
porque escribí porque escribí estoy vivo.

(Now that, perhaps, in a calm year,/I can think; poetry helped me in this;/I could not be happy, that was denied to me,/but I wrote./. . ./I wrote, my writing was like a weed/with bitter flowers but flowers nevertheless/the daily bread of the dry lands,/a hard shell of thorns and roots./From life I took all these words/like a child takes trinkets, or pebbles by the river;/magical things, perfectly useless/but they renew their enchantment over and over again./. . ./Because I wrote I was not in the executioner's house/nor was I carried away by the love of God/nor did I allow men to become gods/nor did I offer my pen to anyone/nor did poverty seem terrible to me/nor power a desirable thing/I neither washed nor dirtied my hands/my best women friends were not virgins/ no Pharisee was ever my friend/nor, despite anger/did I ever want to tear my enemy limb from limb./But I wrote and I die in my own way/because I wrote because I wrote I am alive.)

For Enrique Lihn, then, poetry is a personal testament, a sign of life in the most literal sense. To have a voice even when that voice speaks only of doubt; to maintain a distance from the world and a sense of self, however besieged and insecure it may be. These are the elements of integrity; and that integrity, that minimal wholeness of the self, shot through with rage and despair, is the only inheritance of the Romantic promise. Lihn and Parra found the lyric persona all too human, and the Baudelairian journey to another metaphorical realm an illusion. There is for them no metalanguage, no higher truth – and that understanding is the beginning of knowledge. But the procedure of metaphor, whereby a movement is effected by analogy towards a level of freedom from constraint – linguistic, moral or social – is not available; metonymy – naming the part for the whole – is a trap too, for the wholeness that is alluded to is also unattainable. Neither Lihn nor Parra identify the individual experience as in any sense capable of generalization; its uniqueness, then, without the counterpoint of typicality, makes it futile and unrepeatable and thus profoundly isolating. It becomes a poignant pastiche of the Romantic notion of universality. To have written, to have made a sign, is a single act and all the evidence that poetry can here provide.

Tempus Fugit

Though in relation to a different current in poetry, the Mexican poet José Emilio Pacheco (b. 1939) shares the sense of the transitory and fragile quality of experience that occupies the core of Lihn's poetry. At a very early stage Pacheco developed a tone more characteristic of poetry in English than in Spanish, a register of understatement so hard to achieve in the rhetorical Hispanic tradition. It serves to convey a sense of sombre certainty wrapped in a decorum both linguistic and moral. In a sense, it is the discipline of language itself that increasingly provides an order in a world whose disorder is belied in the unpretentious quality of much of his work. Yet beneath it is a radical and negative perception. As José Miguel Oviedo puts it, 'The certainty of the transitory nature of things fills this poetry with a radical despair [desconsuelo]; it bears witness to a process of destruction that inexorably touches everything.'[40] Yet the air of resignation is not always prevalent. In an early work, 'El reposo del fuego' (Where the fire rests)[41] Pacheco explores and laments the imminent apocalypse that engulfs all life.

> El mundo en vilo azota sus cadenas.
> La tempestad desciende.
> Y yo, sin nombre,
> busco un rastro fugaz, quiero un vestigio;

algo que me recuerde, si he olvidado,
que a veces, en la tarde sin memoria,
presencié en derredor, vi en el silencio
la secreta eficacia con que el polvo
devora el interior de los objetos

(The world wildly thrashes its chains./The tempest descends./And I,
who am without a name,/seek a fleeting trace, I want a sign;/something
that reminds me, if I have forgotten/that sometimes, in the evening
without a memory,/I did witness around me, I did see in the silence/the
secret efficiency with which the dust/devours the inside of things)

This dust and fire leave behind only a scorched surface of the earth
and a memory of fire – 'everything is forgetfulness and shadow and
unfolding'. Yet at the point of most radical despair, at the lowest point
of helplessness,

Porque he extraviado aquí todas las claves
para salvar al mundo y ya no puedo
consolar consolarte consolarme.

(Beause I have lost here all the keys/that might save the world and I can
no longer/console console you console myself.)

there is once again 'desenlace y recomienzo' (unfolding and a new
beginning). That new beginning is in fact an act of rediscovery of an
ancient and still present Mexico under the city streets, the continually
re-emerging ruins of Tenochtitlán. That recurring presence will
emerge again later, in the exploration of the 'destiny full of holes' that
was imposed in 1968.

There is in all Pacheco's work a density and compactness of expres-
sion that contradicts an often prosaic appearance; it is an economy
that seems to derive from a cool and critical distance on the one hand,
and a conservation of poetic energy on the other, as if only the breath
contained in these brief outbursts of humanity could survive the
process of deterioration and the dispiriting failure of grand truths.

No amo mi Patria. Su fulgor abstracto
es inasible.
Pero (aunque suene mal) daría la vida
por diez lugares suyos, ciertas gentes,
puertos, bosques de pinos, fortalezas,
una ciudad deschecha, gris, monstruosa,
varias figuras de su historia,
montañas
(y tres o cuatro rios)

210

(I do not love my Motherland. Its abstract brilliance/is beyond my reach./ But (though it sounds bad) I would give my life/for ten of its places, some people,/ports, pinewoods, forts,/a broken grey and monstrous city,/some figures from its history,/mountains/(and three or four rivers))

We do not, it seems, choose the location of our survival, nor the conditions under which it may occur, but words at least may offer a modest protest, or a single act of 'rebellion against the inevitable'.[42]

In *No me preguntes cómo pasa el tiempo* (Don't ask me how the time goes by)[43] Pacheco's irony has grown more acerbic, his detachment replaced by a sense of tragedy. Yet the overpowering feeling is of impotence, of painful isolation and of the self-reproach that stems continually therefrom. Poetry, he says (in 'crítica de la poesía' – a critique of poetry) 'sirvió alguna vez' (had its uses once) but

> Quizás no es tiempo ahora:
> nuestra época
> nos dejó hablando solos.

(Perhaps this is not the time:/our time/has left us talking to ourselves)

Some part of the barely repressed anger that underpins the book must come from the experience to which it bears implicit testimony – the massacre of students on 2 October 1968 in the Square of Tlatelolco.[44] Pacheco's beautiful reworking of the Cantares Mexicanos (Songs of the Mexican)[45] lament the collapse and destruction of the Aztec world:

> Ah yo nací en la guerra florida,
> yo soy mexicano.
> Sufro, mi corazón se llena de pena:
> veo la desolacion que se cierne sobre el templo
> cuando todos los escudos se abrasan en llamas.
>
> En los caminos yacen dardos rotos.
> Las casas están destechadas.
> Enrojecidas tienen sus muros.
> Gusanos pululan por calles y plazas.
>
> Golpeamos los muros de adobe
> y es nuestra herencia
> una red de agujeros.
>
> Esto es lo que ha hecho el dador de la Vida
> allí en Tlatelolco.

(Ah, I was born in the war of flowers,[46]/I am a Mexican./I suffer, my heart fills with sorrow;/I see the desolation that grips the temple/as all the shields are consumed in flames.//On the streets lie broken darts./The houses are without roofs./Their walls are turned red./Worms crawl through streets and squares.//We strike at the adobe walls/and our destiny is/a network of holes.//This is what the giver of Life has done/ here in Tlatelolco.)

Three poems follow concerning the experience of 1968. Like Octavio Paz in his comments on the event,[47] Pacheco is struck by its confirmation of a cyclical history ('(1968 (I)'), its fearful indication of a future still to be formed – 'Página blanca, al fin, en que todo es posible . . .' (A white page, where everything is possible in the final analysis . . .) – couples with a sense of irrevocable closure in the third of the poems. Here language, form and ideas combine in their sense of transience and their desire for continuity with the given and repeated past and the fearsome empty future. Poetry's promise is insight or elevation; Pacheco offers neither, only the record of his own sense of guilt and a belief in the expression of contingency that is at the core of all poetry. Thus, increasingly, Pacheco offers 'versions' or recreations of the poetry of others; but despite the rage and the careful and delicate reworking of the poetry of the past, the central voice is still full of shame at the ephemeral nature of the business of poetry itself – engulfed by the global village on the one hand and the fragility of things on the other.

> A mi sólo me importa
>   el testimonio
> del momento que pasa
>   las palabras
> que dicta en su fluir
>   el tiempo en vuelo.
>
> La poesía que busco
>   es como un diario
> en donde no hay proyecto
>   ni medida.

(The only thing that matters to me/is the testimony/to the passing moment/the words/set out in its constant flow/by a time in flight.//The poetry I seek/is like a newspaper/in which there is neither a project/nor a measure.)

In Central America the dense and obscure poetry of the finest of the poets says much of the difficulties in sustaining literary activity under a succession of ruthless military dictatorships. Exile and exclusion are a prevalent note in this body of writing, which spans periods of transformation elsewhere in Latin America and has a direct resonance in other later poets of the region. In Cardenal, for example, are clear and acknowledged echoes of his mentors José Coronel Urtecho and Pablo Antonio Cuadra.[48] In Roque Dalton (1933–75) and Claribel Alegría (b. 1924), writing in El Salvador, are glimpses of Juan Cotto (1900–38) and Pedro Geoffroy Rivas.[49] It is logical that a note of hermeticism and isolation should emerge from a region whose early attempts at social change had met the most brutal and sustained repression. This served only to emphasize and underscore the backwardness and poverty of the Central American economies and their impotence in the face of the strategic designs of the United States upon them.[50] Without a working class of any significance, and thus without a collective movement to express its needs, the cause of national liberation had assumed a leading role in the politics of the region in the early thirties.[51] But the struggles of Sandino and Farabundo Martí had both ended in bloody repression and the intellectuals of this world spoke with the voice of an absent class. Urtecho and Cuadra were conservatives in politics, while Salomón de la Selva (1893–1959) was linked to Sandino and often spoke on his behalf. But as they withdrew both physically and aesthetically in the thirties into their jungle fastnesses, the two great precursors of the vital poetic culture of Nicaragua could share none of the communal spirit that describes so much of today's Nicaraguan poetry under the visionary influence of Ernesto Cardenal.

The poetry of these Nicaraguans is obscure and difficult, often impenetrable in its anarchic experimentation with the limits of language. In a sense it is a poetry that corresponds to the European avant garde of the twenties; yet it extends into and reconnects with the resurgent separatism of the forties poets, and the poets of *antipoesía*. The central experience of exile and a defence of humanism is the paradoxical point of contact both with *antipoesía* and with the rediscovery of the popular idiom in the work of their outstanding acolyte Ernesto Cardenal.[52]

> Toda tierra y ser y mar y elemento
> robustecen el límite, al corazón penetran,
> y llevan hacia el mundo, rebotando la vida,
> la múltiple unidad transcendente del hombre.
> La materia es tan dúctil como el torso de la esposa

se alimenta la frente como del pez de la entraña
en el oro y el sol, en la rosa y la rueda.
En el hombre se inscriben la marea y la savia,
la respiración y el temblor de los metales,
la inconsciencia mineral de los motores,
el brusco corazón de los pistones y los árboles.

(All earth and being and sea and elements/strengthen the limits, pene-
trate the heart,/and take us towards the world, bouncing with life,/to the
multiple transcendent unity of man./Matter is as malleable as the torso
of the wife,/the forehead takes its nourishment like the stomach of the
fish/from gold and salt, the rose and the wheel./On man are inscribed
tide and sap,/breath and the trembling of metal/the mineral unconscious
of engines,/the sharp heart of pistons and trees.)

This strange movement between man and nature, between plants and
technology, is a movement between a primitive undeveloped material
and a potentiality, a human potential, locked in the substance of
nature. Like those of Paz, Cuadra's poems are often profoundly erotic
because sex is a meeting of the most deeply human and the most
natural of responses; it is also an act of overcoming the physical limits
of self and environment: 'Buscamos lo inasible y también lo cercano/y
nos duele la prisa y también la lentitud.' (We seek the unattainable and
also what is nearby/and we are hurt by speed but also by the
slowness.)

There is in Cuadra's work a process of returning to origins not
dissimilar to Neruda's, but the results are very different. Cuadra
points ahead to the vernacular history of Cardenal's 'Hora Cero' (Zero
Hour) rather than the high abstract rhetoric of Neruda. In Cuadra
denunciation and history mix indistinctly with snatches of song and
simple words of ordinary life. There is a sense that his jungle occupant
is small, afraid and uneasy, and in a living relationship with the nature
around him. Yet in that natural substance is not the rosebud that Darío
found there, but the potential form of the future – engines and pistons.

Urtecho was a contemporary of Cuadra's and shared his formative
role in the creation of Vanguardia, the key group of poets and writers
in 1920s Nicaragua. Undoubtedly both were in contact with and
knowledgeable about developments in poetry elsewhere in Latin and
North America.[53] Yet their assimilation of these techniques and
insights was undoubtedly profoundly affected by the specificity of
Nicaragua. Urtecho's is a more diverse and in ways more radical
poetry, whose variety of technique and assault upon structure and

semantics represents not so much a revolutionary gesture as an act of personal defiance against the structures of writing and of thought that used to limit the creative possibility of the poet. In his earliest work he issued a challenge to the pervasive influence of his fellow countryman Rubén Darío:

> Burlé tu león de cemento al cabo.
> Tu sabes que mi llanto fue de lágrimas
> y no de perlas. Te amo.
> Soy el asesino de tus retratos.
> Por vez primera comimos naranjas.
> . . .
> Tu que dijiste tantas veces 'Ecce
> Homo' frente al espejo
> y no sabías cual de los dos era
> el verdadero, si acaso era alguno.
> (¿te entraban deseos de hacer pedazos
> el cristal?) Nada de eso
> (mármol bajo el azul) en tus jardines
> – donde antes de morir rezaste al cabo –
> donde yo me paseo con mi novia
> y soy irrespetuoso con los cisnes.[54]

(In the end I cheated your cement lion./You know my weeping was tears/and not pearls. I love you./I am the murderer of your portraits./We ate oranges for the first time./. . ./You who so often said 'Ecce/Homo' in front of the mirror/and who you didn't know which of the two was/the real one, if either of them was./(Did you ever feel a desire to smash/the glass?) None of that/(marble under the blue) in your gardens/ – where in the end you prayed before dying – /where I walk with my girlfriend/and have no respect for swans.)

This humanization of Darío, and the tone of gentle irreverence lay the ghost of the grand style. For Urtecho all material that has a place in human experience has a place in poetry; all language through which human beings seek to communicate is legitimate in the exploration of the limits of understanding. In this he anticipates and inspires Cardenal in his elaboration of a poetic method Cardenal called 'exteriorismo'. Urtecho's wonderfully rich 'Pequeña biografía de mi mujer' (Minimal biography of my wife) is long, discursive, associative and unstructured, complex in the multiple directions of a life, full of admiration and a sense of wonder at this woman who in the end, despite her versatility and breadth of experience is

Una mujer extraordinaria
Una mujer como inventada por un poeta
Una mujer casada con un poeta
Una mujer por eso mismo verdadera
Una mujer verdadera mujer
Una mujer sencillamente
Una mujer

(An extraordinary woman/The sort of woman a poet might invent/A woman married to a poet/For that very reason real/A woman real woman/A woman simply/A woman)

The isolation of both the poet and his partner in the world, their fragile survival on the margins recalls and echoes Cuadra. This fierce individualism is defiant and ironic. But what is remarkable about it at the same time is that it leads neither of these strange and provocative poets towards a refuge in a transcendental language, but into folklore, into children's song at times, into a bare and primitive world of language. Their contemporary and less well known colleague Joaquín Pasos (1914–47) echoed this human fragility, this ordinary survival in his long and complex 'Canto de guerra de las cosas' (War song of things), where he is both resigned and angry, prosaic and redemptive.

Cuando lleguéis a viejos, respetaréis el oro,
si es que llegáis a viejos,
si es que entonces quedó algún oro.
El agua es la única eternidad de la sangre.
Su fuerza, hecha sangre. Su inquietud, hecha sangre.
Su violento anhelo de viento y cielo,
hecho sangre . . .

(When you get old you will respect gold,/if you ever reach old age,/if there is any gold left by then./Water is the only eternity of blood./Its power, made blood. Its restlessness made blood./Its violent desire for wind and sky/made blood . . .)

But it ends with man overwhelmed by a material world:

He aquí la ausencia del hombre, fuga de carne, de miedo,
días, cosas, almas, fuego.
Todo se quedó en el tiempo. Todo se quemó allá lejos.

(We are left with the absence of man, a flight of flesh, of fear/days, things, soul, fire./Everything was left behind in time./Everything burned up far away.)

Others, in very different circumstances, reached a similar despair-

216

ing conclusion – this final reduction to the 'absence of man'. Without the confidence of Octavio Paz, whose scepticism about human contingency was counterbalanced by a conviction that culture provided other and more enduring perceptions, the loss of history represents an absolute loss. The human is reduced to the immediate, and in an increasingly radical despair, poetry enacts and affirms that disappearance. Words announce their own demise, their own absolute contingency, and in that sense the absence of meaning. All that is left is the sensation, the sound, the fleeting appearance of the word. And beyond that is silence. The radical paradox of a poetry enunciated in silence is the key motif of Jorge Eielson,[55] the Peruvian poet whose work is sparse and minimal yet which has had a lasting impact (contradictory though that may seem) on younger poets in his country.

> Labro los astros a mi lado oh hielo!
> y en la mesa de las tierras el poema
> que rueda entre los muertos y, encendido, los corona,
> pues por todo va mi sombra tal la gloria
> de hueso, cera y humus que me postra, majestuoso,
> sobre el bello césped, en los dioses abrasado.
>
> Amo, así este cráneo mío, en su ceniza, como al mundo
> en cuyos fríos parques la eternidad es el mismo
> hombre de mármol que vela en una estatua
> o que se tiende, oscuro y sin amor, sobre la yerba.

(I work the stars by my side, oh ice!/and on the table of earths the poem/ that wanders among the dead and, alight, crowns them,/for my shadow passes through everything like glory/of bone, wax and humus that leaves me majestically prostrate/on the beautiful lawn, burnt in the gods.//So I love this cranium of mine, in its ashes, as I love the world/in whose cold parks eternity is the same/man of marble who watches from his statue/or who lies, dark and loveless, on the grass.)

His contemporary Carlos Germán Belli[56] has perhaps a greater sense of irony, a wit cutting through a no less radical despair.

> HA LLEGADO EL DOMINGO
>
> y procedo a desollarme como a un oso:
> me desenfundo
> y exprimo el sucio overol que cubre mi sangre

Caen entonces al fondo de la tina
goterones de sudor frío
pelos erizados
pelos entreabiertos por el miedo

Y de inmediato un verde cesped reemplaza mi antiguo piel

(SUNDAY HAS ARRIVED//and I proceed to skin myself as I would a
bear:/I unsheathe myself/and squeeze out the dirty overall that covers
my blood//Then on the bottom of the bathtub fall/heavy drops of cold
sweat/erect hairs/hairs half-open with fear//And straight away a green
lawn replaces my old skin)

Without transcendence or metaphysics, and without a concept of
culture as a substitute for God, radical individualism leads inexorably
to the denial of humanity, the poignant self-destruction of man – or his
transformation into object, into pre-social substance. And poetry then
adopts the language of silence as its apotheosis.

The alternative direction finds transcendence not in an external
force or truth, but in the evolution and growth of humanity itself.
Poetry has been the expression of radical lyrical separation. But it is not
inherent in the form. And the contemporary poetry of Latin America
offers too a very different chronicle, an epic reappropriation of history
and a rediscovery of the lyric self as a collective voice.

Neruda's *Canto General*

The third book of Pablo Neruda's *Residencia en la tierra*[57] is entitled
'España en el corazón' (Spain in my heart). Although it was begun as
the third segment of a continuous poetic trajectory, the Spanish Civil
War marked a watershed, a fundamental change in direction. Out of
Spain came a new poet and a new poetry, a poetry of engagement with
history whose traumatic beginnings are recorded in 'Explico algunas
cosas'. The change, however, pointed in two distinct directions:
towards a directly political poetry, on the one hand, and a 'poetry of
testimony' on the other. That testimony made of the poet a collective
spokesman, a representative voice. In that sense Neruda moved
towards that identity with a public that Guillén had elaborated
through the *son* form. But Neruda did not immediately move towards
the vernacular, the language of speech and social communication. His
poetic voice was still rhetorical and celebratory, its public statement
assuming ritual form. That is why Neruda's overtly declamatory
poetry remains fundamentally unsatisfactory, and why those state-
ments of personal conviction and rage remain his best works. The

extraordinary and ambitious *Canto General*[58] embraces both registers. Compare 'Explico algunas cosas' for example, with the pamphlet-poem 'Sanjurjo en los infiernos' (Sanjurjo in hell):

> Como fósforo queman sus riñones
> y su siniestra boca de soldado
> traidor se derrite en maldiciones . . .

(Like a match his kidneys burn/and the sinister mouth of a treacherous/ soldier dissolves into curses . . .)

This is perilously close to abuse, and too distant in its received and trite images to carry the passion of Neruda's finest work. It, and other contingent poetry, provoked a severe reaction from his contemporaries – indeed Baciu reports the publication of a *Defensa de la poesía* by a group of Chilean Surrealists in 1939 which specifically denounced the pernicious influence of Neruda on a younger generation. But there is more than a suggestion here that the conflict as presented was between 'political' and 'pure' poetry. Neruda had other detractors too, however, some of whom attacked him from the left, or for reasons that seemed largely personal. Pablo de Rokha seemed to qualify on both counts.[59]

The question, of course, is not whether politics belongs in poetry; the collective social experience of human beings is the material of all poetry, even when it is denied. But there is a profound and important difference between the presentation of political slogans or programmes, which is not the stuff of poetry, and the assimilation of lived experience into political analysis – the encounter between 'the social fact and the inviolability of the self' – that is poetry's proper content.[60] In that respect, the central core of *Canto General* has a clear perspective, but it is not a programmatic manifesto. The poem is often described as epic, usually referring to its length rather than its content. Yet the term is appropriate. An epic literature is a 'literature of foundation', the record of a heroic *human* struggle to draw order out of chaos, to give human form to inert nature. At one level the procedure of the poem corresponds to the evolution of Neruda's own poetic method; on the global scale, it represents the emergence of the human out of the animal and vegetable. What is crucial to it is that that process is the result of *labour*, the transformation of the material environment by human beings pursuing purposes which at first exist only in the creative imagination.[61] For Marx, and thus for Marxists, that is the dialectical source of historical process. And by analogy, art and literature are both the elaboration in consciousness of alternative possibili-

219

ties and the activity whereby those possibilities are realized.[62] Later, under a capitalist division of labour, that creative activity in the world becomes the province of a few, separated individuals, while the bulk of those who labour do so at the behest and under the control of others. Their activity loses its creative impulse – and their labour is alienated from their consciousness.

The power of *Canto General* is that it locates the history of Latin America in a continuous process of conscious material transformation – the most completely human act. Thus that nature which had imprisoned man and rendered him impotent and without continuity in *20 Poemas* is now rediscovered *in its relationship to man*. Nature, in other words, ceases to be inert matter when it is made the material of the act of creative transformation, when human purposes are carved out of stone. It is in this process that history begins and that the human is differentiated from the animal and vegetable realms – not existence *in* nature (however unsatisfactory that existence) but the harnessing of that nature to human purposes. It is that transformation, and that concept of history, that the *Canto General* records. Furthermore, the process is teleological and magnificently progressive. In that sense, it has been argued, Neruda rediscovered the philosophy of the Enlightenment; he was a thinker in a great Jacobin, radical *bourgeois* tradition. That charge seems unreasonable, but he is undoubtedly *historicist*, seeing the dynamics of history as an autonomous process impelling humans forward on an inexorable road towards fulfilment. In that sense, he could be accused of a lack of the dialectical insight of a Vallejo; but that does not detract from the power and conviction of this extraordinary celebration of the *making* of history. That construction occurs within the mould of a progressive European vision of history which is *universal* – and makes few concessions to a radical nationalist perception of that history. And yet, in the end, the protagonist of this great epic is a nation, a pan-American nation, and the universal history it celebrates is that of the forging of *nations*. It is not therefore an epic of class, not the founding epic of a proletarian history; but it does place the act of production, and the force of labour, firmly at the centre of that history.

The core of that new vision of both Latin America and the place of the poet within that history is to be found in the magnificent sequence called 'Las alturas de Macchu Picchu', Part 2 of the *Canto General*. In his journey to the ancestral Inca city of Macchu Picchu,[63] Neruda embarked on a double 'venture to the interior'[64] – into himself and into the Latin American past. What he found in a sense in both journeys was the presence of the human, the collective, in himself and in that

220

history. He recalled the individual confronting a world in flux who provided the central voice of the first two books of *Residencia*; he re-evoked the solitary urban wanderer of 'Walking around'.

> Cuántas veces en las calles de invierno de una ciudad o en
> un autobús o un barco en el crepúsculo . . .
> me quise detener a buscar la eterna veta insondable
> que antes toqué en la piedra . . .

> (How often in the winter streets of a city or on/a bus or a boat at dusk . . ./
> I have wanted to stop and look for the eternal bottomless vein/that once I
> touched in the stone . . .)

He still searches for the ineffable, the essential of life that is beyond time and history – 'lo indestructible, lo imperecedero, la vida' (the indestructible, the imperishable, life). At the end of the fourth part of the poem, having faced death, contingency, the absence of others to give comfort and refuge, the urban and mountain deserts without food or sustenance, 'rodé muriendo de mi propia muerte' (I turned and turned dying in my own death). This is the emptying of the self, the loss of any sense of materiality or location – the self without any other reference. What Neruda records here is some of the despair that Vallejo alluded to in his final poems.

In this state of emptiness, of primal innocence, Neruda approached the vast stepped terraces that lead to Macchu Picchu.

> Madre de piedra, espuma de los cóndores.
> Alto arrecife de la aurora humana.
> Pala perdida en la primera arena.
> Esta fue la morada, este es el sitio . . .

> (Mother of stone, foam of the condors./High reef of the dawn of
> humanity./Spade buried in the first sands./This was the dwelling, this is
> the place . . .)

The key to what follows is the 'spade buried in the sands', the memento of the human hand which drew form and structure from the fluid sand. Whose hand it was, and how the work was done is not yet clear; here we see man sharing this environment as an equal with the animals. Yet he is even then, at the dawn of prehistory, distinct. What makes him different is the instrument of labour, the projection of himself and the extension of his own labour power.[65] That world, perplexingly, has gone, returned to dust; and yet the mark of man remains, not only as evidence of the past presence of humans, but as a prophecy of what may come again as history is again set in motion. At the end of the seventh section the discovery is made that 'El reino

221

muerto vive todavía' (The dead realm is still alive) and the great condor of the Andes now flies across the face of a clock, a clock that marks the beginning of real time. The list that follows details in a cataract of substantives the elements of the new construction. Now the material exists and the city stands once again on the threshold of history. But it is man alone that can harness the resources and transform them into history, for the entry of man into nature is the very meaning of the word.

> ¿Piedra en la piedra, el hombre, dónde estuvo?
> ¿Aire en el aire, el hombre, dónde estuvo?
> ¿Tiempo en el tiempo, el hombre, dónde estuvo?

(Stone on stone, and where was man?/Air on air, where was man?/Time on time, where was man?)

The man he refers to is nameless and without distinction – the builder and maker of this magnificent structure. He is the buried slave, the poor beggar of the city:

. . . en los campos, veo un cuerpo, mil cuerpos, un hombre, mil mujeres,
bajo la racha negra, negros de lluvia y noche,
con la piedra pesada de la estatua:
Juan Cortapiedras, hijo de Wiracocha,
Juan Comefrio, hijo de estrella verde,
Juan Piesdescalzos, nieto de la turquesa,
sube a nacer conmigo, hermano.
. . .
Mírame desde el fondo de la tierra,
labrador, tejedor, pastor callado;
domador de guanacos tutelares:
albañil del andamio desafiado:
aguador de las lágrimas andinas:
joyero de los dedos machacados . . .
. . .
Yo vengo a hablar por vuestra boca muerta.
A través de la tierra juntad todos
los silenciosos labios derramados
y desde el fondo habladme toda esta larga noche . . .

Dadme la lucha, el hierro, los volcanes.
Apegadme los cuerpos como imanes.
Acudid a mis venas y a mi boca.
Hablad por mis palabras y mi sangre.

222

(In the fields I see a body, a thousand bodies, a man, a thousand women,/beneath the black wind, black with rain and night,/with the heavy stone of the statues:/John Stonecutter, son of Viracocha,/John Eatcold, son of the green star,/John Barefoot, grandson of the turquoise,/ come up and be born with me, my brother./. . ./Look at me from the depths of the earth,/worker, weaver, silent shepherd,/trainer of lead guanacos:/daring labourer on the scaffolding,/waterer of Andean tears,/ jeweller of the crushed fingers/. . ./. . ./I come to speak though your dead mouth./Across the earth gather together all/your silent spilt lips/ and from the very depths speak to me throughout this long dark night . . .//Give me the struggle, the iron, the volcanoes./Hold your body tight against me like a magnet./Come to my veins and to my mouth./Speak through my words and through my blood.)

'I come to speak through your dead mouth' marks a new direction in Neruda's poetry. The indisputable core of his earlier work was the self – irrespective of whether that self was Neruda or a persona – whose consciousness provided both the living centre of all things and the only durable element in a world of flux and arbitrary change. *This* speaker is a spokesman, a representative of collective experience, and the protagonist of this history is a collective of workers and producers who have drawn this human world out of matter. They begin as an obscure and undifferentiated crowd, marching bowed through the night like 'the heavy stone of statues'. But through the lines that follow they come alive, invoked and encouraged by the poet, and begin to forge the world. The poem is transformed into an appeal, a call to action; the poet himself is not so much creator as enabler, the historical and mythic memory of an unfulfilled potential in the past. In this sense the first creative act occurs in language (the idea) but is *realized* in the material world of nature. Man creates himself collectively out of the raw material of nature. The word is not itself the creative act but rather the catalyst – 'Speak *through* my words and my blood'. Here Neruda celebrates and enters history. That is the epic sense of the *Canto General* – and the reflection upon the poetic act itself that it offers. The poem is sometimes wild and often inconsistent, sometimes abandoning the collective act of creation for a more familiar assertion that only an elite of individuals can reshape the world. Nonetheless, the overwhelming sense of the poem, and its real significance as it develops is of a heroic process of change, progress and completion. It is human beings who make history through their actions upon the world.

If Neruda adopts this new protagonist as the central actor of his poetry, the material life is the source of its language.

América no invoco tu nombre en vano.
Cuando sujeto al corazón la espada,
cuando aguanto en el alma la gotera,
cuando por las ventanas
un nuevo día tuyo me penetra,
soy y estoy en la luz que me produce,
vivo en la sombra que me determina,
duermo y despierto en tu esencial aurora . . .

(America, I do not invoke your name in vain./When I tie the sword to my
heart,/when I withstand the water dripping on my soul,/when through
the windows/your new day penetrates me,/I am and I exist in the light it
produces in me,/I live in the shadow that determines me,/I sleep and
wake in your essential dawn . . .)

Most importantly, perhaps, the *Canto General* introduces into Latin
American poetry a new language, an idiom of public rhetoric. The
poem presumes a relationship with a mass audience, and makes itself
accessible to them. It was not, of course, a language of speech or the
popular culture as enshrined in many of the writings of Nicolás
Guillén. But neither was it a poetic language of the sort that Paz
represented as the essential language of poetry – defined by its
universality and its origin outside history. *Canto General* mingles grand
visions of the past and future of Latin America, poems of denunciation
(like 'La United Fruit Co' or 'La Anaconda Mining Co'), poems of
heroic biography ('Cuauhtemoc') and anti-heroic horror ('Alvarado').
This is a panorama of Latin America's history, a tableau of its protag-
onists. It is also a search for a language of public utterance, a democra-
tic language of shared values. There are popular forms – the 'cueca'
(the traditional dance of Chile) is invoked to attest to the presence of
an oral tradition, for example, in the testimony to the heroism of
'Manuel Rodríguez'. But essentially the *Canto* is a reassuring chronicle
of historical progress, a 'national epic' in the truest sense. That nation
is broadly painted, and inclusive of all those who have forged an
identity in a struggle against the main enemy of that constructive
process – the foreign imperialisms who have seized and taken power
over the destiny of the continent. There are heroes, leaders, intellec-
tuals within this grand alliance of forces devoted to the forging of
nationhood, but the nature of that nation is not problematic. It is
presented as continuous from past to present, Cuauhtemoc and
Manuel Rodríguez its originators and pioneers. What is different and
radical is that the anonymous proletarian builder of this world figures
with equal rank and status here. There is something moving and

uplifting about this compassionate alliance, but it is far yet from speaking through the joint experience of the exploited. They are spoken for and to – but they have not yet found their own voice.

The poet, however, has found a role and an idiom – the witness bearing testimony, the omnipresent chronicler of the history of consciousness. He exists within the poem as an individual whose personal experience has formed part of that general life; but he is also another speaker, who identifies with the diversity of historical experience.

> Detrás de los libertadores estaba Juan
> trabajando, pescando y combatiendo,
> en su trabajo de carpintería o en su mina mojada.
> Sus manos han arado la tierra y han medido
> los caminos.
>   Sus huesos están en todas partes.
> Pero vive. Regresó de la tierra. Ha nacido . . .
> Lo ataron, y es ahora decidido soldado.
> Lo hirieron, y mantiene su salud de manzana.
> Le cortaron las manos, y hoy golpea con ellas . . .

(Behind the liberators stood John/working, fishing and fighting,/in his carpentry shop or his damp mine./His hands have ploughed the earth and measured/the roads./His bones are everywhere./But he lives. He returned from the earth. He was born . . ./They tied him down and today he is a determined soldier./They wounded him, and he keeps his apple health./They cut off his hands, and today he strikes out with them. . .)

There is a tension here which Neruda has not resolved, and for which he would be criticised by subsequent generations. While speaking *on behalf of* the masses, and assuming their voice and idiom, he has nonetheless remained within the frame of high art and rhetoric and retained the metaphorical mode with its implicit promise of transcendence. Yet what poetry elevates and celebrates is the experience of material life of daily existence. But this is not to say that imagination should be renounced nor vision eschewed for some narrow realism. On the contrary, the transcendent possibility is embedded in the concept of poetry itself. The question is where can that potential be realized, in what social and cultural location, and by whom? Who shall be the protagonist of this act of transformation? It is, as Benjamin has put it,[66] the 'this-sidedness' of that potential that marks a social poetry rather than its simple declarations of historical optimism. Its power stems not merely from a vision of an unrealized possibility, but from an ability to identify in the lived experience of living social forces the seeds from which that future may grow. It is that that marks the reappropriation of history.

7

The Architects of Construction:
Poetry and the Politics of
Development in Post-war Brazil

The Poet as Architect

'Fábula de um arquiteto'

A arquitetura como construir portas,
de abrir; ou como construir o aberto;
construir, não como ilhar e prender,
nem construir como fechar secretos;
construir portas abertas, em portas;
casas exclusivamente portas e tecto.
O arquiteto: o que abre para o homem
(tudo se sanearia desde casas abertas)
portas por-onde, jamais portas-contra;
por onde, livres: ar luz razão certa.

2.

Até que, tantos livres o amedrontando,
renegou dar a viver no claro e aberto.
Onde vãos de abrir, ele foi amurando
opacos de fechar; onde vidro, concreto;
até refechar o homem: na capela útero,
com confortos de matriz, outra vez feto.[1]

('Fable of an architect': Architecture as the building of doors,/for open-ing; or as the building of openness;/constructing, not as isolating and confining,/nor constructing as shutting away secrets;/constructing open doors, within doors;/houses that are doors and roof, nothing else./The architect: he who opens up to man/(everything could be made good from open houses)/doors through-which, never doors-against;/through which, free: air light certain reason.//2. Until, with so many freenesses

227

frightening him, he gave up bringing to life in the clear and open./Where
there were spaces to open, he began walling in/opaquenesses to close;
where there was glass, concrete;/until he had shut man in: in the chapel
womb,/with comforts of the mother church, foetus again.)

Drummond's homage to Chaplin had pointed optimistically, in 1945,
to the liberating, creative possibilities of human labour, to the capacity
of man to transform his 'ofício' or 'trade' from the instrument of his
alienation under an oppressive class system, into a tool for modelling
the world in his own image and thus, in the company of his fellow-
workers, to discover a new and independent collective consciousness.
Art, like any other kind of labour, possessed the power to reveal and
construct alternative forms of expression and communication which
could cut through the seemingly monolithic structures that are
imposed from above on the mass of individuals and order their lives.

Yet the next thirty years of economic expansion were to witness, on
a massive scale, the denial of that dream of social and spiritual self-
emancipation. Despite the fall of Vargas and a degree of political
liberalization immediately after the war, the repressive labour legisla-
tion installed under the Estado Novo remained largely intact. Tragi-
cally, though, the most influential intellectual and ideological currents
of the period, while apparently at odds with each other, were essen-
tially in agreement about the need to sacrifice the independent,
specific interests of Brazil's exploited classes to the process of national
development. For that class-consciousness was substituted a national-
popular identity, whose immediate struggle was the liberation of
Brazilian capitalism from imperialist domination. The disastrous
consequences of such a strategy revealed themselves in the early
1960s, when the social contradictions inherent in the development
process began to assume a political form, and the best organized
sectors of the new popular movement began to demand reforms and a
share in the spoils. The military coup of 1964, and the dictatorship
which followed, violently disabused them of any illusions about the
ability of a 'democratic' anti-imperialist alliance with the national
bourgeoisie to bring about their liberation. What these events proved
instead was that whatever form it takes, capitalist development
demands of necessity that the exploited classes sacrifice their identity,
their labour and their interests to the logic of accumulation and
competition.

João Cabral de Melo Neto's 'Fable of an architect', from the early
1960s, indicates how central the whole issue of post-war construction,
with all of the contradictions outlined above, was to the culture and

particularly the poetry of these years. Counterposed to Drummond's optimistic conception of the human capacity for constructing forms of communication, exploration and liberation, is a vision of how those powers could instead be turned against humanity, to imprison, blind and deny all true development. In presenting this picture of a crafts-man confronted with and intimidated by the infinite possibilities of his craft, transformed from the architect of openness and illumination into the builder of a self-enclosed, regressively cloistered cell of human habitation, Cabral seems to encapsulate the entire spirit of poetic debate and practice in the 1950s and 1960s.

On the surface there is a strong resemblance between the poetry of this period and that of the 1920s and 1930s. The Concretists, who assumed a leading role at the forefront of the new wave, saw them-selves as the inheritors of the Modernist tradition, taking it to its logical conclusion; for them the 1920s were a rehearsal for the 1950s and 1960s. However, it is not by chance that, in their highly selective evaluation of Modernismo, the Concretists chose as their precursor the poet Oswald de Andrade, rather than Mário, Drummond or any of the other leading figures of the movement. Although Oswald's experi-mentation with poetic form clearly appealed to them, what really lay behind their identification with the author of the *Brazil-wood Poetry Manifesto* was his naïve optimism that he could embrace the contradic-tions of Brazilian culture and synthesize them effortlessly into an integrated whole. It was not so much the revolutionary implications of Oswald's dialectical theory which interested them as its celebration of the imminent birth of a new national culture, a 'poesia de exportação' (poetry for export) that they believed was realized in their own work.

For the Concretists, modernization was not problematic or ambi-guous. On the contrary, the perspective which overshadowed this period was one of uncritical identification with national capitalist development. Its effect was to falsely polarize the debate about poetry between two mutually exclusive extremes: on the one hand, their own view of poetry as a 'pure', autonomous and self-referring practice, the construction of objective, utilitarian forms or aesthetic 'commodities', reproducing the mechanisms of mass production and consumption characteristic of industrial capitalism; and on the other hand, what they saw as the historically 'obsolete' poetry of subjective expression, communicating individual or collective experience on the assumption of a direct, transparent path linking reality and language.

With one or two notable exceptions, the debate tended to be accepted on the terms set out by the Concretists. The practitioners of Poema Processo (1967), for instance, took the semiotic and visual features of Concretismo to their ultimate conclusion, substituting two- or three-dimensional images for the written word. Others, such as Neoconcretismo, Tendência and the later Concretismo itself, attempted to reconcile these structuralist principles with the demands of social commitment which were raised by the political upturn prior to 1964. Still others, in particular the contributors to Violão de Rua (Street Guitar), rejected formalism altogether in favour of a poetry of propaganda, versifying historical, journalistic and political themes using popular oral forms, such as the traditional *cordel* ballads of the Northeast, and a language of revolutionary denunciation and exhortation.

What they all assumed, regardless of their position within the debate, was, first, an unproblematic view of the relationship between language and reality; rather than attempting to grapple, critically and consciously, with the uncertainty of that relationship as Drummond had done, they either dismissed it as totally meaningless or accepted it unquestioningly. Secondly, they assumed an equally uncritical view of the relationship between the poem and the reader, who existed as a passive object to consume or be persuaded by the text. Thirdly, arising out of this, was the implicit view that a common poetic language was not to be forged out of the active dialogue between poet, reader and society, but was rather to be given, either in the form of the Concretists' self-justifying structures, or in the revolutionary rhetoric and folkloric language of the poetry of protest.

In this way, the Concretists successfully divorced the idea of a transformative poetic vision from the wider cultural relations between individual, society, language and ideology. Útopia might be defended in the rhetoric of protest or in the search for 'revolutionary' poetic forms, but rarely was it actively fought for or built by challenging traditional linguistic expectations, structures of thought or the relationship between text, author and reader. Yet it was the very crisis in that relationship – for whom was the poet writing? – which formed the hidden agenda for poetry during the 1950s, '60s and '70s. While the poets of the 1930s and early '40s had sought to embrace and communicate the experience of society as a whole, they never openly confronted the problem of their audience which, it was taken for granted, remained a tiny minority of the educated middle class. The massive shift of people into the cities during the post-war years of modernization, which raised the urban population from 30 to 70 per cent, was accompanied by the emergence of a cultural industry increasingly dominated by the state and by the mass media; both posed an inescapable challenge to the writers of poetry.

The post-war avant-garde movements responded by repudiating the subjective lyrical tradition, which they identified with bourgeois individualism. The individual voice of personal experience was abandoned in favour of the anonymity of either pure formal abstraction or political denunciation. The potential new audience, in the meantime, whether viewed as consumers or as alienated workers, was reduced to the status of a silent, faceless object, whose own ambiguous, messy, yet authentic experiences and reactions to modernization were hardly ever permitted to contaminate the 'objectivity' of the poem. The two dominant conceptions of poetic practice in this period, the formalism of the Concretists and the didactic protest poetry of Street Guitar, therefore mirrored each other in their denial of the independent consciousness of the working-class audience for whom their work was supposedly intended. Only in a few, exceptional cases were the real protagonists of the modernization process, the rural and urban masses suffering the contradictions between development and underdevelopment, between capital and labour, ever contemplated as the possible subject of their own emancipation.

Crisis and Retreat

Procura a ordem
que vês na pedra:
nada se gasta
mas permanece.

Essa presença
que reconheces
não se devora
tudo em que cresce.

Nem mesmo cresce
pois permanece
fora do tempo
que não a mede . . .

Procura a ordem
desse silêncio
que imóvel fala:
silêncio puro.

De pura espécie,
voz de silêncio,
mais do que a ausência
que as vozes ferem.

231

(Seek the order/which you see in stone:/nothing is used up/but remains./
/That presence/which you recognize/does not consume/everything in
which it grows.//Nor does it even grow/for it remains/outside of time/
which does not measure it . . .//Seek the order/of that silence/which
speaks, motionless:/pure silence.//Pure in kind,/voice of silence,/more so
than the absence/which voices wound.) (From 'Pequena Ode Mineral'
(Little Mineral Ode), *O Engenheiro* (1942–45), by João Cabral de Melo
Neto)

The 'mineral order' which João Cabral (b. 1920) invited his reader to
seek out in the last years of the war stands in marked contrast to
Drummond and Mário de Andrade's vision of a flower of rebellion and
human solidarity born out of the mud. Whereas Mário and Drum-
mond glimpsed the seeds of liberation in the hidden structures that
are crystallized within human experience, however oppressive, for
Cabral redemption was to be found, instead, outside of that exper-
ience, in the realm of pure objects. The mineral realm offered an
irreducible permanence and self-sufficiency, against the disorder and
decay of human mortality; the order of stone was the alternative to the
chaotic oblivion of the soul which is dispersed and lost like strands of
hair or spoken words.

Cabral soon afterwards implicitly acknowledged the futility of such
a pursuit of 'pure objectivity', and went on to explore instead how
human beings intervene in that world of objects. Nevertheless, his
initial, extreme statement of the problem defines a crucial moment in
the history of Brazilian poetry. Mário de Andrade, Drummond and
other poets of the 1930s had forced Modernism out of its aristocratic
isolation and had invited it to embrace 'the feeling of the world', to
fuse subject and object, and discover social being through individual
being. Now, however, this integration between subject and object,
individual and society, seemed to have collapsed; poetic language had
lost its power as a collective voice able to speak of a common exper-
ience. The entire Modernist project, which had confronted the contra-
dictions within and between the cultural practices of the intellectual
and artistic elite and the diverse cultural reality lived by Brazilian
society at large, now came under attack from a new post-war genera-
tion, whose watchwords were formal classicism, metaphysical pro-
fundity and universalism. The so-called '45 Generation repudiated the
experimentalism, the popular sympathies and socio-political commit-
ment associated with the Modernists; Drummond, for example, was
berated for his alleged inability to write a sonnet.

It is worth remembering, nevertheless, that many of the Modernist
poets themselves moved in just this direction, and that some of the

leading figures of the avant-garde movements of the 1950s, such as the Concretist brothers Haroldo (b. 1929) and Augusto de Campos (b. 1931), João Cabral and Ferreira Gullar (b. 1930), were products of the same generation. In fact, the latter's common concern with form and objectivity reflects a much more general crisis within Brazilian culture and ideology.

The crisis had its roots in the 'democratic interlude' which followed the end of the war and of the Estado Novo. In 1945 Vargas had been forced to stage free elections, issue a new constitution and release communists, trade-union activists and other political prisoners. But his removal failed to produce the structures of a new bourgeois democratic order. Power was now disputed between two essentially conservative forces: on the one hand were Vargas's newly created parties, the PSD, representing his support amongst a sector of the landowning oligarchy, and the PTB, the voice of the right-wing, 'yellow' trade unionists, or *pelegos*; and on the other, the anti-nationalist UDN which, after the departure of its liberal wing, represented a bloc embracing the traditional export sector, the new bankers, conservative professionals and small businessmen.

The left, meanwhile, offered no significant reformist, let alone revolutionary, alternative to this stark choice. While the Communist Party could enjoy a brief period of legality, the independent working-class organization on which its influence depended was in tatters, and still had to deal with the corporativist trade-union legislation left untouched by the Estado Novo. The CP's own confusion and disarray was exposed when groups of workers began to set up underground factory committees and to organize strikes in defiance of the state-run union bureaucracies. Having called for a programme of national unity around Vargas in alliance with his Brazilian Labour Party (PTB) the CP now found itself outlawed again under the Dutra government and thus forced to put aside its policy of restraint and support the growing strike movement, which culminated in the 'greve dos 300 mil' in 1953, paralysing São Paulo for twenty-six days.[2]

The shift to aestheticism and universal values in poetry was thus symptomatic, less of a self-conscious conservative reaction than of an ideological vacuum, a sense of isolation, insecurity and uncertainty in the face of an unknown future, underscored by a loss of confidence in the ability of collective social institutions to offer any radical way forward. The '45 Generation had no coherent ideological programme, only a concern with order and stability; their formalism thus seems to respond to a need to leave monuments of permanence in a world where nothing endures. It is not difficult to see a continuity between

this monumentalism and the pure, abstract formalism of the Concre-
tistas, even though the latter considered themselves radical opponents
of the '45 Generation. What is perhaps less obvious is the extent to
which the early poetry of João Cabral and Ferreira Gullar emerged out
of the same fear of oblivion.

Ferreira Gullar's *A luta corporal* (The bodily struggle) (1950–53) is one
of the two poetic landmarks of the pre-Concretist period, the other
being Cabral's *O Engenheiro* (The Engineer) (1942–45). The central
problem which Gullar confronted in *The bodily struggle* is whether
language, and poetry in particular, can offer a means of coming to
terms with the knowledge of mortality. Consciousness forces the poet
to recognize himself as perishable flesh and blood, yet, like the
cockerel which defiantly if impotently crows in the face of death, he
cannot suppress the animal urge to assert himself, to cry out his
existence, however impotent and alone he is. The instinctive struggle
with mortality thus restores to language its primitive function as a
material expression of his being, futile yet necessary:

> Vê-se: o canto é inútil.
>
> O galo permanece – apesar
> de todo o seu porte marcial –
> só, desamparado,
> num saguão do mundo
> Pobre ave guerreira!
>
> Outro grito cresce
> agora no sigilo
> de seu corpo; grito
> que, sem essas penas
> e esporões e crista
> e sobretudo sem esse olhar
> de ódio
>   não seria tão rouco
> e sangrento.[3]
>
>   (from 'Galo galo' –
>   Cockerel cockerel)

(It is obvious: his song is useless.//The cockerel remains – despite/all his
martial bearing – alone, helpless,/in some courtyard of the world./Poor
warrior bird!//Another cry grows/now in the hidden recesses/of his
body; a cry/that, without those feathers/and spurs and crest/and espe-
cially without that look of hatred,/would not be so hoarse/and bloody.)

As the book progresses, however, Gullar seems to ask whether a
more conscious assumption of his mortality is possible, through which
language can be transformed from a mere instinctive utterance into a

means of regaining a true knowledge of the world. Deliberately consuming his awareness of mortality as if, like coal, it were the concentrated linguistic accumulation of his experience, and devouring himself ferociously in a kind of continual suicide, he seeks to take control of the process and to forge a space of defiance and rebellion. More than anything else, Gullar conveys the awful solitude of the individual who is struggling in this way with his knowledge, yet cannot, or will not, seek any sense of continuity through the lives of others:

> As minhas palavras esperam no subsolo do dia; sobre elas chovera, e sóis bebidos trabalham, sem lume, o seu cerne; tempo mineral, eu as desenterro como quem desenterra os meus ossos, as manhãs calcinadas – carvões!
> queimo-as aqui; e esta fulguração já é nossa, é luz do corpo
>
> construo uma nova solidão para o homem; lugar, como o da flor, mas dele, ferocíssimo!; como o silêncio aceso; a mais nova morte do homem
> construo, com os ossos do mundo, uma armadilha; aprenderás, aqui, que o brilho é vil; aprenderás a mastigar o teu coração, tu mesmo
> ('Carta do morto pobre', 1 – Poor dead man's letter, 1)

> (My words wait in the subsoil of the day; it had rained on them, and swallowed suns are working, without fire, at their core; mineral time, I dig them up like one who digs up my bones, the charred mornings – lumps of coal!/I burn them here; and this blazing flash is ours, it is the light of our body//I build a new solitude for man; a place, like that of the flower, but his, oh so fierce!; like silence on fire; man's newest death/I build, with the bones of the world, a snare; you will learn, here, that radiance is wretched; you will learn to chew your heart, yourself)

If Gullar's 'bodily struggle' represents the defiant assumption of his biological mortality, he remains doubtful about the possible contribution of language and poetry to this process. For language, far from permitting knowledge, seems instead only to distance us from that which it names, to estrange from us our most sensual experiences:

> Maçã?
> Sirvo-me deste nome como dum caminho para não te tocar, cousa, fera, objeto vermelho e súbito . . .
>
> (estas palavras como a tua cor, fruta, são as nossas acrobacias, o nosso pobre jogo. O que somos é escuro, fechado, e está sempre de borco. Falamos, gesticulamos, soluçamos, puerilmente, em torno dele – que não nos ouve nem nos conhece . . .) ('Carta do morto pobre', 4)

> (Apple?/I make use of this name like a path to avoid touching you, thing,

beast, red, sudden object . . ./(these words like your colour, fruit, are our somersaults, our poor game. What we are is dark, closed, and always face down. We speak, gesticulate, sob, puerilely, around it – which does not hear or know us. . . .)

In the closing pages of the book, where Gullar's prose-poetry degenerates into an increasingly unpronounceable, multilingual babble, this crisis of faith in the expressive capacity of artistic language begins to take a graphic form, anticipating the formalist path which he and others would pursue during the next few years.

There is a striking similarity between the problems concerning Gullar in *The bodily struggle* and those which preoccupied Drummond in the books published between 1948 and 1959 – *Novos Poemas, Claro Enigma, Fazendeiro do Ar* and *A Vida Passada a Limpo*. 'Contemplação no banco' (Contemplation on the bench), for example, reveals the critical shift in artistic faith which had taken place since *The Rose of the People*. Whereas Drummond's confidence in the power of language to communicate a collective experience was previously qualified by a sceptical mistrust, that balance has now been reversed – the poetry is dominated by suspicion and uncertainty as to the possible existence of order in the world and the ability of art to reveal it, while the struggle for expression has become a lonely necessity, an alternative to despair – 'Increasingly the poems become forms which the poet creates because he can do nothing else.'[4] Thus the poet who, in the urban landscape of 'The flower and the nausea', caressed the rose in intimate communion with his vision of liberation, can now only anticipate its birth in some uncertain future beyond the realm of poetry and language:

> Meu retrato futuro, como te amo,
> e mineralmente te pressinto, e sinto
> quanto estás longe de nosso vão desenho
> e de nossas roucas onomatopéias . . .[5]

(My future portrait, how I love you,/and sense your mineral coming, and feel/how far you are from our vain designs/and our harsh onomatopoeias . . .)

Drummond, now in middle age, feels his mortality as in inability to leave any mark on the world but some insubstantial structure which neither contains nor supports anything real. 'A sculpture of air', shaped naked and abstract by his hands 'for the man I'll never be'. The many long and complex poems of this period movingly express this fear and the struggle to recover, if only fleetingly, a moment of stability, a flash of communication, love or freedom before it is lost to the flux of destruction and death. At the same time, these compositions dare to ask whether the very construction of artistic forms, rather than providing a defence against decay and death, does not in fact conceal a deeper emptiness and loss. One of the most expressive examples of this dilemma is 'Escada' (Stairway), whose architectural imagery and structure capture so suggestively the spirit of this contemporary crisis in Brazilian poetry:

> Na curva desta escada nos amamos,
> nesta curva barroca nos perdemos.
> O caprichoso esquema
> unia formas vivas, entre ramas.
> Lembras-te, carne? Um arrepio telepático
> vibrou nos bens municipais, e dando volta
> ao melhor de nós mesmos,
> deixou-nos sós, a esmo,
> espetacularmente sós e desarmados,
> que a nos amarmos tanto eis-nos morridos.

> E mortos, proscritos
> de toda comunhão (esta espira
> é testemunha, e conta), que restava
> das línguas infinitas
> que falávamos ou surdas se lambiam
> no céu da boca sempre azul e oco?

(At the turn of this stairway we loved each other,/at this baroque bend we lost each other./The capricious scheme/united living forms, amidst branches./Do you remember, flesh? A telepathic shiver/ran through the municipal wealth, and running rings around/the best of us, left us alone, adrift,/spectacularly alone and disarmed,/so that from so much loving each other here we are made dead.//And dead, proscribed/from all communion in the century (this turn of the stairway/is witness, and account), what remained/of the countless tongues/that we spoke or that deafly licked each other/in the roof of the always blue and hollow mouth?)

The form of the spiral staircase is reflected in an undulating sequence of six-, ten- and twelve-syllable lines and preterite, imperfect and present tenses, which lead the reader through the twists and turns of reconstituted experience, memory and loss. At first sight, the staircase seems to offer a monument of stability within which the poet is able to fix the briefly remembered experience of an erotic encounter. However, as we are drawn downwards into the baroque complexity of the building, this illusory point of permanence is lost in the dialectical tension between the spiral turns of the staircase and its vertical axis, between the images of sexual communication and monumental silence, or between the forces of love/life and death. By the closing lines of the poem, past and present have been fused into a single eternity of loss, as that brief affirmation of human life is discovered buried in the foundations, leaving the poet to devour himself in his solitude:

> E se este lugar de exílio hoje passeia
> faminta imaginação atada aos corvos
> de sua própria ceva,
> escada, ó assunção,
> ao céu alças em vão o alvo pescoço,
> que outros peitos em ti se beijariam
> sem sombra, e fugitivos,
> mas nosso beijo e baba se incorporam
> de há muito ao teu cimento, num lamento.

(And if today this place of exile walks/its hungry imagination tied to the crows/of its own feeding,/stairway, oh assumption,/in vain do you raise your milk-white neck to the sky,/that other breasts might kiss in you/ without shadows, and fleetingly,/but our kisses and slaver have long since/been incorporated into your cement, in a lament.)

Poetry is reduced to an almost blind struggle with the materials of language and a chaotic reality – 'this inconclusive country,/of unformulated rivers/and perplexing geography' ('Aliança') – which offers only the briefest and rarest encounters or 'alliances'. Outside those moments, the poet's work resembles that of a magician, 'tecendo fios de nada,/moldando potes de pura/água, loucas estruturas/do vago mais vago, vago.' (weaving threads of nothingness,/shaping pots out of pure/water, crazy structures/of the vaguest, vaguest vagueness), or drawing cities, flowers, experiences out of an invisible bag, uncertain whether his creations have the substance of reality or whether they are pure illusion. In the words of 'Elegia' (Elegy), 'já não sei se é jogo, ou se poesia' (I no longer know whether it's a game, or whether it's poetry). Drummond's 'Fazendeiro do ar' (Farmer of the air) records the crisis of a poet still coming to terms with the disintegration of the old post-colonial agricultural world as one of its disinherited sons, yet trapped within its legacy, deprived as he is of the faith in the possibility of a new, free social order, which the collective struggles of the pre-war years had inspired.

New Beginnings? Popular Fronts and the Poetics of Construction

For a younger generation, less weighed down by that memory yet by the same token without any clear vision of the future, the structures of poetry were not to be sought in the past, but would have to be created afresh, out of nothing. Hence Cabral's emphasis on the artistic process as 'A luta branca no papel' (The blank struggle on the paper), and his choice of the engineer as a model for the artist in the new era of post-war reconstruction. In contrast to Drummond's introspective interrogation of past subjective experience, or Gullar's aggressive assumption of his biological nature, Cabral's engineer dreamed of 'clear objects',

> superfícies, tênis, um copo de água.
>
> O lápis, o esquadro, o papel:
> o desenho, o projeto, o número:
> o engenheiro pensa o mundo justo,
> mundo que nenhum véu encobre.
> ('O Engenheiro' – The Engineer)

(surfaces, tennis, a glass of water.//The pencil, the quadrat, the paper;/ the design, the plan, the number:/the engineer thinks of a world of precision,/a world that is not cloaked in any veil.)

Trained as a statistician by the mathematician-poet, Joaquim Cardozo (1897–1978), Cabral was one of that post-war generation of professional technicians – architects, designers, landscape artists and draughtsmen – whose skills were so vital to the building of the new industrial society, and with whom the Concretists would seek to identify their own project. However, even at this early moment in his work, despite his unequivocal rejection of the subjective world and its randomness in favour of the rational geometric forms of the world of objects, Cabral acknowledged a dynamic principle at work in the process of construction. The silent, monumental immobility of the 'mineral order' in the 'Little mineral ode' had now been invaded by a spirit of organic, living growth:

> (Em certas tardes nós subíamos
> ao edifício. A cidade diária,
> como um jornal que todos liam,
> ganhava um pulmão de cimento e vidro).
>
> A água, o vento, a claridade,
> de um lado o rio, no alto as nuvens,
> situavam na natureza o edifício
> crescendo de suas forças simples.

239

(On some afternoons we'd climb up/the building. The daily city,/like a newspaper that everyone read,/was acquiring a lung made of concrete and glass).//The water, the wind, the clear air,/the river on one side, the clouds up above,/located a place in nature for the building/growing from its own simple forces.)

By the time of *Psicologia da composição* (Psychology of composition) (1947), Cabral had reached a more fully developed conception of poetic construction, not as the mere reproduction of existing forms, but as a conscious and difficult struggle to breathe life into the inert, dispersed material of language – 'Cultivating the desert/like an orchard in reverse' – through the creative agency of human labour:

> Não a forma encontrada
> como uma concha, perdida
> nos frouxos areais
> como cabelos:
>
> não a forma obtida
> em lance santo ou raro,
> tiro nas lebres de vidro
> do invisível:
>
> mas a forma atingida
> como a ponta do novelo
> que a atenção, lenta,
> desenrola,
> aranha: como o mais extremo
> desse fio frágil, que se rompe
> ao peso, sempre, das mãos
> enormes.

(Not the form that's found/like a shell, lost/in the loose sandbanks/like strands of hair://not the form obtained/through some holy or unusual impulse,/a shot at the glass hares/of the invisible://but the form reached/ like the end of a ball of wool/which your attention slowly/unravels,// spider: like the very, very end/of that fragile thread, that always/breaks, under the weight of your/huge hands.)

By the mid 1950s, though, the developmentalist fervour of the Kubitschek administration and its accompanying cultural ideology imposed a different interpretation of the metaphor of construction. The most influential intellectual current of the decade was associated with the ISEB institute, whose leading figures, such as Roland Corbisier and Álvaro Vieira Pinto, followed in the footsteps of the philosophers and sociologists of the Frankfurt School. They applied the Hegelian concepts of alienation and the objectification of the spirit to

240

the contemporary state of Brazilian culture and argued that Kubits-chek's programme of rapid industrialization offered the prospect that the country might overcome its colonial inheritance of underdevelopment and cultural dependence. In the process, a true civil society or Brazilian 'people' was being constituted for the first time, whose legitimate representatives were the intellectuals; by transforming and developing his world, the Brazilian was transforming himself and realizing his hitherto alienated being.[6]

This theory of Brazilian culture, which identified the 'people' with the nation and its intellectual leaders, and the struggle for national liberation with the process of capitalist development, paralleled and echoed the popular front strategy adopted by the Communist Party. Even after Vargas's suicide in 1954, the Communist Party put its faith in the national bourgeoisie as the key revolutionary, anti-imperialist force in society. Thus it supported the candidacies of Juscelino Kubits-chek and João Goulart in the presidential elections of 1955, and of General Lott and Goulart again in the elections of 1960. This pursuit of the popular front survived the party split which followed the Soviet invasion of Hungary in 1956 and the subsequent exposure of Stalin's crimes. It was put to its most critical test, though, under the presidencies of Jânio Quadros and João Goulart, the first of whom adopted austerity measures aimed at both workers and the middle class, while the latter depended upon the cooperation of the popular and trade union movement to push through 'reformas de base' (grassroots reforms). The POLOP (Organização Revolucionária Marxista-Política Operária) emerged in 1961 to criticize the Stalinist reformism of the PCB and the Goulart government, but it had little mass influence and could offer no real alternative leadership. For others convinced of the bankruptcy of class collaboration, the example of the Chinese and Cuban revolutions suggested other options. The Partido Comunista do Brasil, created out of a split with the PCB in 1962, turned to armed struggle in the countryside, and in 1966 Carlos Marighela left the Party to pursue his own variant of guerrilla warfare focused on the cities. The Communist Party's faith in the revolutionary, anti-imperialist character of the national bourgeoisie thus led to the tragic abandonment of any political struggle based on the independent power of the working class whose organization had been built up during the 1950s, and left that class without any effective leadership during the dark years of military rule that were to follow.[7]

The Popular Front substituted capitalist development as the prime agency of historical change, and the national bourgeoisie rather than the working class as the subject of the revolutionary transformation of

241

society. It was precisely this distortion of Marxism, and its cultural equivalent in the work of the *isebianos*, which a new group of poets writing in the review *Noigandres* (1952–58) began to apply to the practice of poetry. Augusto and Haroldo de Campos, Décio Pignatari (b. 1927) and, for a brief period, Ferreira Gullar, were the leading figures of the Concretist movement, which broke formally with the '45 Generation in 1956 and produced its 'Pilot-Plan' or manifesto in 1958. As the following extract from an essay of 1960 suggests, Concretismo sought to celebrate the spirit of capitalist production symbolized by the construction of the new federal capital, Brasília:

> Meanwhile, our country, which has just given the world the highly significant example of the construction, in the deep West, of a new capital which is at once a mark of avant-garde architecture and urban design, more perhaps than any other, offers the conditions for the production and consumption of an art that is truly contemporary, because, as aesthetic information, it is commensurate with today's man.[8]

Within this modern order, 'today's man' existed above all as a consumer, demanding a utilitarian function of art, one attuned to his collective, impersonal, rationalized experience of labour as an industrial worker. If we are to believe Décio Pignatari,

> The worker loves the machine – while charitable intellectuals cry out in protest against it and against the mechanization of man, without ever having got close to the problem. There are problems, and most serious they are too, but the only people who can teach us anything useful about the subject are those who have tried to solve them from the premises of the industrial revolution.[9]

Given the worker's industrial mentality and sensibility, his 'love' of the machine, the task of the poet must be to produce 'objetos-bens-de-consumo' (consumer-good-objects) which would be the equal of rationally planned and produced industrial commodities.[10] This promise of an impersonal, rationally constructed poem-product would be the Concretists' contribution to the struggle of workers against the capitalist system:

> A worker who works a part on the lathe doesn't inscribe on it his name or his revolt. The rational lucidity of the machine teaches him to understand the basic irrationality of capitalist relations of production: he constructs buildings out of *rayban* glass and knows that he will never be able to fly in them. And he knows too that he will only be able to put an end to social injustices through clear and united ideas and actions. . . . The worker wants a rational poem, which will teach him to act and think

242

as the machine teaches him – and if he likes roses, he is bound to prefer real ones, for the allegorical ones are fortunately dead in his positive sensibility.[11]

If the objective was the widest possible accessibility and distribution of these commodities, then the industrial poetry must work with a minimal artistic vocabulary, the equivalent of Ogden's Basic Vocabulary of 850 words. Whereas the linguistic sophistication of modernists such as Joyce or Guimarães Rosa had unashamedly highlighted the restricted range of their audience, the Concretists' poetry of 'mass production' therefore rested upon a populist assumption about its readership (the 'user'), which was expected to respond unanimously to the object set before it in accordance with the rules implicit in the poem's own structure:

> The concrete poem, says the pilot-plan, is a 'useful object', a *Gebrauchsgegenstand*, an object to be used. This involves an uncommon responsibility for the user. It relies upon the user using the poem correctly, exhausting it of all its possibilities. Of course faults may occur in the construction of the poem, to the extent that it even actually fails. The user will have to discover this too; but before deciding that the object has failed, he must be absolutely sure that he has followed the instructions correctly – that he has understood and obeyed the rules truly provided by the structure of the poem and that he is not obliging it to do that for which it was not designed.[12]

Underlying the Concretists' mechanical view of the 'worker-reader' as an uncritical consumer of the artistic product, was a denial of any problematic or dialectical relationship between language, individual and society. Language, rather than constituting the dynamic arena of our apprehension and expression of experience, was suspended from that reality in a state of autonomy. The notion that art might communicate or express anything outside of itself belonged to the pre-industrial culture of individual self-expression, whereas modern mass society demanded a universal artistic language; the significance of the modern poem would not derive from its ability to yield up a given philosophical or experimental 'message', rather the poem's only 'meaning' would be that of its own structure, which would determine a limited number of possible, and simultaneous, readings.

In the case of Pignatari's 'terra' (land) (1956), for instance, these might include the horizontal and diagonal readings of the keyword 'terra' and its constituent elements ('ter' – have, 'erra' – err, wander), the recognition of three major configurations of these elements and their visual characteristics, and the discovery of an 'error' beginning in line seven: the term 'ara' (plough), introduced into the apparently regular, continuous flow of the keyword from line to line by the action of the central 'furrow' ploughed diagonally through the 'field' of the text:

```
ra terra ter
rat erra ter
rate rra ter
rater ra ter
raterr a ter
raterra terr
araterra ter
raraterra te
rraraterra t
erraraterra
terraraterra¹³
```

Concretismo thus saw itself as the culmination of a particular tradition within modernist thought, poetry and music, which embraced Gestalt theory, the serial compositions of Schoenberg, Webern et al., the experimental poetry of e.e. cummings, Mallarmé's *Un Coup de Dés*, Apollinaire's *Calligrammes* and the studies made by Ezra Pound and Fenollosa of the ideograms of Chinese script, not to mention Brazilian 'precursors' such as Oswald de Andrade and João Cabral. The common denominator identified by the Concretists was the tendency away from a strictly discursive, representational art and the expression of a personal voice, towards the creation of self-contained structures which referred only to themselves, and whose significance lay in the communication of a totality that was qualitatively different from the mere sum of its component parts. Hence the increasing approximation of Concretist poetry to the visual arts, the emphasis on the disposition of the poem in space, the interest in typographical resources, such as colour – the material of Concretist art was no longer words, but 'elementos verbivocovisuais' (verbivocivisual elements). To sum up, then,

> The concrete poem – to use an observation by Gomringer on the 'constellation' – 'is a reality in itself, not a poem about . . .'. Since it is not linked to the communication of contents and uses the word (sound, visual form, content load) as the material of composition and not as a vehicle for interpretations of the objective world, its structure is its true content. Only on the historical-cultural level will we be able to find a relationship between the concrete poem-object and a content external to it: a relationship, however, which, once again, will be a relationship of structures. Thus the 'physiognomy of our time' (the industrial revolu-

tion, the techniques of journalism and advertising, the theory of communication opened up by cybernetics, etc.) will be the likely structure of content related to the content-structure of the concrete-poem, and not this or that object, this or that subjective sensation, gleaned from the external or internal world of the poet . . .[14]

In effect, this last distinction returns us to the central ideological question raised above, the Concretists' uncritical identification of their project with that of post-war capitalist development. For Haroldo de Campos, the only relationship between the Concretist poem and historical reality was the structural affinity between the principles governing the construction of the commodity-poem and those on which the modern technological order was based. By assimilating and synthesizing experimental developments within Western modernism, Concretismo had taken up the task faced by the national bourgeoisie, that of 'technological reduction', 'in which is recorded the understanding and mastery of the process of elaboration of an object, which allow for an active and creative use of foreign technical experience'.[15] It had succeeded in creating what Oswald de Andrade had aspired to in his *Brazil-wood Poetry Manifesto* – 'uma poesia de exportação' (a poetry for export).

By the mid to late 1960s the Concretists could certainly claim to have exported and internationalized their movement. The first National Exhibition of Concrete Art in 1956 was subsequently taken to Japan and Europe, where it attracted new followers such as the Scottish poets Ian Hamilton Finlay and E.G. Morgan.[16] In 1964 London's *Times Literary Supplement* devoted two special issues to the Concretists and related avant-garde currents, and in the following year the Austrian Ernest Jandl presented a recital of Concrete poetry in the Royal Albert Hall.[17] The movement was not received so warmly in some quarters, however; in June 1965 an exhibition of Concretist work in Oxford was destroyed by a mob of conservative students.

Nevertheless, while it appeared to inhabit an objective, ideologically neutral world, manufacturing a rational art for the new mass society, Concretismo in fact reflected and reproduced the prevailing relations of power and production. When the Concretists triumphantly announced the arrival of a 'poetry for export' and a universal art 'of the people', they were really offering the people nothing less than a mirror-image of a world in which their labour, their destiny and their consciousness were not their own.

Indeed, to read a Concretist poem, like Augusto de Campos' 'iniciomeiofim' (beginningmiddleend), is a disheartening experience, for one is not being invited to participate actively and critically in a process of communication. Instead, the possibilities of communication are predetermined by the internal relationships between the various 'verbivocovisual elements' of the poem. In the end, the reader must accept the rules of the poem's structure and consume it, or be excluded by it; however complex and sophisticated it is, that structure remains inert, immune to interrogation and dialogue, as monumentally sterile and inhuman as the bureaucratic planned architecture of Brasília which was its inspiration. Isolated, like the government palaces of the federal capital, from the historical process whose contradictions were now being played out in the industrial centres of the south and in the forests and cattle estates of the North and Northeast, it was safe from the disturbing reality of lived experience, with its incessant compulsion to doubt and challenge received explanations of the world.

```
início
meio      início
fim       meio      início
no        fim       meio
fim       no        fim
meio      fim       no
início    meio      fim
          início    meio
                    início[18]
```

Already in 1957, at least one member of the movement, Ferreira Gullar, had begun to find this level of formal abstraction intolerable, as the rural and urban trade-union movement revealed how the development process was in reality riven with conflict, cruelty and struggle. For the next five years or so, Gullar led a loose dissident grouping of 'neo-Concretist' poets, whose manifesto rejected the Concretists' mechanical analogy for art in favour of that of a living organism, and reasserted 'the independence of artistic creation in the face of objective knowledge'. The few textual examples from the group are not easily distinguished from those of the mainstream Concretists, however, unlike the work of *Tendência*, which was active in the state of Minas Gerais during the same period and sought to apply certain of the Formalist innovations to a linguistic material drawn from historical and social themes.

In 1961, the Concretists gave their answer to those who increasingly accused them of an alienated abstentionism from the urgent issues that had been raised by the recent political upturn. For the next four years the Concretist middle period of 'committed poetry' relaxed the stricter principles of pure objectivity and 'synthetic-ideographic logic' in order to explore the subversive potential of Formalist experimentation. Décio Pignatari's 'Coca-cola' for instance, took a contemporary advertising slogan – 'beba coca cola' (drink coca-cola) – symbolic of the 'Americanization' of the Brazilian economy and culture, and by deconstructing and mutilating its key elements, transformed a triumphant statement of economic imperialism into an infantile babble suggestive of disintegration and corruption:

beba	coca	cola
babe		cola
beba	coca	
babe	cola	caco
caco		
cola		

$$c \quad l \quad o \quad a \quad c \quad a^{19}$$

(drink coca cola/dribble cola [glue]/drink coca [coke]/dribble glue broken bit/junk/junk/glue/sewer)

While the political impact of such texts is debatable, the fact remains that these attempts to introduce ideological 'meaning' into the objective structure of the poem left unaltered the deeper alienation which surrounded the Concretist project; the bleak alienation to which it consigned the reader who, denied the exercise of any critical consciousness, was reduced to the combined roles of operator and consumer of the poem, eternally reproducing and assimilating the structures of the new socio-economic order.

Facing the Formalist Challenge

It was really only in 1962 that any significant alternative conception of poetry appeared to confront the formalist challenge laid down by the Concretists. Before that date, and roughly contemporaneous with the rise of Concretismo, the lyrical imagination of a more traditional generation of poets, most notably Vinicius de Moraes, was inspired by a new wave in samba composition and performance which revolutionized the history of Brazilian popular music – Bossa Nova. The arrival of Bossa Nova is commonly dated from the recording in 1958 of 'Chega de saudade' (Can't take this longing), which began a rich collaboration between Vinicius, the classically trained pianist and composer Tom (Antônio Carlos) Jobim and the singer-guitarist, João Gilberto:

Vai, minha tristeza
E diz a ela
Que sem ela não pode ser
Diz-lhe numa prece
Que ela regresse
Porque eu não posso mais sofrer.
Chega de saudade
A realidade é que sem ela
Não há paz, não há beleza
É só tristeza, e a melancolia
Que não sai de mim, não sai de mim
Não sai.[20]

(Go on, blues of mine/And tell her/There's no way I can be without her/ Tell her in a prayer/To come back/'Cause I can't go on suffering./Can't take this longing/It's a fact that without her/There's no peace, no beauty/ Just these blues, and this heartache/That won't leave me be, won't leave me be/Won't leave me be.)

Vinicius's sensual, conversational style matched perfectly the mood of this new wave, reflecting in its own way the changed economic and social conditions of the post-war boom – the optimism and well-being of an expanded, affluent middle-class and student population – yet was also flexible enough to adapt to the musical demands of the form. For Bossa Nova turned away from the simple binary rhythm of the traditional samba and the operatic style and orchestral sound of the prevailing *samba-canção* or ballad. In their place it introduced a sophisticated counterpoint between the complex syncopation and improvisatory chromatic harmonies of the instrumentalists (either a small, chamber-jazz line-up or simply the solo guitar) and, integrated into this sound, the delicate, intimate 'cool' delivery of the solo voice, epitomised by João Gilberto.[21] There were immediate affinities with parallel developments in North American jazz, in particular the 'cool' sound of post-war Be-bop. Bossa Nova achieved international acclaim following the 1963 collaboration between João and Astrud Gilberto, Tom Jobim and saxophonist Stan Getz on 'Garota de Ipanema' (The Girl from Ipanema), also from the Jobim/Vinicius partnership. 'Desafinado' (Off-key) (Jobim/Newton Mendonça), another highly successful composition, with its difficult, falling intervals and playfully defensive lyrics, captured this mood of novel sophistication, the 'modern', subtly dissonant sound of the new wave:

Se você disser que eu desafino, amor,
Saiba que isto em mim provoca imensa dor.
Só privilegiados têm ouvido igual ao seu.
Eu possou apenas o que Deus me deu.

Se você insiste em classificar
Meu comportamento de antimusical,
Eu mesmo mentindo devo argumentar
Que isto é bossa nova, é muito natural.

(If you say that I sing off-key, my love,/Let me tell you that this really
hurts./Only lucky people have an ear like yours./I've just got the one
God gave me.//If you insist on classifying/My behaviour as unmusical,/
I'll have to tell a lie and argue/That this is the latest trend, it's quite
natural.)

By now, however, popular song was being increasingly viewed as a
potential vehicle for a more political message. Brazil had entered the
critical years of the Goulart administration, whose populist/nationalist
leanings, especially so soon after the 1959 Cuban Revolution, seemed
to many to represent a response to the reformist demands of an
increasingly confident popular and trade-union movement. The chief
focus of radical cultural activity during these years was the CPCs, or
Popular Culture Centres, linked to the National Students' Union
(UNE), which itself was dominated by the politics of the Communist
Party. Ferreira Gullar, now completely disassociated from the Concre-
tist movement, was one of those who assumed a leading role in the
activities of the CPCs and in the development of a theoretical framew-
ork for the new cultural avant garde, which he set out in *A Cultura posta
em questão* (1965) (Culture under question) and *Vanguarda e Subdesenvol-
vimento* (1969) (Avant garde and Underdevelopment).

Central to the approach of the CPCs was the distinction they made
between the traditional 'folkloric' culture of the masses, which was
considered to be a product of false consciousness and therefore
beneath consideration, and the popular culture born out of the trans-
formation and realization of political consciousness. They assumed a
gulf between the existing cultural reality of the masses, lacking class or
national consciousness, and the revolutionary consciousness and
culture to which they could aspire, a gulf reflected in the relationship
between the CPC intellectual or artist and his audience. Rather than
emerging from within the ranks of the class and its experience of
oppression and struggle, as in Gramsci's conception of the 'organic
intellectual', the intellectual-artist of the CPCs would 'go amongst the
people', bringing to the masses a revolutionary culture already elabor-

249

ated within the vanguard organization. As the accompanying text to a recording of protest songs produced by the CPC put it: 'the composer becomes the enlightened interpreter of the feelings of the people, prompting them to realize the causes of many of the difficulties with which they are struggling.'[22] Working from the maxim 'outside political art there is no popular art', the artists of the CPCs excluded the actual experiences of individual lives engaged in the daily, partial defeats and victories out of which any social revolution is made, and opted instead for archetypal dramas of class and imperialist conflict played out by representative types – the student, the priest, the worker, the bourgeois, etc. – which were devoid of inner life and authenticity. Formal, aesthetic considerations were relegated to a narrowly utilitarian status, and otherwise dismissed as a distraction from the business of political action.[23]

The poetry of this movement was published in the three volumes of *Violão de Rua* (Street Guitar) (1962–63), which brought together established poets, such as Joaquim Cardozo, Vinicius de Moraes and Cassiano Ricardo, some of those who had been involved in other avant-garde movements, such as Ferreira Gullar and Affonso Romano de Sant'Anna (b. 1937), as well as a younger generation. Moacyr Félix de Sousa's 'A fala irritada' (Angry speech) is typical of the denunciatory, rhetorical style of so many of these texts, which report the fact of class struggle and announce the impending revolution, but rarely suggest how the battle with the dead weight of backward ideas and the construction of a revolutionary social movement are actually mediated through the lives of individuals:

> Mais devagar, meus senhores,
> isto é um processo histórico.
> Modéstia, meus caros, modéstia
> e um pouco de consciência
> em não chamarem de autores
> palradores
> do que a milhares de anos de vida
> custou sangue, morte e muitas dores.
> Quando vier, ó carreirista
> da política e das letras,
> com a sua teoriazinha na mão
> – como se fosse um buquê
> para enfeitar sua vida
> no jornal ou na TV –
> saiba disto:

>   atrás de você,
>   empurrando você,
>   causando você,
>   afirmando você,
>   negando você,
>   transcendendo você
>   existe a fábrica
>   – e seu chão
>   ligado ao motor das almas
>   que compõe uma nação . . . etc. etc.[24]

(Slow down, good sirs,/this is a historical process./Modesty, dear sirs, modesty/and just enough consciousness/so that you don't call yourself authors/you people who prattle on/about something which for thousands of years of life/has cost blood, death and a lot of pain./When you get here, oh careerist/of politics and letters,/with your little theory in your hand/ – as if it were a bouquet/to adorn your life with/in the paper or on the TV – /know this:/behind you,/pushing you./causing you,/ affirming you,/denying you,/transcending you/there is the factory/ – and its floor/connected to the engine of souls/which makes up a nation.)

The drama of an awakening class consciousness is more effectively rendered in Vinicius de Moraes's ballad 'O operário em construção' (The worker in construction), which avoids the triumphalist rhetoric so common in the Street Guitar poetry. Instead, Vinicius takes up the key theme of the period, construction, following the building worker's transformation from the alienated instrument of his labour into a conscious subject capable of saying 'no!' to his oppression and discovering within himself the creative power of the collective:

>   Foi dentro da compreensão
>   Desse instante solitário
>   Que, tal sua construção
>   Cresceu também o operário
>   Cresceu em alto e profundo
>   Em largo e no coração
>   E como tudo que cresce
>   Ele não cresceu em vão.
>   Pois além do que sabia
>   – Exercer a profissão –
>   O operário adquiriu
>   Uma nova dimensão:
>   A dimensão da poesia.

(It was within the comprehension/Of that solitary instant/That, like his

251

building/The worker also grew/He grew in height and depth/In breadth and in his heart/And like everything that grows/He did not grow in vain./For besides the thing he knew/ – How to carry out his trade – /The worker acquired/A new dimension:/The dimension of poetry.)

The traditional ballad, especially the *cordel* ballad of the Northeastern interior, was the most typical form adopted by the poets of Street Guitar as a means of grounding their propagandistic message in a framework of 'popular' authenticity. There is, of course, an irony in the appropriation of this form by the protest poets, given the distinction drawn by the intellectuals of the CPCs between the 'alienated' traditional culture of the masses and the consciously 'revolutionary' culture which was the object of their own activities. Certainly, the characteristic format of the *cordel* ballad was a drama played out by the stock social types of the rural Northeast – the peasant, the ranch-owner and the bandit – or an allegorical tale of foolish ambition, sinful transgression or perdition, whose outcome normally served to confirm an extremely conservative Christian morality and social hierarchy, spelt out in the closing lines by the narrator.[25] The approach of the poets of Street Guitar was essentially to substitute their own dramas of class conflict for the traditional narratives of struggle between Good and Evil, and to replace the concluding conservative 'lesson' of the tale with a revolutionary moral of their own. In Ferreira Gullar's 'João Boa-Morte' (John Good-Death), for example, the exploited peasant João prepares to kill himself and his family for want of any other solution to their misery, until he is met by a member of the Peasant League, who persuades him of the need to build a united struggle against their common oppressor, the landowner. The ballad ends with an invitation to follow their example:

E assim se acaba uma parte
da história de João.
A outra parte da história
vai tendo continuação
não neste palco de rua
mas no palco do sertão.
Os personagens são muitos
e muita a sua aflição.
Já vão todos compreendendo,
como compreendeu,
que o camponês vencerá
pela força da união.

252

Que é entrando para as Ligas
que ele derrota o patrão,
que o caminho da vitória
está na revolução.²⁶

(And so ends a part/of John's story./The other part of the story/is to be
continued/not on this street-stage,/but on the stage of the backlands./
The characters are many/and great is their distress./Now they are all
beginning to understand,/just as he understood,/that the peasant will
overcome/through unity./And that it is by joining the Leagues/that he
will defeat the boss,/that the path to victory/lies in revolution.)

Yet, by simply inserting this revolutionary content into the didactic,
moralistic framework of the traditional ballad, the Street Guitar poets
left unchallenged a deeper obstacle to the transformation of conscious-
ness – the complex relationship between language and ideology.
Because the protest poet viewed his putative peasant or working-class
audience as a passive vessel of *false* consciousness, and not the subject
of a *contradictory* consciousness, he felt compelled to leave no room for
doubt or ambiguity. That audience, like the Concretists' 'consumer-
reader', was denied the opportunity to learn through the critical
exercise of its own imagination, to explore the 'open doors' of which
Cabral spoke in his 'Fable of an architect', and construct its own
possible solutions to the problems it faced.

Severino's Journey

It is surely significant, then, that the most celebrated and durable
adaptation of the traditional ballad-form associated with the protest
poetry of this period should be Cabral's own *Morte e Vida Severina*
(Death and Life of a Severino), written in 1956 and therefore long
before the emergence of the Street Guitar movement. The text became
one of the most popular works to be staged by the radical theatre
movement under the dictatorship after it was set to music by Chico
Buarque de Hollanda. It is not difficult to see why, considering its
uncompromising depiction of the intolerable conditions suffered by
the Northeastern peasantry, its reminders of the simple political and
economic facts, such as the monopoly of landownership, which
explain that oppression, and its implicit appeals for agrarian reform. In
his introduction to the poem, Severino explains that, along with
countless others, he has inherited his name, and the harsh condition it
denotes, from their common subjection to the tyranny of the local

253

patriarch; the shared identity of all those for whom he stands is unequivocally rooted in the reality of class oppression:

> Somos muitos Severinos
> iguais em tudo na vida;
> na mesma cabeça grande
> que a custo é que se equilibra,
> no mesmo ventre crescido
> sobre as mesmas pernas finas,
> e iguais também porque o sangue
> que usamos tem pouca tinta.
> E se somos Severinos
> iguais em tudo na vida,
> morremos de morte igual,
> mesma morte severina:
> que é a morte de que se morre
> de velhice antes dos trinta,
> de emboscada antes dos vinte,
> de fome um pouco por dia
> (de fraqueza e de doença
> é que a morte severina
> ataca em qualquer idade,
> e até gente não nascida).[27]

(We Severinos are many/the same in every part of our lives:/in the same large head/that is so hard to balance,/in the same swollen belly/on the same spindly legs,/and the same too because the blood/we use up has little colour in it./And if we are Severinos/the same in every part of our lives,/we die the same death,/the same severino death:/which is the death you die/from old age before you're thirty,/from an ambush before you're twenty,/from hunger a little every day/(with weakness and illness/the severino death/strikes at any age,/even the unborn)).

But what sets this account of peasant migration apart from the political morality tales of Street Guitar is its refusal simply to depict unproblematically a leap of consciousness from desperate isolation and resignation to revolutionary unity and resolve. Instead, the reader is carried with the protagonist along a journey of disillusionment, whose own material and ideological contradictions leave them both at the end of the poem with nothing but their own experience and imagination from which to create a new meaning for their existence. Rather than merely replacing the structures and language of the traditional ballad with those of a pure, 'revolutionary' popular culture, Cabral parodies and subverts those structures and language. In doing so, he is implicitly recognizing that there are the only cultural resources available to the peasant or worker to understand his/her world, and that it is only out of these resources that a new consciousness can be constructed.

The narrative framework for *Death and life of a Severino* is the *auto de natal*, one example of the Luso-Brazilian tradition of one-act morality plays, whose subject is the nativity story, the journey of pilgrimage culminating in the spectacle of Christ's birth and the celebration of the renewal of life and hope on earth. If the deeply rooted religious faith of the Northeastern peasant derived one form of consolation and hope from this Christian drama, another promise of salvation lay in the journey of migration from the drought-ridden semi-desert of the *agreste*, via the sugar-plantations of the *zona da mata* to the coastal, industrial city of Recife. To these two central structural devices Cabral adds further metaphors suggestive of life, renewal and hope: the imagery of agriculture and work in general; the 'rosary' of Severino's journey, whose thread is the course of the river Capiberibe from the interior to the sea, its beads the towns and villages along the way, and the river itself, as a life-giving source of fertility and the dynamic flux of human existence.

However, the irony on which the poem's drama depends lies in the denial of all these symbols of hope and regeneration by the reality of Severino's journey. Each stage of his migration contradicts the assumption that the historical and geographical journey from *sertão* to coast, from semi-feudal social and economic relations, primitive pastoral agriculture, through the wage-labour system of the plantation, to the relatively advanced capitalist conditions of the modern industrialized city, is necessarily accompanied by material and social improvement for the majority. Instead he meets only evidence of death, whether the murder of Severino Lavrador (Severino the Farmer) by the anonymous 'bird-bullet' which 'queria voar mais livre' (wanted to fly more freely) and so add another peasant plot to the rancher's swollen estates, or the death of the plantation-worker swallowed up by the soil, which now ironically promises to clothe and shelter him and provide the plot of land which was never his in life:

> – Agora trabalharás
> só para ti, não a meias,
> como antes em terra alheia.
> – Trabalharás uma terra
> da qual, além de senhor,
> serás homen de eito e trator.

255

> – Trabalhando nessa terra,
>   tu sozinho tudo empreitas:
>   serás semente, adubo, colheita.

(Now you'll work/just for yourself, not as a sharecropper,/like before on someone else's land./You'll work a plot of land/of which you'll be, not just master,/but harrower and tractor too./Working on this land,/you alone will do all the hiring:/you'll be the seed, the fertilizer, the harvest.)

Severino's farming skills are redundant in a world where the only busy trades are those profiting from death itself – the doctor, chemist, mourner, pall-bearer and gravedigger – and where, as the professional mourner tells him, 'Esses roçados o banco/já não quer financiar' (The bank won't finance/these plots any more). The rosary of his journey is repeatedly broken as the river dries up and Severino questions the very point of his migration, realizing that 'nessa viagem que eu fazia,/ sem saber desde o Sertão, meu próprio enterro eu seguia' (on this journey I've been making,/from the backlands, without realizing it, I've been following my own funeral).

The discovery that life is a process of erosion, that human beings are continually ground into dust and swept inexorably into the sea, prompts Severino to contemplate suicide as he arrives at the slums on the mudflats of Recife. José, the carpenter, can provide no comforting answer to his question as to whether there is any purpose in attempting to resist the tide, to search for a bridge across the river, or simply abandon oneself to the ocean of death. Instead, Cabral allows the structure of the nativity story itself to offer its own ambiguous response. The conversation is interrupted by the announcement that a son has been born to José, and the slum-dwellers proceed to celebrate the event with the meagre resources at their disposal, offering gifts which parody those of the Wise Kings and remind us of the harsh future in store for the child: crabs to teach it to crawl about on the mud in search of a living, newspaper to provide a blanket and the ironic promise of 'education'. An alternative future is predicted by a gypsy, who sees the child exchanging the black mud of the river-bank for the black grease of the factory, once again mocking the illusion of material progress:

> Não o vejo dentro dos mangues,
> vejo-o dentro de uma fábrica:
> se está negro não é lama,
> é graxa de sua máquina,

coisa mais limpa que a lama
do pescador de maré
que vemos aqui, vestido
de lama da cara ao pé.
E mais: para que não pensem
que em sua vida tudo é triste,
vejo coisa que o trabalho
talvez até lhe conquiste:
que é mudar-se destes mangues
daqui do Capiberibe
para um mocambo melhor
nos mangues do Beberibe.

(I don't see him on the mud-flats,/I see him inside a factory:/if he's black it's not with mud,/it's with the grease from his machine,/something cleaner than the mud/of the tidal fisherman/we see here, clothed/in mud from head to toe./There's more: lest you think/that all is sadness in his life,/I can see something which his labour/may yet perhaps win for him:/ to move from these mud-flats/here on the Capiberibe/to a better shack/ on the mudflats of the Beberibe.)

Yet the 'spectacle of life', whose celebration is integral to the narrative structure adopted by Cabral, presents a stubbornly resistant challenge to the despair which his parodic approach otherwise seems to impose. On the one hand, this spectacle suggests an impersonal, mechanical dynamic: 'vê-la desfiar seu fio,/que também se chama vida,/ver a fábrica que ela mesma;/teimosamente, se fabrica' (to see it unravelling its thread,/which is also called life,/to see the factory which it/obstinately makes of itself). Although pale and sickly, the new-born child has 'the mark of a man', and 'the machine of a man/already beats incessantly within him'. At the same time, the child's beauty resides in his creative potential, in his capacity to affirm possibilities where previously none seemed to exist, to renew and revive what was old or exhausted:

– é tão belo como um sim
numa sala negativa.

– É tão belo como a soca
que o canavial multiplica.
– Belo porque é uma porta
abrindo-se em mais saídas.
. . .
– Ou como o caderno novo
quando a gente principia.

   – É belo porque com o novo
   todo o velho contagia.
   – Belo porque corrompe
   com sangue novo a anemia.

(he's as beautiful as a yes/in a room that says no.//He's as beautiful as the
second cutting/which multiplies the cane-fields./Beautiful because he is
a door/opening up into more ways out./. . ./Or like the new exercise
book/when you're just beginning.//He's beautiful because he infects/
everything old with his newness./Beautiful because he corrupts anae-
mia with new blood.)

This notion of a creative human capacity allows for a positive re-
evaluation of Severino's own function within the drama of the poem;
for although disabused of his innocent faith in salvation through his
'pilgrimage' to the coast, Severino's very identity as a farmer means
that he does not simply suffer the process of erosion passively, but is
engaged in a permanent struggle to wrest a living out of his harsh
environment. His condition, like that of all the thousands of other
Severinos for whom he stands, is 'a de abrandar estas pedras/suando-
se muito em cima,/a de tentar despertar/terra mais extinta' (that of
softening these stones/by sweating and sweating over them,/that of
trying to bring to life/land that is ever more exhausted).

Such images – the door opening up new paths, the fresh exercise
book waiting to be filled, the erosive power of the river and the
struggle to awaken life from the dead silence of stone – suggest that
there is a profound link between the more overtly social concerns of
poems such as *Death and life of a Severino*, the wider body of Cabral's
work and his conception of poetry itself. His approach to composition
has been described as a process of 'dual calcination', first reducing to
ashes the memory of lived experience and then transmuting that
mineral substance into an organic linguistic form. 'To João Cabral the
verse resembles an organism which lives off the dead germs of
subjective experience.'[28] Although only achieved through an emi-
nently rational effort of will, Cabral's concept of the construction of the
poem is clearly far from the abstract intellectualism of the Concretists
or the mechanical propagandism of the protest poets. It implies a
labour of the mind whose discipline arises, not from an adherence to
preconceived formulae of composition, but out of the struggle
between language and consciousness. This was precisely the principle
which Cabral identified in the work of the artist Miró:

   This appreciation of creative labour as a pure activity also necessarily
   means leaving the initiative to whatever may emerge from that struggle

between the constructive hand and the hard, irreducible material. . . . But, above all, this appreciation of the doing itself, this locating of the labour in itself, this departing from the actual conditions of the labour and not from the demands of a previously crystallized substance, has, in the explanation of Miró's work, another utility. This concept of labour, above all by virtue of that initial openness and emptiness, allows the artist to exercise a minute and permanent judgement on every slightest result to which his labour gives rise.[29]

The best of Cabral's poetry works through just such a dialectical process whereby language and consciousness are continually brought to reflect on one another, challenging the received associations of the metaphor and opening up new, ever richer layers of meaning. In 'Uma faca só lâmina' (A knife all blade), for instance, Cabral defies his reader to content herself with a univocal interpretation of the metaphor; the title is just one of a complex of paradoxically negative images – the knife that is all blade, the invisible bullet or the ticking clock lodged in the flesh – which revolve around and indirectly reveal the core of the poem, the vital motor or 'irritant' of human want and desire. 'Estudos para uma bailadora andaluza' (Studies for an Andalusian dancer, from *Quaderna* (1956–59), meanwhile, explores a number of metaphorical possibilities suggested by the image of the flamenco dancer, developing and modifying their meanings by a series of questions and negations, until a new synthesis is achieved. Cabral begins with the imagery of fire: the dancer's movements and gestures resemble flames, as if her flesh, ablaze with energy, were hungry for its own consumption. Yet there is a difference: she alone is capable of igniting that fire from nothing with an inner spark of inspiration. Other sections focus on her steps, whose staccato precision seems to transmit a coded message from an invisible telegraph-line, or which root her body like a living tree in the earth; and on the evolution of the dance itself, the statuesque symmetry of the poses with which she begins and ends her performance, and the essential core which is finally revealed like the ripe fruit of the maize plant emerging clothed yet naked from within its foliage. In another study on the same theme, the subject is the very relationship between the dancer and the dance which is explored through the metaphor of the rider and her mount:

> Subida ao dorso da dança
> (vai carregada ou a carrega?)
> é impossível se dizer
> se é a cavaleira ou a égua.

259

Ela tem na sua dança
toda a energia retesa
e todo o nervo de quando
algum cavalo se encrespa.

Isto é: tanto a tensão
de quem vai montado em sela,
de quem monta um animal
e só a custo o debela,

como a tensão do animal
dominado sob a rédea,
que ressente ser mandado
e obedecendo protesta.

Então, como declarar
se ela é égua ou cavaleira:
há uma tal conformidade
entre o que é animal e é ela,

entre a parte que domina
e a parte que se revela,
entre o que nela cavalga
e o que é cavalgado nela,

que o melhor será dizer
de ambas, cavaleira e égua,
que são de uma mesma coisa
e que um só nervo as inerva,

e que é impossível traçar
nenhuma linha fronteira
entre ela e a montaria:
ela é a égua e a cavaleira.

(Mounted on the back of the dance (is she carried or does she carry it?)/
it's impossible to say/whether she is the rider or the mare.//She pos-
sesses in her dance/all that taut energy/and all that vigour such as when/
some horse tosses and rears.//That's to say: both the tension/of someone
mounted in the saddle,/someone mounted on a beast/and who can
hardly subdue it,//and the tension of the beast/subdued beneath the
reins,/which resents being controlled/and obeys under protest.//How
then, can one state/whether she is the mare or the rider:/there is such a
conformity/between that which is the animal and that which is her,//
between the part in control/and the part which rebels,/between the thing
in her that is riding/and the thing in her that is being ridden,//that it
would be best to say/of them both, rider and mare,/that they are part of

THE ARCHITECTS OF CONSTRUCTION

the same thing/and that a single nerve innervates them,//and that it is
impossible/to draw a dividing line/between her and her mount: she is
the mare and the rider.)

Implicitly, then, Cabral refuses to see his reader simply as a passive
'consumer' of the poem's structure: 'The consumer is, here, an active
party. For the man who reads wants to read himself in what he reads,
he wants to find himself in that which he is incapable of doing
himself.'[30] By provoking a critical attitude to the linguistic structures
through which we apprehend the world, he seeks to transform and
liberate the reader's consciousness. An authentic collective language
capable of expressing the experience of the community can therefore
neither be appropriated uncritically from the past, nor assimilated as a
ready-made consumer-commodity or political programme. Rather it
must be forged through a dynamic and open-ended dialogue between
the poet, the text and the reader, in which the perception of error, of
false meaning, is the key to new understanding.

While Cabral's sense of formal clarity and his objective rationalism
seem on the surface to be inspired, like that of the Concretists, by the
spectacle of post-war urban construction, the critical edge of his poetry
springs out of the knowledge that such construction involves a merci-
less battle with the hard, irreducible rural landscape of stone surround-
ing the city. At the heart of Cabral's poetry is a precarious, dynamic
struggle between form and communication, matter and conscious-
ness, city and *sertão*; what we recognize in his poems is the transforma-
tive and liberating agency of human labour, which is not content
simply to reproduce the inherited structures of the world, whether
they be the archaic semi-feudal institutions of the Northeastern interior
or the new economic order of the technological age, but continually seeks
to alter them in accordance with its own needs and aspirations.

All of this makes Cabral's poetics an implicit but powerful critique of
the naïve optimism of the Concretists, of their uncritical faith in the
necessarily progressive nature of a culture founded upon the mecha-
nics of the industrial production line. The construction of the modern
capitalist export economy was instead shown to be problematic,
concealing beneath its hygienic rationalism the systematic marginali-
zation of the rural labourer and peasant, and the alienation of the
worker. And it was the predicament of the peasant *lavrador* and the
migrant worker that provided the linguistic and thematic material for
the only other organized and conscious challenge to the Concretist
perspective – the movement called Praxis.

261

Praxis

Mário Chamie (b. 1933) launched the work of the Praxis group in 1962, with the publication of *Lavra Lavra* (Ploughing Ploughing), a collection of poems written between 1958 and 1959. It set in motion the long and often bitter debate with the Concretists which continues to smoulder and occasionally erupt thirty years on. Today, Chamie judges the main contribution of Praxis to have been its resistance to the Concretists' battle for the reification of the word, and its redemption of poetic language as living, historical actuality.[31] Even before *Ploughing Ploughing*, Chamie's sense of the dialectical relationship between language and historical process was in evidence in at least one composition of 1958. 'Migradores' (Migrants) suggests how the false dichotomy set up by the Concretists, between a poetry expressive of human experience and one concerned with its own internal structures, could be overcome. As Chamie says of Praxis, 'The crucial step which it takes is that of not working on themes. What is proposed is to raise problems',[32] problems simultaneously linguistic and historical.

In the case of 'Migrants', the problem or 'field of aesthetic enquiry' is the predicament of the peasant farmer forced to migrate to the city. This 'field of inquiry' supplies the text with a given range of vocabulary, and in particular with a number of key words whose lexical, semantic and morphological potential can be explored and developed. Thus the verb *esfalfar-se* ('to exhaust oneself') gives rise to a group of related terms – *asfalto* (asphalt), *ar* (air) and *arfar* (gasp) – which lead to a questioning of the option of urban migration as a solution to the peasant's condition:

> Que? Muito quereis ser civis
> de esfalfado arfar sobre o asfalto
> falto de ar pairado ao nível
> do espaço como a azul sensível?
>
> Não. Quanto quereis pedregosos lavra-
> dores? Sempre lavrais em côres
> disfarçadas na seara dos cereais
> o ódio elementar e a mansa dor
> das rêses lamberosas dos calos
>
> camponêses.
>
> Aprendei o ordenho, a grama, o pasto
> e nada busqueis do solo sarjo e gasto.
>
> Mesmo

o pneuma ático do poema e efígie
morreram, migraflores, n'alma *civilis* . . .[33]

(What? Ye would really be civilians/gasping exhausted on the asphalt/
short of breath hovering at the point/where the air meets the tangible
blue?//No. How much do ye want stony [farmers] ploughmen/of pain?
Ye always plough, in colours/disguised in the fields of corn,/the elemen-
tal hatred and gentle pain/of your licking cattle, your//peasant calluses.//
Learn the milking, the grass, the pasture/and seek nothing from the
ragged worn-out soil.//Even the Attic breath [pneumatic] of the poem
and effigy/have died, migrating flowers, in the civilian soul . . .)

By the time of *Ploughing Ploughing* the principles with which Chamie
had been experimenting had been developed into an elaborate theory
explained in some detail in the 'didactic manifesto' *Poema-Praxis*.[34]
Chamie's first point was that the significance of the word in the poem
arises out of three factors which react together: the relative autonomy
of words as 'living bodies' within the 'defence field' of the poem,
where they are revealed as 'univocal signs'; their connotative relation-
ship (*mobilidade inter-comunicante*) with other elements in the same
linguistic field, taking into account the relative intensity and impor-
tance given to the word by its place on the 'black space' of the printed
page – this relationship gives rise to the dialectical flux of the poem:
'univocal (isolated) word – multivocal word (in connotation) – univo-
cal word (the poem)'; and, finally, the 'internal framework of mean-
ings', a web of semantic connections set up within and between the
different fields of the poem by a number of key words belonging to
similar or identical phonetic and syllabic groups. Thus 'Debulha-
mento' (Threshing) presents seven versions of the same structural
configuration, some of whose elements (for example, *o homem, o grão, se
faz, espiga*) remain identical from section to section, some of which are
related by assonance (*Ver não visto aviva, Perder o siso arrisca, Quer se o
risco aviva*) or by identical suffixes (*descasca, desvela, desvenda, descose*).
The successive modulations of the matrix pattern are built up, allow-
ing multiple dimensions of the core 'problem' to be explored, rather in
the manner of Cabral's 'Studies for an Andalusian dancer'. In this case,
the 'problem' is the threshing of the harvested grain in search of the
ripe fruit of the peasant's labour; the action brings into play a whole
complex of contradictions and tensions – between expectation and
deception, hope and suspicion, security and risk, industry and exploi-
tation, containment and violence – which mark this moment in the life
of the peasant. (Only two sections of the poem are cited below by way

of illustration, although clearly the text must be read in its entirety to appreciate fully Chamie's approach):

Perder o siso arrisca
o homem:
não pense.
Massa de cal
se faz na casa;
ponta de dedo
o grão
descasca.
Perder o siso arrisca.
No monte espiga esconde.
Mais
montante a mente enreda
a malha.

Estar no núcleo abriga
o homem:
não fuja.
Planta de pé
se faz no corte;
ponta de dedo
o grão
descose.
Estar no núcleo abriga.
No catre espiga entope.
Tenso
com fome o homem acolhe
a fome.

(To lose his cool puts the man/at risk:/don't think./A lump of lime is forming in his house:/his finger-tip/husks/the grain./To lose his cool would be a risk./In a heap he hides the ears of corn./The pile/grows higher, his mind gets entangled in the mesh of his threshing.//Lying in the nucleus gives/the man shelter: don't run away./The seedling is planted/at the moment of cutting: his finger-tip/shells/the grain./Lying in the nucleus gives shelter./Ears of corn stuffed in his cot./Tense/and hungry the man greets/his hunger.)

As the ambiguous complexity of this example suggests, Chamie expected an active and critical participation on the part of the reader to explore and reconstruct for him/herself the rich potential offered by the poem's 'internal framework of meanings'. Praxis was thus an attempt to acknowledge the dynamic function of poetic language, based on an open-ended interaction between the structural space of the text in its relative autonomy, the wider contextual framework and the conscious, creative role of the reader. It is this recognition of the dialectical relationship between language, world and individual, which counterposed Praxis so radically to the Concretist project. As Chamie argued, by working from its own *pre-established* structures, rather than those given by the conditions of real human experience, the Concretist poem was far more subjective and conservative than its defenders claimed: 'If there is a *revolution* in that poem, it is *in* and *for* literature, never *in* and *for* the context, whose structures remain intact.'[35] By contrast, the writing (and reading) of the praxis-poem, as an active mediation between the 'area of aesthetic enquiry' (the world) and the structure of the composition (the text), represents a form of knowledge, a critical act of learning, the subjectivization of objective reality without which there can be no consciousness and therefore no revolutionary action. Interesting parallels can be drawn between this approach and the methods of popular literacy and education being developed during the same period by Paulo Freire, in which the learner was transformed into the subject of the learning process, constructing a unique 'grammar' and vocabulary out of the material of his or her own experience.[36]

The work of João Cabral and Mário Chamie indicated that there was a way out of the sterile debate between the pure formalism of the Concretists and the didactic propagandism of the protest poets. An independent perspective was available, which could combine a critical approach to structure, language and the reader – text relationship with a vision of social transformation, in which the self-transformation of individual consciousness could play a central part. Yet this perspective remained largely isolated, for the cultural movement of the late 1950s and early 1960s remained under the sway of ideas which subordinated the subjective role of the individual to the blind process of national development. And, although during the first four years after the military coup of 1964, left-wing cultural and intellectual activity was permitted to continue in relative freedom, the possibility of creating a bridge between that movement and the wider masses of the working-class popular movement was destroyed by the imprisonment or exile of key labour leaders.[37] It could equally be argued that the opportunity to build such a relationship had already been sacrificed before the coup, as the Communist Party leadership of the Goulart years had effectively disarmed any independent, revolutionary challenge on the part of the rising wave of organized labour. The consequent defeat of that movement led the disillusioned poets of the generation to abandon any faith in the viability of collective utopian projects, and the

Concretists were once again able to occupy the cultural vacuum, pushing forward their perspective as the only coherent 'radical' theory of art. As long as no other effective leadership was available to challenge the entire model of development now being pursued in the country, the Concretists could pose as cultural revolutionaries, whilst remaining the spokesmen of capitalist models of artistic construction. Left with this legacy of ideological confusion and political isolation, the next two generations of poets – the Tropicalists and the Marginals – would now have to face the challenge of responding to the brutal experience of the dictatorship and its particular brand of 'capitalismo selvagem'.

8

Speaking Aloud:
The Re-entry into History

Cuba: The Poet in the Vanguard

In myth and in reality the echoes of the Cuban Revolution were heard throughout the Americas. The entry of the 26th July Movement into Havana on the first day of 1959, and the overthrow of the regime of Fulgencio Batista, was not recognized at first as an event of great significance, but its impact was soon felt both in Latin America and in the very heartland of imperialism.[1] On the one hand, it served to crystallize liberal thinking in the United States and to focus a more general critique of the Cold War around issues of social justice and the right to progress. Within Latin America, the Cuban Revolution served to break the trauma of United States omnipotence so dismally reaffirmed in Guatemala in 1954. In that year[2] the United States through a surrogate overthrew the reforming regime of Jacobo Arbenz. The key movers in the conspiracy were the Dulles brothers, both of whom were in the leadership of the US administration while simultaneously employed by the United Fruit Company, which had long seen Guatemala as its own terrain. The destruction of the Arbenz regime confirmed both the intimate association between business and the US government that served it and the capacity of that government to dictate policy as well as the pace and direction of change in the region. The democratic opening of the late forties seemed now to be ending in the most painful fashion.[3]

In any event, the period of democracy had produced a political crisis whose effects ran through the following decade. Through the forties the Communist parties of Latin America collaborated in popular front alliances which often involved cooperation with the most recalcitrant regimes – with Batista in Cuba and Somoza in Nicaragua for example.[4] The logic of a hegemonic theory of 'stages of development' within these parties led not only to coexistence but to active collaboration in capitalist development throughout Latin America. Stalinism rewrote the communist tradition in nationalist terms, spoke of 'socialism in one country' and abandoned the leading role of the working classes in the struggle for socialism. The Arbenz government in Guatemala, of which the Communist Party were active supporters, was a manifestation of that policy as well as of its real limitations, for the Latin American bourgeoisie and its representatives clearly were not prepared to take the anti-imperialist struggle into the arena of confrontation where the initiative would move to the mass organizations. That was the fundamental reason why Arbenz surrendered so quickly to the US-backed troops led by Castillo Armas.

In the aftermath of Guatemala, the revolutionary socialist tradition seemed to have nothing more to say to the exploited and oppressed of Latin America. For many, that tradition was now identified with a corrupt Stalinism, and only in Bolivia[5] had it given way to a Trotskyism which stood in the authentic heritage of the October Revolution of 1917. Elsewhere populism prevailed, winning to itself the mass base which the Communist parties had largely lost.

The contradictions were still present, of course, and visible to those who cared to see them. Yet among many poets there was, as we have seen, a mood of despair veiled by a withdrawal into the autonomous realm of poetry, or a radical cynicism exemplified by Nicanor Parra. In the absence of any organized social force capable of enacting change they were faced once again, for the most part, with the alienating experience of modernization. This entailed the growth of cities in chaotic and haphazard fashion, the widening contradiction between country and city, the apparently inescapable anachronism of a combined and uneven development that enabled poverty to coexist with modern wealth. That combination of vision and the complete lack of any sense of the nature or source of the agent of change brought a deepening disillusionment and despair, and produced an art and a literature whose density could be explained, as Marcuse spoke of modern art in the period of Nazism, as a deliberate obscurity developed to protect the humanist core – the redemptive promise of all art – from the invasion of a crushing immediate reality.[6] This was the period when the ideas represented by Octavio Paz, which emphasized the 'withdrawal from history' as an *essential* characteristic of poetry, held undoubted sway.

It is often suggested that the period was dominated by the exuberant historicism of Neruda, but in fact that is far from the reality. Both Neruda and Cardenal wrote their sweeping celebrations of history during the fifties; yet it was only after 1959 that they were recognized and acknowledged as the voice of a new epoch. Only in the sixties was the audience that these poems implied present in an organized form. This is not to say that Neruda was not widely read or well received; but it does suggest that the audience for poetry remained relatively restricted whatever the implied public to whom the words were addressed. The prophetic power of art on the one hand, and its power to create a collective consciousness on the other, were perhaps lost in the period of modernization and the Cold War. The Cuban Revolution placed on the agenda again a possibility that Latin America could conduct and control its own history, could re-enter history. Hence the extraordinary symbolic significance of Castro's assertion that 'history will absolve me'.[7]

The ideological framework of that recuperation of history, however, was shaped by the political culture that prevailed. The guerrilla theory of revolution given credibility by the Cuban experience had its parallel, in the early sixties in particular, in the visionary utopianism of the theology of liberation. Both articulated the redemptive promise in terms of the 'optimism of the will',[8] where the power of the will was offered as the determining factor in revolutionary change – as if material conditions were the product of neglect or subjective factors. Against that Gunder Frank's pathbreaking concept of 'the development of underdevelopment'[9] revealed with aggressive clarity that underdevelopment was not 'a failure to develop' but an active component of an international system, and that it deepened and extended as the global structure expanded. It was, in other words, the product of a *relationship of forces* rather than a condition of consciousness; thus it was the system itself that had to be attacked in any attempt to resolve the problems of socio-economic backwardness. A commitment to growth and national development was not sufficient in itself; it was not simply a matter of hastening the pace of an inexorable progress. Development could only be achieved to the extent that the dynamics of the global system could no longer reproduce and deepen that relationship of inequality.

Gunder Frank's theories were the product of the post-Cuba phase, when the possibility of a revolutionary transformation of this relationship of inequality was placed on the historical agenda again. The Marxist precept is that 'man makes history but not in circumstances of

269

his own choosing'. The new concept of revolution in Cuba, however, in rejecting the determinism of Stalin's 'stages theory', argued with maximum optimism that those conditions could be overcome by will and self-sacrifice. This voluntaristic vision of change and revolution was enshrined in a version of the history of the Cuban Revolution – the guerrilla struggle victorious over a powerful state – and of its chief protagonist, the 'heroic guerrilla'.[10] The prophecy and the redemption came together in a secular version of an essentially religious myth; poetry resumed its visionary role. And the poet became an exemplary figure, the resurrection of the Romantic ideal of the artist-hero, the bearer and personification of a 'new man' or woman whose activity and personal example were revolutionary propaganda. It is that which explains the curious phenomenon of a 'guerrilla poetry' which is characteristically lyrical and visionary rather than in any sense political.

The central issue was that the Cuban Revolution specifically accorded a key role to culture. In Cuba itself, the significance of cultural struggle was as it had been in 1917 in Russia.[11] The revolution could not offer a solution to material need – it could only redistribute scarcity; that was its first problem. Secondly, the development of the revolution itself had put the majority of Cuban workers in an essentially passive role in the overthrow of a state realized not by mass insurrection but in a confrontation between a crumbling state and an organized guerrilla force.[12] The mass mobilization of the population behind the revolutionary project, therefore, had to occur after the event, and on the basis of a general commitment to the strategies and objectives of the revolution. Further, this had to be achieved without significant immediate material improvement in the general standard of living. The consolidation of revolution, therefore, would take place at the ideological level.

Making of the New Man

In his 'Man and socialism in Cuba',[13] Che Guevara articulated a theory of the 'new man' which replaced the notion of material gain with a general idea of human development – the creation of a 'new man' and relationships based not on gain or profit, but on cooperation and solidarity. Material incentives would be replaced by moral incentives, the actuality by the vision. The general strategy of a revolution of the will led by an exemplary new man (the guerrilla fighter) was persuas-

270

ively represented in the poetry, the graphic art, the song and the film of the Cuban Revolution. What were the main lines of force of this new culture? First and foremost, it was a committed art that set out to make real or make possible the promised future.

The art of the Cuban Revolution had two functions: to mobilize activity around immediate tasks, and to establish the vision of a new world and a new man. There were those, inside and outside Cuba, who argued that the former was a improper function for poetry – and that argument was at the root of the case against Heberto Padilla.[14] The second function seemed less problematic, as the work of Cintio Vitier and Fernández Retamar showed. The redemptive, prophetic conception arose out of a meeting of several traditions – religion, the politics of the guerrilla, Marxism. The question that had to be addressed, however, was to what extent such poetry was ideological and tendentious, to what extent its particular selection of elements led to a falsification of a contradictory reality veiled by a future promise.

When Fidel Castro addressed the gathering of Cultural Workers in April 1961,[15] he coined the famous phrase 'within the revolution everything, outside the revolution nothing'. The interpretation placed on that varied considerably in the years that followed, however; by 1971 a similar congress heard that the concept of a revolution which signalled creative freedom and the right to experimentation in art had been supplanted by a far more instrumental conception of an art *serving* the revolution.[16] Central, of course, was the extent to which serving the revolution in fact meant serving the state, and since the identity of both was beyond question it seemed equally clear that a poetry devoted to the achievement of material purposes was one which would speak with an 'official' voice. Certainly critical voices were stilled after 1971 in all areas of Cuban society; and while many of those who denounced that lack of creative freedom spoke from the right and simply used the issue to attack the revolutionary perspective as a whole, there were those for whom the denial represented a betrayal of that very perspective.[17]

Between 1959 and 1961 the Cuban Revolution clearly saw its survival in a continuing relationship with liberal opinion in the United States and within Cuba itself. It emphasized openness and consensus, and the Cuban leadership made a much-publicized visit to New York to appeal to the United Nations for the right to self-determination. But the US state resisted; Eisenhower imposed an embargo on Cuba's main source of foreign income – sugar – and the Cubans turned to Russia for help and support. That relationship, and the renewed dependence of Cuba on an external power, was uneasily conducted throughout the sixties.[18]

The political tradition which gave birth to the Cuban Revolution was deeply hostile to Stalinism and a declared enemy of the Communist parties. The radical nationalism which informed the 26th of July Movement placed the intelligentsia in the leadership of the political movement, saw it as a representative of the broad mass of the oppressed and exploited, and made a virtue of its lack of an organic connection with the working-class movement. That disconnection was encapsulated in the myth of the heroic guerrilla, who raised principle above interest, and who held only moral capital in the society. Standing above the contending classes, and thus above material interest, the new protagonist of history could speak without equivocation of the future.

> Che tú lo sabes todo,
> los recovecos de la Sierra,
> el asma sobre la yerba fría
> la tribuna
> el oleaje en la noche
> y hasta de que se hacen
> los frutos y las yuntas
>
> No es que yo quiera darte
> pluma por pistola
> pero el poeta eres tú.
> (Miguel Barnet: 'Che')

(Che you know everything,/the corners of the mountains,/asthma over cold grass/platforms/waves in the night/and even what/the fruits and teams of oxen are made from//I don't want to exchange/your pistol for a pen/yet you are the one who is a poet.)

It is the *guerrillero*, then, who can represent the 'general interests' of society and the consensus of nationhood in a period when no other class is powerful enough to defend and pursue its class interests.

It was that vision that informed arguments about culture and relationships between the state and the artists as expressed by Fidel Castro in his 1961 *Words to the intellectuals*. Consciousness must first be transformed, material considerations superseded by higher, moral, values, and the necessity of sacrifice on the road to economic development and independence acknowledged and celebrated.

Por esta libertad de canción bajo la lluvia
habrá que darlo todo.
Por esta libertad de estar estrechamente atados
a la firme y dulce entraña del pueblo
habrá que darlo todo.
. . .
No hay más camino que la libertad.
No hay otra patria que la libertad.
No habrá más poema sin la violenta música de la libertad
(Fayad Jamis: (Por esta libertad' – For this freedom)

(For this liberty to sing beneath the rain/we may have to give every-
thing./For this freedom to be closely tied/to the firm sweet innermost self
of the people/we shall have to give everything/. . ./There is no road but
freedom./There is no other country but freedom./There is no poem
without the violent music of liberty)

'It is the 21st century man whom we must create, although this is
still a subjective and unsystematic aspiration.'[19] In that process, the
new intelligentsia would play an *organic* role, rather than a critical one,
transforming consciousness and creating a new vision. The object was
twofold; to win the intellectuals and their allies to the advocacy of the
Cuban cause, and to win the battle of ideas on the construction of the
new state. The battle had to be won against the aggression of an
international capitalism intent on isolating and if possible destroying
Cuba; but it also turned against another enemy with whom Castro's
relationship was difficult and paradoxical throughout the decade – the
Communist Party and its Russian mentor. What Che Guevara in
particular represented was a deep resistance to the residual theories of
Stalinism, which argued the need to pass through inescapable stages
of growth and development. His argument seemed close to a theory of
permanent revolution, of the need to extend the revolution beyond
national boundaries and assert its internationalism.[20] Guevara's image
has been used (among many other purposes) to symbolize the inter-
nationalist character of the Cuban Revolution and to offer a strategy
for confronting the subjugation of small nations to the mighty laws of
the world economy. Yet in 1968, a year after Guevara's death, the
Russian invasion of Czechoslovakia provided an occasion for Castro to
acknowledge the failure of the strategy of spreading the revolution,
and to accept Cuba's membership of the Soviet power bloc and the
harsh laws of economic development under capitalism.
Nevertheless, the impact of Cuban culture on Latin America was

associated in those years with optimism and vision, with a promise of redemption which the Christian poet Cintio Vitier found fulfilled in Cuba. In his 'Viernes Santo' (Good Friday) the ambiguous object of the poem could be Christ or the *guerrillero* – the qualities evoked and celebrated are the same in either case, as is the anticipated paradise.

> Los que piensan en el prójimo
> y lo ayudan y trabajan para él
> son tus discípulos:
> no importa que lo ignoren . . .
> Olvidado por unos y por otros,
> desconocido, estás
> pendiente de tus hijos
> y tus palmas
>   (ellas saben
> como echa ramos una cruz):
> en el fruto,
>   en el sudor,
> en la ignorancia,
> en el olvido de Tí Mismo
>
> que es la Materia de la Realidad.

(Those who think of their fellow man/and help him and work for him/are your disciples;/it doesn't matter whether they know it or not . . ./ Forgotten by many/unknown, you/watch over your children/and your palms/(they know/how a cross can grow branches):/in the fruit/in the sweat,/in the ignorance,/in Forgetting Oneself//that is the substance of reality.)

Here the imagery of Good Friday is interwoven with the virtue of self-sacrifice and voluntary anonymity which is the current emphasis. The Christ figure becomes the hero of the harvest or the armed struggle.

'Tengo' – I have

The most moving and compassionate evocation of the Cuban Revolution is also its most deeply personal. Once again it is Nicolás Guillén who is able to address the real sense of freedom and hope through the voice that has consistently marshalled his poetic thoughts. This singer of the people's songs, the Cantaliso of earlier work, now walks the streets of the new Cuba and experiences a kind of quiet joy.

Cuando me veo y toco,
yo, Juan sin nada no más ayer,
y hoy Juan con todo,
y hoy con todo,
vuelvo los ojos, miro,
me veo y toco
y me pregunto cómo ha podido ser.

Tengo, vamos a ver,
tengo el gusto de ir
yo campesino, obrero, gente simple,
tengo el gusto de ir
(es un ejemplo)
a un banco y hablar con el administrador,
no en inglés,
no en señor,
sino decirle compañero como se dice en español.

Tengo, vamos a ver,
que siendo un negro
nadie me puede detener
a la puerta de un *dancing* o de un bar.
O bien en la carpeta de un hotel
gritarme que no hay pieza
una mínima pieza y no una pieza colosal
una pequeña pieza donde yo pueda descansar.

Tengo, vamos a ver,
que ya aprendí a leer
a contar,

tengo que ya aprendí a escribir
y a pensar
y a reir.

Tengo que ya tengo
dónde trabajar
y ganar
lo que me tengo que comer.
Tengo, vamos a ver,
tengo lo que tenía que tener.[21]

(When I look at myself and touch myself,/me, John with nothing until yesterday,/and today John with everything,/and today with everything,/ I look around and see,/I see myself and touch myself/and I ask myself how it could have happened.//I have, let's see now,/I have the pleasure of going,/me, peasant, worker, an ordinary man,/I have the pleasure of going/(it's just an example)/to a bank and speaking to the manager,/not

275

in English,/not in sir,/but to say comrade to him as we say in Spanish.//I
have, let's see,/that being black still/no-one can stop me at the door of a
dancehall or a bar./Or in the entrance to a hotel/shout at me that there
are no rooms;/just a small one not a huge room,/a little room where I can
rest.//I have, let me see,/that I have learned to read/to count,//I have that I
have learned to write/to think,/to laugh.//I have that I have/somewhere
to work/and earn/the food I need./I have, let's put in this way,/I have
what I had a right to have.)

This is the title poem of a collection published in 1964. It embraces
poems of denunciation and rage, and quasi-elegiac poetry like the
piece devoted to Eduardo García, killed during the invasion of the Bay
of Pigs in 1961. It includes a number of powerful anti-American satires,
and a range of expressions of celebration and joy. But 'Tengo' itself is
the most deceptively profound of all, and the piece most closely in
continuity with the finest of his earlier work. The voice here could be
that of Cantaliso or the anonymous black inhabitants of Havana's
slums. What is certain is that it is vernacular; in many ways the most
important feature of the poem is the recuperation of language ('to
speak to the manager, but not in English, not in sir'). The alienation of
language and of the self are one and the same thing; in a colonial
culture the estrangement of selfhood is the most traumatic and painful
facet of external domination. With the single exception of the phrase
'un ancho resplandor', which belongs in a more lyrical mode, the rest
of the poem is resolutely prosaic. It is built around an intensification of
a feeling of joy and liberty that stems above all from the right to speak,
to name the world. Other poets, like Ernesto Cardenal, found in Cuba
the realization of many utopian aspirations.[22] But for Guillén the key
feature of utopia was a freedom to speak, to name the self and recover
a sense of wholeness, of the sum of those parts ('I see myself and touch
myself'). The language of speech, of democracy, marks the line
beyond which 'Tengo' may now step. And in that sense it is pro-
foundly different from the prophetic tone of much Cuban poetry. The
characteristic lyricism of much post-1959 writing, and above all of the
songs of Cuba, is here matched by a simplicity and directness of
articulation which makes the fulfilment of the self a present possi-
bility. And the marked modesty of the aspiration means that it can be
expressed through the language of lived experience.

The significance of 'Tengo' is that it points to the development
which in a way brought the wheel full circle – from the withdrawal of
poetry from Modernismo onwards, to the recuperation of the public
voice in poetry. Even private experience may now become the material
of shared insight and emotion. The public voice need not be the

rhetorical utterance of global statement; the greatest of public poets encounter the public world at a point of personal contact with it. And as the wider reality impinges on the self, that interface is the location of poetry. Of course, this is neither a prescription nor a formula. But it does represent a profound movement from the literature of private anguish, or of withdrawal and the autonomy of form, to a writing of collective experience. And the achievement of that public voice is realized in both form (and language) and in content. That is what is enshrined in the term 'poesía conversacional' (conversational poetry), coined by Roberto Fernández Retamar.[23]

Undoubtedly the new generation of Cuban poets expressed their devotion to and enthusiasm for the new society. The old school of writers, many of whom had spent much of the previous decade in exile, now returned and added their supportive voices to the transformation of political culture. Cintio Vitier and Roberto Fernández Retamar represented the intellectuals of a previous generation; they were also the stalking horses among their own class of the alliance that Castro sought with liberal and democratic opinion beyond Cuba. Retamar's essay 'Caliban'[24] provided the intellectual scaffolding for their argument.

> Those intellectuals who consider themselves to be revolutionary must break their ties with their own class (the petty bourgeoisie in many cases); they must also break their ties of dependency with the metropolitan culture that gave them its culture, its language, its conceptual and technical apparatus.[25]

More intensely and personally, Retamar expressed his own position in the poem 'El otro' (The other one):

> Nosotros los sobrevivientes,
> ¿A quienes debemos la sobrevida?
> ¿Quién se murió por mí en la ergástula?
> ¿Quién recibió la bala mía,
> La para mí, en su corazón?
> ¿Sobre qué muerto estoy yo vivo,
> Sus huesos quedando en los míos,
> Los ojos que le arrancaron, viendo
> Por la mirada de mi cara,
> Y la mano que no es su mano,
> Que no es ya tampoco la mía,
> Escribiendo palabras rotas
> Donde él no está, en la sobrevida?[26]

(We, the survivors,/to whom do we owe our survival?/Who died for me on the scaffold,/who received my bullet/the one meant for me, in the heart?/At the expense of which dead person am I alive/his bones remaining behind in mine/The eyes they tore out of him, seeing/through the look on my face,/and the hand that is not his hand/yet which is not mine either/writing broken words/where he no longer is, among the survivors?)

This is a classic statement of petty bourgeois guilt, a self-flagellation whose central theme is the individual isolation of the intellectuals. It seems then that Retamar's call to slough off the impact of imperialist culture involved a double movement. On the one hand, the intellectuals should renounce their individuality, their isolation won at the expense of others; and on the other, they should contribute to the creation of a new language, a new culture of independence. As editor of the influential magazine *Casa de la Americas*, Retamar has been in a position to influence directly the construction of the new culture. Much of his post-1959 work has fallen into the category of 'contingent poems' or 'pamphlet poems', mobilizing and agitating around immediate issues. Other poems have the quality of testimony, a confession and an expiation so often repeated among the poets of his generation. Against the dead language of the 'ruins' of a European culture, Retamar sets the process of *construction* of a new world out of the elements of national and popular culture. This is the central motif of his 'conversational poetry', overcoming the gulf between literary and social language, between archaeology in the classic cultures and the construction of the new. The adventurous graphics of the magazine Retamar edits, the challenging originality of Cuban poster art, were important symbols of the process of *renewal* to which the Cuban Revolution was devoted. The role of poetry in it was to renounce its strangeness, its separateness as a mode of activity, its 'making strange'. Instead, 'conversational poetry' sets out to make the world familiar, knowable.

This is summarized in Retamar's poem 'Con las mismas manos' (With the same hands):

Con las mismas manos de acariciarte estoy construyendo una escuela.
Llegué casi al amanecer, con las que pensé que serían ropas de trabajo
Pero los hombres y los muchachos que en sus harapos esperaban
Todavía me dijeron señor.
       Están en un caserón a medio derruir,
Con unos cuantos catres y palos: allí pasan las noches
Ahora, en vez de dormir bajo los puentes o en los portales.
Uno sabe leer, y lo mandaron a buscar cuando supieron que yo tenía
   biblioteca . . .

... me eché a aprender el trabajo elemental de los hombres
Luego tuve mi primera pala y tomé el agua silvestre de los trabajadores
Y fatigado, pensé en tí . . .
　　　　　¡Qué lejos estábamos de las cosas verdaderas
Amor qué lejos – como uno de otro!

(With the same hands I caressed you with I am building a school./I arrived just before dawn, with what I thought would be working clothes/But the men and boys who waited there in their rags/Still called me sir./They are in a half-ruined house,/With a few camp beds and some sticks of furniture; that's where they spend their nights./Now, instead of sleeping under bridges or in doorways./One of them can read and they called him when they discovered I have some books. . ./. . . I began to learn the basic work of people/Then I got my first spade and I drank the wild water of the workers/And then, tired out, I thought of you. . ./How far we were from the real things/how far, my love – as far as we are from one another!)

Here the personal guilt is overcome by submergence in the general will. The workers are idealized and shadowy, models of the oppressed (but not the highly unionized workers of pre-revolutionary Cuba) who once 'slept under bridges and in doorways'. These figures belong to the general category of 'the poor', an appropriate symbol for an equivalent national oppression. These are the representative beneficiaries of an independent national state, reconstructing a world out of the ruins of their own past. The individual consciousness of the middle-class intellectual, and its contradictions, are lost and suffused in the general experience.

This pattern is repeated in many of the poets of the revolution and after; there are few doubts or confusions, few confrontations between past aspirations and present realities. At the level of ideology, material conflict is overcome in an act of will constantly reaffirmed in this poetry of utopian affirmation.

The case of Heberto Padilla illustrates some of the central contradictions in the artist's relationship with the Cuban state.[27] In 1967 Padilla was awarded the Casa de las Americas literary prize for his volume of poetry *Final del juego* (The game is over); it was published with a preface from the Union of Cuban Writers which denounced the poet for his rejection of the revolution and his scarcely veiled complaint that his creative freedom had been compromised. Padilla himself was quite explicit; the title poem, for example, established the characteristic tone of the whole volume.

279

¡Al poeta, despídanlo!
Ése no tiene aquí nada que hacer.
No entra en el juego.
No se entusiasma.
No pone en claro su mensaje.
No repara siquiera en los milagros.
Se pasa el día entero cavilando.
Encuentra siempre algo que objetar.

¡A ese tipo despídanlo!
Echen a un lado al aguafiestas,
a ese malhumorado
del verano,
con gafas negras
bajo el sol que nace.
Siempre
le sedujeron las andanzas
y las bellas catástrofes
del tiempo sin Historia.

(Get rid of the poet!/He's got no business here./He doesn't play his part./ He doesn't get enthusiastic./He doesn't make his message clear./He doesn't even acknowledge miracles./He spends his whole day vacillating./He always finds something to object to.//Get rid of that so and so. /Shove the killjoy aside/the bad tempered sod./In summer/wearing dark glasses/as the sun rises/Always/seduced by the ups and downs/and the heroic failures/of time outside History.)

The literary debates that emerged around the Padilla case provided an opportunity for right-wing liberals like Mario Vargas Llosa to dissociate themselves finally from Cuba and its revolutionary example. In the period since then both Padilla (who has since left Cuba) and Vargas Llosa have made it very clear that their attitudes stemmed from a political difference with Cuba and have become active spokespersons for the right. Nonetheless, there were others whose unease was real and well-founded. While the right of intellectuals to occupy a place beyond social criticism is very questionable, public debate and criticism of the direction of the social process is an indispensable element of any genuine movement towards socialism. The attack on Padilla was a sign of a more general suppression of criticism and concentration of power in Cuba. The writers and artists who came to the defence of Padilla, however, did not address the wider issue of democratic control throughout the society, and thus exposed themselves to a withering assault from the 'official' intellectuals of the regime, whose accusations of elitism and special pleading thus found an echo.[28] Oscar Collazos's debate with Vargas Llosa, for example, left little doubt as to the expectations of a new generation of intellectuals of the revolution. The Uruguayan writer Mario Benedetti, long associated with Cuba, in his major anthology of revolutionary poetry called *Poesía trunca*,[29] argued that now 'Poets don't write *for* the people but rather *from* the people.'[30] This criticism of the distance of some artists from the concerns of the masses was echoed by Fidel Castro at the 1971 Education and Culture Congress.

> For us, a revolutionary people involved in a revolutionary process, we evaluate cultural and artistic creations in terms of their usefulness for the people . . . Our evaluation is political. There can be no aesthetic value without human content.[31]

Clearly, this declaration was directed against Padilla and his demand for a right to lyrical autonomy. But there was another and very different perspective on the issue, that serving the revolution and serving the state were not always the same thing, and that veiling the contradictions within that revolution could not contribute to the deepening of a revolutionary self-awareness. The authority of the state that inherited the revolutionary mantle, however, ensured that such artistic independence within the revolution would be automatically equated with the elitism of a Padilla.

The Guerrilla Poets

In Cuba, as we have seen, poetry actively participated in the creation of a mythology and a martyrology of revolution. It was to do so again in Nicaragua. Through the 1960s, the myth of the *guerrillero* was central to the maintenance of the Cuban state and the firm base of social support on which it rested. That consensus was achieved and sustained, in part, by the cohesion created and recreated by a persistent foreign menace (the fact that nothing so unifies a nation as an external aggressor is a lesson the United States have never learned), and in part by the creation of a shared symbolic language around which that construction of national unity could be achieved.[32] The *guerrillero* provided the core of that symbolic discourse, uniting in the person some of the key elements of Cuban ideology. The *guerrillero* represented a sacrifice – the willing suffusion of the individual in the collective – to which Padilla raised such deep objections. He represented too the renunciation of material benefit as the consequence of revolution; instead the surplus produced was essentially a moral capital, the creation of a new man, a living embodiment of that politics

281

of the will in which men could cease to be the objects and become the protagonists of their own history.

Hundreds of young idealistic revolutionaries, full of courage and selflessness, raised the guerrilla banner in the other republics of Latin America.[33] They did so with staggering ingenuousness and an apparently limitless self-abnegation; they were imbued with a sense of the redemptive power of the revolutionary will and expressed it in a lyric form that recalled and reactivated the myth of the Romantic hero, the Ulysses of old whose will and commitment brought him out of the conditions of his life into confrontation with a greater force – destiny, history, evil. In a sense, too, it resolved the bitter dilemma of the radical intelligentsia caught between a pusillanimous bourgeoisie and a demobilized working class, and without a social force to whose aspirations it could attach its visions and its radicalism. Now the intellectuals could celebrate their isolation as a virtue, as a condition of purity, and represent that oft-repeated unity of the nation in the face of imperialism.

It was a new exile; not this time an exile within the new city, like that of Belli or Parra, but a return to the mountains, the prehistory of Latin America, to forge its history again. This was not rural Latin America, peopled by an impoverished agricultural proletariat and a peasantry equally dependent on the pervasive multinational companies that largely controlled the distribution of agricultural goods. This was a countryside free of social relations, an empty utopia from which the assault could be launched upon the world.

> Hacia
> las blancas montañas
> que me esperan
> debo viajar nuevamente.
> . . .
> Viaje rotundo y solo:
> ¡Qué difícil es dejar
> todo abandonado!
> ¡qué difícil es vivir
> entre ciudades y ciudades,
> una calle,
> un tranvía,
> todo se acumula,
> para que sobreviva
> la eterna estación
> del desencanto!
> . . .

No es que yo quiera
alejarme de la vida,
sino que tengo
que acercarme hacia la muerte . . .

(Towards/the white mountains/that await me/I must go./. . ./A round
journey and a lonely one:/it is so difficult/to leave everything behind!/It
is so difficult to live/between city and city,/a street,/a tram,/everything
accumulates/to ensure the survival/of the endless season/of disillusion-
ment!/. . ./It isn't that I want/to leave life behind,/it's just that I must/
come face to face with death . . .)

This poem, called 'Nuevo Viaje' (A new journey), is by Javier Heraud
(1942–63),[34] killed like so many of the very best of his contemporaries
at an early age, sacrificing himself in a naïve confrontation with the
combined counter-guerrilla forces of Latin America's rulers. Heraud
died in 1963, in his native Peru; he was 21 years old. His work has a
characteristic style – brief lines, sustained nature imagery, and the
words carried by a consistent speaker, the young idealist travelling full
of wonder through a world he is just beginning to discover. His long
poem 'El río' (The river), for example, has a quality of innocence and
openness; the poet is a river enriching and nourishing a landscape of
primal innocence. In 'El poema' he returns to his own origins and
those of his culture, to the place of emptiness, to begin again:

> . . . tendremos que llegar al mismo
> nacimiento del camino, rehacer todo,
> volver con pasos lentos desparramando
> lluvias por los campos,
> sembrando trigo con las manos,
> cosechando peces con nuestras
> interminables bocas.
> . . .
> Mejor hubiera sido naufragar
> y no llegar,
> porque ahora tenemos
> que hacerlo con las manos:
> construir palabras como
> troncos, no implorar ni
> gemir sino acabar,
> terminar a golpes con la tierra muerta.

(. . . We shall have to reach the very/beginning of the road, make
everything anew,/return slowly spreading/rain across the fields,/sowing
corn by hand/harvesting the fish with our ever-open mouths/. . ./It
would have been better to be wrecked/and never arrive,/because now

we must/make it with our hands;/build words the size of/tree trunks, neither implore/nor whine nor come to an end,/but blow by blow have done with this dead land.)

There is no sense in Heraud of the real world that exists, the living and complex social relations that have made of this landscape the scenario of exploitation and struggle; it is as if the poet were the explorer and discoverer of virgin earth. But that is metaphor – the land is culture and consciousness, the sense of the political space as an *absence*, an emptiness to be filled. Such a vision is deeply and movingly idealistic; it is also apolitical and dehistoricizes the real context of struggle, replacing it with a place of exemplary martyrs and mythic possibilities. That very innocence gives the poetry an intense and moving quality, but it reveals too a concept of political action severed from any *social* force.

The Guatemalan poet and political leader Otto René Castillo also died young and horribly. Like Heraud, Castillo was a revolutionary and a youthful victim of the violence of counter-insurgency. Born in Guatemala in 1936 he was tortured and murdered in 1967 in the last moments of a guerrilla struggle which had acquired more strength and support than most of the other similar attempts in Latin America.[35] Castillo's vision, in common with most of those who came to be called the 'guerrilla poets',[36] rested on a single overpowering motif – love. The central motivations of his life and work were sacrifice, personal commitment and abnegation, as well as a kind of joy in living perilously engaged in a reckless gamble with death. His 'art of poetry' was simply summarized:

> Hermosa encuentra la vida
> quién la construye hermosa.
> Por eso amo en tí
> lo que tú amas en mi:
> la lucha por la construcción
> hermosa de nuestro planeta.

(Life is beautiful for those/who construct it in beauty./That is why I love in you/what you love in me:/the struggle for the/beautiful construction of our planet)

This is a profoundly lyric vision, in which the poet is an exemplar of emotion and compassion. His early work centres on a love affair, the lover obscure and unnamed; indeed the love itself is defined by its abandonment, by the distance between the loves, by the sense of exile and nostalgia that prevails in the work. Like Edgardo Tello[37] ('Las puertas de la esperanza' – The gates of hope), Heraud and others, the *guerrillero*'s sacrifice is exemplified in the renunciation of love, as if this were the most telling evidence of self-denial. The recompense is the suffusion of the self in the collective, though that collective is mystical and abstract. Writing of Berlin ('Nuestro amor' – Our love), Castillo explains:

> Pero yo no sólo escribo estas palabras,
> También hombre escribo, lucha, libertad.
> Ellas están tan unidas a nosotros,
> tan nacidas con nosotros,
> que todo nuestro amor no tendría sentido,
> perdería su derecho a ser,
> si ellas no nos unieran para siempre.
>
> Puentes son ellas sobre el abismo del tiempo.

(But I don't write these words only,/I also write man, struggle, freedom./ The words are so close to us,/born so near to us,/that all our love would be meaningless,/it would lose its right to exist,/if we were not joined forever by them.//They are bridges across the chasm of time)

His leaving is inevitable and presented as the fulfilment of love; to learn love for the community and to renege on selfhood is the first and most significant act of transition to the guerrilla struggle.

> Me voy,
> pero no te preocupes
> si tardo un poco en el regreso.
> Un día en otoño me verás llegar
> De lejos, con polvo aún en los cabellos.

(I'm going,/but don't worry,/if it takes a while before I return./You'll see me coming one autumn day/from a distance you'll see me, the dust still in my hair)

Thus in what is Castillo's best poem, 'Vámonos patria a caminar' (Let us walk together, my country), the specific self gives way to the exemplary 'I'. The lyric mode gives way to the epic mode, wrenching form from nature, marching across the wastes and imprinting the human presence upon them. The lyric elegy gives way to the epic song and the personal love of young lovers yields to the love of the *guerrillero* for a new interlocutor – the 'patria'.

Para que los pasos no me lloren,
para que las palabras no me sangren,
    canto.
Para tu rostro fronterizo del alma
que me ha nacido entre las manos;
    canto.
Para decir que me has crecido clara
en los huesos más amargos de la voz;
    canto.
Para que nadie diga tierra mía,
con toda la decisión de la nostalgia:
    canto.
Por lo que no debe morir, tu pueblo:
    canto.

Me acompaña emocionado el sacrificio de ser hombre,
para que nunca baje al lugar donde nació la traicion
del vil que ató su corazon a la tiniebla, negándote . . .

(So that my steps should not weep/so that my words should not bleed,/I sing./For your frontier face of the soul/born in my hands/I sing./To say that you have grown clear and bright/in the most bitter bones of my voice/I sing./So that no one shall ever say, my country,/with all the decisiveness of nostalgia/I sing./For what should never die, your people/ I sing//The sacrifice of being a man fills me with emotion,/so that I shall never go down to the place where treason was born/the treason of the scoundrel that tied his heart to the darkness, denying you . . .)

The Nicaragua of Ernesto Cardenal

The Sandinista National Liberation Front (FSLN) has produced an unusually rich vein of poetry – indeed Nicaragua seems proportionally better endowed with poets than almost any other country in Latin America. Why this should be is a complex and difficult question, but the irony is that the answer almost certainly has to do with Nicaragua's backwardness. The extreme weakness of the Nicaraguan bourgeoisie, even in Central American terms; the failure of its attempt at national development under the brief regime of Zelaya (brought down in 1911); the persistence of impoverished and isolated peasant communities;[38] all these factors combined to produce a culture in which the oral traditions persisted side by side with the fragments of a metropolitan culture. No sense of the totality of things, of the nature of a wider world was available to provide the underpinnings of the novel; no autonomous past towards which the Nicaraguan bourgeoisie could look for an independent utopia. It was in that respect the most completely subaltern middle class whose best-known representative was buried in the subsidiary mythologies of other sectors of the bourgeoisie.

For those who followed Darío, as we have seen, that problem also proved to be the central unspoken drama of their work. How else to explain the breadth and individual power of Nicaragua's 'Vanguardia' group,[39] on the one hand, or on the other its characteristic but unusual immersion in popular culture. Pablo Antonio Cuadra and José Coronel Urtecho, for example, withdrew into a pre-social world in the search for origins, and sought it in the most recondite elements of speech and popular culture. Yet they took with them an extraordinarily eclectic range of forms and techniques, from the automatic writing to which Urtecho was sometimes devoted, to a close reading of Whitman, to a fascination with Apollinaire and his ideographic poems. Both Cuadra and Urtecho spoke of the need to create a 'tradition' or a 'cultural identity', but one that would necessarily be composed of fragments from elsewhere. This gathering of elements gave Nicaraguan poetry its inchoate and unpredictable character, its radical individuality in the very diversity of those who arbitrarily came together under the heading of 'Vanguardia'. Politically, their postures varied, though all were agreed it seemed on the necessity for a return to that pre-formed world, that world of primal sludge and cultural formlessness out of which through the ups and downs[40] a sense of self could perhaps be formed. Urtecho tried to draw on the ideas of Action Française and produce some corporate vision enshrined briefly in Somoza; Cuadra too was drawn briefly to that reactionary utopia though he resolved his posture in a radical individualism laced with nationalism. Alfonso Cortes, for his part, fell into madness in the late twenties and remained estranged from the world until his death in 1969.[41] His poetry is strange and disturbing, its classical forms belied by the refusal of its thoughts and concerns to be contained within any discipline.

> Un trozo azul tiene mayor
> intensidad que todo el cielo,
> yo siento que allí vive, a flor
> del éxtasis feliz, mi anhelo.
>
> Un viento de espíritus, pasa
> muy lejos, desde mi ventana,
> dando un aire en que despedaza
> su carne una angélica diana.

Y en la alegria de los Gestos
ebrios de azur, que se derraman . . .
¡siento bullir locos pretextos,
que estando aquí de allá me llaman!

(A piece of blue is more/intense than the whole sky,/I feel that there lives, on the surface/of an ecstasy of joy, my desire.//A wind of spirits, passes/far away, from my window/producing a wind in which the angelic fanfare/leaves its flesh behind.//And in the joy of Gestures/drunk with blue, that melt away . . ./I hear the bubbling of crazy pretexts/ which, though I am here, call to me from over there!)

The bizarre linguistic anarchy of the poem, its absence of any concrete reality and its immanent sense of place and time, make it strange and disturbing, as words and forms that seem recognizable here come apart in something close to lucid incoherence.

This variety of expression and concern was the most impressive feature of a poetic movement that produced a new generation of Nicaraguan poets, including Ernesto Cardenal.[42] Cardenal assimilated the range of elements in the work of his mentors, and took to heart Ezra Pound's injunction to let no form of language or expression be alien to poetry.[43] Most crucially Cardenal set his writing in the context of public utterance and progressively sought out the form of his writing in the structures of collective communication in their fullest diversity. He came to call it 'poesía exteriorista', a language of poetry already characterized by his contemporary Carlos Martínez Rivas as

> Poetry suddenly speaking the language of everyday life, accessible to the tram driver, the tradesman and the schoolgirl . . . Its simplicity is an effort against literature, of elaborate forms of expression . . . the genuine and sufficient poetry of the word bread, without wordplay, without subtlety, without metaphor . . .[44]

In the introduction to his anthology of Nicaraguan poetry,[45] Cardenal added his own definition of what 'exteriorista' poetry was, describing it as a peculiarly Nicaraguan poetic practice. The coincidence of views and responses to language among other poets outside Nicaragua, like Roque Dalton and Francisco Urondo among others, suggests that this diction is not so confined. What is certain is that it is developed and rich in the Nicaraguan tradition, and that Cardenal himself is almost certainly its most profound and vital representative. He described it as

> poetry created with the images of the outside world, the world we see

and touch . . . Exteriorismo is an objective poetry, narrative and anecdotal, composed of the elements of real life and with concrete things, with proper names and precise details and accurate data and figures and facts and popular sayings . . .[46]

There are two issues here; first, the recovery of a poetic diction still embedded in popular culture but lost from the poetic tradition. That diction is not simply the vernacular, the language of speech; it is in the fullest sense the language of collective experience, or rather the multiplicity of codes and symbolic systems through which ordinary people shape and define their lives. This is not to exclude vision or romance or emotion, of course; but it does reject the priority given in what Cardenal calls 'interiorista' poetry to a language of distance from everyday experience, and to a poetic language whose symbolic codes represent a disengagement from the varieties of social experience. That refinement and dehistoricizing of language is what Cardenal most specifically rejects. Similarly, his references to objectivity do not imply any absence of commitment, or solidarity or judgement. The rhetoric of Cardenal's poetry is shot through with denunciation and exposure, just as it evokes a different and better world in a language of prophecy and utopia. The 'objectivity' to which Cardenal refers is in contrast to 'subjectivity' – that the locus of the vision of the language is a collective experience, and the central voice a representative one. Even if there is an individuated spokesperson at its core, that person's vision is shared and recognizable, and connected linguistically and experientially with the collective.

This points in turn to the third component of exteriorismo – its historicism. As in Walt Whitman,[47] it is a central feature of Cardenal's poetry – and of all those within this framework of practice – that images and objects are enumerated in voluminous and rich array. They are not necessarily ordered or explained, nor is their relationship to one another necessarily logical or sequential. Yet this 'naming' of the world represents an act of discovery and appropriation, a writing of history. The richness and variety of image serves to name possibilities and potentialities, to point by enumeration and analogy to the enormous power lying hidden in the world. For so much of this world is hidden in the shadows.

Cardenal's wonderful 'Hora Cero' (Zero hour)[48] brilliantly illustrates this dynamic and vital process. Cardenal's previous work, *Epigramas*[49] was full of self-parody, quizzical explorations of the interweaving of adolescent love and political idealism.

Me contaron que estabas enamorada de otro
y entonces me fui a mi cuarto
y escribí este artículo contra el Gobierno
por el que estoy preso,

(They told me that you loved another/so I went to my room/and wrote an article denouncing the government/which has landed me here, in jail)

or

Uno se despierta con cañonazos
en la mañana llena de aviones.
Pareciera que fuera revolución:
pero es el cumpleaños del tirano.

(You wake to the sound of cannon/and the morning is full of aeroplanes./It sounds like a revolution;/actually, it is the tyrant's birthday)

But by the time he wrote 'Hora Cero', Cardenal had emerged from a long process of personal exploration and reassessment in America, where he was a member of the Gethsemane community directed by the outstanding North American poet Thomas Merton. In his two years of contemplative enclosure, Cardenal was not permitted to engage in creative writing, but he was able to set out his meditations on moral and religious questions later published as *Vida en el amor* (A life of love) (1970). These essays and explorations located Cardenal firmly within the radical reassessment of Catholic doctrine called the 'theology of liberation'. Here he established a direct analogy between communism and the Kingdom of God, saw the Christian obligation as centrally concerned with the struggle for social justice and for the definitive liberation of mankind, and assessed Christian witness to involve a self-denying commitment to the cause of the poor and the oppressed. It was those unequivocal testimonies that shaped and directed the life of Ernesto Cardenal thereafter, leading him eventually (to the great wrath of the incumbent Pope) to participation in the Sandinista government of Nicaragua as Minister of Culture.[50]

Returning to Nicaragua, Cardenal's *poetic* dilemma seemed also to have been resolved. His voice spoke now with the conviction of solidarity, and he issued the most forceful of condemnations. But he did so from the shadows where the alternative community, the hitherto voiceless one of the poor and oppressed, was to be found:

San Salvador bajo la noche y el espionaje
con cuchicheos en los hogares y pensiones
y gritos en las estaciones de policía.
El palacio de Carías apredreado por el pueblo.
Una ventana de su despacho ha sido quebrada,
y la policía ha disaparado contra el pueblo.
Y Managua apuntada por ametralladoras
desde el palacio de bizcocho de chocolate
y los cascos de acero patrullando las calles.

¡Centinela! ¿Qué hora es de la noche?
¡Centinela! ¿Qué hora es de la noche?

(San Salvador under the night and the spies/whisperings in cheap hotels
and student halls/and screams from the police stations./Carias's palace
is stoned by the people/A window in his office has been broken/and the
police have opened fire on the people./And Managua under the
machine-guns/pointing from the chocolate biscuit palace/and the steel
helmets patrolling the streets.//Watchman, what of the night?/Watch-
man, what of the night?)

This opening section of the poem provides a bitter commentary on
the history of a region so often subject to the whim of tyrants. But it
also contains a warning and a prophecy in the quotation from the Book
of Isaiah – for in the shadows is a silent waiting army, just outside the
glare of the searchlights sweeping the palaces. The Biblical analogy,
the insistence on the fact that these are 'palaces', reinforces the sense
of their fragility and of the temples under siege. The group in the
shadows is the central protagonist of all Cardenal's poetry; the exper-
ience is organized through their discourse, their revelation – it is the
voice of the community. The community has its past, its time of unity:

Los campesinos hondureños traían el dinero en el sombrero
cuando los campesinos sembraban sus siembras
y los hondureños eran dueños de sus tierras
Cuando había dinero
y no había empréstitos extranjeros . . .

(The Honduran peasants brought their money in their hats/when the
peasants sowed their own land/and the Hondurans owned their own
land/When there was money/and there were no foreign loans . . .)

But between that authentic past (and the issue is not one of whether it
had actual historical existence) and its re-establishment in the utopia
of the future, there intervenes a process of deprivation, loss of lan-
guage, loss of memory. The cacophony of the 'official language' steals

291

meaning and integrity from language itself, which becomes a closed and empty code.

> La United Fruit Company
> con sus revoluciones para la obtención de concesiones
> y exenciones de millones en impuestos de importaciones
> y exportaciones, revisiones de viejas concesiones
> y subvenciones para nuevas explotaciones,
> violaciones de contratos, violaciones
> de la Constitución . . .

> Corrompen la Prosa y corrompen el Congreso. . .

(The United Fruit Company/with its revolutions to obtain concessions/and exemptions of millions in import imposts/and exports, revisions of ancient concessions/subventions for new exploitation,/violations of contracts, violations/of the Constitution . . .//They corrupt the language like they corrupt the Congress . . .)

It is through that corrupted language that the story of Central America is told, with rage and bitterness. But with the second part of the poem comes an abrupt change of register; here the tone is prophetic and lyrical, corresponding to the visionary possibility enshrined in the central figure of Augusto César Sandino. It is clear that Sandino has the power here of a redeemer, and the incorruptibility of a Messiah:

> Había un nicaraguense en el extranjero
> un 'nica' de Niquinohomo . . .
> Y tenía economizados cinco mil dólares
> Y no era ni militar ni político

(There was a Nicaraguan abroad/a 'nica' from Niquinohomo . . ./And he had saved up 5000 dollars/and he was neither a soldier nor a politician)

Arriving in Nicaragua, Sandino finds the struggle has already been betrayed by Moncada:

> [Sandino] pasó tres días, triste, en el Cerro del Común,
> triste, sin saber que hacer.
> Y no era político ni militar.
> Pensó y pensó y se dijo por fin:
> Alguien tiene que ser.
>> Y entonces escribió su primer manifiesto.

([Sandino] spent three days, sadly, on the Common Mountain,/sad, not knowing what to do./He was neither politician nor soldier./He thought

and thought, and in the end he said to himself:/Someone has to do it/and
then he wrote his first political manifesto)

Sandino[51] waged a seven-year struggle against imperialism,
deserted by his erstwhile liberal allies and relying for the most part on
the peasantry and the workers of the Atlantic coast for his support.
When the US marines against whom he was fighting were finally
withdrawn from Nicaragua, in February 1933, Sandino renounced the
armed struggle and withdrew to Wiwili to establish an agricultural
cooperative. Recalled a year later to Managua, he was betrayed and
murdered; his death was organized by the man who initiated a forty-
three-year dynastic tyranny over Nicaragua with the vigorous and
consistent support of the United States who described him as 'a son of
a bitch but our son of a bitch'. Politically Sandino was an eclectic,
hostile to revolutionary socialism and drawn by the amalgam of
elements encapsulated in Aprismo. He was above all a revolutionary
nationalist; one, however, whose example rather than his ideas was
his most enduring inspiration. For Cardenal, Sandino is a contempor-
ary reincarnation of the Wandering Jew, the exile lost in the shadows
who represents a whole community in exile from its own world and its
own history. 'Hora Cero' thus fulfils a series of functions: a reincorpo-
ration of the past into the language of popular speech, and a rediscov-
ery of Sandino as national hero who crystallizes myths of both a
nationalist and a religious character. The symbolic code into which
Cardenal places Sandino is that of a revivified Catholicism whose
central theological tenets have been rewritten into a popular tradition,
removed from the realm of high culture and enshrined in this trans-
cendent metaphysical persona.

The third part of the poem describes utopia; it bears a remarkable
resemblance to Sandino's community at Wiwili, a community later to
be rediscovered in Cardenal's work in the Inca empire of Tahuantin-
suyu[52] and in the Cuba of the early sixties.[53] In this third part the cycle
of nature, and the implicit harmony between man and environment
represents the ideal state of equilibrium:

> En abril, en Nicaragua, los campos están secos.
> Es el mes de las quemas de los campos,
> del calor, y los potreros cubiertos de brasas,
> y los cerros que son de color de carbón . . .
>
> En mayo llegan las primeras lluvias.
> La hierba tierna renace de las cenizas.
> Los lodosos tractores roturan la tierra.
> Los caminos se llenan de mariposas y de charcos,

y las noches son frescas, y cargadas de insectos,
y llueve toda la noche. En mayo
florecen los malinches en las calles de Managua.
Pero abril en Nicaragua es el mes de la muerte.
En abril los mataron.

(In April, in Nicaragua, the fields are dry./It is the month of burning the fields,/of heat, and fields covered in bonfires,/and the mountains that are the colour of coal . . ./In May the first rains come./The young grass is reborn out of the ashes./The muddy tractors turn over the earth./The roads fill with butterflies and puddles,/the nights are cool and full of insects,/and it rains through the night. In May/the malinches flower in the streets of Managua./But April in Nicaragua is the month of death./ They killed them in April.)

The idyll is brutally interrupted, the cycle broken by violent death. Cardenal is here referring to the so-called April Conspiracy, a plot to kill Somoza which was betrayed. Many of the conspirators were subsequently brutally murdered. Cardenal himself was part of the conspiracy, but unlike his friend Adolfo Báez Bone, Cardenal escaped death when his hiding place remained undiscovered by Somoza's National Guard. Having previously devoted a lament to him, in 'Hora Cero' Cardenal absorbs Báez Bone into a pantheon of heroes and martyrs enshrined in the figure and the name of Sandino:

El pueblo no creía que había muerto
    (Y no había muerto).
Porque a veces nace un hombre en una tierra
    que es esa tierra.
Y la tierra en que es enterrado ese hombre
    es ese hombre.
Y los hombres que después nacen en esa tierra
    son ese hombre.
Y Adolfo Báez Bone era ese hombre.

La gloria no es la que enseñan los textos de historia:
es una zopilotera en un campo y un gran hedor

Pero cuando muere un heroe
    no se muere:
sino que ese heroe renace
    en una Nación.

(The people did not believe he had died/(And he had not died)./Because sometimes a man is born in a land/and he is that land./And the earth where that man is buried/is that man./And the men who are later born in the land/are that man./And Adolfo Báez Bone was that man.//Glory is not what the history textbooks talk about;/it is vultures circling above in a field and a terrible smell.//But when a hero dies/he does not die;/he is reborn/in a Nation.)

The nation is 'the thin man, the barefoot man, the man on the bicycle, the black man, the man with a long nose, the man in yellow . . .' – the anonymous crowd in the shadows. From his hiding place in this final part of the poem, the poet is a witness, delivering condemnations of this society and prophesying a world where the fragments will be reunited in one body, the alienation overcome in solidarity, the community that is the silent protagonist of history restored. If the world of Somoza is one where the terrors of technology combine to silence and terrorize the people of the shadows, the poem's language and form offer a voice to the silent community, rediscovered in the past and promised for the future, and the language is the utopian incantation of a future world, a kind of public meditation on the inevitability of future liberation.

For Cardenal, that redemption will be achieved in the social world and not in the hereafter:

> The kingdom of heaven is a kingdom – or as we should say nowadays a republic – that is, a social order. The kingdom of heaven is social, an ecclesia, a community, a spiritual marxism . . . It is a kingdom without subjects, a democratic kingdom . . .[54]

If the subject of this new world is the community, the language of that community is presaged in the poetry of Cardenal, which is also a democratic language, elaborating and enumerating the depth and variety of human experience, actual and potential; it is declamatory and prophetic. This is a narrative poetry in its sense of history, and a visionary language in its exploration of potentialities.

> The creator did not want us to be independent of one another and self-sufficient.

> The whole universe is a song, a song in chorus, a festive song, of the wedding feast . . . We are still in the darkness awaiting the bridegroom, but we already see the light far away and hear singing in the night.

Out of 'Hora Cero' arose the development of Cardenal's poetry and his political development through the subsequent two decades. His *Salmos* (Psalms) of 1965 evoke a militant god, a bitter and relentless opponent of oppression. It is the avenging god that speaks with the voice of a community still in exile, re-evoking the circumstances of the writing of the psalms which express that pain and isolation of a marginalized and persecuted minority. But here too the form is

295

profoundly significant – for the psalm is a collective incantation, chorally enacted, whose protagonist is the community of exiles.[55] The *Salmos* draw together the denunciation and the prophecy, and the deep alienation experienced by modern man in a world of technology that has wrenched him violently from his harmonious relationship with the earth.

> Escucha mis palabras oh Señor
> Oye mis gemidos
>
> Escucha mi protesta
> Porque no eres tú un Dios amigo de los dictadores
> ni partidario de su política
> ni te influencia la propaganda
> ni estás en sociedad con el gangster . . .
> Castígalos oh Dios
> malogra su política
> confunde sus memorándums
> impide sus programmas.
> . . .
> Al que no cree en la mentira de sus anuncios comerciales
> ni en sus campañas publicitarias ni en sus campañas políticas
> tú lo bendices
> Lo rodeas con tu amor
> como con tanques blindados.

(Hear my words oh Lord/Hear my sighs/Hear my protest/For you are not a God that is a friend to the dictators/nor are you a supporter of their politics/nor are you influenced by their propaganda/nor do you associate with gangsters . . ./Punish them oh Lord/destroy their policies/create confusion in their messages/block their programmes/. . ./To those who do not believe in the lies of their advertisements/nor in their publicity campaigns nor their political campaigns/to those give your blessing/ surround them with your love/as you would surround them with armoured cars).

Cardenal's appeal is to an avenging god intervening on behalf of a suffering people. But there are two registers here; of passive suffering and pain (Psalm 5) and of rage and resistance (Psalm 57) – 'El Dios que existe es el de los proletarios' (The God that exists is the God of the workers) is how it ends, challenging god to expose his class allegiances and place himself emphatically on the side of the oppressed and the exploited. The note of defiance and struggle becomes increasingly central and the warning to those who seek to stand back from that struggle is that they thus become accomplices to the crime. This is the message of two fine poems, 'Murder Inc' and 'Oración por Marilyn

Monroe'. Both focus on the tragic victims of repression and brutality; but both are also victims of the indifference of their fellow man. Monroe was found dead, with her hand on the telephone.

> Señor
> quienquiera que haya sido él que ella iba a llamer
> y no llamó (y tal vez no era nadie
> o era Alguien cuyo número no está en el directorio de Los Angeles)
> ¡contesta Tú el teléfono!

(Lord/whoever it was that she was going to call/and did not call (and perhaps it was no one/or it was Someone whose number is not in the Los Angeles Telephone Directory)/You answer the telephone!)

Cardenal's world does not admit of objectivity or indifference – there is no refuge from one's own humanity, except by losing it. That has been the hallmark of Cardenal's personal conduct; it is also the moral power of his poetry as well as its guiding aesthetic principle. There can be no separate language of poetry, just as there can be no separate realm of experience whose prevailing moral categories are different. There is for Cardenal no absolution from human responsibility, not for God or man. Thus the appeals and the revelations are firmly rooted in the language and reality of day-to-day experience; high moral issues, questions of theology, existential and psychological dilemmas and tensions are all resolved in the public arena, in the part of each of us that belongs in collective experience. If poetry is celebration, revelation or epiphany, it does not and cannot exist in a separate realm – for all of these are features of social existence. After the Nicaraguan Revolution of 1979, that was the continuing message Cardenal offered, for example, in his Letters to José Coronel Urtecho and to Monseñor Casaldáliga:

> Uno siente la soledad de ser sólo individuos.
> Tal vez mientras le escribo Usted ya fue condenado.
> Tal vez yo después estaré preso.
> Profeta allí donde se juntan el Araguaia y el Xingú
> y también poeta
>   Usted es voz de los que tienen esparadrapos en la boca.
> No es tiempo ahora de crítica literaria.
> Ni de atacar a los gorilas con poemas surrealistas.
> ¿para qué metáforas si la esclavitud no es metáfora
> ni es metáfora la muerte en el Río das mortes
> ni lo es el Escuadrón de la Muerte?

(One feels the solitude of being only an individual./Perhaps while I am writing to you you have already been condemned./Perhaps I will be imprisoned later./Prophet, where the Araguaia and the Xingú meet/and a poet too/you are the voice of those whose mouths are closed with tape./Now is not the time for literary criticism./Nor is it a time to attack the military with surrealist poems./Why metaphors when slavery is no metaphor/nor is death on the Rio das mortes/nor the Death Squads?)

This is Cardenal's clearest rejection of metaphor, of poetry that offers refuge or solace, an otherness in poetic language. Restating his doctrine of exteriorismo, Cardenal welcomes public speech and utterance into the frame of poetry, formally abandons the individuality of the poetic hero and assumes the mantle of a public poet, a crier of the collective cause, an exemplary speaker of the shared experience. At its heart is the concept of selflessness, of renunciation as the hallmark of commitment.

As Minister of Culture, Cardenal (through Mayta Jiménez[56]) advocated and espoused the poetry workshops which offered such exciting evidence of the potential creativity of every human being. Yet the criticism that emerged of the project addressed precisely the issue of selflessness, of the flattening of specific experience into a reiteration of the common in a language of extreme simplicity. What his critics claimed was that these very features of the shared public emotion concealed and suppressed the tension and conflict, the doubt and dilemma out of which growth and exploration was born. It was, in a word, in danger of becoming a new dogma and betraying the creative and critical assimilation of the social self that marked the finest political poetry. And here perhaps the work of Roque Dalton, poet and political leader of El Salvador, provided a powerful comparator.

Roque Dalton: Speaking Aloud

In a declaration of principles produced by the multiple authors he created to be his alter egos, Roque Dalton (1935–75)[57] made clear that

> the poet can only be to the bourgeoisie
> SERVANT
> CLOWN or
> ENEMY

It is clear that Dalton was unremittingly their enemy. The weapons that Dalton employed in his unstinting battle against the complacency of the bourgeoisie were irony and a language of denunciation and exposure rooted in the everyday. Dalton's contemporary, Ernesto Cardenal, identified what he called 'exteriorista' poetry, a poetry that was, in his words, 'impure', deriving from the range of daily experience and the language of speech. It was a vernacular quite distinct from the lyric terms of a subjectivist poetry of private refuge. For Dalton, the poet's obligation was to speak aloud, to make the common experience and the private experience accessible to a public that approached poetry collectively.[58] It was therefore the conditions of reception of the poetry, and not simply the intentions of its author, which made this 'conversational' poetry both new and revolutionary. It was revolutionary not in the sense that it spoke directly for the proletarian cause, but rather in that it overturned the isolation of culture, the gulf between vision and act, between the possibility of a world transformed and its realization.

> En la garganta de un beodo muerto
> se quedan las palabras que despreció la poesía.
>
> Yo las rescato con manos de fantasma
> con manos piadosas es decir
> ya que todo lo muerto tiene la licuada piedad
> de su propia experiencia.
>
> Furtivamente os las abandono:
> feas las caras sucias bajo el esplendor de las lámparas
> babeantes sobre su desnudez deforme
> los dientes y los parpados apartados esperando el bofetón
>
> amadlas también os digo. Reñid a la poesía
> la limpidez de su regazo.

(In the throat of a dead drunkard/the words that poetry scorned are left behind.//I rescue them with ghostly hands/that's to say with compassionate hands/for everything that's died has all the liquid pity/of its own experience.//I pass them on to you, furtively;/the dirty faces are ugly in the bright light of the streetlamps/they dribble over their deformed nakedness/they squeeze their teeth and eyelids anticipating a slap.//I say to you, love them too. Be critical of a poetry whose/apron is so clean.)

This is a manifesto for an impure poetry. The ugliness it calls on poets to recognize is not a lack of beauty, not deformity or horror, but the contradictory and painful experience of living people. Seeking the limpid beauty of the perfect image, the line of language denuded of that contact with the real is a betrayal both of the solidarity of which this poetry is an expression and a denial of the language that does have a history and a continuity not in art but in experience. That is its 'liquid pity', its compassion for the pain of those who 'expect a slap in the face' or whose 'faces are dirty under the streetlamp'. Earlier in the same collection Dalton asked '¿Para quién deberá ser la voz del poeta?' (Who should the voice of the poet be for?) 'La angustia existe./El hombre usa sus antiguos desastres como un espejo.' (Anguish does exist./Man uses his past disasters as a mirror.) That man has two faces; the frightened, lonely person for whom 'la cama es un sepulcro diario/ no tiene un cobre en el bolsillo/tiene hambre/solloza' (this bed is a daily tomb/he hasn't a penny in his pocket/he is hungry/he sobs). But the other face is visionary, the promise of redemption existing within the harsh reality of labour and exploitation:

> parten las piedras como frutas obstinadas en su solemnidad
> cantan desnudos en el cordial vaso del agua
> bromean con el mar lo toman jovialmente de los cuernos
> construyen en los páramos melodiosos hogares de la luz
> se embriagan como Dios anchamente
> establecen sus puños contra la desesperanza
> sus fuegos vengadores contra el crimen
> su amor de interminable raíces
> contra la atroz guadaña del odio.

(they break stones like obstinately solemn pieces of fruit/they sing naked in the cordial glass of water/they make jokes with the sea and grab it cheerfully by the horns/on the barren plains they build melodious homes full of light/they get drunk, like God, enthusiastically/they raise their fists against despair/build their fires of revenge against crime/set their love with its endless roots/against the awful Reaper and his scythe)

This is Roque Dalton the visionary, the humanist who recognizes in his poetry the creative potentiality that lies buried in the 'ugliness' of everyday living. Paradoxically, this is his version of beauty in art – the reconciliation of vision and reality. Sometimes Dalton's sense of irony, the absurdity of such a dream in the face of the appalling and brutal reality of his own country, El Salvador, must seem a kind of madness, as he converses with a madman whose vision is not unlike his own.

Me contaste que tu padre era un pequeño mar.

Que los angeles son unos estupidillos
pero por las noches hacen mucho daño con sus uñas de cola de cometa.

Me contaste que en tu casa la lluvia naufraga
y tus hermanas castran furiosas los almendros.
Me contaste que los sedientos son la gran esperanza.

(You told me that your father was a little ocean.//That angels are just stupid little people/but at night they do a lot of damage with their nails like comet's tails.//You told me that even the rain comes to grief in your house/and that your sisters furiously castrate the almond trees./You said that the thirsty are our great hope.)

There are several faces to the poetry of Dalton; but the overpowering sense is of his pained and enraged humanity. His own vulnerability, his joyful sensuality, the self-deluding romanticism of his youth are enshrined in a poetry of real sensual joy and gentle self-mockery. It is a note in his early work, and one that reappears when, having escaped from imprisonment in El Salvador, Dalton found himself in lengthy exile, wandering between Prague, Mexico and Havana. The prison experience is recorded in *Taberna y otros lugares* (A tavern and other places);[59] it is an emotional record of conviction and commitment. But it is also an experience of isolation, of internal exile, and of loss.

> Hoy cuando se mueren los amigos
> sólo mueren sus nombres.
>
> Cómo aspirar, desde el violento pozo,
> abarcar más que las tipografías,
> resplandor de negruras delicadas
> flechas hasta las íntimas memorias?

(Today when your friends die/it is only their names that die.//How can we aspire, from the violent dungeon,/to embrace any more than the letters on the page,/the brilliance of delicate blackness/arrows that point to our most intimate memories?)

What is most moving about this and Dalton's other poetry is the honesty and directness, not just of its language, which never conceals emotion or confusion behind deceit, but of its personal quality. The abstraction does not figure in his gentle ironies; the generality of politics appears only as a sardonic counterpoint to the limitations within which individuals must work. Yet it is those very limitations which confirm Dalton's profound idealism; what makes his human beings heroic is not their distinction from their fellows, but rather their typicality, their representative vulnerability. He reserves his scorn for the bourgeois and the petty bourgeois, like the 'Mecanógrafo' (The typist) who looks neither to left nor right but seeks only the means to evade his social self or the collective responsibility that that entails. Indeed it seems only the poorest and the least powerful who are the bearers of the force and power of history – even when they do not see themselves in such grand terms. 'La segura mano de Dioś' (The sure hand of God) illustrates the point. The instrument of collective revenge against the old military dictator Hernández Martínez is a burglar surprised in the act of theft who strikes out blindly against the elderly proprietor of the house he is stealing from. He does not know him at all. Yet he is the avenger on behalf of the tens of thousands of equally anonymous individuals who suffered and died at the hands of the bloody scourge of the 1932 peasants uprising;[60] they are the vanguard of history. For history works *through* this archetypal victim, and he joins the ranks of those many nameless figures in the landscape of Dalton's country.

> Phillips O'Mannion los ojos y el recuerdo llenos de su Irlanda natal
> murió ayer en la calle las manos crispadas junto al pecho
> sin pronunciar una palabra
> sin alarmar a nadie
> como quien paga por la vida poco precio
>
> Al estarle enterrando se rompieron las cuerdas
> y el féretro cayó de golpe saltándose la tosca tapa de pino
>
> Su compañera – los labios despintados –
> le echó el primer puñado de tierra directamente en el rostro

(Phillips O'Mannion his eyes and memory full of his native Ireland/died yesterday in the street his hands stiff across his chest/without saying a word/and without alarming anyone/like someone who pays a low price for his life//When they were burying him the ropes broke/and the coffin fell abruptly, bursting open the crude pine lid//His lover, her lipstick smudged,/threw the first handful of earth into his face).

Figures like this are in some sense the public envisaged in Dalton's poetry, when he counsels against an excess of abstract vision. The poet's task is to 'examine the present' and 'raise to the category of poetry the contradictions, disasters, defects, customs and struggles of today's society'. This is not to say that Dalton advocates a poetry without vision, without the conviction of redemption – though he is gently ironic about his own youthful idealization of the actuality of struggle, of its heroic grandeur in 'Buscándome lios' (Looking for trouble):

> La noche de mi primera reunión de célula llovía
> mi manera de chorrear fue muy aplaudida por cuatro
> o cinco personajes del dominio de Goya
> todo el mundo ahí parecía levemente aburrido
> tal vez de la persecución y hasta de la tortura diariamente soñada.

Fundadores de confederaciones y de huelgas mostraban
cierta ronquera y me dijeron que debía
escoger un seudónimo
que me iba a tocar pagar cinco pesos al mes
que quedábamos en todos los miércoles
y que cómo iban mis estudios
y que por hoy íbamos a leer un folleto de Lenin
y que no era necesario decir a cada momento camarada.

Cuando salimos no llovía más
mi madre me riñó por llegar tarde a casa.

(The night of my first cell meeting it was raining/and the way the rain ran off me won me the applause of four/or five figures straight out of Goya/everyone there seemed slightly bored/perhaps with the persecution and the torture they thought about every day.//Founders of confederations and leaders of strikes were/a little hoarse and they said I should choose/a pseudonym/that I would have to pay five pesos a month/that we'd agreed to meet on Wednesdays/and how were my studies going/and today we were going to read one of Lenin's pamphlets/and that it wasn't necessary to say comrade all the time.//By the time we came out it wasn't raining any more/and mother told me off for being home late.)

But there is another purpose at work here, which connects Dalton's revolutionary commitment with his poetic strategies. As a poet he has set out to demystify the act of poetry, to seek its roots in the contingencies of everyday life, to see the noble acts of historical transformation in the anti-heroic mode of the struggles for everyday survival. His characteristic self-mockery is also a critical riposte to the exclusively abstract grand mode of Neruda et al. It is in that sense that Dalton's work can find roots and sources in the resolutely anti-revolutionary work of Nicanor Parra. Dalton's constant references to 'ugliness' and 'dirt' are reminders of a literary practice whose object, like Mayakovsky's, is 'to pull the republic out of the mud', and is prepared to risk immersion in the swamp too. Discarding over and over again the conceptual and elevated aestheticism of his conservative precursors, Dalton's task *as a poet* is to mobilize and move his public to a consciousness of the action it is already engaged in.

In that sense, Dalton's is not a party literature (as John Beverley suggests in an excellent essay[61]) but an authentic revolutionary poetry whose protagonist is the revolutionary subject itself, the working class, and whose form and language have their source in the actual and potential experience of that subject.The consequence is a poetry prosaic in its eschewing of a specific language of poetry and anti-heroic in its critique of the hero who acts *on behalf of* the masses.

Increasingly his emphasis on his own contingency, his own imperfection is the very basis of his representativity. Yet it is also a challenge to other political and philosophical traditions.

The guerrilla poets of the sixties reproduced a vision of revolutionary change derived directly from the concept of 'Guevarism'. At its heart the exemplary self-sacrifice of the revolutionary stood as surrogate for an inactive mass – though the sacrifice was given in their name. Enclosed in imprisoning structures of social organization and culture, the masses were unable to act, and the spurned and derided bourgeoisie was too cowardly and dependent upon its imperialist masters to act independently. Into this breach stepped the heroic guerrilla, breaking the paralysis and acting on behalf of the society as a whole. This vision of the *guerrillero* as the embodiment of the revolutionary will infused the guerrilla poetry of the revolutionary generation of the sixties, Heraud, Castillo, Gordillo, etc. Their courage and self-denial are beyond question; most of these poets died in demonstration of their unswerving conviction. Yet their sacrifice alone did not produce mass action, only an expanded gallery of martyrs to fuel the demonology of repression and death.

There can be little doubt that Dalton's poetry carries a critique of this absence of the collective, of this substitution of revolutionary will for a mass movement. Later that debate would explode in the organization which he had formed and led and result in his tragic and wasteful death at the hands of his own comrades.[62] But there was another level of critique implicit in his writing too; a rejection of a mechanical and deterministic vision of the process of change towards socialism. Love, sensibility, a different pattern of human relations both individual and collective were the objective of this struggle:

> A quienes te digan que nuestro amor es extraordinario
> porque ha nacido de circunstancias extraordinarias
> díles que precisamente luchamos
> para que un amor como el nuestro
> (amor entre compañeros de combate)
> llegue a ser en El Salvador,
> el amor más comun y corriente,
> casi el único.

(When people say that our love is extraordinary/because it was born out of extraordinary circumstances/tell them we are fighting precisely/so that a love like ours/(the love of comrades in the struggle)/becomes in El Salvador/the most common kind of love/almost the only kind.)

At the level of both politics and culture, Dalton's poetry therefore addresses two different traditions: the petty bourgeois individualism of the lyric poet, and the rigidities of Stalinism. What they have in common is their exclusion from the process of creative transformation. What is called 'conversational poetry' – though the concept of a 'democratic' poetry seems preferable – locates the collective at the heart of poetic language. This means recuperating the traditions of popular culture, the patterns and rhythms of speech, the alternative history told in the oral myth, and moulding the redemptive revolutionary vision out of the material of everyday life. The process is not reductive, but expansive. It is also deeply problematic.

Despite Dalton's frequent professions of his dedication to the generation of such a language and such a form, he never resolved entirely his own contradictions. That is of course to be expected. Yet his work as a poet did generate 'a new kind of revolutionary sensibility'; further, Dalton began to write the history of that sensibility, in his history of El Salvador[63] and his recording of the experiences of *Miguel Mármol*,[64] both of which represent an activity in what might be called 'political archaeology' – the rediscovery and recuperation of a hidden history, a repressed voice accustomed to expression only in ironic and indirect form and now given form and location in an insurgent culture.

It is in this sense that John Beverley can see in Dalton and Ernesto Cardenal the process of creation of a 'national-popular culture' and its instrument in a new poetry of the vernacular. What is significant is that in this new culture poetry is not only no longer a marginal and esoteric form; it becomes the privileged mode of expression, drawing together in a single form the oral culture, speech, the daily documents of public language in all its manifestations, and the music and words of popular song. The centrality of rhythm and rhetoric (as opposed to image and metaphor) *relocates* poetry in the public discourse, seeks to regenerate the shared language of collective experience and to reunite the popular creative imagination (enshrined as Dalton and Cardenal among others have shown in the secret history of their countries) and the act of social transformation which is the highest cultural expression – revolution as the *festival* of the oppressed.

305

9

Voices from the Silence:
Poetry and Dictatorship in Brazil

The Refuge of Postmodernism

In January 1968, exponents of Poema Processo, the last of Brazil's self-consciously avant-garde movements, publicly announced the 'end of literature' when, on the steps of Rio's Municipal Theatre, they tore up texts by those authors considered representative of the poetic establishment, such as Drummond and Cabral. The statement marked a logical extension and completion of the Concretist project, which had itself entered its third, 'semiotic' phase in 1964, and signified the final repudiation of discursive, verbal poetic language in favour of a disposable, object-poetry of performance and immediate consumption. In December of the same year, in the wake of a strike wave and widespread political protest against the dictatorship, General Costa e Silva shut down the Federal Congress, issued the Ato Institucional No.5, suspending habeas corpus for political detainees, and began the systematic use of censorship, torture and political assassination.

These events were not unconnected. In fact they marked the convergence of developments within Brazilian poetry and politics whose common objective was the silencing of private and public voices that sought to express interests and experiences incompatible with the new orthodoxies of cultural and economic 'development'.

The military takeover of 1964 had put paid to the popular-nationalist aspirations of a radical sector of the bourgeoisie and its allies within the labour and popular movements. It imposed an alternative strategy for Brazilian capitalism – its complete integration into the world economy. However, the first few years of the dictatorship were occupied primarily with the consolidation of the regime and, although

307

they saw a drastic strengthening of presidential powers, the abolition of existing political parties, the imprisonment of key trade-union activists and the annulment of the political rights of over four and a half thousand individuals, certain pseudo-democratic mechanisms were retained, such as proportional elections and an official opposition party.

During this period, the cultural avant garde and the intellectual protest movement centred in the universities were permitted to continue their activities relatively unimpeded. Nevertheless, the failure of Concretismo and the Popular Culture Centres to engage their imagined audiences in any meaningful dialogue, added to the initial measures of the regime, meant that this movement was already cut off from any wider social base amongst the general population. That isolation was reflected in the Concretists' deepening excursions into experimentation with the manipulation of verbal 'codes' and images, and the complete abandonment of any critical questioning of the capitalist discourse of development.

This begs the question of why, throughout the years of the dictatorship and even today, the Concretist project has continued to exercise such a powerful influence on successive generations of poets, including the Tropicalistas of 1967/8, the group surrounding Paulo Leminski (1945–90) in the southern state capital of Curitiba, and younger artists such as Eduardo Kac who since 1983 has been pioneering the development of three-dimensional 'holo-poems' using the new technology.[1] A clue to the explanation can be found in Augusto de Campos's 'Póstudo' (Posteverything), which rekindled the flames of the debate when it was published in January 1985:

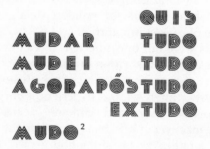

(I WANTED/TO CHANGE EVERYTHING/I CHANGED EVERYTHING/
NOWPOSTEVERYTHING/EXEVERYTHING [I STUDY]/I CHANGE [(I AM) SILENT])

Soon after its appearance the poem was subjected to a minute and exhaustive analysis by Roberto Schwarz.[3] Amongst other things, Schwarz unmasked the vacuous pretension of its subject's claim to the definitive act of transformation, to have had, literally, the 'last word' on an all-encompassing, monumentally abstract and ultimately meaningless 'everything'; empirical reality had been suppressed, and the act of transformation reduced to an aimless ritual of change for change's sake, reflecting once again the blind cycles of capitalist development.

But it is one thing to deconstruct and expose the superficial radicalism of the formalist avant-garde project, and another to explain its longevity and continued acceptance amongst such a broad layer of the cultural community in Brazil. Concretismo threw up a formidable challenge to the discursive and figurative tradition within Brazilian Modernism, that much is undeniable. But just as important, in claiming so arrogantly and aggressively to have superseded that tradition it struck a local chord with the international mood of apocalyptic agnosticism and aestheticism which came to be known in the 1980s as Postmodernism. The key features typically attributed to the Postmodern aesthetic found an unmistakeable echo in the theoretical language of Concretismo: the idea, taken over from semiotics and poststructuralist philosophy, of simulation, our inability to talk of a world independent of our representations of it, to distinguish between some elusive and perhaps non-existent 'basic reality' and its image; consequent upon this, the sensation of schizophrenia and the abolition of the coherent individual subject; the loss of interpretative depth, of reliable points of ideological reference, the collapse of the Grand Narratives of historical analysis, indeed the 'end of history' itself; the fondness instead for montage and collage, the assemblage of fragments from different discourses and media, for pastiche and the endless recycling of infinite styles, and the self-reflexive, self-conscious nature of aesthetic activity, by which the form and process of artistic production become the subject of the work itself.[4]

However, as Alex Callinicos has shown, although couched in a superficially new philosophical language, these are all essentially motifs common to the mainstream of Western Modernism of the first half of the century, or even to the Romantic critiques of the Enlightenment project which emerged in response to the experience of capitalist industrialization.[5] Ironically, by appropriating those Modernist motifs in order to justify what they claim to be a radical historical break, denoted by the prefix 'post', those who defend the idea of a distinctive Postmodernist aesthetic have betrayed instead its continuity with the

Modernist tradition. In a parallel and contradictory manner, the Concretists have repeatedly pointed to Modernist 'precursors' of their own project, such as Oswald de Andrade, while claiming to have broken with tradition and to have 'changed everything'.

If there is something distinctive about this latest phase of Modernism, inside Brazil and beyond, it is what Fredric Jameson has termed 'the waning of affect',[6] or the loss of the radical impact of avant-garde art in the post-war period, its growing inability to shock; and, at least in part a explanation for this change, its ideological pessimism and political conservatism, its abandonment of any belief in the possibility of a radical, let alone revolutionary, transformation of society. The most enthusiastic advocates of the Postmodernist culture, as well as those more critical observers like Jameson, for whom Postmodernism is nevertheless an inescapable 'cultural dominant' forcing one to suspend ideological judgement or moral denunciation,[7] have grounded their descriptions of these and the other features of the new culture in an analysis of what they perceive to be a moment of fundamental social and economic change. Whether it is the post-Fordism of *Marxism Today*'s 'New Times',[8] or Jameson's Third Machine Age, the era of 'multinational capital', the common features of the analysis are the replacement of the classical pattern of capitalist commodity production by an economy typified by the new computer and media technology, in which the *re*production of information and images predominates; and, related to this, the blurring of the traditional categories of social class and the emergence instead of a whole range of specifically targeted consumer groups democratically circulating and participating in this market of image-commodities, whose interest resides not in their use-value but in their stylistic connotation. Again, one is reminded strikingly of the Concretists' vision of a post-utopian world of consumers and poem-commodities (see Chapter 7).

Acceptance of this description of late-twentieth-century society is possible only by wilfully ignoring the emergence and expansion of massive new centres of manufacturing production around the world, not least in Brazil itself (the basic material demands of human beings for food, housing and transport not having diminished); the real impact which successive crises in this increasingly integrated global economy since the end of the long post-war boom have had on the societies of both the developed and developing world, where exposure to a proliferating wealth of media images has served to underline the deepening material impoverishment of the majority and their exclusion from many areas of the consumer market; and the rise since the late 1970s of new labour movements based on the proletariats of the newly industrializing countries, amongst them the CUT trade-union federation and Workers' Party of Brazil.[9]

If such realities are absent from most descriptions of the Postmodern age, then perhaps, as Callinicos argues, it is because Postmodernism is not in fact the dominant cultural logic of the late twentieth century, but rather the ideological expression of a specific political subject, the 'children of Marx and Coca Cola'.[10] The apologists of Postmodernism are, in the first place, typically members of a social layer – the newly expanded salaried middle class of professionals and managers, recognizable by their 'overconsumptionist' lifestyle – which benefited from the boom periods of the 1970s and '80s, whilst being cushioned from the worst effects of recession. Secondly, they are characteristically drawn from that generation of intellectuals radicalized and often won to revolutionary politics by the period of international turmoil which in Europe culminated in the May–June 1968 events of France, the general strike and student occupations, but which also embraced the Vietnam War, the American and Northern Irish civil rights movements, the Portuguese Revolution of 1974-75, the Soviet invasion of Czechoslovakia, the last of the national liberation struggles in Africa, and the guerrilla movements of Latin America, Brazil included. In the absence of any thoroughgoing socialist revolution in the wake of this political upturn, faced with the spectacle of retreat and even brutal military repression in the cases of Brazil and Chile, as Western capitalism reasserted its self-confidence, and lacking any ideological or organizational means of coming to terms with this defeat, most of this disillusioned generation of 1968 took refuge in the prosperity afforded by professional and managerial careers, in the politics of social democracy, and in the inward-looking aestheticism of Postmodernism.

If such was the trajectory of many European and North American intellectuals, in Brazil the scale of the defeat and ensuing repression following the 'phoney war' of 1964–68 left even fewer options open to the radicals of the post-war avant-garde and Street Guitar movements. The 1968 'coup within the coup' ushered in a quite different political and cultural atmosphere riven with ambiguities and contradictions. The new repressive measures which became the hallmark of the Médici presidency were designed to ensure favourable conditions for a second wave of industrial growth based on massive multinational investment. This was the period of Brazil's 'economic miracle' when cheap oil, a burgeoning transport and power infrastructure and new

311

engineering and manufacturing industries supported a booming export market and growth rates in double figures. Direct physical repression was the key to containing working-class resistance to the brutal exploitation on which the miracle depended, and which saw the real value of the minimum wage fall by 25 per cent between 1963 and 1973. A basis of political consensus was meanwhile cultivated amongst an increasingly affluent middle class, which supplied the regime with its managerial and technical staff and which was rewarded with access to the new consumer market.

The cultural policy of the dictatorship reflected this two-pronged strategy, combining a modernization and expansion of those mass media industries which offered the greatest potential for social control, such as television and cinema, with selective censorship of individual works and artists.[11] Thus,

> During the period '64–80 censorship is defined not so much by a veto on all and any kind of cultural product, but acts primarily as a selective repression which makes impossible the emergence of certain types of thought or artistic works. Plays, films, books are censored, but not the theatre, the cinema or the publishing industry. The repressive act affects the specificity of the work but not the generality of its production.[12]

The grotesque contradictions of the Miracle, therefore, were manifested in a deepening gulf between the working-class victims of the economic boom and its middle-class beneficiaries, in particular its intellectual and cultural left wing. Outright repression and censorship existed alongside the newly expanded but highly controlled cultural arena centred on the public spectacle with access to a subjugated mass audience. Given these conditions, and the paralysis of any organized mass challenge to the regime, the appeal of the formalist project during subsequent years is more comprehensible as a 'postmodernist' alternative to social and political marginalization from the new cultural environment of the Miracle. Students of Concretism typically found careers in advertising and the media, where the manipulation of sign and image could be put to the service of commercial gain. Interestingly enough, parallels can be found amongst the erstwhile poets of Street Guitar; Affonso Romano de Sant'Anna, for example, has combined an academic career pioneering structuralist approaches to Brazilian literary criticism, with poetry commissions for football and motor-racing videos sponsored by the Globo network, and collaborations on similar projects with Citibank, Embratel and IBM.[13]

The Tropicalist Euphoria

However, these were by no means the most significant responses in poetry to the experience of the Economic Miracle and the years of uninterrupted crisis which followed. It was the explosion of a new wave in popular music, Tropicalismo or Tropicália, which first confronted the nightmarish carnival of a modernization carried out at the point of a bayonet, yet dared to do so with humour and spontaneity, unworried by theoretical debates about formalist aesthetics or revolutionary popular culture. As early as 1967, the Northeastern singer and songwriter Caetano Veloso (b. 1942) had greeted the bewildering kaleidoscope of the international urban landscape with his award-winning 'Alegria, Alegria' (Joy, Joy). Stripped of all that might tie him to any previous cultural identity, the song was his only guide through this fragmented world of infinite possibilities:

> caminhando contra o vento
> sem lenço sem documento
> no sol de quase dezembro
> eu vou
>
> o sol se reparte em crimes
> espaçonaves guerrilhas
> em cardinales bonitas
> eu vou
>
> em caras de presidentes
> em grandes beijos de amor
> em dentes pernas bandeiras
> bomba e brigitte bardot
>
> o sol nas bancas de revista
> me enche de alegria e preguiça
> quem lê tanta notícia?
> eu vou
>
> . . .
>
> por entre fotos e nomes
> sem livros e sem fuzil
> sem fome sem telefone
> no coração do brasil
> ela nem sabe até pensei
> em cantar na televisão
> o sol é tão bonito
> eu vou
>
> sem lenço sem documento

313

nada no bolso ou nas mãos
eu quero seguir vivendo
amor
eu vou
por que não? por que não?[14]

(walking into the wind/without a handkerchief without my papers/in
the nearly midsummer sun/I go//The sun scatters into crimes/spaceships
guerrilla wars/into lovely scarlet lobelias/I go//into faces of presidents/
into great kisses of love/into teeth legs flags/bombs and brigitte bardot//
the sun on the magazine stands/fills me with joy and laziness/who reads
all that news?/I go//. . ./through photos and names/without books with-
out a rifle/without hunger without a telephone/in the heart of brazil/she
doesn't even know I even thought/of singing on the TV/the sun is so
lovely/I go//without a handkerchief without my papers/nothing in my
pockets or in my hands/I want to go on living/love/I go/why not? why
not?)

With the launch of the Tropicália movement in 1968, following the
release of the collaborative album *Tropicália ou Panis et Circensis*, a
collective expression was found for this ambiguous celebration of the
new order. Abandoning the restrained sophistication and intimacy of
Bossa Nova, the Tropicalistas instead uninhibitedly embraced the
instrumental sound and style of international commercial rock music.
They forced Brazilian popular music and poetry out of the isolation of
the clubs, universities and Popular Culture Centres literally into the
public arena of the concert hall and television screen and into the mass
market of the recording industry. Appropriately enough, it was the
spectacle of Carnival, so often exploited propagandistically by the
regime as a popular endorsement of the Miracle, which provided the
typical metaphorical setting for this rediscovery of the Modernist
melting-pot of cultural contradictions. Consider Torquato Neto's
'Geléia Geral', the 'total Brazilian Jam, announced in the National
Daily' beneath a joyful tropical sun, or Caetano Veloso's 'Tropicália',
for example,

> Sobre a cabeça os aviões,
> sob os meus pés os caminhões,
> aponta contra os chapadões
> meu nariz.
> Eu organizo o movimento,
> eu oriento o carnaval,
> eu inauguro o monumento
> no planalto central
> do país.

314

Viva a bossa-sa-sa
viva a palhoça–ça-ça-ça-ça.[15]

(Aeroplanes overhead,/lorries beneath my feet,/my nose/points towards the table-land./I organize the movement,/I steer the carnival,/I inaugurate the monument/on the central plateau/of the country./Long live the new wave-ave-ave/long live the thatched hut-hut-hut-hut-hut.)

Nevertheless, this depiction of the Brazilian Carnival hardly confirmed the image of social harmony and wellbeing, free from contradictions, that was being projected by the dictatorship. Instead these lyrics juxtaposed symbols of modernity and underdevelopment, primitive tradition and multinational technology, in an undifferentiated mélange, whose simultaneous effect of parody and kitsch was more than reminiscent of the poetry and manifestos of Oswald de Andrade:

> é a mesma dança na sala, no Canecão, na TV
> e quem não dança não fala
> assiste a tudo e se cala.
> Não vê no meio da sala
> as relíquias do Brasil:
> doce mulata malvada,
> um elepê de Sinatra,
> maracujá, mês de abril,
> santo barroco baiano,
> superpoder de paisano.

(it's the same dance in your front-room, on the stage of the Canecão, on the TV/and anyone who doesn't dance can't speak/they watch it all and keep quiet./They don't see in the middle of the room/the treasures of Brazil:/a sweet wicked mulatto girl, a Sinatra LP,/passion-fruit, the month of April,/a Baroque saint from Bahia,/a superpower in plain clothes.)

Brasília, the 'monument on the central plateau' which was the centre of the regime's operations and the symbol of its power and success, sheltered in its shadows a more sinister reality:

> o monumento não tem porta
> a entrada é uma rua antiga estreita e torta
> e no joelho uma criança sorridente feia e morta
> estende a mão

(the monument has no gate/the entrance is an old narrow and twisted street/and on its knee a smiling child ugly and dead/stretches out its hand).

The parallels with the *Brazil-wood Poetry* and *Cannibalist Manifestos*

315

were not lost on the Concretists. In 1967 Augusto de Campos had introduced Caetano Veloso to their own work and that of Oswald de Andrade, whose play *O Rei da Vela* (The candle king) was staged in the same year by the Teatro Oficina (Workshop Theatre) as part of a radical revival of the cannibalist aesthetic. The Concretists' paternalist adoption of the Tropicalist cause as yet another means of giving social legitimation to their formalist project, achieved a degree of success. The Tropicalistas even incorporated some of the innovations of the post-war avant-garde tradition into their lyrics. Gilberto Gil and Caetano Veloso's 'Batmacumba', for instance, depicted graphically the shape of a bat to produce a fusion of 'Batman' and 'macumba', the symbols of a globalized American mass culture and the rhythms and mysticism of Afro-Brazilian religion:

> batmacumbaieiê batmacumbaobá
> batmacumbaieiê batmacumbao
> batmacumbaieiê batmacumba
> batmacumbaieiê batmacum
> batmacumbaieiê batman
> batmacumbaieiê bat
> batmacumbaieiê ba
> batmacumbaieiê
> batmacumbaie
> batmacumba
> batmacum
> batman
> bat
> ba
> bat
> batman
> batmacum
> batmacumba
> batmacumbaie
> batmacumbaieiê
> batmacumbaieiê ba
> batmacumbaieiê bat
> batmacumbaieiê batman
> batmacumbaieiê batmacum
> batmacumbaieiê batmacumba
> batmacumbaieiê batmacumbao
> batmacumbaieiê batmacumbaobá[16]

The Tropicalistas' refusal to adopt any clear ideological position at this stage, indeed their uninhibited acceptance of the multinational culture as a progressive advance on a national tradition which had

316

tended to folklorize the country's underdevelopment, certainly seemed to echo the Concretists. Those who had been involved in the activities of the Popular Culture Centres and the student struggles of the National Students' Union, closed by the regime in 1965, now found themselves marginalized from these cultural developments and could do no more than criticize from the sidelines. Meanwhile, songwriters such as Chico Buarque de Hollanda (b. 1944) who both dared to register a sense of loss at the rupture with the national cultural tradition and to voice less ambiguous fears about the social implications of the process, found themselves branded reactionaries by both camps. Chico Buarque's 'Essa moça tá diferente' (That girl's changed), from a 1970 album, recorded the alienation felt by one attached to the 'old-fashioned' samba tradition, and whose lover (and audience) had, with a touch of insincerity, updated their tastes:

> Essa moça tá diferente
> Já não me conhece mais
> Está pra lá de pra frente
> Está me passando pra trás
>
> Essa moça tá decidida
> A se supermodernizar
> Ela só samba escondida
> Que é para ninguém reparar
>
> Eu cultivo rosas e rimas
> Achando que é muito bom
> Ela me olha de cima
> E vai desinventar o som
>
> Faço-lhe um concerto de flauta
> E não lhe desperto emoção
> Ela quer ver o astronauta
> Descer na Televisão[17]

(That girl's changed/She don't know me no more/She's way out ahead/ She's leaving me behind//That girl's made up her mind/To get ultra-up-to-date/She only dances samba in secret/So's no one will see//I grow roses and rhymes/And reckon it's pretty good/She looks down on me/ And goes and disinvents the sound//I play the flute for her/And don't move her at all/She just wants to see the astronaut/Landing on the TV)

Chico Buarque's 'Construção' (Construction), meanwhile, from the following year, depicted a drama symbolic of the paradox of development – the building-worker as the victim of modernization, who falls from the scaffolding into the street and dies 'na contramão atrapalhando o tráfego/o público/o Sábado' (in the wrong lane holding up the traffic/the public/that Saturday). In a formal approach that suggests certain affinities with the technique of Poesia-Praxis, Chico Buarque used here a reiterative structure based on anaphora and a repertoire of interchangeable complementary terms. Rising to a climax swept along by the dissonant crescendo of the orchestral backing, the composition gave a new intensity to this ironic drama of the reification and ritualization of human life and the tragic inevitability of death under such conditions:

> Amou daquela vez como se fosse a última/ o último/ máquina
> Beijou sua mulher como se fosse a última/ a única
> E cada filho seu como se fosse o único/ o pródigo
> E atravessou a rua com seu passo tímido/ bêbado
>
> Subiu a construção como se fosse máquina/ sólido
> Ergueu no patamar quatro paredes sólidas/ mágicas/ flácidas
> Tijolo com tijolo num desenho mágico/ lógico
> Seus olhos embotados de cimento e lágrima/ tráfego
> Sentou pra descansar como se fosse sábado/ um príncipe/ um pássaro
> Comeu feijão com arroz como se fosse príncipe/ o máximo
> Bebeu e soluçou como se fosse um náufrago/ máquina
> Dançou e gargalhou como se ouvisse (fosse) música/ o próximo
>
> E tropeçou no céu como se fosse (ouvisse) um bêbado/ música
> E flutuou no ar como se fosse um pássaro/ sábado
> E se acabou no chão feito um pacote flácido/ tímido/ bêbado
> Agonizou no meio do passeio público/ náufrago
>
> Morreu na contramão atrapalhando o tráfego/ público/ sábado[18]

(He made love that time as if it were the last/as if he were the last/as if he were a machine/He kissed his wife as if she were the last/the only one/ And each of his sons as if they were the last/the prodigal son/And crossed the street with his timid/drunken walk//He climbed the building as if it were a machine/solid/He erected on the platform four solid/ magical/flaccid walls/Brick by brick in a magical/logical design/His eyes dulled with cement and tears/traffic/He sat down to rest as if it were Saturday/as if he were a prince/a bird/He ate his beans and rice as if he were a prince/the greatest/He drank and sobbed as if he were ship-wrecked/a machine/He danced and laughed out loud as if he could hear music/as if he were the next//And stumbled in the sky as if he were a drunk/as if he could hear music/And floated in the air as if he were a bird/as if it were Saturday/And came to grief on the ground like a flaccid/ timid/drunk parcel/He breathed his last in the middle of the promenade/ shipwreck.//He died in the wrong lane holding up the traffic/the public/ that Saturday)

It has been argued that the Tropicalistas' posture of cultural canni-
balism (like that of Oswald de Andrade in his time) actually mirrored
the economic policy of the 1964 government and its planning minister
Roberto Campos, in its commitment to the project of import-substitu-
tion via the manufacture of modern export commodities.[19] Yet lyrics
such as those discussed above indicate just how precarious was the
ideological 'neutrality' briefly sustained by Tropicalismo. It was cir-
cumscribed on the one hand by the commercial conditions imposed by
a state-dominated recording and television industry, and on the other
by the international political atmosphere of 1968 and its revolutionary
challenge to the prevailing order. Despite its initial rejection of any
form of political commitment, the movement's carnivalesque libertar-
ianism, its parodic irreverence and unprejudiced openness to all
stylistic and thematic influences, inexorably turned Tropicalismo into
a focus of middle-class unease and opposition to the monolithic
authoritarianism of the regime. In September of that year, Caetano
Veloso found himself defending that idea of freedom in the theatre of
Rio's Catholic University, when his performance of 'É Proibido Pro-
ibir' (It's Forbidden to Forbid), inspired by the slogans of the Paris
students, ended in a battle with a hostile, booing audience. Soon
afterwards he, along with the other chief representatives of the move-
ment, Chico Buarque and Gilberto Gil, became the direct victims of
state censorship, imprisonment and forced exile.

New Voices from the Shadows

The key factor in the movement's demise was the collapse of the very
economic 'miracle' upon which the Tropicalist euphoria had been
founded. Oil prices trebled in 1974, and between 1973 and 1975
economic growth fell catastrophically from 14 to 5.6 per cent. A
balance of payments deficit provoked external borrowing which led by
the end of the decade to an accumulated foreign debt of US$45 billion.
The consensus between the military and Brazil's industrial bourgeoi-
sie disintegrated, while a wider layer of the middle class, disaffected
by the recession and psychologically and physically scarred by the
experience of imprisonment and torture, demonstrated its feelings by
deploying a massive vote for opposition candidates in elections to the
Senate. And, while Generals Geisel and Golbery courted international
respectability by promising to reform some of the cruder aspects of the
regime, in many ways the post-1974 government was even more
repressive than that of Médici.

The single most memorable poetic testimony to these years was Ferreira Gullar's *Poema Sujo* (Dirty Poem), written in exile in Buenos Aires between May and October 1975. After the closure of the Popular Culture Centres in 1965 and a period in prison in December 1968, Gullar was forced into hiding for a year because of his activities as a member of the Communist Party. Fleeing to Argentina in 1971, he then travelled to Europe and the Soviet Union before returning to Latin America, where in 1973 he witnessed and narrowly escaped the fate of the many thousands who were butchered in the National Stadium of Santiago de Chile during Pinochet's coup against the Allende government.[20] The *Dirty Poem* was composed in the wake of these events, and it is a courageously ambitious affirmation of the power of memory to resist the obliteration of social identity by the violence of political terror and economic upheaval. The 'filthy', frail mortality which he evokes in the opening section is no longer the existential solitude of *The bodily struggle*, written in the early 1950s; instead it is the anatomy of collective experience of an entire city whose fragments he witnessed and which now, dispersed over time, he attempts to reconstitute in his imagination as he travels back to the decaying home of his wartime childhood, São Luis do Maranhão:

> e era dia
> como era dia aquele
>   dia
>   na sala de nossa casa
> a mesa com a toalha as cadeiras o
>   assoalho muito usado
> e o riso claro de Lucinha se embalando na rede
>   com a morte já misturada
>   na garganta
> sem que ninguém soubesse
>   – e não importa –
> que eu debruçado no parapeito do alpendre
>   via a terra preta do quintal
>   e a galinha ciscando e bicando
>   uma barata entre plantas
>   e neste caso um dia-dois
>   o de dentro e o de fora
>   da sala
> um às minhas costas e outro
> diante dos olhos
> vazando um no outro
> através de meu corpo

dias que se vazam agora ambos em pleno coração
de Buenos Aires
    às quatro horas desta tarde
    de 22 de maio de 1975
    trinta anos depois[21]

(and it was day/as it was day that/day/in our living room/the table with
its cloth the chairs the/wooden floor worn to a shine/and Lucinha's
bright smile rocking in the hammock/with death already poised/at her
throat/with no one's knowledge/ – and it doesn't matter – /that I leaning
on the porch sill/saw the dark earth of the backyard/and the chicken
scratching and pecking at/a cockroach among the plants/and in this case
a double-day/inside and outside/of the living room/one at my back the
other/before my eyes/ebbing one into the other/through my body/days
both now ebbing in the very heart/of Buenos Aires/at four in the
afternoon/22 May 1975/thirty years later)

The effort to discover a continuity in this social history must
contend with the sensation that the flux of time is itself uneven,
reflecting the different rhythms moving the intimate lives of indivi-
duals and classes, the minute details of family tragedies, poverty,
betrayals and murders, the processes of putrefaction, fermentation,
copulation and the labour of the butcher, the farmer, the street vendor
and the factory worker. Like the polluted river Anil (recalling Mário de
Andrade's 'Meditation on the river Tiête'), absorbing and respiring the
fluids and vapours of the lives through which it goes on flowing, the
poet sustains the memory of the community as living actuality con-
veyed through his material being which its experiences have touched:

Desce profundo o relâmpago
de tuas águas em meu corpo,
    desce tão fundo e tão amplo
    e eu me pareço tão pouco
pra tantas mortes e vidas
        que se desdobram
no escuro das claridades,
        na minha nuca,
no meu cotovelo, na minha arcada dentária
    no túmulo da minha boca
        palco de ressurreições
inesperadas
    (minha cidade
    canora)
    de trevas que já não sei
    se são tuas se são minhas
mas nalgum ponto do corpo (do teu? do meu corpo?)

321

(Lightning from your waters penetrates/my body deeply,/penetrates so
deeply and completely/and it seems that I'm so small/for so many lives
and deaths/that unfold/in the darkness of clarity/in the nape of my
neck,/in my elbow, in the roof of my mouth/stage of unexpected/
resurrections/(my song-bird/city)/of darkness maybe yours maybe mine/
I no longer know/but in some part of the body (of your body? of mine?))

In the closing pages of the poem the voices of the community are
heard still echoing through 'that intricate labyrinth/of walls rooms and
courtyards,/of bathrooms, of patios, of back yards' in a 'mortal illumi-
nation/mouthed with timelessness'.

Gullar's testimony of faith in the survival of community was excep-
tional in these years of fear and isolation. The relatively prolific poetic
activity of the period was symptomatic of other things. On the one
hand, events such as the 1972 Expoesia I exhibition in Rio's Catholic
University, or the 'Poemação' happening in the Museum of Modern
Art in 1973 suggested that the cycle of self-renewal of the formalist
avant-garde projects had exhausted itself.[22] On the other hand, the
emergence of a number of semi-clandestine publications, such as
Navilouca (Crazyship), indicated that the process of stylistic miscege-
nation and syncretism initiated by the Tropicalistas was being taken in
a new direction.

By 1976, with the publication of the anthology 26 Poetas Hoje (26
Poets Today) edited by Heloísa Buarque de Hollanda, it was clear that
the authority of the avant-garde movements had ended. The illusion
of ideological neutrality fostered by the post-Concretist generation
and to some extent by the Tropicalistas was now definitively torn
away. A new, self-consciously 'marginal' community of poets found
themselves forced by the repressive political conditions to rediscover
an audience by adopting alternative means of production and distri-
bution of their work. In the process they began to recreate individual
poetic voices which could register the reality of the dictatorship at the
level of language and personal experience. Also known as the mimeó-
grafos (state control of the publishing industry obliged them to resort to
unsophisticated, small-scale printing and copying methods) the Mar-
ginals sought out their readers individually in cinema queues, bars,
theatre foyers and bookshops, distributing their work by hand, or
attempted to reach a wider readership via the anonymity of the
'postcard-poem'. Their compositions characteristically defied traditio-
nal assumptions of structural coherence and consistency, often to the
point of obscurity. They shared an autobiographical fascination with
the minute detail of an alienated daily existence composed of frag-
mented and often sordid events and objects, a world of contingent

subjective experience whose ever-present but unspoken determinant was the anonymous social atmosphere of crisis and repression. Take Afonso Henriques Neto's 'Das unhas cotidianas' (From my daily fingernails), for example:

> Pulmões de petróleo e nicotina e rádio.
> Nabos maduros
> minas
> abortadas.
> Montanha primordial
> minério dos automóveis intestinos de lata
> de um morro havido
> apocalipse de fatos.
> Canções ardendo no subsolo
> vazio labirinto das máquinas.
> Beterrabas maduras
> secaram-se sob
> há um sol seco.
> Apocalipse de fetos.
> Imantadas televisões radares
> colmeias do global acampamento
> lá fora cá dentro
> barbas e deserdados ossos da impostura
> se condenam:
> confessionários de moscas.
> Oh liberdade dos aptos
> que papéis monstruosos
> músculos das trucidadas árvores
> circulam no empedrado vento
> signos do nada ao nada?
> Martelem os d(m)entes computadores tortos
> oh tantos porcos suando.
> Frutas: legumes: fumaça
> podre mar zumbidor
> por que lado consolar a bomba?
> Sapatos no chão.
> Jogo-os pela janela
> (na rua, pulmões)
> ligo o chuveiro
> saio.[23]

(Lungs of petroleum and nicotine and radio./Ripe turnips/chicks/with abortions./Primordial mountain/mineral ore of cars intestines of tin/from a hill that used to be/apocalypse of facts./Songs burning in the subsoil/ empty labyrinth of machines./Ripe beetroots/have dried up beneath/ there's a dry sun./Apocalypse of foetuses./Magnetized televisions

323

radars/hives of the global village/out there in here/beards and disinher-
ited bones of fraud/condemn themselves:/confessionals of flies./Oh
freedom of those who are fit/what monstrous papers/muscles of but-
chered trees/blow around in the petrified wind/signs of nothing into
nothing?/Teeth (minds) twisted computers let them pound away/oh so
many swine sweating./Fruits: vegetables: smoke/rotten buzzing sea/
from which angle can we console the bomb?/Shoes on the floor./I throw
them out the window/(in the street, lungs)/I turn on the shower/and go
out.)

The central themes and characteristics of the poetry of the last
twenty years have emerged at the interface between those social and
cultural conditions. A community at once atomized by and absorbed
into the anonymity of a totalitarian political order and the inescapable
forces of a global capitalist economy on the one hand; on the other, the
artistic legacy of an impersonal formalism and public rhetoric which
registered both the euphoria and the grotesqueness of the shared
experience of modernization, but which was incapable of imagining
alternative forms of human solidarity, that is, of imagining a future
beyond the new 'postmodern' order. Much of the output of the
Marginal generation seemed to confirm the fears of those observers for
whom the proliferation of an undifferentiated mass of poetic voices all
documenting an identical collective experience would do no more
than *reflect* the anonymity of that experience, while failing to transcend
the banality of that world.[24]

However, the recent publication of a number of re-editions and
complete works of poets associated with or moulded by the experience
of the Marginal generation[25] has revealed that out of the post-Miracle
crisis there has emerged a consistent body of work, a gathering of
genuinely individual voices committed not only to the task of register-
ing the reality of contemporary Brazilian life but also to a critical and
conscious dialogue with the Modernist tradition as a whole on a
number of issues, such as the crisis of the poetic subject, the difficulty
of communication, the autonomy of the artistic and linguistic object,
and the relationship between language and power.

Francisco Alvim (b. 1938) is one of those who best illustrate this
return to a dramatic sense of history, to the notion of the poem as the
utterance of a conscious subject (although not necessarily that of the
poet himself), revealing through his dialogue with others the disorder
and discontinuity of social relations under an oppressive regime in
crisis. Many of the compositions from *Passatempo* (Pastime) (1974), for
instance, take the form of theatrical meetings or conversations in
which powerless individuals become the victims of sinister transac-

tions. 'Muito obrigado' (Thank you very much) depicts an anonymous encounter in a doctor's surgery: the smooth-tongued doctor extracts a sample of blood from his patient, who uneasily feels the needle seek out the vein 'right up to my armpit' and then receives in exchange a document with the threateningly conspiratorial comment, 'Sua experiência nos pode ser muito útil' (Your experience could be of great use to us).[26]

On other occasions, the drily ironic tone of these interviews is exchanged for the more emotional urgency of a violent encounter, as in 'Anamnese' (Anamnesis) from *Lago, Montanha* (Lake, Mountain) (1981):

> Meu deus do céu
> que situação
> eu não merecia isto
> ai minha mãe morta
> dá vontade de abrir tudo
>
> Pelo amor de deus
> deixa eu ir
> não não vai não
> você está me matando
> é mas ali você não vai
>
> Faz isso não meu irmão
> fica quietinho meu irmão
> que sujeira
>
> Vou me levantar
> e eu vou deixar?
>
> Não faz isso
> você me mata
>
> Não me bata
> Bato
>
> Não me mate
> Mato

(Dear God in heaven/what a situation/I didn't deserve this/oh my dead mother/it makes you want to open everything up//For the love of God/let me go/oh no you're not going anywhere/you're killing me/right but you're not going over there//Don't do that brother/keep nice and still brother/what a mess//I'm getting up/you think I'm going to let you?// Don't do that/you'll kill me//Don't hit me/I will/Don't kill me/I will)

When not engaged in these dramatic dialogues, the voices of

Alvim's poetry are witnesses to a fragmented, disarticulated historical time, the isolated subjects of episodes which acquire meaning only in the context of the compositions which surround them, suggesting the reconstituted totality of social experience. *Passatempo, Lago, Montanha* and *Dia sim, dia não* (On and off, day to day) (1978) are full of these brief utterances and observations, whose natural, colloquial language recalls the early work of Oswald de Andrade, Drummond or the Bandeira of 'Pequena notícia tirada de um jornal' (Little report taken from a newspaper). As with the Modernist poets of the early 1920s, the juxtaposition of public and private events suggests both an alienation and an unavoidable interference between the two levels of existence, as the individual seeks refuge in the subjective:

> Amanhã sai o recesso
> depois cassações
> eleições indiretas
> tudo combinadinho
> tudo combinadinho
> é mas agora eu vou é
> cuidar da vida
> ('Véspera' – The night before)

(Tomorrow it's the end of the recess/then the annulment of political rights/indirect elections/all ticketty-boo/all ticketty-boo/right but now what I'm going to do is/mind by own business)

However, these gestures of casual or defiant withdrawal are deceptive, betraying a they do a sense of weakness and desperate impotence in the face of a political reality which brutally invades the domestic world. In 'Mamãe' (Mummy), for example,

> Pra mim chega.
> Seus cães policiais não vão mais farejar meu jardim
> nem sacudir as pulgas do meu tapete voador.
> Seu arame farpado não vai mais cercar vaca nenhuma.
> Nunca mais vou medir os dias nem as pesadas noites
> pela batida de um coração que apodrece.
> E vê se não esquece
> de retirar os corpos as manchas de sangue
> os mapas irregulares que me destinam
> a um país ocupado.
> Chega de tímpanos estourados
> chega de perder os dentes.
> Vê se dá uma basta nesse fodido medo.

As paredes revestidas
o algodão nos ouvidos
nada disso pode isolar o berro
o ruído animal que arrepia pêlos e espinha
gravado em cavernas abismos
gargantas.
Chega de carne moída chega de vida engasgada.
Hoje todo o seu povo
vivos e mortos famintos e doidos raivosos
faz as malas abre as veias
e volta pra casa de mamãe.

(I've had enough./Your police-dogs aren't going to sniff around my garden any more/or shake the fleas out of my flying carpet./Your barbed wire isn't going to pen up any cow again./Never again will I measure the days or the heavy nights/by the beating of a rotting heart./And see you don't forget/to take away the bodies the bloodstains/the irregular maps that have me destined/for an occupied country./No more burst eardrums/no more losing my teeth./See if you can put a stop to that fucking fear./The soundproofed walls/the cotton-wool in your ears/none of that can isolate the bellowing/the animal noise that makes your hair stand on end, a shiver run down your spine/engraved in caves abysses, throats./No more flesh beaten to a pulp no more living a choked up life./Today all your people/living and dead hungry and crazy raging/are packing their bags opening up their veins/and going home to mummy.)

One of the most exciting responses to this violation of the private realm of experience by the reality of public life has been the emergence of a generation of female poets, whose confidence in their own creative power, in the possibility of 'transforming life into words',[27] is symptomatic of the increasing prominence of Brazilian women in the struggle for democracy and self-emancipation over the last fifteen years. In the work of Adélia Prado (b. 1935), this faith in the redemptive power of a courageous engagement with life takes a predominantly religious form. In the composition entitled 'Guia' (Guide) from *Bagagem* (Baggage) (1976), she repeats the phrase 'A poesia me salvará' (Poetry will save me), explaining that through poetry she is better able to understand the meaning of Christ's passion, as the immanent revelation of the sublime in the day-to-day suffering of human flesh: 'A Deus não temo./Que outra coisa ela é senão Sua Face atingida/da brutalidade das coisas?' (I do not fear God./What is [poetry] but His Face struck/by the brutality of things?)[28] Therefore, she protests, 'Se o que está prometido é a carne incorruptível,/é isso mesmo que eu quero' (If what is promised is incorruptible flesh,/that is just what I want) ('A Catecúmena', The Catechumen); and poetry, that 'splendid chaos' of 'dark places' residing in the interstices between the meaning-less, inert particles of language, is a form of communication with that pure existential experience:

> A palavra é disfarce de uma coisa mais grave, surda-muda,
> foi inventada para ser calada.
> Em momentos de graça, infreqüentíssimos,
> se poderá apanhá-la: um peixe vivo com a mão.
> Puro susto e terror.
>
> ('Antes do nome' – Before the name)

(The word is a disguise for something more serious, deaf-and-dumb,/it was invented to be silenced./At moments of grace, so, so rare,/you can grasp it: a live fish with your hand./Pure fright and terror.)

Life, almost sufficient in itself, is to be grasped and lived in all its raw carnality. As a woman, assuming that commitment means a conscious and courageous rejection of the male poet's traditional posture of ironic withdrawal and self-concealment, a posture Prado identifies with the persona of Drummond's 'Seven-sided poem', which she confronts in 'Com licença poética' (With poetic licence):

> Quando nasci um anjo esbelto,
> desses que tocam trombeta, anunciou:
> vai carregar bandeira.
> Cargo muito pesado pra mulher,
> esta espécie ainda envergonhada.
> Aceito os subterfúgios que me cabem,
> sem precisar mentir.

(When I was born a slender angel,/of the kind that blows trumpets, announced:/go on and carry your flag./A very heavy burden for woman, that still bashful species./I accept the subterfuges that befit me,/without the need to lie)

Instead, she defiantly shoulders that burden, taking on her destiny of desire, pain and self-realization: 'Vai ser coxo na vida, é maldição pra homem./Mulher é desdobrável. Eu sou.' (Go on and be lame in life, that's a man's curse./Woman can unfold and show herself. So can I.) The drama of awakening to experience, and simultaneously awakening language to give that experience form and meaning, is also a central theme of Orides Fontela's *Alba* (Dawn) (1983). For Fontela (b. 1940), the daughter of working-class parents (her father was illiterate), the act of artistic creation, of writing, is identified with that first moment of human consciousness at dawn, a moment renewed every day, when eyes are opened to the sun's rays and 'the violence of images in time' ('Alba'), and the waking senses of her being lie at the threshold of life: 'Branco/sinal oferto/e a resposta do/sangue:/ AGORA!' (Blank/sign offered up/and the response of your/blood:/ NOW!)[29] Without that human intervention, as she suggests in 'Reflex-os' (Reflections), the wordless image of life that stares back in the mirror remains blank, devoid of identity or meaning, 'no one/no one'. Thus, the transformation of life into words involves a necessary violation of the pure, self-sufficient moment of being pursued by Adélia Prado. Whereas Prado's poetry seeks to overcome the separation between art and life, not so much *representing* the world and human utterances as *invoking* them, in Fontela's work the artifice of poetry is cause for celebration, the affirmation of her, and our, capacity to recreate the world in our image:

> Humanizar o cisne
> é violentá-lo. Mas
> também quem nos dirá
> o arisco esplendor
> – a presença do cisne?
>
> Como dizê-lo? Densa
> a palavra fere
> o branco
> expulsa a presença e – humana –
> é esplendor memória
> 　　　　　e sangue.
>
> 　　　　　E
> 　　　　　resta
> não cisne: a
> 　　　　　palavra
> – a palavra mesmo
> 　　　　　cisne.

(To make the swan human/is to violate it. But/then again who will tell us/ of its wild splendour/ – the presence of the swan?//How can one tell of it? Densely/the word wounds/the whiteness/expels that presence and – human – /it is splendour memory/and blood.//And/there remains/not the swan: the/word// – the actual word/swan.)

Self-consciousness about the artistic process, and the creative role of the poet as a subject and communicator of experience, took other forms, too, in the women's writing of the period. For Ana Cristina César (1952–82) the diary and letter offered alternative vehicles for exploring the dialectic between private and public lives, as well as for reconstructing a new and original relationship with the reader. More than simply a poetic idiom, the diary and letter constitute a dramatic space of their own, in which the poet is paradoxically distanced from herself while allowing the reader privileged access to an autobiographical universe whose painful intimacy blurs the boundaries between fiction and reality, poetry and prose. Like a drama within a drama, the subject of these confidences is typically the minute vicissitudes of interpersonal contact and communication, and the complex relationship between physical sensation and psychological mood, exploring another dimension of that interface between the objective and subjective worlds. Consider 'Arpejos' (Arpeggios), from the collection 'A teus pés' (At your feet), published in 1982, a year before the poet's suicide:

1

Acordei com coceira no hímen. No bidê com espelhinho examinei o local. Não surpreendi indícios de moléstia. Meus olhos leigos na certa não perceberam que um rouge a mais tem significado a mais. Passei pomada branca até que a pele (rugosa e murcha) ficasse brilhante. Com essa murcharam igualmente meus projetos de ir de bicicleta à ponta do Arpoador. O selim poderia reavivar a irritação. Em vez decidi me dedicar à leitura.

2

Ontem na recepção virei inadvertidamente a cabeça contra o beijo de saudação de Antônia. Senti na nuca o bafo seco do susto. Não havia como desfazer o engano. Sorrimos o resto da noite. Falo o tempo todo em mim. Não deixo Antônia abrir sua boca de lagarta beijando para sempre o ar. Na saída nos beijamos de acordo, dos dois lados. Aguardo crise de remorsos.

3

A crise parece controlada. Passo o dia a recordar o gesto involuntário. Represento a cena ao espelho. Viro o rosto à minha própria imagem sequiosa. Depois me volto, procuro nos olhos dela signos de decepção. Mas Antônia continuaria inexorável. Saio depois de tantos ensaios. O movimento das rodas me desanuvia os tendões duros. Os navios me iluminam. Pedalo de maneira insensata.[30]

(1: I woke up with an itch in my hymen. I examined the spot with a little mirror on the bidet. I didn't come across any signs of something wrong. My untrained eyes no doubt can't see that an extra patch of rouge has an extra meaning. I put some ointment on it until the skin (rough and withered) shone. Upon which my plans of cycling to the Arpoador point likewise withered. The saddle might revive the irritation. Instead I decided to devote myself to some reading.//2: Yesterday in the reception I inadvertently turned my head against Antônia's kiss of greeting. I felt the quick puff of breath of her surprise in my neck. There was no way of undoing the misunderstanding. We smile for the rest of the evening. I talk about myself the whole time. I don't let Antônia open her caterpillar's mouth forever kissing the air. On the way out we kiss in agreement, on both cheeks. I await an acute crisis of remorse.//3: The crisis seems to be under control. I spend the day remembering that involuntary gesture. I perform the scene in the mirror. I turn my face towards my own eager image. Then I turn round and look for signs of disappointment in her eyes. But Antônia remains inexorable. I go out after all those rehearsals. The turning of the wheels relieves my stiff tendons. The ships illuminate me. I pedal wildly.)

The ambiguities and paradoxes opened up by Ana Cristina César's dramatic use of the autobiographical voice are confronted more explicitly in 'Fogo do fiel' (Fire of the faithful), where the private world of correspondence appears as an indispensable and defiant arena of collective 'therapy' and self-discovery in the midst of a sterile urban landscape, 'an industrial desert of mouths that cannot be questioned':

26 de março.
Preciso começar de novo o caderno terapêutico. Não é como o fogo do final. Um caderno terapêutico é outra história. É deslavada. Sem luvas. Meio bruta. É um papel que desistiu de dar recados. Uma imitação da lavanderia com suas máquinas a seco e suas prensas a vapor. Um relatório do instituto nacional do comércio, ríspido mas ditoso, inconfessadamente ditoso. Nele eu sou eu e você é você mesmo. Todos nós. Digo tudo com ais à vontade. E recolho os restos das conversas, ambulância. Trottoir na casa. Umas tantas cismas. O terapêutico não se faz de inocente ou de rogado. Responde e passa as chaves. Metálico, estala na boca, sem cascata. E de novo.

(26th march./I must start the therapeutic notebook again. It's not like the final conflagration. A therapeutic notebook is another story. It's insolent. Gloves off. Kind of raw. It's a piece of paper that's stopped giving messages. An imitation of a laundry with its driers and steam presses. A report from the national institute of commerce, curt but happy, unconfessedly happy. In it I am me and you are yourself. Us all. I say everything with as many alases as I like. And I gather up the remains of conversations, an ambulance. Indoor trottoir. A few musings. The therapeutic notebook doesn't play the innocent or hard-to-get. It answers and hands over the keys. Metallic, it explodes in your mouth, without a cascade. And once more.)

The poetry of Sebastião Uchoa Leite (b. 1935) offers a sharp contrast to the confessional intimacy of Ana Cristina César. His sardonic, elliptical style seems intent on questioning, concealing and even denying the reality of the self as a viable subject for the poem. *Antilogia* (Anthilogy) (1972–79) is inhabited instead by anti-beings, the poisonous, self-consuming serpents of the poet's own creation, or the diabolical alter egos of a gothic underworld, whose fictional existence is 'larger than life' but simultaneously threatened by oblivion:

> antes que eles destruam vocês
> atenção amigos ocultos
> drácula
> nosferatu
> frankenstein
> mr. hyde
> jack the ripper
> m – o vampiro de dusseldorf
> monstros do mundo inteiro:
> uni-vos![31]
>
> ('V Internacional')

(before they destroy you/attention occult friends/dracula/nosferatu/ frankenstein/mr. hyde/jack the ripper/m – the vampire of dusseldorf/ monsters of the world:/unite!)

As such, this short collection represents one phase or dimension of a continually evolving dialogue concerning two of the key problems raised by Modernism: the autonomy of art and language as self-referring sign-systems and the consequent unviability of a poetry of subjective expression or metaphorical 'meaning'. What makes Uchoa Leite's work so compelling is his ruthless determination to pursue these problems through to their ultimate and most disturbing implications, offering what seems superficially to be a form of artistic nihilism, whilst in fact inviting the reader to confront honestly the risks and consequences of abolishing the metaphorical link between art and reality. Thus, in 'Biografia de uma idéia' (Biography of an idea), the writing of poetry is mercilessly depicted as a vacuous, futile exercise, in which language and ideas seem condemned to devour each other and themselves in a kind of semiotic prison:

> ao fascínio do poeta pela palavra
> só iguala o da víbora pela sua presa
> as idéias são/não são o forte dos poetas
> idéias-dentes que mordem e se remordem:

os poemas são o remorso dos códigos e/ou
a poesia é o perfeito vazio absoluto
os poemas são ecos de uma cisterna sem fundo ou
erupções sem larva e ejaculações sem esperma
ou canhões que detonam em silêncio:
as palavras são denotações do nada ou
serpentes que mordem a sua própria cauda

(the fascination of the poet for the word/is only equalled by that of the viper for its prey/ideas are/aren't the strong point of poets/teeth-ideas that bite and bite at themselves:/poems are the remorse of codes and/or/ poetry is the perfect absolute void/poems are echoes of a bottomless tank or/lava-less eruptions and spermless ejaculations/or cannons that detonate in silence:/words are detonations of nothing or/ serpents that bite their own tail)

In his next collection, *Isso não é aquilo* (This isn't that) (1979–82), Uchoa Leite extends his critical examination of this paradoxical notion of the poem as simultaneously material and immaterial, a linguistic sign-system dangling precariously from some possibly fictional 'real world'. 'Vamos destruir a máquina das metáforas?' (Shall we destroy the metaphor machine?) he asks in 'A Morte dos simbolos' (The Death of symbols), only to denounce elsewhere the ideological intention of a discourse which, whilst disowning all claims to meaning, is busy occupying the citadels of linguistic power:

eles discursam
eles mentem
no lugar da mensagem
mas essa história de códigos
confundidos com linguagem
nada tem a ver
eles dizem que são funcionários
mas o discurso é claro:
que tem o poder do espaço
tem o espaço do poder
('Os críticos panópticos' – The Panoptic critics)

(they hold forth/they lie/where there should be a message/but that business about codes/confused with language/has got nothing to do with it/they say they are functionaries/but the discourse is clear:/he who holds the power of space/holds the space of power)

But Uchoa Leite does not confine himself exclusively within the abstract, cerebral realm of these discussions. In a number of compositions the abolition of metaphor and the consequent crisis of meaning is implicitly linked to the problematic idea of Postmodernist culture, in which the disarticulated images of social and political history as reported in the mass-media world of global capitalism have become indistinguishable from the imaginary universe of popular mythology or cinema. Consider 'Questões de método' (Questions of method), for example:

um monte de cadáveres em el salvador
– no fundo da foto
carros e ônibus indiferentes –
será isso a realidade?
degolas na américa central
presuntos desovados na baixada
as teorias do state department
uma nova linha de tordesilhas
qual a linha divisória
do real e do não real?
questão de método: a realidade
é igual ao real?
o homen dos lobos foi real? o panopticum
o que é mais real: a leitura do jornal
ou as aventuras de indiana jones?
o monólogo do pentágono ou
orson welles atirando contra os espelhos?

(a heap of corpses in el salvador/ – in the background of the photo/ indifferent cars and buses – /can that be reality?/beheadings in central america/stiffs spawned in the suburbs of Rio/the theories of the state department/a new tordesillas line/which is the dividing line/between the real and the non-real?/a question of method: is reality/the same as the real?/was the wolf-man real? was the panopticon?/what is more real: reading the newspaper/or the adventures of indiana jones?/the monologue from the pentagon or/orson welles shooting at mirrors?)

If there is an alternative to Uchoa Leite's stark, sombre vision of this Postmodernist crisis, it is to be found in the work of Armando Freitas Filho (b. 1940). As with Alvim, César and Uchoa Leite, the material of Freitas Filho's poetry is the fragmentation and elusiveness of the self, the alienation of language from reality, and the defence of human experience against the anonymity of a seemingly ahistorical world where everything and everyone is sucked into the aimless, meaningless cycles of economic growth and crisis. What marks him out, though, is his playful linguistic inventiveness, his manipulation of pastiche, the catch-phrase, the slang expression, cliché, proverb and pun, in other words the linguistic stuff of our contemporary global culture. It is this ludic quality which denotes not only a preparedness to grasp the nettle and confront the artistic problems identified above, but also an optimistic faith in the idea that language can provide the moments of collective recognition which will make some sense of life in a world where 'all that is solid melts into air'.

Thus the most consistent subject of his poetry is the struggle of an alienated, schizophrenic self to hold on to memory and identity when these are continually threatened by the disintegrating flux of a blind history. 'Mr. Interlúdio' (Mr Interlude), from *À mão livre* (Freehand) (1975–79),[32] for example:

> Quem sou você
> que me responde
> do outro lado de mim?
> Quem é que passa
> invisível
> pelo espaço da sala
> e vai
> do meu corpo
> a este outro,
> em emulsão ou emoção instantânea,
> feito como eu mesmo,
> de repente,
> em noite antiga
> e não perde
> nessa viagem
> o tempo que perdi,
> e, no entanto,
> os dias que me fizeram
> estão ali
> correndo em suas veias?

(Who am you/who answers me/from the other side of me?/Who is it who wanders/invisibly/through the space of the room/and goes/from my body/to this other one,/in an instantaneous emulsion or emotion,/made like myself,/suddenly,/on a previous night/and does not lose/in that journey/the time I lost,/and yet,/the days that made me/are there/ running through his veins?)

Paradoxically, though, as his 'Cidade maravilhosa' (Marvellous city) suggests, the solitary individual may discover a point of solidarity as he recognizes a common cultural language amidst the news headlines, street signs, show titles and neon advertisements of the global urban landscape:

335

Aqui estão os rótulos
rasgados do meu rosto,
as máscaras,
     as marcas,
as letras do meu nome,
com todos os erres,
com todos os erros,
em garranchos
pichados no cimento,
nos cartazes,
e nas caligrafias de neon:

Motel de Mel Não Há Vagas
Os Desaparecidos
Homens Trabalhando

Na frente de todos
O Rei do Mau gosto
usa o seu rosto

A Stripper sem Script
se incendeia
sob o sol do Mangue

Assegure Sua Fartura
no Carné Futuro
de Baby Doll

Aqui estamos nós,
     enfim,
João e Maria
feitos um para o outro
no acaso das calçadas:
neste banco nos beijamos,
neste jardim nos devoramos,
nesta rua nos deixaram
joão
     e maria
nos perdemos
     com a roupa do corpo
     com a casa nas costas
na floresta
     dos dias,
(índio) e (indigentes)
atravessando as veredas da avenida
sob a paixão do sol.

(Here are the torn/labels of my face,/the masks,/the marks/the letters of

336

my name,/with all the rrrs,/with all the errors,/scrawled in pitch on the concrete,/on the posters,/and in the neon calligraphy://*Honeymoon Hotel No Vacancies/The Disappeared/Men At Work//In front of everyone/The King of Bad Taste/wears his face/The Stripper without a Script/sets herself on fire/ beneath the sun of the Mangue//Be Sure of Satisfaction/In Baby Doll's/Next Appointment Book//*Here we are,/at last,/John and Mary/made for each other/in that chance meeting on the sidewalks:/on this bench we kissed,/ in this garden we devoured each other,/in this street they left us,/john and mary/we got lost/with the clothes on our backs/in the forest/of the days,/(Indian) and (indigent)/crossing the lanes of the avenue/beneath the passion of the sun.)

Freitas Filho's awareness of the contradictory nature of contemporary mass culture – its ability to a congregate millions of individuals around a whole number of familiar, shared experiences, yet also, by the same token, its tendency to render those experiences anonymous, banal and alienated – is what gives his poetry a sense of living tension as he searches for those moments of collective discovery and understanding. So he could write of 'All of us/naked/short-circuited', plugged into a summer seascape as if into the same output socket of a giant psychedelic cinema and audio system, and sharing 'the regained sensation/of the gaze of someone leafing for the first time/through an atlas, and who discovers/on a double page, the Mapa-Mundi/the wide-open space that life/has on Earth to fly'.[33] Yet just a few years later, in 3 × 4 (1981–83),[34] it is as if he was living only what had already been lived, recorded, digested and written. The technological world of the modern apartment is switched on, but has become a putrefying still-life which 'I can't turn off'. The bloody horrors of the death squads in the city suburbs have been assimilated into a no-man's land of media mythology devoid of moral, political or historical context:

> . . . O Terrorama da Baixada
> anunciando seus cadáveres:
> secos, súbitos, recortados
> impressos em preto e branco
> com todas as letras garrafais
> dos jornais que são só manchetes
> ou cartazes, sem maiores explicações.

(The Terrorama of the Suburbs/advertising its corpses:/curt, sudden, cut out/printed in black and white/with all the letters in large type/from the newspapers that are just headlines/or posters, without further explanation.)

Freitas Filho's consciousness of this very 'postmodernist' loss of reference, the impossibility of a unique, individual experience that is not subsumed into the infinitely repeatable structures of mass consumer capitalism, led him back, interestingly enough, to the very problem raised twenty or more years previously by the Concretists. How to genuinely 'make it new', how to create the future without simply reproducing the ready-made phrases of the past, without refracting or filtering experience through the inherited media of our common culture?

> Passar a limpo os cinco sentidos.
> Apagar com sono e borracha
> para usar – todos
> novos em folha
> de novo:
> sem luvas, óculos, fones
> perfumes de meio ambiente
> e com a boca livre de lembranças.

(To start afresh again with your five senses./To erase with sleep and rubber/so as to use them – all of them – /fresh on a fresh/page:/without gloves, glasses, telephones/environmental perfumes/and with your mouth free of memories.)

Is art nothing less than an eternal reflection of its own image, like two mirrors or photocopying machines facing each other? Or is there a 'before' which escapes the reflection of the mirror or the image of the photograph, 'which picks up the trail and departs/but leaves no trace/ or fingerprint'; or which even defies and subverts that image-making process, like light invading the developer's dark-room? In the closing few poems of the book, Freitas Filho makes an approximation to what he sees as his task as a poet who, like the 'detetive do olhar' (detective of the gaze), in the blinking of an eye, tracks down the fleeing criminal hidden behind the optical illusion; or that other, African, hunter who hunts with blank bullets 'for I only want souvenirs/that are not images'. The effort to redeem human experience from the oblivion of history without petrifying it and emptying it of all communicative power remains a precarious venture, the perfect crime which, sooner or later, may be found out:

338

Preposições: antes, até, após
por quanto tempo
este crime ficará perfeito
fora de foco entre dois fogos
depois dos disparos
no espaço durante
onde
        tiro no escuro
retratos ou a vida do que
num instante, escapa do registro
do desejo, do livro de ocorrências
e queima o filme, o nu, a confissão
no estúdio, still, então
vira vã estátua de vácuo
contra o fundo infinito
sem assinatura?

(Prepositions: before, until, afterwards/for how long/will this crime remain perfect/out of focus between two lines of fire/after the shots/in space during/where I shoot in the dark/photos or the life of what/in an instant, escapes the register/of desire, the book of happenings/and burns the film, the nude, the confession/in the studio, a still, then/turns into a vain statue of emptiness/against the infinite unsigned/background?)

If there is anything that is shared by the gathering of voices which has emerged since the crisis in Brazil, it is a commitment to that precarious venture. Out of the political and formalist orthodoxies of the dictatorship, Brazilian poetry has begun the slow task of rediscovering the art of dialogue, a dialogue with the new forms and expressions through which modernity is being experienced in the lives of individuals, and with the many traditions of writing thrown up in response to that experience during the course of the twentieth century. In the words of Armando Freitas Filho, any future project for Brazilian poetry must accept precisely those libertarian qualities of openness, plurality and informality which the Marginals redeemed from the early Modernists after the formalism of Concretismo had sought to stifle them. Such a project

Can only be of consequence if it is multiple, if it is heretical . . . the more heresy it has, the more assemblages, collages, pre-collages, influences of all kinds, which are today called postmodernist art . . . the more miscegenation, the more incestuous that project is, the more it can gather pluralities and discordant voices, as moreover Modernism did. Modernism is the parameter, the model to be followed and surpassed, because Modernism summoned up utterances, different voices, different moments, incorporated them all and gave them all a meaning.[35]

339

What now remains to be seen is whether the new poetry can open up that dialogue to the exciting expressions of collective organization, struggle and vision which have been growing steadily in other spheres of Brazilian society since the late 1970s, and can in this way contribute to the imagination and construction of a self-conscious, independent movement of the immense majority, whose hitherto unheard voices will speak and, in the realization of their words, bring about a new world.

10

Conclusion:
Against Exile

Words from Outside

The linked experiences of exile and struggle shape the poetry and song of the last decade. The end of exile and the reorientation of the mass struggle will produce a new writing whose character it would be futile to predict. But in the world emerging from the terrified silence of the dictatorships of the eighties the first process will be one of accounting – 'Nunca más' (Never again), the report on the dirty war in Argentina pronounced. That will be the keynote. For those who have lived in exile, wherever they were forced to spend it, reintegration must pass through the squaring of accounts, the lifting of veils, the search for a common language with those who in many cases have replaced the language of politics with a general rhetoric of resistance and rejection. That rejection and denial, its rage and its pain, are the material of a new poetry. Yet it cannot simply excise the language and politics of an earlier time. They are its past, the history after all of the movement itself, and without it it will be unable to identify the origins of its pain or the forces that can reshape the world.

The refusal to build walls around experience, however painful or bitter, is anticipated in the sardonic piece by Mario Benedetti[1] 'Contra los puentes levadizos' (Against drawbridges). Written in the seventies, it is an anticipation of the withdrawal that exile may provoke.

> que entren amor y odio y voz y gritos
> que venga la tristeza con sus brazos abiertos
> y la ilusión con sus zapatos nuevos
> que venga el frío germinal y honesto
> y el verano de angustias calcinadas

que vengan los rencores con su niebla
y los adioses con su pan de lágrimas
que venga el muerto y sobre todo el vivo
y el viejo olor de la melancolía

que baje el puente y que se quede bajo

que entren la rabia y su ademán oscuro
que entren el mal y el bien
y lo que media
entre uno y otro
o sea
la verdad ese péndulo
que entre el incendio con o sin lluvia
y las mujeres con o sin historia
que entre el trabajo y sobre todo el ocio
ese derecho al sueño
ese arco iris

que baje el puente y que se quede bajo

(Let in love and hate and shouting and voices/let sadness in with its arms open/and illusions with their new shoes/let in the germinal honest cold/the summer of scorched suffering/let bitternesses come with their fog/and farewells with their bread of tears/let in the dead man and above all the living /and the old smell of melancholy//let down the bridge and keep it down//let rage in and its dark gesture/let good and evil in/and what mediates/between them/that is/truth that pendulum/let in the fire with or without rain/let women come with or without a history/let labour in and leisure above all/that right to dream/that rainbow//let down the bridge and keep it down)

Benedetti anticipates that most persistent quality of the poetry and song of the last decade – the naming of the world. Metaphor gives way to an accumulation of experience, rich and diverse, contradictory and perplexing. This is the process of rewriting history, or *rediscovering* history in a sensual, lived world; it is the *making* of that world as an act of human creativity which is celebrated here. Juan Gelman, the Argentine poet, found 'history' too:

Estudiando la historia,
fechas, batallas, cartas escritas en la piedra,
frases célebres, próceres oliendo a santidad,
sólo percibo oscuras manos
esclavas, metalúrgicas, mineras, tejedoras,
creando el resplandor, la aventura del mundo,
se murieron y aún les crecieron las uñas.

(Studying history,/dates, battles, letters written on stone,/famous say-
ings, military heroes smelling of saintliness,/I only see dark hands/
enslaved, metalworking, mining, weaving,/creating the light, the
world's adventure,/they died and their nails are still growing.)

It is the same discovery that Neruda made, but in an era about to
face the all-embracing silence of the state of siege, in which the
Uruguayan authorities banned certain words from public utterance
and the plagues of forgetfulness affected whole societies forced to
deny their own most recent and remembered past. In response poetry
becomes public remembrance as well as personal certainty. Doubt will
infiltrate both the public and the private realm, but that very doubt
belongs to the public domain.[2]

There is no doubt that the experience of the late seventies and early
eighties produced a profound despair among many poets. The with-
drawal into self became in many cases the creation of an alternative
geography, a curious universe of historical as well as geographical
analogies producing a kind of pastiche upon the explorations of an
earlier decade. No longer a world to win or conquer, rather a world to
defy and evade. The body itself became the alternative landscape,
silence the space of separation. Glimpses of this new and painful
direction were to be found in Alejandra Pizarnik, in Rosario Murillo
and Gioconda Belli. Other writers – Claudia Lars and Claribel Alegría
of El Salvador, for example – were drawn out of their private lyric
world by the events and transformations to which they were subject. It
is no coincidence that women poets predominate here, when the
body, sexuality and the private self become both the locus of oppres-
sion and a means of liberation.

> Afuera hay sol
> No es más que un sol
> pero los hombres lo miran
> y después cantan.
>
> Yo no sé del sol.
> Yo sé la mediodía del ángel
> y el sermón caliente
> del último viento.
> Sé gritar hasta el alba
> cuando la muerte se posa desnuda
> en mi sombra.

Yo lloro debajo de mi nombre . . .
Yo agito pañuelos en la noche
y barcos sedientos de realidad
bailan conmigo.
Yo oculto clavos
para escarnecer a mis sueños enfermos.

Afuera hay sol.
Yo me visto de cenizas.[3]

(It is sunny outside/It is only a sun/but men look at it/and then sing.//I know nothing of the sun./I know the angel's melody/the intense sermon/of the last wind./I know how to shout until dawn/when death stands naked/in my shadow.//I weep beneath my name. . ./I wave handkerchiefs in the night/and ships thirsty for the real world/dance with me./I hide nails/to tear at my sick dreams.//It is sunny outside./I wear only ashes.)

In her poignant 'Exilio' (Exile), Pizarnik embraces 'only what flows away/like lava'. Adrift and without support in the world, only her words keep her from despair, though her ultimate suicide suggests it was not enough. It is doubly curious then that where the cage Pizarnik refers to in her earlier poem are the real bars of the cage, as they are for the women poets jailed in Chile, then the same sense of isolation produces anger and pain, yes, but also a sense of returning, of a living landscape beyond the place of exile and incarceration.

¡Me llevan!
¡Me sacan!
laberintos recorridos
puertas que suenan,
cerrojos que se abren
    Me toman
    Me suben
    Me encierran
Por la ventanilla diminuta,
a través de la rejilla
contemplo,
    aferro a mis retinas
lo hermoso del día
Te siento tan cerca sin poder alcanzarte
naturaleza prohibida . . .[4]

(They're taking me!/They're taking me out!/labyrinths I have travelled before/doors that close,/locks that open/They take me/They take me up/They lock me in/Through the tiny window/through the bars/I see/I press

against my retina/the beauty of the day/I feel you so close though I
cannot reach you/forbidden nature . . .)

Gioconda Belli,[5] from her 'Exilio', speaks with the same desperate
register as those who at the same time were finding how deep was the
sense of grief and loss that came with looking back on a Chile, an
Argentina and a Uruguay locked in their respective silent dirty wars.

> Esto es el exilio
> este tenerme que inventar un nombre,
> una figura,
> una voz nueva.
> Este tener que andar diciendo
> de dónde soy
> qué hago aqui.
> Esto es el exilio
> esta soledad clavándose en mi carne
> y este tiempo vacío. . .

(This is exile/this having to invent a name for myself,/a face,/a new
voice./This having to go around saying/where I'm from/what I'm doing
here./This is exile/this solitude biting into my flesh/and this empty time
. . .)

With the Nicaraguan Revolution of 1979, Belli with others celebrated
the return of the light, the emergence of Cardenal's community out of
the shadows. She stands with the crowds in Revolution Square and
watches the tyrant depart. Yet there is in Belli a hurt and poignant
sense of doubt and hesitancy:

> Claro que no somos una pompa fúnebre,
> a pesar de todas las lágrimas tragadas
> restamos con la alegría de construir lo nuevo
> y gozamos del día, de la noche
> y hasta del cansancio
> y recogemos risas en el viento alto . . .
>
> Huyendo como prófugos
> vemos cómo nacen arrugas en la frente
> y nos volvemos serios,
> pero siempre por siempre
> nos persigue la risa . . .

(Of course we're not a funeral procession/despite the tears we've
swallowed/we're here with the joy of constructing something new/and
enjoying the day and the night/and even the weariness/and we're
collecting laughter on the high wind . . .//Fleeing like fugitives/we watch

how lines emerge on the brow/and we become serious,/but always and forever/it is laughter that pursues us . . .)

There is uncertainty here as to how far it is possible to throw off the pain of the past. Belli's subsequent writing returns to the anguish of loss, of disappointed desire, of loneliness. These are the 'problems of transition':

> Amo a un hombre.
> Sé que él me ama,
> pero grandes soledades y distancias que mi mano no alcanza
> nos separan.

(I love a man./I know he loves me,/but solitudes and distances that I cannot reach over/separate us.)

The new world is full of uncertainties –it is after all a society in movement towards a new and as yet undefined future. The public optimism, the absence of doubt in public discourse, make it all the more difficult to confront the residues of individual fear. It is in many ways a poetry that is more authentic, though not necessarily more deeply felt, than those poems of love and revolution in which a new generation has expressed without any hesitation the identity of public and private self.[6] Yet the youngest Nicaraguan poets still cling to a lyric voice that accepts the separation of self and world.

> Huye mi razón
> como mariposa temerosa
> hacia la alambrada azul del crepúsculo
> y en alguna parte oscura y sensitiva
> duele una canción lloviendo
>   entre sombra fugaces,
> se alborotan pájaros salvajes
>   prisioneros de jaulas,
> lloran dulces flores silvestres
>   pisoteadas
> Cómo me duele el mundo habitado
> por locos y extraños pasajeros
> inocentemente culpables.[7]

(My reason flees/like a fearful butterfly/towards the blue wire fence of dusk/and in some dark and sensitive place/a song hurts, raining down/among fleeting shadows,/wild birds become agitated/imprisoned in their cages,/sweet wild flowers weep/crushed underfoot/I feel such pain from a world inhabited/by mad and strange travellers/who are guilty in their innocence.)

346

Reclaiming the Future

The last decade, then, has unfolded between the poles of exile and struggle. Yet there is hope and optimism even in exile and alienation; and there is also doubt, uncertainty and unanswered questions in the heart of the struggle. It is these elements that constitute the continuity and the fulfilment of the movement towards a public voice and the renunciation of lyrical exclusion which we have tried to trace. The challenges of belonging to history, of its enumeration and reappropriation, place at the heart of poetry a public voice and a common concern, the very opposite of the *withdrawal from history* which for Octavio Paz is the central condition of poetry.

The focus is Central America and the experience of the southern cone. This is not to suggest that fine poetry is not produced elsewhere of course, but rather that the central questions concerning the movement of history arise and are tested in those regions. Central America produces more than its share of poets and singers. Clearly the generally low literacy levels in the region, coupled with the weakness and subordination of the local bourgeoisie, both ensured the persistence of an oral culture and produced little in the way of a bourgeois self-expression. Poetry, particularly a popular poetry not necessarily located in the lyric voice, was thus the most appropriate form for the tentative vocabulary of a new self-consciousnes. While there is no single form characteristic of the region, there is a prevailing register. In Nicaragua, the echoes of Cardenal are unmistakable; there is intensity of expression but an absence of metaphor, and there is an overpowering identity between the individual subject and the destiny of the community as a whole – the fulfilment of the concept of 'solidarity' articulated by Ernesto Cardenal in his work as a poet and as minister of culture in the Sandinista government. There is a utopian tone to the poetry of the poetry workshops as they echo the special rhetoric of Nicaraguan political discourse with its self-consciously poetic language. Tomás Borge, minister of the interior, gave speeches that were lyrical disquisitions full of references to a future of fulfilment and love. The words are echoed in their turn in the songs of the revolution, which often take their lyrics from poetry or political speeches. The emotive and powerful 'No pasarán' (They shall not pass), using the echoes of Spain in 1936, was written by Gioconda Belli; she herself says it is far from her best poem, but takes pride in the public resonance it acquired in the era of national defence against US imperialism.

This poetry of revolution represents the construction of a history and a sense of community. Its keynotes of sacrifice and selflessness

347

anticipate the community of equals that will issue from revolution. But these words also serve to some extent to veil a more contradictory and problematic present, where inequality has persisted, and the revolution has survived through compromise and postponement. This does not devalue the poetry – it is as legitimate for it to participate in the construction of a culture as in its destruction and rejection. But at the point where it veils the reality, distracting attention from the complexity of public experience, it approaches the realm of ideology. The line is hard to draw, but poetry does and should enshrine a critical appropriation of the real, not as abstraction, but as lived experience. It is in this sense that the heterodox work of Rosario Murillo and Gioconda Belli seems, in a sense, more convincing and authentic – and to strike a note whose absence in Cuba we have already noted.[8] In Central America, of course, the dream is to the fore – it is the intrusion of the real that is sometimes absent.

In El Salvador, that criticism does not seem apposite, perhaps because the general level of political consciousness is higher, perhaps because the class nature of the struggle was so much clearer as it evolved through the last decade. There is a maturity of understanding in the best of Salvadorean poetry, a balance of rage and insight in the work for example of Claribel Alegría, different but as profound as the wonderful irony of Roque Dalton. Like the much older Claudia Lars, the predominant note in Alegría's poetry was an increasing distance and alienation from her own class ('El abuelo' – The grandfather) and the oppressive experience of exile, of distance from the elements that could resolve a different identity. It is not far from the experience of Gioconda Belli in Mexico City prior to 1979, and echoes the persistent image of an oppressive silence that is a focus for the writing of Rosario Murillo.

What Central America has produced is a political poetry of a distinct kind, a poetry without artifice which seeks in its very simplicity to reproduce the putative consciousness of the revolutionary protagonist, the rural guerrilla. The problem is that the picture of the subject of the Central American revolution is too limited, too specific. El Salvador, for example, has experienced a struggle which has for several of the last ten years evolved in liberated rural zones. Yet the political character of that movement is still given by an urban experience, of workers' organization and mass mobilization in the cities. And the completion of that revolution will hinge on its resuming that character. It is, in brief, a rising of workers and peasants – yet its image is overwhelmingly that of a rural community fighting for its existence. Poetry and song, of course, are instruments of mobilization and propaganda, and very properly so. But the troubled and critical voice of a Geoffroy Rivas, for example, is absent in the nascent literary culture of an El Salvador in struggle. The question is: are the poets necessary to the unfolding of the struggle? Clearly not, if they are perceived as Paz sees them as detractors from that struggle, their *absence* being their defining characteristic. But if we see the poet as embedded in and responsive to a public demand, a witness and the bearer of a collective voice, then clearly the poets are central to the process. Today, the pressing task is the creation of community built around concepts of love and solidarity whose source is often religious. In the construction of a new society, however, new and different relationships will be forged whose complexities and contradictions will require a matching exploration in poetry and song.[9]

The simplicity of form in the work of Lars and Alegría, for example, provides a note of immediacy, of personal intensity. Both these poets, having wrestled in much of their work against the impositions of their own class, testify to the urgency of the immediate tasks, and their own self-effacement: 'I was slow to hear the rebels footsteps/and the live burial of any prison./Today I am ashamed of the years wasted/in the comfortable refuge/of the deaf.'[10]

Out of the Night

Clearly, however, there is a different direction to be discerned elsewhere in the continent. The poetry of exile produces a rejection of the prevailing discourse at home, the new language of repression and abstract nationalism that shrouds the reality of the military regimes. Here, naming the world passes first through a process of *dis*integration, taking apart and ironizing discourses. At the heart of that procedure is a contradiction, however, as the process of deconstruction of that kind of society involves in turn a dismembering of the self, a cannibalizing of the individual as an act of defiance. Art breaks the conventions, challenges the wholeness of discourse, fragments both language and speaker. It is difficult to conceive in principle of a more private pursuit – yet it is part of the process to which this book is devoted. It does form part of a public poetry; after all, the esoteric discourse of poetry and art is not saved from the ruthless coercive operation. The point, however, is that the private pain is rehearsed in the public domain, in a language of collective experience. The restrictions on poetic language are dispensed with and all discourses and areas of knowledge are embraced – there occurs a kind of negative enumeration. At the same time the current of a poetry of the street, the language of public argument and polemic is, as it is in Urondo and Gelman, the medium of shared experience.

By the early eighties that language, dismembered and disconsolate, gives way to another language, a poetry of absence, remnants of the past. As Horacio Salas put it in his 1985 volume *Gajes del oficio* (Hazards of work)[11]

> muchos hombres
> en determinados momentos de la historia (casi siempre digamos)
> deben abandonar el edificio en llamas
> para no consumirse como los volúmenes de Alejandría
> o terminar con dos balas en la nuca y las manos atadas en la espalda.
> Con la ropa que pudieron salvar del bombardeo
> los refugiados recorren los caminos en largas caravanas
> perseguidos por las ametralladoras de las cazas
> quemados por la luz de las bengalas
> por las pestes el hambre y el saqueo
> Y todavía con cicatrices y temblores que agitan la memoria
> arriban a cuidades lejanas . . .

> (many men/at certain moments in history (we could say almost always)/ have to just abandon the burning building/not to be consumed like the books of Alexandria/or end up with two bullets in the back of the neck and hands tied behind the back./With the clothes they could save from the bombing/the refugees travel along the roads in long columns/ persecuted by the machine-guns of the hunt/burned by the flares/by plagues hunger and pillage/And still with scars and tremors that move the memory/they reach the foreign cities . . .)

The flat matter-of-fact tone is characteristic of much of the poetry in exile, as if the brute facts of expulsion and loss were sufficient in themselves, too awful to grasp as emotion and presented then as fact, event. Others speak of the emotion, the loss of self, the withdrawal and despair – an alternative universe from the details of reality. The radical separation between self and world is the most ravaging component of exile, and is echoed in the poetry of the time. There are refuges – in nostalgia, in the enactment of the past, in the constant reminder that it was once otherwise; utopia is located in the past, and recalled above all through song.[12] The present is a topic, but in Chile that present is repression and torture, and the key memory is recent pain. That is the prevailing note of the new poetry. Yet it is subversive, for it asserts the existence of a collective memory of which the poems are fragments – and in the reading, the private assimilation, there can be a secret meeting and reconstruction, a public world reconstructed in the dense and private imagery of poetry and song.

350

This new register is captured in two small volumes published in 1987 by the Chilean poet Raul Zurita, *Purgatorio* and *Canto a su amor desaparecido*. Here the voices of emptiness and disintegration combine with the deep and searing lament for the lost and tortured. Nothing so dominates the centre of consciousness of a generation of Chileans than the systematic torture and brutalization of nearly twenty years of military rule. There is no escape from that collective memory. The issue is where the pain of it can be assuaged, and what can be rescued and recreated out of the terrible grief that the poets share. In a sense the heroic mode of the songs and poetry that commemorate the achievements of the Allende period seems curiously inappropriate to the new and younger generation for whom the opportunity to shape their own world was for over a decade almost absent. The external Chile, the Chile of political memory, belongs to a different code. It seems, however, that the more dense and painfully contradictory voices of Zurita and the singer-songwriter Patricio Manns say more to the current generation.

Purgatorio (Purgatory) is a location in logic and thought, a memory emptied of anything other than the remotest echoes of a past. The prehistory of this strange journey through the objective and mythic deserts of Chile is a violation, the denuding of a human being of whose biography we have only fragments, numbered randomly to underline how much of that history has already disappeared. We know that what it has left behind are an intense self-loathing ('Me he aborrecido tanto estos años' – I have hated myself so much in these years). Yet there is some residual sense of self, despite the humiliation and the pain.

> Destrocé mi cara tremenda
> frente al espejo
> te amo – me dije – te amo
>
> Te amo a más que nada en el mundo

(I destroyed my tremendous face/before the mirror/I love you – I said to myself – I love you//I love you more than anything in the world)

The other, and the reference points of language, are lost. The dehumanization is almost absolute, and the desert of the following sections is both an external and an interior landscape of devastation and absolute loss.

351

MI PROPIA MENTE EL DESIERTO DE CHILE
te creías que era poca
cosa enfilarse por allá para
volver después de su propio
nunca dado vuelta extendido
como una llanura frente a nosotros

(MY OWN MIND THE DESERT OF CHILE/you thought it was no big/deal to
walk out that way and then/come back after your own/never turned
back stretched/like a plain before us)

The noise of baaing sheep out there is the noise of our own souls, and
Chile, the nation the community is 'el más allá de la vida' (the other
side of life). All that is left are words overwritten on other documents,
like the computer printouts of the final part which carry the legend 'mi
mejilla es el cielo estrellado' (my cheek is the starry sky), and beneath
at the end, 'Yo y mis amigos, MI LUCHA' (My friends and I/MY
STRUGGLE).

Language, experience, memory, geography lose their coherence in a
poetry of found objects and fragments. Only the 'I', the meeting point
remains, dismembered but alive. The landscape of Chile is a symbolic
desert occupied by animals who are only their sign. The radical
pessimism of this vision is not absolute; the final word is struggle, after
all. Zurita's other 1987 volume, however, is both more absolutely
despairing and more complex in its response. Words crowd the pages
and although the speakers are not identified there are, in *Canto a su
amor desaparecido* (Song to a disappeared lover), a multitude of voices, a
chorus of pain. The field of crosses stretches before the speaker, and he
looks across the 'galpones', the edifices of burial niches where one of
the voices speaks and lies in purgatory with his lover, lamented,
missed and wanted. The alternative typeface permits a cumulative
chorus of other voices to echo and confirm the communal despair. The
symbol of the 'desert' recurs in these 'Desiertos de amor' (Deserts of
love or Bereft of Love). Yet the second part is not mere enumeration,
naming of common pain, a registering of the dead and the wounded
across the world. It is also a reconstruction of a common experience of
love – it is still love even though it has been lived in pain and distress –
and a kind of resurrection in the word. 'No queda nada. Pero muerta te
amo' (There is nothing left. But even in death I love you).

La generación sudaca canta folk, baila rock, pero todos se están murien-
do con la vista vendada en la barriga de los galpones
En cada nicho hay un país, están allí, son los países sudamericanos.
Grandes glaciares vienen a recogerlos.

(The generation of the south sings folk songs, dances to rock music, but all are dy-/ing with their eyes covered in the belly of the burial niches/In every niche there's a country, they are there, they are the countries of South America./Great glaciers are coming to collect them.)

The search through all these places of the dead yields a common history, a shared dread, and the affirmation of all that is in the final words of assertion 'Sí dice' (Yes he says) and the dedication to the people who have been part of the work and also 'to the grass, the air, the sky, the beloved trees'. With love the landscape returns, and with it a possibility of reconstruction.

It is at this point, then, that the radical and pained individualism of Zurita meets the voice of those like Patricio Manns whose dense and complex songs and poetry have caught the irony and the rage of the years of exile. As the pupil and legitimate inheritor of the finest of Chilean singers, Violeta Parra, Manns attests to the continuity of the critical voice of the 'popular poets' whose work is embedded in the songs of Violeta.[13] On the other, the elliptical and dense quality of his language bears witness to the other experience, of exile and clandestinity. The language of poetry becomes again testimony to the creativity of human imagination, an act of utopian affirmation *and* a medium in which those dreams can both be protected from the corruptions of the world and prepared to be cast into the public domain and transformed there by collective use.

The form and direction of the poetry of the coming decade is unpredictable – as unpredictable as the forms that the popular movement will assume in its coming struggle. It can be said with certainty, however, that poets and writers will emerge who will try to articulate the aspirations of such movements in a way that persuades and convinces those who waver. With the overcoming of exile, the return to a world newly enumerated and appropriated, the private drama may enter into dialogue with the public experience. That is the direction that we have traced as poetry has emerged from its isolation and left behind the closed language of other times. The entry into the public domain can mean many things. For some poets it has meant an increasing immersion in popular culture, as they have moved into television, soap operas and other arenas of popular culture. What has been a realm of consolation on the one hand and alienation on the other is now reoccupied, reappropriated, as a place of rebellion and resistance, but also of knowledge and understanding. Is that the direction of political poetry? It is certainly *one* direction, and one that is particularly clear in the field of music, where many of the new singers have become immersed in dance and popular music where versions of political declamation evolve through music.[14]

There are dangers inherent in these developments. They could lead to a parochialism which denies the deepening integration of the world market and the consequent identity of experience in the face of a common enemy. Equally, they could produce a devaluation of that individual experience which can both enrich the collective and challenge it – the critical function of poetry that we have tried to address. There will always be tension between private desire and public need. But that encounter is the legitimate location for a public poetry that questions the prevailing discourse, but also enters the world of real history and living forces, immersing itself in real living experience. When he remembers his country Patricio Manns 'feels he is rifle and volcano' but he is also a seagull; he is fighter and dreamer. The hope is that from one end of Latin America to the other there has evolved, and continues to emerge, a poetry whose democratic purpose embraces every experience, every memory, every element of a living world whose enumeration and reappropriation begins in the emergence from the secrecy of private language and proceeds upon the gathering of voices.

Notes

Introduction

1. See T. Eagleton, *Literary Theory*; Blackwell, Oxford 1983; in particular the introduction.

2. See for example Steven White, *Culture and Politics in Nicaragua*; Lumen Books, New York 1986; *Hacia una política cultural*, Ministerio de Cultura, Managua 1983; M. Randall, *Risking a Somersault in the Air*, Solidarity Publications, San Francisco 1984.

3. Jean Franco in C. Nelson and L. Grossberg, *Marxism and the Interpretation of Culture*, Macmillan, London 1988, p. 504.

4. 'Poetry is the other voice. Not the word of history or antihistory but the voice that, in history, always says *something else* – the same something since the beginning' in Octavio Paz, *Convergences*, Harcourt Brace, New York 1987, p. 216.

5. See Noe Jitrik, *Las contradicciones del modernismo*, Colegio de Mexico, Mexico 1978.

6. As Williams puts it, the avant-garde artists 'were not the bearers of a progress already repetitiously defined, but the militants of a creativity which would revive and liberate humanity' in R. Williams: *The Politics of Modernism*, Verso, London 1989, p. 51.

7. See F. Fanon, *Black Skin White Masks*, Grove Press, New York 1967.

8. See A. Roa Bastos, 'Fragments of a Paraguayan Autobiography' in *Third World Quarterly* 9(1), January 1987, pp. 212–28.

9. See A. Rama, *Transculturación narrative en América Latina*, Siglo XXI, Mexico 1982, particularly Part I.

10. See the debate between Bloch and Lukács in E. Bloch et al, *Aesthetics and Politics*, Verso, London 1977, pp. 16–59.

11. See below Chapter 8.

12. See his key essay 'A literature of convergences' in Paz, *Convergences*, pp. 217–26.

13. In M. Benedetti, *Antología poética*, Alianza, Madrid 1984, p. 111.

14. See G. Bisztray, *Marxist Models of Literary Realism*, Columbia UP, New York 1978, p. 81.

15. See for example S. Basnett (ed.), *Knives and Angels*, Zed Books, London/New Jersey 1990.

16. See for example M. Crow, *Woman who has Sprouted Wings*, Pittsburgh 1984; also A. Hopkinson (ed.), *Lovers and Comrades: Women's Resistance Poetry from Latin America*, The Women's Press, London 1989.

17. See in this respect Hopkinson (ed.), *Lovers and Comrades*.

1. How to Strangle a Swan

1. For an introduction to that history see Eduardo Galeano, *The Open Veins of Latin America*: Monthly Review Press, New York 1973; Tulio Halperin Donghi, *Historia contemporánea de América Latina*, Alianza, Madrid 1972 or the *Cambridge History of Latin America*, edited in 7 volumes by Leslie Bethell, Cambridge University press, Cambridge 1984.

2. This contradiction is in many ways the starting point for what remains a seminal essay on the Indian and the land, 'La cuestión de la tierra' (The question of the land) in José Carlos Mariátegui, *Siete ensayos de interpretación sobre la realidad peruana*, Lima 1927.

3. A great deal has been written on Modernismo. Particularly useful are J.E. Pacheco (ed.), *Antología del modernismo 1884–1921*, UNAM, Mexico 1970; G. Brotherston, *Spanish American Modernista Poets*, Pergamon, London 1968; Max Henriquez Ureña's standard work, *Breve historía del modernismo*, FCE, Mexico 1962; Noe Jitrik, *Las contradicciones del modernismo*, Colegio de Mexico, Mexico 1978.

4. See, in this respect, W. Benjamin: 'The Work of Art in the Era of its Mechanical Reproduction' in *Illuminations*, Jonathan Cape, London 1970.

5. See the Preface to Darío's *Prosas profanas* in Darío, *Poesías completas*, Aguilar, Madrid 1961; pp. 611–15.

6. See for example J.J. Arrom, *Esquema generacional de la literatura latinoamericana*, Instituto Caro y Cuervo, Bogota 1963.

7. M. Berman, *All That Is Solid Melts Into Air*, Verso, London 1983, p. 24.

8. See H.E. Davis, *Latin American Thought*, Louisiana State University, Baton Rouge 1972 (ch. in particular); L. Zea (ed.), *America Latina en sus ideas*, Siglo XXI/Unesco, Mexico 1986. Also R.L. Woodward, *Positivism in Latin America 1850–1900*, D.C. Heath, London 1971.

9. On colonial Latin America see S.J. and B. Stein, *The Colonial Heritage of Latin America*, OUP, New York 1970. Also Ricardo Palma, *Tradiciones peruanas*

10. See Gwen Kirkpatrick, *The Dissonant Legacy of Modernismo: Lugones, Herrera y Reissig and the Voices of Modern Spanish American Poetry*, Univ. of California Press, Berkeley 1989. Also C.H. Magis, *La poesía de Leopoldo Lugones*, Ateneo, Mexico 1960.

11. This despite the frequent references to Jose Hernández's *Martín Fierro* and the body of 'popular poetry' on which it rested in its turn.

12. Berman, *All That is Solid* p. 15.

13. See ibid. also the critique of Berman by Perry Anderson, 'Modernity and Revolution' in C. Nelson and L. Grossberg, *Marxism and the Interpretation of Culture*, Macmillan, Basingstoke 1988: pp. 317–38.

14. Berman, *All That is Solid* p. 24.

15. J.A. Silva, *Obras Completas*, Bogota 1965.

16. See Berman, *All That Is Solid* ch. 3; W. Benjamin: 'On Some Motifs in Baudelaire': in *Illuminations*, Cape, London 1970: pp. 157–202. See also T.J. Clark, *The Absolute Bourgeois*, Thames & Hudson, London 1973.

17. Benjamin, 'On Some Motifs', p. 160.

18. M. Henriquez Ureña, *Breve historía*, p. 157.

19. A process explored by T.J. Clark, *The Absolute Bourgeois*, and Walter Benjamin (see below) in their exploration of the work of Baudelaire.

20. Cf. A. Sánchez Vázquez, *The Philosophy of Praxis*, Merlin, London 1977, chap. vi.

21. J.K. Huysmans, *A rebours*, Paris 1925.

22. See in this respect Raymond Williams, *The Country and the City*, Hogarth Press, London 1985, chaps 13 and 14. The pastoral could rarely survive the shock of the encounter between the imagined conditions of rural life and the real relations that prevailed there. The *costumbrista* writers, with their picturesque and unchanging rural

scapes, could never write in the same way after John Kenneth Turner and others exposed the horror of social and economic relationships on the working land.

23. K. Marx and F. Engels, *The Communist Manifesto*, Penguin Books, Harmondsworth 1967: 'the bourgeoisie cannot exist without constantly revolutionizing the instruments of production and thereby the relations of production, and with them the whole relations of society.'

24. See introduction to Pacheco, *Antología del modernismo*.

25. See D. Cosío Villegas, *Historia moderna de México: el Porfiriato*, Mexico 1937 and Leopoldo Zea, *El positivismo en Mexico*, Mexico 1968.

26. Their conditions described in John Kenneth Turner's famous piece of investigative muckraking, *Barbarous Mexico*, S.H. Kern, Chicago 1911.

27. See below, p. 11

28. See R. Darío, *Poesías completas*. The Darío bibliography is enormous but see, for example, Noe Jitrik, *Las contradicciones*; and Ángel Rama *Rubén Darío y el modernismo*, Alfadil, Caracas 1970.

29. 'Palabras liminares', pp. 612–13.

30. Ibid., p. 611.

31. Ángel Rama, *Literatura y clase social*, Folios, Mexico 1983, p. 85.

32. Ibid., p. 88.

33. Ibid., pp. 91–2.

34. Published 1888–90: Darío, *Poesías completas*, pp. 574–608.

35. Rama, *Rubén Darío* p. 101.

36. In Marx's words 'Man has lost his identity [in the present-day society], but at the same time he has not only acquired the theoretical consciousness of this loss, he has been driven, out of distress no longer to be evaded, no longer to be ameliorated, utterly imperious – as the practical expression of necessity – to revolt against this inhumanity.' *The Holy Family*; Moscow 1956, p. 52. It is this necessity to which the Modernista movement responds.

37. Rama, *Rubén Darío* p. 134.

38. Cf. Oscar Collazos, *Los vanguardismos en América Latina*, Ed. Península, Barcelona 1977; and J.C. Mariátegui, *El artista y la época*, Ed. Amauta, Lima 1964.

39. In the essay 'El poeta frente a la modernidad' in *Literatura y clase social* referred to above.

40. J. Herrera y Reissig, *Poesías completas*, Aguilar, Madrid 1961.

41. In J.E. Pacheco, *Antología del modernismo*, Tomo I, p. 8.

42. In ibid., p. 88.

43. In ibid., p. 80.

44. Pacheco describes it as a 'a poetry written on tiptoes lest the world awake', *Antología*, p. 86.

45. On this body of writing see J. Brushwood, *Mexico in its novel*, Univ. of Texas Press, Austin 1966.

46. J.E. Rodo, *Ariel*, published in 1900. See edition by G. Brotherston, Cambridge University Press, Cambridge 1967.

47. José Martí has provoked a massive amount of writing, particularly in Cuba. But see especially Angel Rama on Martí; Peter Turton, *José Martí: Architect of Cuba's Freedom*, Zed Books, London 1986. See too R. Fernández Retamar, 'Las letras fieras de José Martí,' the introduction to *José Martí: Antología*, Havana 1980.

48. Heralded in Baudelaire's famous opening poem of *Les fleurs du mal*, and his sardonic reference to his 'Hypocritical reader'.

49. See Benjamin, 'On Some Motifs in Baudelaire', pp. 157–202.

50. Manuel Gutiérrez Nájera, *Poesías completas*, Ed. Porrua, Mexico 1953.

51. Ramon López Vélarde, *Poesías completas*, Ed. Porrua, Mexico 1953. On the work of

357

López Velarde see, for example, Octavio Paz: *Cuadrivio*, Joaquin Mortiz, Mexico 1969, pp. 67–130.

52. E. González Martínez: 'Tuércele el cuello al cisne' in S. Elizondo (ed.), *Museo poético*, UNAM, Mexico 1974, p. 90.

53. On Lugones see particularly Gwen Kirkpatrick, *The Dissonant Legacy*.

54. See Jorge Basurto, *El proletariado industrial en Mexico: 1850–1930*, UNAM, Mexico 1975.

55. He was a considerable influence on many artists of his time. See, for example, J.C. Orozco: *Autobiografía*, ERA, Mexico 1970.

56. R. Williams, *The Politics of Modernism*, Verso, London 1989. p. 71.

57. José Olivio Jimenez, *Antología de la poesía hispanoamericana contemporánea: 1914–1970*, Alianza Editorial, Madrid 1971, introduction.

58. See J.D. Cockcroft, *Intellectual Precursors of the Mexican Revolution*; and J.E. Pacheco, introduction to *Antología del Modernismo*, UNAM, Mexico 1970.

59. J.J. Tablada, *Obras I – Poesía*, UNAM, Mexico 1971.

60. In S. Baciú, *Antología de la poesía surrealista latinoamericana*, Mortiz, Mexico 1974. p. 36.

2. Out of the Prison of Language

1. On Mexico, the revolution of 1910–17 and the origins and development of Mexican nationalism see: A. Gilly, *The Mexican Revolution*, Verso, London 1983; Alan Knight, *The Mexican Revolution*, OUP, Oxford 1987; and James D. Cockcroft, *Intellectual Precursors of the Mexican Revolution*; Univ. of Texas Press, Austin 1968; Arnaldo Córdova, *La formación del poder político en Mexico* ERA, Mexico 1972; P. Gonzalez Casanova, *La democracia en México*, Siglo XXI, Mexico 1967. See also John Reed's *Insurgent Mexico*, International Publishers, New York 1982.

2. See Alfonsina Storni, *Selected Poems*, White Pine Press, New York 1987. See also Conrado Nalé Roxlo y M. Mármol, *Genio y figura de Alfonsina Storni*, EUDEBA, Buenos Aires 1964; Rachel Phillips, *Alfonsina Storni: From Poetess to Poet*, Tamesis London, 1975; S.C.A Andreola, *Alfonsina Storni, vida, talento, soledad*, Plus Ultra, Buenos Aires 1976; Beatriz Sarlo, *Una modernidad periférica, Buenos Aires 1920 y 1930*, Ed. Nueva Vision, Buenos Aires 1988, pp. 78–85.

3. See G. Mistral, *Antología*, Zig Zag, Santiago 1957. Also D.Dana (trans.), *Selected poems of Gabriela Mistral*, Johns Hopkins Univ. Press, Baltimore 1971. See too M. Arce de Vázquez, *Gabriela Mistral: The Poet and her Work*, New York Univ. Press, New York 1964.

4. See J. Elliott, *Antología crítica de la nueva poesía chilena*, Univ. de Concepción, Concepción 1957.

5. José Gorostiza, *Muerte sin fin*, Mexico 1939.

6. The phrase is assumed by Octavio Paz in *Convergences*, Harcourt Brace, New York 1987, p. 224. See also Frederick Stimson, *The New Schools of Latin American Poetry*, Univ. of North Carolina, Valencia 1970.

7. Quoted in C. Slaughter, *Marxism: Ideology and Literature*, Macmillan, London 1980, p. 2.

8. This is from the third of Karl Marx's *Theses on Feuerbach*, in Bottomore and Rubel (eds.), *Karl Marx: Selected Writings in Sociology and Social Philosophy*, Penguin, Harmondsworth 1963. p. 83.

9. On Chile see Luis Vitale, *Interpretación marxista de la historia de Chile*, Prensa Latinoamericana, Santiago 1962.

10. V. Huidobro, *Poesía y prosa*, Aguilar, Madrid 1967.

11. On this period in general see Sarlo, *Una modernidad periférica*. See Thorpe Running, *Borges's Ultraista Movement and its Poets*, International Book Publishers, Michigan 1981; and Oscar Collazos, *Las Vanguardias literarias en AméricaLatina*, Eds Peninsula, Barcelona 1977.

12. See Guillermo Ara, *Suma de poesía argentina*, Part I – Critica, Ed. Guadalupe, Buenos Aires 1970; especially chapter VI.

13. Quoted in F. Stimson, *The New Schools of Spanish American Poetry*, Univ. of North Carolina Press, Valencia 1970. p. 56.

14. See Enrique Lihn, 'Momentos esenciales de la poesía chilena' in *Panorama de la literatura latinoamericana*, Mexico 1967, pp. 189–90.

15. Ibid.

16. 'Altazor o el viaje en paracaídas' in Huidobro, *Poesía y prosa*, pp. 275–89. See too D.M. Gross (trans.), *Selected Poetry of Vicente Huidobro*, New Directions, New York 1981.

17. Alcides Arguedas's *Raza de bronce* for example, was published in 1916, though its imagery of a timeless race of noble savages belonged to a much earlier perception. Romantic visions of Inca and Aztec pasts, enshrined perhaps in the spectacular success of the Peruvian singer Yma Sumac, coexisted with the emerging *indigenista* approach to the indigenous peoples as an oppressed group.

18. See John Berger, 'The Moment of Cubism' in J. Berger, *Selected Essays and Articles*, Penguin, Harmondsworth 1972, pp. 133–64.

19. On these issues see the masterly study of art under Weimar by John Willett, *The New Sobriety: Art and Politics in the Weimar Period 1917–1933*, Thames & Hudson, London 1978.

20. D. Lodge, *The Modes of Modern Writing*, Univ. of Chicago Press, Chicago 1977. p. 89.

21. C. Vallejo, *Obra poética completa*, Alianza Editorial, Madrid 1983. See too Jean Franco, *César Vallejo: The Dialectics of Poetry and Silence*, Cambridge University Press, Cambridge 1976; and James Higgins, *Visión del hombre y de la vida en las últimas obras de César Vallejo*, Siglo XXI, Mexico 1970.

22. Cf. T. Bennett, *Formalism and Marxism*, Methuen, London 1979, chapter 2.

23. Enshrined, of course, in Borges's 'fictions', each explorations of the contingent, accidental quality of language. See for example, 'Tlon Uqbar, Orbis Tertius' in *Ficciones*, Alianza Editorial, Madrid 1971.

24. In Voloshinov's words, 'consciousness itself can arise and become a viable fact only in the material embodiment of signs . . .And nowhere is there a break in the chain, nowhere does the chain plunge into inner being, nonmaterial in nature and unembodied in signs'. N.N. Voloshinov, *Marxism and the Philosophy of Language*, Harvard Univ. Press, Cambridge 1986, p. 11.

25. The concept of 'structure of feeling' was developed by Raymond Williams. See his *Problems in Materialism and Culture*, Verso, London 1980. pp. 22–7.

26. J.C. Mariátegui, *El artista y la época*, Ed. Amauta, Lima 1964 (Obras Completas 6), pp. 29–31.

27. Ibid, p. 31.

28. Ibid.

29. See J.C. Mariátegui, *Siete ensayos de interpretación de la realidad peruana*, Amauta, Lima 1978 (Obras Completas 2), p. 270. The English version, *Seven Interpretive Essays on Peruvian Reality*, was published by University of Texas press in 1971.

30. See Franco, *César Vallejo*, chapter 2.

31. Marx described religion, in his famous phrase, as 'the sigh of the oppressed creature, the sentiment of a heartless world'. See Bottomore and Rubel, *Karl Marx*, p. 41.

32. Published in 1922.

359

33. The term belongs to Lucien Goldmann; see Williams, *The Politics of Modernism*, pp. 11–30.

34. See R. Jakobson, *Huit questions de poétique*, Eds du Seuil, Paris 1977.

35. See, in this respect, David Lodge, *The Modes of Modern Writing*, pp. 77–9, 'Two types of aphasia'.

36. See R. Jakobson, *Huit questions de poétique*, p. 16 passim. See too David Lodge, *The Modes of Modern Writing*, part 2, pp. 73–124; and R. Williams, *Problems*, ch. 4 pp. 65–80.

37. There is an enormous bibliography of critical work on Neruda, and it is invidious to select from it. Nonetheless the work of Alain Sicard is expremely comprehensive: *El pensamiento poético de Pablo Neruda*, Ed. Gredos, Madrid 1981. See also M. Duran, *Earth Tones: The Poetry of Pablo Neruda*, Univ. of Indiana Press, Bloomington 1981. M. Aguirre's *Las vidas de Pablo Neruda*, Grijalbo, Buenos Aires 1973 gives a more intimate vision of Neruda's life and work and Neruda's own memoirs (*Confieso que he vivido*) and published in English as *Memoirs*, Penguin Books, Harmondsworth 1973 gives his own version of himself.

38. See M. Vera Valenzuela, *La política económica de cobre en Chile*, Ed. Universitaria, Santiago 1961.

39. See L. Vitale (ed.), *Obras escogidas de Luis Emilio Recabarren*, Santiago 1965.

40. Neruda's *Obras completas* have been published by Editorial Losada in Buenos Aires in a number of editions. See also *Pablo Neruda, Selected Poems*, edited by Nathaniel Tarn, Penguin Books, Harmondsworth 1977. *Residencia en la tierra* was published in three parts from 1933.

41. Published in 1950 and written between 1947 and 1949.

42. As Benjamin noted in the case of art nouveau, 'The transfiguration of the lone soul was its apparent aim. Individualism was its theory. It mobilized all the reserve forces of interiority' in 'Paris, Capital of the 19th century' in *New Left Review*, 48, March–April 1968, p. 83.

3. The Peanut-eating Poet

1. See Raymond Williams, 'When was Modernism?', *New Left Review*, 175, May/June 1989, pp. 48–52, or *The politics of Modernism: against the new conformists*, Verso, London 1989, pp. 31–5.

2. Mário da Silva Brito, *História do modernismo brasileiro: antecedentes da Semana de Arte Moderna*, Civilização Brasileira, Rio de Janeiro 1978, p. 20.

3. See Alfredo Bosi, *História concisa da literatura brasileira*, Cultrix, São Paulo 1970, pp. 246–62.

4. See Jeffrey D. Needell, *A tropical belle époque: elite culture and society in turn-of-the-century Rio de Janeiro*, Cambridge Unversity Press, Cambridge 1987, pp 10–22.

5. Olavo Bilac, *Poesias*, Edições de Ouro, Rio de Janeiro 1978, p. 9.

6. Mário de Andrade, 'Vicente do Carvalho', *Mestres do Passado – VI, Jornal do Comércio*, 23/8/21, in Silva Brito, *História do modernismo brasileiro*, p. 269.

7. E.g. the Andrades, Augusto Frederico Schmidt, Menotti del Picchia, Cassiano Ricardo and Plínio Salgado.

8. See Sérgio Miceli, *Intelectuais e classe dirigente no Brasil*, 1920–1945, DIFEL, São Paulo 1979.

9. See Neill Macaulay, *The Prestes Column: Revolution in Brazil*, New Viewpoints, New York 1974, and Boris Fausto, 'Society and Politics', in Leslie Bethell (ed.), *Brazil: Empire and Republic, 1822–1930, Part Two: First Republic (1889–1930)*, Cambridge University press, Cambridge 1988, pp. 257–307.

10. The most important precedent for the Modernist debate on the country's social

divisions was Euclides da Cunha's account of the Canudos Rebellion, *Os Sertões (1902)*, *Rebellion in the Backlands* (trans. Samuel Putnam), Chicago 1944.

11. Editorial of revista *Klaxon*, São Paulo, 15 May 1922, in Gilberto Mendonça Teles, *Vanguarda Européia e Modernismo Brasileiro: apresentação dos principais poemas, manifestos, prefácios e conferências vanguardistas, de 1857 a 1972*, Record, Rio de Janeiro 1987, p. 295.

12. 'Eu sou trezentos', *Remate de males*. All citations from poems by Mário de Andrade are taken from *Obras Completas de Mário de Andrade, II – Poesias Completas*, Martins, São Paulo 1966.

13. From *Alguma Poesia* (1930). All citations from poems by Drummond are taken from *Reunião: 10 livros de poesia de Carlos Drummond de Andrade*, José Olympio, Rio de Janeiro 1980.

14. This approach to Brazilian culture closely resembles that proposed in 1873 by the novelist Machado de Assis in his essay 'Instinto de nacionalidade' (Instinct of nationality).

15. *Caramurus* – members of a restoration monarchist faction during Brazil's Regency period (1831–40).

16. All citations from poems by Jorge de Lima are taken from the *Antologia Poética*, José Olympio, Rio de Janeiro 1978.

17. For a survey of these ideas, see Thomas Skidmore, *Black into White: Race and Nationality in Brazilian Thought*, Oxford University Press, New York 1974.

18. Gilberto Freyre, *Casa Grande e Senzala* (1933) (*The Masters and the Slaves.*)

19. See Needell, *A tropical belle époque*, pp. 10–22.

20. All citations from poems by Bandeira are taken from *Manuel Bandeira: Antologia poética*, José Olympio, Rio de Janeiro 1978.

21. All citations from poems by Mendes are taken from *Murilo Mendes: Poesia* org. Maria Lúcia Aragão, Agir, Rio de Janeiro 1983.

22. All citations from poems by Oswald are taken from *Obras Completas* vol. VII: *Poesias Reunidas*, Civilização Brasileira, Rio de Janeiro 1978.

23. Benedito Nunes, 'Antropofagia ao Alcance de Todos' in Oswald de Andrade, *Do Pau-Brasil à Antropofagia e às Utopias: manifestos, teses de concursos e ensaios*, Civilização Brasileira, Rio de Janeiro 1978, pp. xviii–xix.

24. Alceu Amoroso Lima (Tristão de Athaíde), 'Literatura Suicida', *Estudos 1925* in *Estudos Literários*, 2 vols, Aguilar, Rio de Janeiro 1966, vol. I, p. 917.

25. Nunes, 'Antropofagia', pp. xviii–xix.

26. Interview with Péricles Eugênio da Silva Ramos, *Correio Paulistano* 26/6/49, 3a seção, pp. 1–2, also cited in Péricles Eugênio da Silva Ramos, 'O Modernismo na Poesia', *A Literatura no Brasil* ed. Afrânio Coutinho, vol. V, Sul Americana, Rio de Janeiro 1970, p. 46.

27. All quotations from Oswald's manifestoes are translated from *Do Pau-Brasil à Antropofagia e às Utopias: manifestos, teses de concursos e ensaios*, Civilização Brasileira, Rio de Janeiro 1978.

28. 'A Poesia Pau-Brasil. Resposta a Tristão de Athayde', *O Jornal*, 18/9/25, reproduced in *Obras Completas*, vol.X: *Telefonema*, Civilização Brasileira, Rio de Janeiro 1974, pp. 43–51.

29. Cited in Joan Dassin, *Política e Poesia em Mário de Andrade*, Duas Cidades, São Paulo 1978, p. 145.

30. See Claudia Matos, *Acertei no milhar: malandragem e samba no tempo de Getúlio*, Paz e Terra, Rio de Janeiro 1982, pp. 39–59.

31. *Macunaíma: o herói sem nenhum caráter* ed. crítica de Telê Porto Ancona Lopez, SCCT, São Paulo 1978, p. 34; trans. (E.A. Goodland), *Macunaíma*, Quartet, London 1984.

32. Matos, *Acertei no milhar*. pp. 107–27.

33. Citations from *Cobra Norato* are taken from *Cobra Norato e outros poemas*, Civilização Brasileira, Rio de Janeiro 1978.

34. See João Marschner, 'Depoimentos: Oswald de Andrade no cotidiano', *Estado de São Paulo, Suplemento Literário* 24/10/64, p.2; also Raul Bopp, *Vida e Morte da Antropofagia* Civilização Brasileiro, Rio de Janeiro 1977.

35. From 'A raça cósmica', *Martim Cererê (o Brasil dos meninos, dos poetas e dos heróis)*, José Olympio, Rio de Janeiro 1978, pp. 56–7. See also 'Nota da editora', p. ix, and 'Nota à 12a edição', pp. 177-8.

36. See *A Marcha das Utopias* (1953) in *Do Pau-Brasil à Antropofagia*.

37. Davi Arrigucci Jr., 'O humilde cotidiano de Manuel Bandeira', *Enigma e comentário: ensaios sobre literatura e experiência*, Companhia das Letras, São Paulo 1987, pp. 9–27. See also Davi Arrigucci Jr., *Humildade, paixão e morte: a poesia de Manuel Bandeira*, Companhia das Letras, São Paulo 1990.

38. 'Prefácio interessantíssimo' for *Pauliceia Desvairada* in Mendonça Teles, *Vanguarda Européia*, pp. 299–300.

4. Awakenings

1. Quoted in T. Bennett, *Formalism and Marxism*, Methuen, London 1979, p. 45.

2. Raymond Williams, *The Politics of Modernism*, Verso, London 1989, p. 51.

3. 'Not only is the work of art liberated from its previous subordination to cultic ritual and its production transformed from a collaborative, artisanal into an individual practice – changes already under way under the absolute monarchies – but its mode of reception becomes individual . . .' in Alex Callinicos, *Against Postmodernism*, Polity Press, Oxford 1989, p. 52. See too A. Sanchez Vazquez, *Art and Society*, Merlin, London 1977, Part II: 'The Destiny of Art under Capitalism'.

4. On the rise of nationalism in Latin America see T. Halperin Donghi, *Historia Contemporánea De América Latina*, Alianza Editorial, Madrid 1971. On the complex significance accorded to indigenous cultures see Angel Rama, *Transculturación narrativa en América Latina*, Siglo XXI, Mexico 1982.

5. On the early history of the working-class movement in Latin America see P. González Casanova, *Historia del movimiento obrero en América Latina*, Siglo XXI/UNAM, Mexico 1984, 4 volumes. See too Latin American Bureau, *Unity is Strength: Trade Unions in Latin America*, London 1980.

6. See the discussion of Gutiérrez Nájera in Chapter 1 above.

7. See the anthology edited by E. Ballagas, *Mapa de la poesía negra americana*, Pleamar, Buenos Aires 1946.

8. On this period see in particular D. Rock, *Politics in Argentina 1880–1930: The Rise and Fall of Radicalism*, Cambridge Univ. Press, Cambridge 1975.

9. See R.J. Walter, *Student Politics in Argentina: The University Reform and its Effects 1918–1964*, Basic Books, New York 1968.

10. See in this connection B. Sarlo, *Una modernidad periférica, Buenos Aires 1920 y 1930*, Ed. Nueva Vision, Buenos Aires 1988; and John King, *Sur: A Study of the Argentine Literary Journal and its Role in the Development of a Culture*, Cambridge Univ. Press, Cambridge 1986.

11. See Sarlo, *Una modernidad periférica*.

12. See 'Proclama de Prisma' in O. Collazos (ed.), *Los vanguardismos en la América Latina*, Peninsula, Barcelona 1970, pp. 143–5.

13. All poetry would be pared down to its single fundamental element, 'metaphor', See ibid., p. 135.

14. The manifesto appears in ibid., pp. 143–5.

15. Published in Buenos Aires in 1923. On Borges's poetry in general see, among a vast bibliography, C. Cortinez (ed.), *Borges the Poet*, Univ. of Arkansas Press, Feyetteville 1986.

16. See too E. Martínez Estrada, *Muerte y transfiguración de Martin Fierro*, FCE, Mexico 1958.

17. Thus Martín Fierro and his sons and companions, having experienced both exile and the new society, opt again for exile in a disappearing world – a kind of social death in which only the momentary survival of the self is possible.

18. See Jorge Luis Borges, *Obra poética*, Alianza/Emece, Madrid/Buenos Aires 1985, p. 73.

19. See David Viñas, *Literatura argentina y realidad política*, Jorge Alvarez, Buenos Aires 1971.

20. Borges then turns this on its head, using the word 'universal' only in its most ironic sense, and occupying the furthest edges of his own world.

21. Published in 1922. See Sarlo, *Una modernidad periférica*, chap. 2 and F. Masiello, *Lenguaje e ideologia: las escuelas argentinas de vanguardia*, Hachette, Buenos Aires 1986.

22. The paradox is that the dream leads back to reality, as Benjamin pointed out: 'Every epoch not only dreams the next, but while dreaming impels it towards wakefulness' in *Illuminations*, Jonathan Cape, London 1970, p. 88.

23. On Peruvian surrealism see S. Bacíu, *Antología de la poesía surrealista latinoamericana*, Joaquin Mortiz, Mexico 1974, particularly pages 43–9 and 111–16. Also James Higgins, *The Poet in Peru*, Francis Cairns, Liverpool University, 1982, ch II.1 and II.4.

24. J.M. Eguren, 'El andarín de la noche' quoted in S. Baciú, *Antologia* p. 134.

25. On Futurism etc. see J. Willett, *The New Sobriety*, Thames & Hudson, London 1978.

26. Cf. G. List Arzubide, *El movimiento estridentista*, Cuadernos de Lectura Popular, Mexico 1967. See too the general introduction to O. Paz et al., *Poesía en movimiento*, Siglo XXI, Mexico 1966.

27. See Luis leal 'El movimiento estridentista' in O. Collazos *Los vanguardismos*, pp 105–17 and C. Monsivais, 'Los estridentistas y los agoristas' in ibid., pp. 117–24.

28. Nothing so poignantly illustrated the consequences of uncontrolled growth as the Mexico City earthquake of 1986 which produced its own literature by Cristina Pacheco, Humberto Masocchi, Carlos Monsivais and many others.

29. Benjamin, *Illuminations*, p. 84.

30. Ibid., p. 85.

31. Cf. Sarlo, *Una modernidad periférica*, ch. 6 pp. 155–78. See also H. Yanóver (ed.), *Raul González Tuñón*, ECA, Buenos Aires 1962.

32. This refers to Sinclair Lewis's novel *Babbit* whose central character became synonymous with the *homme bourgeois moyen*, the 'average petit bourgeois'.

33. The Platt Amendment to the Cuban constitution allowed the United States to intervene directly in Cuban affairs under several pretexts.

34. In M. Bloch et al., *Aesthetics and Politics*, Verso, London 1977, p. 111

35. Quoted in T. Eagleton, *Marxism and Literary Criticism*, Methuen, London 1976, p. 62.

36. Ibid., p. 72.

37. On Guillén in general see Angel Augier: *Nicolás Guillén* (in 2 volumes), Univ. de las Villas, Havana 1965. See also Keith Ellis, *Cuba's Nicolás Guillén*, Univ. of Toronto Press, Toronto 1983.

38. See for example, E. Ballagas, *Mapa de la poesía*, and Julio Finn, *Voices of Negritude*, Quartet Books, London/New York 1988.

39. See Finn, *Voices of Negritude*, pp. 97–110.

40. Cf. R. Guirao, *Orbita de la poesía negra afrocubana*, Ucar Garcia, Havana 1938.

41. Ellis, *Cuba's Nicolás Guillén*, pp. 63–71.

42. A. Augier, 'Hallazgo y apoteósis del poema – son de Nicolás Guillén' in *Casa de las Americas*, Havana 1982, 132, pp. 36–53.

43. Augier, 'Hallazgo y apoteósis', vol.I. p. 246.

44. See the discussion of this and other issues plus an extensive bibliography edited

by Nancy Morejon, a considerable black poet in her own right. Nancy Morejon (ed.), *Recopilación de textos sobre Nicolás Guillén*, Valoración Múltiple, Havana 1974.

45. See, for the poetry of the period, D. Fitts (ed.), *Anthology of Contemporary Latin American Poetry*, New Directions, Norfolk, Conn. 1942.

46. See Felix Morrow, *Revolution and Counter-revolution in Spain*, New Park, London 1963.

47. See F. Bourricaud, *Power and Society in Contemporary Peru*, Praeger, New York 1970, the standard book on the early period. See also J.C. Mariátegui whose debates with APRA appear in the volume of his writings called *Peruanicemos el Perú*, Ed. Amauta, Lima 1964.

48. See for example C. Caudwell *Illusion and Reality: A Study of the Sources of Poetry*, International Publishers, New York 1970 (first edition 1937).

49. On this period in general see L. Trotsky, *Fascism, Stalinism, United Front*, Bookmark, London 1989.

50. See G. Bisztray, *Marxist Models of Literary Realism*, Columbia Univ. Press, New York 1978, chapter 2, pp. 51–102.

51. Maurice Bowra, *Poetry and Politics*, Cambridge Univ. Press, Cambridge 1966, p. 106.

52. 'The Author as Producer' in W. Benjamin, *Illuminations*, Cape, London 1967, p. 91.

53. See V. Cunningham (ed.), *Penguin Book of Spanish Civil War Poetry*, Penguin Books, Harmondsworth 1980; *Les poètes latinoamericains et la guerre d'Espagne*, CRICCAL, Sorbonne, Paris 1986; M. Rosenthal, *Poetry of the Spanish Civil War*, New York Univ. Press, 1975.

54. See M. Aznar Solet and L.M. Schneider, *II Congreso Internacional de Escritores Antifascistas*, Laia, Barcelona 1979, 3 volumes.

55. See Morrow, *Revolution*; and George Orwell, *Homage to Catalonia*, Penguin Books, Harmondsworth 1970. Orwell wrote his book, of course in 1938, as soon as he returned from Spain.

56. See Orwell, *Homage to Catalonia*, pp. 8–10.

57. For a general history and analysis of the Spanish Civil War, the fullest account is the brilliant narrative history assembled by Ronald Fraser in his *Blood of Spain*, Penguin Books, Harmondsworth 1981.

58. See ibid., pp. 373–83.

59. See Andreu Nin, *Los problemas de la revolucion española*, Paris 1971; and L. Trotsky's arguments with Nin in *The Spanish Revolution*, Pathfinder, new York 1973.

60. As Orwell put it in the famous passage from *Homage to Catalonia*, 'It was the first time I had ever been in a town where the working class was in the saddle.'

61. W.H. Auden's 'Spain' gives a profound sense of the mood of the period – see V. Cunningham, *Penguin Book*.

62. See Fraser, *Blood of Spain*, pp. 294–8 and 454–61.

63. See, for example, J.A. Ramos, *Historia del estalinismo en Argentina*, Ed. Mar Dulce, Buenos Aires, 1962/1969.

64. The war was presented in this way particularly after May 1937, in the wake of the defeat of the social revolution within the Spanish republic. See Orwell's postscript to *Homage to Catalonia*, 'Looking back on the Spanish War'.

65. On Guernica see J. Berger, *Success and Failure of Picasso*, Writers and Readers, London 1980, pp. 164–70.

66. As in some of the celebratory poems of his 1958 collection *Odas elementales*, for example 'Oda a la cebolla' (Ode to the onion) or 'Oda al tomate' (Ode to the tomato).

67. If the artist is reduced to the secondary and occasional role of making propaganda . . . whose role would it be to bear the artist's great traumaturgy of the spirit?'

68. See George Lambie's discussion of this period in Vallejo's life in his Warwick

University PhD thesis *Poetry and Ideology: The Effect of the Politics of the Inter-war Years on César Vallejo*, 1987.

69. Ibid. ch II.

70. See R. Paris et al., *El marxismo latinoamericano de Mariátegui*, Eds de Crisis, Buenos Aires 1973.

71. C. Vallejo, *La vida en Rusia en 1931* Ed Labor, Lima 1965.

72. See Jean Franco, *César Vallejo: The Dialectics of Poetry and Silence*, Cambridge Univ. Press, London 1976, ch. 6.

73. See Rubel and Bottomore, (eds), *Karl Marx: Selected Writings in Sociology and Social Philosophy*, Penguin, Harmondsworth 1963, p. 83.

74. It is often suggested that the long gap between the publication of *Trilce* and of his later work indicated a period of rethinking. It is equally clear that he remained to the end full of doubt despite his general convictions at the level of abstraction.

75. C. Vallejo, *Contra el secreto profesional*, Lima 1975.

76. Lambie, *Poetry and Ideology*, pp. 197-8.

5. The Feeling of the World

1. 'Sentimento do mundo' (1935); all citations from poems by Drummond are taken from *Reunião: 10 livros de poesia de Carlos Drummond de Andrade*, José Olympio, Rio de Janeiro 1980.

2. Antonio Ozai da Silva, *História das tendências no Brasil (Origens, cisões e propostas)*, São Paulo, n/d, pp. 61–8. See also E. Bradford Burns, *A History of Brazil*, Columbia University Press, New York 1980, pp. 398–433.

3. Oswald de Andrade, *Obras Completas* Vol. II, Civilização Brasileira, Rio de Janeiro 1971, pp. 131–2.

4. Andrade, *Obras Completas*, vol. II, p. 133.

5. Mário de Andrade, 'O Movimento Modernista', *Aspectos da literatura brasileira*, Martins, São Paulo 1974, p. 243.

6. Ibid., p. 253.

7. 'Do alto das montanhas de Minas, um terrível libelo contra os novos! – um dos epígonos do modernismo da terra inconfidente considera fracassada toda uma geração de intelectuais', *A Pátria*, 26 May 1931, cited in John Gledson, *Poesia e poética de Carlos Drummond de Andrade*, Duas Cidades, São Paulo 1981, p. 90; the analysis of Drummond's poetry in the present chapter is indebted to the latter study by John Gledson.

8. *71 Cartas de Mário de Andrade*, São José, Rio de Janeiro, n/d, (letter to Carlos Lacerda, 5/4/44), p.90.

9. From 'Solidariedade' (Solidarity). All citations from poems by Mendes are taken from *Murilo Mendes: Poesia* org. Maria Lúcia Aragão, Agir, Rio de Janeiro 1983.

10. All citations from poems by Bandeira are taken from *Manuel Bandeira: Antologia poética*, Jose Olympio, Rio de Janeiro 1978.

11. Irwin Stern (ed.) *Dictionary of Brazilian Literature*, Greenwood Press, New York 1988, p.194.

12. Marta Peixoto, 'The absent body: female signatures and poetic convention in Cecília Meireles', *Bulletin of Hispanic Studies*, LXV, No. 1, January 1988, pp. 87–100.

13. All citations from poems by Meireles are taken from Cecília Meireles, *Obra Poética*, José Aguilar, São Paulo 1967.

14. Peixoto, 'The absent body', p. 92.

15. Eduardo Portella, 'Do verso solitário ao canto coletivo' in Vinicius de Moraes, *Obra Poética*, José Aguilar, Rio de Janeiro 1968, p.19.

16. All quotations from poems by Vinicius de Moraes are taken from Moraes, *Obra Poética*, p. 175.

17. All citations from poems by Jorge de Lima are taken from the *Antologia Poética*, José Olympio, Rio de Janeiro 1978.

6. Retreats and Rediscoveries

1. 'Modern poetry is inseparable from the criticism of language which in turn is the most radical and the most virulent form of criticism of reality': Octavio Paz in *Alternating Current*, Wildwood House, London 1974, p. 4.

2. One example is Luis Mario Schneider, *La literatura mexicana*, CEAL, Buenos Aires 1967, vol. II ch. 3.

3. Paz saw a divergence at the heart of Latin American poetry between a 'poetry of solitude and a poetry of communion' in *Las peras del olmo*, UNAM, Mexico 1965, p. 124.

4. Through his many books of critical essays and review summarized to some extent in *Convergences*, Harcourt Brace, New York 1987.

5. See Ruy Mauro Marini, *Subdesarrollo y revolución*, Siglo XXI, Mexico 1969.

6. See E. Galeano, *The Open Veins of Latin America*, Monthly Review press, New York 1973.

7. See for example Efrain Huerta, *Poemas prohibidos y de amor*, Siglo XXI, Mexico 1980.

8. The indigenous question, the Indian community, the alternative vision of a future based on non-industrial culture remained central to the writing and explorations of such key figures as José Maria Arguedas and Ciro Alegria, major figures of Peruvian literature, for example.

9. Particularly in his extremely influential novel *Manhattan Transfer* (1928).

10. See, for example, his *Leyendas de Guatemala*, published in 1957.

11. Cf. C. Anglade and C. Fortin (eds), *The State and Capital Accumulation in Latin America*, Macmillan, London 1990 (2 volumes which examine the process country by country, as well as providing more general essays).

12. See on US responses to Guatemala and more generally on Central America Jenny Pearce's seminal *Under the Eagle*, Latin American Bureau, London 1981.

13. That spirit is caught in the so-called guerrilla poetry of the time, and in the memoirs of the participants like Hector Béjar Rivera (Peru 1965), Omar Cabezas (*Fire on the mountain*) and many others.

14. CF. E. Mallea, *Historia de una pasión argentina*, Espasa Calpe, Buenos Aires 1951 (4th edition, published 1940).

15. Cf. M. Gonzalez, 'Ernesto Cardenal's Zero Hour' in *Readings in Spanish and Portuguese Poetry for Geoffrey Connell*, Dept of Hispanic Studies, Glasgow University, 1985, pp. 47–66.

16. E. Cardenal, 'Salmo 43' from *Salmos*; in *Nueva antología poética*, Siglo XXI, Mexico 1983, p. 97.

17. Cf. Paul W. Borgeson, *Hacia el hombre nuevo: poesía y pensamiento de Ernesto Cardenal*, Tamesis Books, London 1984; and the excellent PhD thesis by J.J. Lyons, *Ernesto Cardenal: The Poetics of Love and Revolution*, Kings College, London 1988.

18. Published in 1937.

19. See J. Bernard, 'Myth and Structure in Paz's "Piedra del sol"' in *Symposium*, 21, 1967, pp. 5–13.

20. In Paz, *Alternating Current*, p. 67.

21. *Las Peras del olmo*, p. 124.

22. See O. Paz, *Claude Lévi-Strauss o el nuevo festín de Esopo*, Siglo XXI, Mexico 1967.

23. It is clear that Octavio Paz is not only an important poet but the dominant influence on Latin American poetry criticism for the last thirty or so years. See for

example his *Alternating Current* and *Convergences*, both previously referred to and both translated by Helen Lane.

24. Paz's definition of poetry, offered in his numerous essays and articles, specifically rejects conversational poetry from the canon he establishes there. Many of the arguments offered in this volume are intended to refute that definition.

25. Spender's Spanish writing can be found in V. Cunningham (ed.) *Penguin Book of Spanish Civil War Poetry*, Penguin Books, Harmondsworth 1980. His disillusionment with Spain is expressed in much of his subsequent work but see particularly his essay in *The God that Failed*,

26. In C. Tomlinson (ed.) *Octavio Paz*, Penguin, London 1979. This very good anthology contains a bilingual version of 'Himno entre ruinas', pp. 20–23.

27. Published by UNAM in Mexico.

28. Cf. T. Eagleton, *Literary Theory*, Basil Blackwell, Oxford 1983, pp. 92–4. See too F. Chiles, *Octavio Paz*, Peter Lang, New York/Berne 1987, p. 15.

29. See for example his lecture *The Scope of Anthropology*, Cape, London 1967.

30. J. Rulfo, *Pedro Páramo*, FCE, Mexico 1955.

31. See O. Paz, *The Collected Poems: 1957–1987*, edited by Eliot Winberger, Paladin Poetry, London 1988, the fullest collection. For the earlier work see the anthology *Libertad bajo palabra*, FCE, Mexico 1968.

32. Cf. O. Paz on 'El surrealismo' in *Las peras del olmo*, pp. 165–83 in reference to Latin America, as well as S. Baciu, *Antología de la poesía surrealista latinoamericana*, Joaquin Mortiz, Mexico 1974. On the principles of surrealism more generally see F. Rosemont, *André Breton and the First Principles of Surrealism*, Pluto Press, London 1978.

33. See introduction by José Miguel Ibañez-Langlois to to N. Parra, *Antipoemas*, Seix Barral, Barcelona 1976.

34. See I. Meszaros, *Lukács's Concept of Dialectics*, Merlin Press, London 1972, pp. 41–5.

35. Cf. Peter Wollen, 'Eisenstein's Aesthetics' in *Signs and Meaning in the Cinema*, Secker and Warburg, London 1969.

36. Nicanor Parra, *Antipoemas* (an anthology), Seix Barral, Barcelona 1976. See too E. Grossman, *The Antipoetry of Nicanor Parra*, New York Univ. Press, New York 1975.

37. See Chapter 10, note 13.

38. See E. Lihn, *This Endless Malice*, translated by W. Witherup et al., Lillaburlero Press, Northwood Narrows NHNH, 1969; and *The Dark Room and Other Poems*, translated by J. Cohen, New Directions, New York 1978.

39. See Gonzalo Rojas, *Contra la muerte*, Ed. Universitaria, Santiago 1964. Also Nelson Rojas, *Estudios sobre la poesía de Gonzalo Rojas*, Novo Scholar, Madrid 1984.

40. J.M. Oviedo, *Escrito al margen*, Instituto Colombiano de Cultura, Bogota 1983, p. 123.

41. Pacheco's poetry is gathered in *Tarde o temprano*, FCE, Mexico 1980.

42. Oviedo, *Escinto al margen*, p. 128.

43. Mortiz, Mexico 1969.

44. See Elena Poniatowska's account through the voices of witnesses and participants in the events of that day in *La noche de Tlatelolco*, ERA, Mexico 1971.

45. 'Manuscrito de Tlatelolco' in Pacheco, *Tarde o temprano*, pp. 65–70. These poems were the last written in the Nahua language by the singers and historians of the Aztec nation. They were present to the end to record the destruction of their society.

46. The Aztec term for the ritual encounters preceding battle as well as the battle itself.

47. In his *Posdata* (Postscript), Siglo XXI, Mexico 1970. (The book is a 'postscript' to his 1949 essay 'The Labyrinth of Solitude').

48. See Ernesto Cardenal (ed), *Poesía nicaraguense*, Ed. Nueva Nicaragua, Managua 1981.

49. Cf. Roberto Armijo and R. Paredes (eds), *Poesía contemporánea de Centroamérica*, Libros de la frontera, Barcelona 1983.

50. The fullest examination of that relationship is in James Dunkerley, *Power in the Isthmus*, Verso, London 1988.

51. See ibid., chapters 3 and 4.

52. On Salomon de la Selva see Cardenal, *Poesía nicaraguense*, pp. 38–52.

53. On the significance of the Vanguardia group which brought these poets together see F. de Asís Fernandez, introduction to *Poesía política nicaraguense*, Ministerio de Cultura, Managua 1986.

54. José Coronel Urtecho, 'Oda a Rubén Darío', in *Pol-la D'Ananta Katanta Paranta*, Eds UNAN, Managua 1970.

55. See A. Escobar (ed.), *Antología de la poesía peruana*, Ed. Nuevo Mundo, Lima 1965. See too J.M. Oviedo, 'Jorge Eielson; una negación radical', in pp. 253–61.

56. See A. Escobar, *Antología*.

57. Published in 1950 and to be found in P. Neruda, *Obras completas*, Losada, Buenos Aires 1973. For a good introduction see R. Pring Mill, *Pablo Neruda: A Basic Anthology*, Dolphin Book Co, Oxford 1975. Of p. IV.

58. P. 36.

59. See P. de Rokha, *Neruda y yo*, Santiago, n.d.

60. See Alan Bold, introduction to *Penguin Book of Socialist Verse*, Penguin Books, Harmondsworth 1970.

61. See the study of this specific aspect of Neruda's work in M. Litt thesis by R. Romero, Glasgow University, 1991.

62. Cf. A. Sánchez Vázquez, *The Philosophy of Praxis*, Merlin, London 1977, particularly ch. vi.

63. Refuge of the last Inca rebellion, Macchu Picchu was 'lost' in the Andean fastnessnes until its 'rediscovery' by Hiram Bingham in 1911. Since then it has acquired enormous symbolic significance in the reappropriation of Inca Peru, and great economic significance, until recently at least, in the generation of tourist income.

64. Just as Baudelaire and his contemporaries had embarked on a similar journey in the late, nineteenth century; see W. Benjamin, 'Paris – Capital of the 19th century', in *Illuminations* p. iv.

65. As Marx put it, 'Nature builds no machines . . . These are products of human industry, natural material transformed into organs of the human will over nature . . .The power of knowledge objectified'; K. Marx, *Grundisse*, Penguin, Harmondsworth 1973, p. 706.

66. See W. Benjamin, 'The Work of Art in the Age of Mechanical Reproduction', in *Illuminations*.

7. The Architects of Construction

1. Unless otherwise indicated, citations from poems by Cabral are taken from João Cabral de Melo Neto, *Antologia Poética*, José Olympio, Rio de Janeiro 1979.

2. Antonio Ozai da Silva, *História das tendências no Brasil (Origens, cisões e propostas)*, São Paulo, n/d, chs 4 and 5. See also E. Bradford Burns, *A History of Brazil*, Columbia University Press, New York 1980, pp. 435–504.

3. All citations from poems by Gullar are taken from Ferreira Gullar, *Toda poesia (1950–1980)*, José Olympio, Rio De Janeiro 1987.

4. John Gledson, *Poesia e poética de Carlos Drummond de Andrade*, Duas Cidades, São Paulo 1981, p. 242.

5. All citations from poems by Drummond are taken from *Reunião: 10 livros de poesia de Carlos Drummond de Andrade*, José Olympio, Rio de Janeiro 1980.

6. Renato Ortiz, *Cultura brasileira e identidade nacional*, Brasiliense, São Paulo 1986, pp. 45–61.

7. Ozai da Silva, *História das tendências*, chs 4 and 5.

8. Haroldo de Campos, 'Contexto de uma vanguarda', *Teoria da poesia concreta: textos críticos e manifestos 1950–1960*, Duas Cidades, São Paulo 1975, p. 149.

9. 'Construir e expressar', *Teoria da poesia concreta*, p. 123.

10. Décio Pignatari, 'Forma, função e projeto geral', *Teoria da poesia concreta*, p. 108.

11. 'Construir e expressar', p. 123.

12. Claus Clüver, 'Reflexões sobre os Ideogramas Verbivocovisuais', *Poesia Concreta* – 30, Salvador, Código 11, 1986, n/p.

13. Décio Pignatari, *Poesia, pois, é Poesia 1950–1975*, Brasiliense, São Paulo 1986, p. 111.

14. Haroldo de Campos, 'Poesia Concreta-Linguagem-Comunicação', *Teoria da poesia concreta*, p. 151.

15. 'Contexto de uma vanguarda', p. 151.

16. See Mary Ellen Solt, *Concrete Poetry: A World View*, Indiana University Press, Bloomington 1968.

17. See *Times Literary Supplement* 29 March, 6 August and 3 September 1968.

18. Augusto de Campos, *Poesia 1949–1979*, Brasiliense, São Paulo 1986, p. 102.

19. Pignatari, *Poesia*, p. 113.

20. Vinicius de Moraes, *Obra Poética*, José Aguilar, Rio de Janeiro 1968, pp. 535–6. All subsequent citations are from this edition.

21. See Ruy Castro, *Chega de saudade: a história e as histórias da Bossa Nova*, Companhia das Letras, São Paulo 1990, and José Ramos Tinhorão, *Pequena história da musica popular: da modinha ao tropicalismo*, Art Editora, São Paulo 1986.

22. Text accompanying *O povo canta* ed. CPC da UNE, cited in Tinhorão, *Pequena história da musica popular*, p. 238.

23. Ortiz, *Cultura brasileira*, p. 63.

24. Moacyr Félix, *Invenção de crença e descrença*, Civilização Brasileira, Rio de Janeiro 1978, pp. 148–9.

25. See William Rowe and Vivien Schelling, *Memory and Modernity: Popular Culture in Latin America*, Verso, London 1991, pp. 84–97.

26. All citations from poems by Ferreira Gullar are from *Toda poesia (1950–1980)*, José Olympio, Rio de Janeiro 1987.

27. Citations from *Death and Life of a Severino* are taken from João Cabral de Melo Neto, *Morte e vida severina e outros poemas em voz alta*, José Olympio, Rio de Janeiro 1980.

28. Benedito Nunes, *João Cabral de Melo Neto*, Vozes, Petrópolis 1974, p. 43.

29. João Cabral de Melo Neto, *Joan Miró* (Cadernos de Cultura), Ministério de Educação, Rio de Janeiro 1952, in Nunes, *João Cabral*, p. 186.

30. João Cabral de Melo Neto, 'Poesia e Composição – A inspiração e o Trabalho de Arte' (Conferência pronunciada na Biblioteca do Clube Brasileiro de Poesia), *Revista Brasileira de Poesia*, VII, April 1956, in Benedito Nunes, *João Cabral*, p.194.

31. Interview with the author, São Paulo, 9/8/88.

32. Mário Chamie, 'Poema Praxis: um evento revolucionário', *Instauração Praxis I: manifestos, plataformas, textos e documentos críticos – 1959 a 1972*, Quíron, São Paulo 1974, p.111.

33. Citations from poems by Chamie are taken from *Objeto Selvagem*, Quíron, São Paulo 1977.

34. Chamie, *Instauração Praxis I*, pp. 21–45.

35. Mário Chamie, 'Literatura-Praxis (por uma consciência de leitura)', *Instauração Praxis*, pp.71–2.

36. See Paulo Freire, *Pedagogia do oprimido*, Paz e Terra, Rio de Janeiro 1987.

37. Roberto Schwarz, 'Cultura e política, 1964–69', *O pai de família e outros estudos*, Paz e Terra, Rio de Janeiro 1978, p.62.

8. Speaking Aloud

1. That impact may be traced in the United States in, for example, Huberman and Sweezy, *Cuba: Anatomy of a Revolution*; and Scheer and Zeitlin, *Cuba: An American Tragedy*; as well as C. Wright Mills, *Listen Yankee*, 1960. On its impact in Latin America see John Gerassi, *The Great Fear*; Hector Béjar Rivera's *Peru 1965*; and in Richard Gott, *Rural Guerrillas in Latin America*, Penguin, London 1965; and in the writings of Regis Debray, i.e. *Revolution in the Revolution*, Penguin, London 1968. See too C. Mesa Lago (ed.), *Revolutionary Cuba* for the first period and for the past decade Jean Stubbs' *Cuba: The Test of Time*, Latin America Bureau, London 1989. A recent very thorough critical look at Cuba's history since 1959 is Jeanette Habel's *Cuba: Revolution in Peril*, Verso, London 1991.

2. For an account of the coup against Arbenz, see S. Schlesinger and S. Kinzer, *Bitter Fruit*, Anchor/Doubleday, New York 1983.

3. Cf. Jenny Pearce, *Under the Eagle* Latin American Bureau, London 1981; and see P. Gonzalez Casanova (ed.), *América Latina: Historia de medio siglo*, Siglo XXI, Mexico 1981.

4. On the Cuban experience in that respect see H.M. Enzensburger, 'PCC: Anatomy of a Party' in *Raids and Reconstructions*, London 1976. Also J. O'Connor, *Origins of Socialism in Cuba*, Cornell University Press, Ithaca 1970.

5. See James Dunkerley, *Rebellion in the Veins*, Verso, London 1984, chs 1 and 2.

6. See Phil Slater, 'The Aesthetic Theory of the Frankfurt School' in *Cultural Studies*, no. 6, Autumn 1974, pp. 174–211.

7. Castro's famous 1953 speech from the dock, after the failure of the assault on the Moncada barracks. See *History will Absolve Me*, Jonathan Cape, London 1967.

8. Expressed and developed by Che Guevara, particularly in his 'Man and Socialism in Cuba' (1965) and in the context of the debates about the economy in the early sixties, his 'On the Budgetary System of Financing'. Both are in J. Gerassi (ed.), *Venceremos*, Weidenfeld, London 1970. See too the interpretation of Guevara offered by Regis Debray in his *Revolution in the Revolution*. The theological restatement of a similar vision is encapsulated in the writings of *Camilo Torres: Revolutionary Priest*, Penguin, London 1964.

9. See A. Gunder Frank, *Capitalism and Underdevelopment in Latin America*, Monthly Review Press, New York 1967. His theories are placed in context by Ian Roxborough in *Theories of Development*, and recently readdressed in Petras and Morley, *U.S. Hegemony under Siege*, Verso, London 1990, ch 1.

10. See Mike Gonzalez, 'The Culture of the Heroic Guerrilla: The Impact of Cuba in the Sixties' in *Bulletin of Latin American Research*, Vol. 3, no. 2, 1984, pp. 65–76.

11. See L. Trotsky, *Literature and Revolution*, Bookmarks, London 1991.

12. See K.S. Karol, *Guerrillas in Power*, London 1971. See too Habel, *Cuba*; and P. Binns and M. Gonzalez, *Cuba, Castro and Socialism*, Socialist Workers Party, London 1983.

13. In Gerassi, *Venceremos*, pp. 536–53.

14. See below for a fuller discussion of the Padilla case.

15. The speech is reprinted under the title 'Palabras a los intelectuales', 1961.

16. Speech to the Congress of Education and Culture, Havana 1971.

17. Guillermo Cabrera Infante has become one of the most vocal and visible critics from the right. He left Cuba after the suppression of his brother's film 'PM' in 1961, and now lives in London as a naturalized British citizen. See too Tad Szule, *Fidel: A Critical Portrait*, William Morrow, New York 1986. For a more general critique see Habel, *Cuba*.

18. See on this issue N. Miller, *Soviet Relations with Latin America 1959–1987*, CUP, Cambridge 1989, ch. 3.

19. Che Guevara, *Man and Socialism in Cuba*, Pathfinder Press, New York 1978, p. 18.

20. A view reinforced, for example, by Michel Lowy in *La pensée de Che Guevara*, François Maspero, Paris 1971.

21. Nicolás Guillén 'Tengo' in *Tengo*, Havana 1964.

22. See his *En Cuba: 1972*. See also, for example, Enrique Lihn's *Escrito en Cuba*, 1967.

23. See R. Fernandez Retamar, 'Poesía conversacional' in *Panorama de la literatura latinoamericana*, Mexico 1969.

24. R. Fernández Retamar, *Calibán y otros ensayos*, Ed. Diogenes, Mexico 1972.

25. Ibid., p. 83.

26. This and other poems from Fernández Retamar's *Poesía Reunida*, Havana 1966.

27. All the documents and debate were published in *Index on Censorship*, 1 (1), 1972. See too Lourdes Casal, *El caso Padilla: literatura y revolución en Cuba*, Eds Nueva Atlantida, New York 1972. See also articles on the topic by Antoni Kapcia and Pedro Perez Sarduy in *Red Letters*, no. 15, Summer/Autumn 1983, pp. 11–34.

28. The debate is published in a small book with a very long title: *Literatura en la revolución y revolución en la literatura*, Siglo XXI, Mexico 1971, with an additional comment by Julio Cortazar.

29. M. Benedetti (ed.), *Poesía trunca: poesía latinoamericana revolucionaria*, Visor, Madrid 1980.

30. Ibid., p. 10.

31. Quoted in S. Menton, *Prose Fiction of the Cuban Revolution*, Univ. of Texas Press, Austin 1975. See also Lisandro Otero, 'La funcionalidad de la cultura' in *Casa de las Americas*, Havana, Sept–Oct. 1971.

32. See Francios Maspero, introduction to Habel, *Cuba*, La Brèche, Paris 1989 (French edition).

33. Their tragic experience is recorded in Gott, *Rural Guerrillas*, though it is not analysed in those terms there.

34. Javier Heraud, *Poemas*, Havana 1970.

35. Otto Rene Castillo, *Poemas*, Havana 1971.

36. See Ed Dorn and C. Brotherston (trans.), *Our Word*, Cape Goliard press, London 1968. Also Roberto Márquez (ed.), *Latin American Revolutionary Poetry*, Monthly Review Press, New York/London 1974; and Benedetti, *Poesía trunca*.

37. His work appears in the Benedetti anthology pp. 359–78.

38. On the peasantry see Joseph Collins, *What Difference Could a Revolution Make?*, San Francisco 1982. Despite the wealth of writing on Nicaragua after 1979, there is still very little on the history of Nicaragua. But see G. Selser, *Sandino*, Mexico 1980, and on background to the revolution R. Harris and C. Vilas, *Nicaragua: A Revolution Under Siege*, Zed, London 1985.

39. On Vanguardia and on Cardenal in general see the PhD thesis by J.J. Lyons, *Ernesto Cardenal: The Politics of Love and Revolution*, Kings College, London 1988. See also E. Cardenal, introduction to his own edition of *Nueva poesía nicaragüense*, Madrid 1949.

40. See Stephen White, *Culture and Politics in Nicaragua*, Lumen Books, New York 1986, part I: 'Poets of the Vanguardia', pp. 8–36.

41. See Cardenal, introduction to *Nueva poesía nicaragüense*.

42. Born in 1925, Ernesto Cardenal's work has passed through a number of quite distinct phases though with a consistent direction culminating in his immersion (as Minister of Culture) in the experience of the Sandinista revolution. *Nueva antología poetica*, Siglo XXI, Mexico 1983 (4th edition) provides a well chosen and comprehensive selection.

43. See J.P. Sullivan (ed.), *Ezra Pound*, Penguin, Harmondsworth 1970, and in particular the essay 'A few don'ts', pp. 41–5.

44. E. Cardenal (ed.), *Nueva poesía nicaragüense*, p. 95.

45. Ibid.

46. Quoted in Paul W. Borgeson, *Hacia el hobre nuevo: poesía y pensamiento de Ernesto Cardenal*, Tamesis Books, London 1984, p. 100.

47. See G.W. Allen (ed.), *The New Walt Whitman Handbook*, New York 1975. See also F. Alegria, *Walt Whitman en Hispanoamérica*, Ed. Ctudium, Mexico 1954. It is worth noting too that Cardenal coedited and translated with Urtecho, an anthology of North American poetry: *Antología de la poesía norteamericana*, Madrid 1963.

48. Published in 1961.

49. *Epigramas*: first published 1961, though clearly writen much earlier.

50. *Vida en al amor*, published in English as *Love*, New York 1981, provides the fullest insight into Cardenal's interpretation of his religious obligations. Its practical projection into the work of the Ministry of Culture of the Sandinista government is the most eloquent expression of the consequences of Cardenal's Christian vision: its expression, developing his earlier ideas, is found in *La santidad en la revolución*, 1976. Through the Ministry, clearly, Cardenal set out to forge the Christian community envisaged in his prophetic poetry – though there was considerable argument about his understanding of it. See for example Steven White, *Culture and Politics*.

51. The best among the welter of recent largely hagiographic writings about Sandino are G. Selser, *Sandino*, Mexico 1978; and S. Ramirez (ed.), *El pensamiento vivo de Sandino*, Managua, 1982.

52. 'Economía de Tahuantinsuyu'.

53. *En Cuba*, 1972.

54. *Love*, p. 135.

55. See Borgeson, *Ernesto Cardenal*, ch iii.

56. See Robert Pring Mill's writing on workshop poetry, as far as I am aware the most searching and well-informed approach to this experience. His 'The "workshop poetry" of Sandinista Nicaragua' adds to his earlier piece 'Mayra Jiménez and the rise of Nicaragua's "poesía de taller"' (1983). M. Lopez Vigil, *de la insurrección a la resurrección* (Bilbao, 1981) offers one anthology and some have been published in English as *Poems of Love and Revolution*, London 1984.

57. Roque Dalton, *Poesía* (selected by Mario Benedetti), Casa de las Americas, Havana 1980.

58. See R. Dalton, 'Poesía y militancia en América Latina' in *Art on the Line*, I, 1981. Quoted in Nick Caistor, 'Roque Dalton', in *Red Letters*, 15, Summer/Autumn 1983, pp. 36–7.

59. Included in *Poesía*, pp. 117–224.

60. On this incident and its implications for the history of El Salvador, see Thomas P. Anderson, *Matanza: El Salvador's Communist Revolt of 1932*, Lincoln, Nebraska, 1971. It is part of the experience recounted with such power in Roque Dalton's *Miguel Mármol*, San José 1977.

61. Cf. J. Beverley and M. Zimmerman, *Literature and Politics in the Central American Revolutions*, Univ. of Texas Press, Austin 1990.

62. The issue is more fully discussed in Jenny Pearce, *Promised Land*, Latin American Bureau, London 1986, pp. 122–39 and in particular on Dalton's death, ibid, pp. 130–31.

63. *Las historias prohibidas de Pulgarcito*, Siglo XXI, Mexico 1974.

64. See above note 60.

9. Voices from the Silence

1. See 'No MIS, a poesia do futuro', *Folha de São Paulo*, 1 August 1985.

2. *Folhetim*, 27 July 1985.

3. Roberto Schwarz, 'Marco histórico', *Que horas são?: ensaios*, Companhia das Letras, São Paulo 1987, pp 57–66.

4. See, for example, Michael Newman, 'Revising Modernism, representing Postmodernism', *Postmodernism*, ICA Documents, Free Association Books, London 1989, pp. 95–154.

5. Alex Callinicos, *Against Postmodernism: A Marxist Critique*, Polity Press, Oxford 1989, pp. 9–28.

6. Fredric Jameson, 'Postmodernism, or The Cultural Logic of Late Capitalism', *New Left Review*, No. 146, July/August 1984, pp.61–2.

7. Jameson 'Postmodernism', pp.85–6.

8. See R. Murray, 'Life after Henry (Ford)', *Marxism Today*, October 1988.

9. See David Beecham and Ann Eidenham, 'Beyond the Mass Strike: Class, Party and Trade Union Struggle in Brazil', *International Socialism*, 2: 36, Autumn 1987, pp.3–48.

10. Callinicos, *Against Postmodernism*, pp.162–71.

11. Flora Sussekind, *Literatura e Vida Literária: polêmicas, diários e retratos*, Jorge Zahar, Rio de Janeiro 1985, p.13.

12. Renato Ortiz, *Cultura brasileira e identidade nacional*, Brasiliense, São Paulo 1985, p.89, also cited in Sussekind, *Literatura*, p.20.

13. Interview with the author, Rio de Janeiro, 25 July 1988.

14. Paulo Franchetti and Alcyr Pécora (orgs), *Caetano Veloso* (Literatura Comentada), Abril Educação, São Paulo 1981, pp.44–5.

15. Franchetti and Pécora, *Caetano Veloso*, p.46.

16. Cited in Armando Freitas Filho, 'Poesia vírgula viva', *Anos 70* ed. Armando Freitas Filho, Heloísa Buarque de Hollanda, Marcos Augusto Gonçalves, vol 2: *Literatura*, Europa Empresa, Rio de Janeiro 1979–1980, p.91.

17. Cited in Adélia Bezerra de Meneses, *Desenho mágico: poesia e política em Chico Buarque*, Hucitec, São Paulo 1982, pp.32–3.

18. Bezerra de Meneses, *Desenho mágico*, pp.151-8 (accompanied by an excellent analysis of the poem).

19. José Ramos Tinhorão, *Penquena história da música popular: da modinha ao tropicalismo*, Art Editora, São Paulo, 1986.

20. See Leland Guyer, 'Ferreira Gullar: an introduction', *Dirty Poem: poema sujo by Ferreira Gullar*, Lanham, University Press of America, New York/London 1990, pp.5–7.

21. *Dirty Poem: poema sujo*, pp.64–7. All citations and translations, with some modifications, are from this edition.

22. Freitas Filho. 'Poesia vírgula viva', p.102.

23. Heloísa Buarque de Hollanda (ed.), *26 poetas hoje*, Labor do Brasil, Rio de Janeiro 1976, p.89.

24. See Iumna Maria Simon and Vinicius Dantas, 'Poesia ruim, sociedade pior', *Novos Estudos* CEBRAP, São Paulo, No. 12, June 1985.

25. See, for instance, the *Claro Enigma* series edited by Augusto Massi for Duas Cidades.

26. All citations from poems by Alvim are taken from *Poesias reunidas*, 1968–1988, Duas Cidades, São Paulo 1988.

27. Antonio Candido, referring to Orides Fontela, cited in Leda Tenório da Motta's introduction to *Artes e oficios da poesia*, org. Augusto Massi, Porto Alegre, Artes e Ofícios, 1991, p.8.

28. All citations from poems by Adélia Prado are taken from *Bagagem*, Rio de Janeiro, Imago, 1976.

29. All citations from poems by Orides Fontela are taken from *Trevo* (1969–1988), Duas Cidades, São Paulo 1988.

30. All citations from poems by Ana Cristina César are taken from *A teus pés*, Brasiliense, São Paulo 1988.

31. All citations from poems by Uchoa Leite are taken from *Obra em dobras* (1960–1988), Duas Cidades, São Paulo 1988.

32. Armando Freitas Filho, *À mão livre (1975–1979)*, Nova Fronteira, Rio de Janeiro 1979, pp.45–6.

33. Armando Freitas Filho, *Longa vida (1979–1981)*, Nova Fronteira, Rio de Janeiro 1982, pp.103–4.

34. Armando Freitas Filho, *3 × 4 (1981–1983)*, Nova Fronteira, Rio de Janeiro 1985, p.97.

35. Interview with the author, Rio de Janeiro, 13 August 1988.

10. Against Exile

1. See M. Benedetti, *Antología poética*; Alianza Editorial, Madrid 1984.

2. See A. Roa Bastos, 'Fragments from a Paraguayan Autobiography' in *Third World Quarterly*, Vol. 9 no. 1 London, January 1987, pp. 212–8 and in the same issue 'Thresholds of Identity: Literature and Exile in Latin America', pp. 229-45.

3. See A. Pizarnik, *Textos de sombra y últimos poemas*, Ed. Sudamericana, Buenos Aires 1982. On her work see Susan Bassnett, 'Speaking with Many Voices: The Poems of Alejandra Pizarnik' in S. Bassnett (ed.), *Knives and Angels*, Zed Books, London 1990, pp. 36–51.

4. Belinda Zubicueta; 'Sin poderte alcanzar' in *Poesía prisionera: escritura de cinco mujeres encarceladas*, Bruno Serrano, Santiago 1988.

5. Gioconda Belli, *Amor insurrecto*, 1984; and *De la costilla de Eva*, Ed. Nueva Nicaragua, Managua 1987. See also the selection in F. de Asís Fernandez, *Poesía política nicaragüense*, Ministerio de Cultura, Managua 1986. See too Patricia Murray, 'A Place for Eve in the Revolution' in Basnett, *Knives and Angels*, pp.176–98.

6. Cf. *Poems of Love and Revolution*, NSC, London 1983.

7. Marianella Corriols, 'Geometría de la mujer' in *Panorámica de de la literatura joven de Nicaragua*. Union de Escritores ATC, Managua 1986, p. 47.

8. See D. Craven, *The New Concept of Art and Popular Culture in Nicaragua. . .*, Edwin Mellen Press, Lewiston, 1989.

9. See A. Hopkinson (ed.), *Lovers and Comrades*, Women's Press, London 1989; and G. Yanes et al, *Mirrors of War: Literature and Revolution in El Salvador*, Zed Press, London 1985.

10. See Yanes et al, *Mirrors of War*, p. 107.

11. Cf. Thorpe Running, 'Responses to the Politics of Oppression by Poets in Argentina and Chile', in *Hispania*, 73, March 1990, pp. 40–49.

12. The Chilean Nueva Canción movement was a vital component of a living mobilization for change in Chile, whatever the contradictory visions their songs enshrined, or their different life experience from those on whose behalf they sang. In the aftermath of the Chilean coup of 11 September 1973, those songs became part of a different and complex process. On the one hand the groups who sang the songs of Chile in Europe, like Inti Illimani and Quilapayun, were part of an active solidarity movement, whose object was to raise the cry of protest and rejection against the new Chilean regime of Augusto Pinochet. On the other, it contributed to the elaboration of a myth of democracy undermined by conspiracy which in turn veiled the much more profound class struggle whose most extreme expression was the coup itself. Struggle and combat combined with a kind of nostalgia which in some ways denied the possibility of struggle in the here and now.

13. Violeta Parra is a figure of enormous stature in every area of Latin American culture. Her poetry is song in the first instance, yet stands as literature in its own right. She was an original voice yet also a collector, who reappropriated and gave legitimacy anew to the songs of the popular tradition. She was a craftswoman and artist, who taught one generation of artists and learned from another. Yet there was a tension in the movement that quite rightly saw her as its predecessor, founder and outstanding contributor. It was a tension between the translation of popular experience for a more

374

politicized and probably largely middle-class audience on the one hand, and on the other the need to remain embedded in a living popular/folk culture which was itself evolving and being transformed in the context of the political process in Chile – and producing its own new forms. The first tended to freeze the folk form, the latter to press it towards continual change. While Violeta herself uneasily spanned the two areas, her brother Roberto remained a popular poet par excellence, and her children Angel and Isabel the main representatives of the Nueva Canción movement, Cf. I. Parra: *El libro mayor de Violeta Parra*, Eds Michay, Madrid 1985.

14. The issue is the subject of a vast potential literature of its own. What is clear is that the logic of the search for a public voice leads into the forms and vehicles which dominate the public arena. Music, declamatory poetry of one sort or another, popular ritual of many kinds are just such an arena. It led some singers in Peru, for example, meeting in 1977, to consciously relinquish 'political' music to become singers in a popular tradition which was, at least in its inheritance, largely apolitical. But then the Portuguese revolution was set in motion by a sentimental ballad of local nostalgia called 'Grandola' and the traditional song 'Flor de retama' (Heather flower) gave the Peruvian singer Martina Portocarrero the means by which to denounce the massacre of miners by the Peruvian government. In the end, perhaps, the criterion must be that the voice be heard and understood, and that that alone should determine form!

Bibliography

Spanish America

1. Poetry

Adan, Martin, *Obre poética 1928–71*. Inst Nacional de Cultura, Lima 1971.

Agosin, Marjorie, trans. Naomi Lindstrom, *Women of Smoke*, LA Literary Review Press, Pittsburgh 1988.

—— trans. Cola Franzen, *Brujas y algo más/Witches and other Things*. LA Lit. Review Press, Pittsburgh 1986.

—— trans. Cola Franzen, *Zones of Pain*, White Pine Press, New York 1988.

Alegria, Claribel, trans. Carolyn Forche, *Flowers from the Volcano*, Univ. of Pittsburgh Press, Pittsburgh 1982.

—— trans. Darwin Flakoll, *Woman of the River*, Univ. of Pittsburgh Press, Pittsburgh 1989.

Belli, Gioconda, *Amor insurrecto*, Managua 1984.

—— *De la costilla de Eva*, Ed Nueva Nicaragua, Managua 1987.

—— trans. John Lyons, *Nicaragua under Fire*, Warwick Greville, London 1989.

—— trans. Steven White, *From Eve's Rib*, Curbstone Press, Willimantic, Conn. 1989.

Benedetti, Mario, *Antología poética*, Alianza Editorial, Madrid 1984.

Borges, J.L., *Obra poética 1923–67*, Emece, Buenos Aires 1967.

—— *Obras completas 1923–72*, Emece, Buenos Aires 1974.

—— *Obra poética completa*, Alianza/Emece, Madrid/Buenos Aires 1985.

—— trans N. Thomas de Giovanni, *Selected Poems: 1923–67*, Dell Publishing, New York 1969.

—— trans. Alastair Reid, *The Gold of the Tigers: Selected Later Poems*, Dutton, New York 1977.

Cardenal Ernesto, *Nueva antología poética*, Siglo XXI, Mexico 1983.

—— *El estrecho dudoso*, Ed Nueva Nicaragua, Managua 1985.

THE GATHERING OF VOICES

—— *Tocar el cielo*, Ed Nueva Nicaragua, Managua 1981.

—— *Evangelio, pueblo y arte*, Eds Loguez, Salamanca 1983.

—— trans R. Pring Mill, *Marilyn Monroe and Other Poems*, Search Press, London 1975.

—— *Love*, Crossroad Books, New York 1981.

—— trans M and C. Altschul, *Homage to the American Indians*, Johns Hopkins Univ. Press, Baltimore 1973.

—— trans Dinah Livingstone, *The Music of the Spheres*, Katabasis Seabury Press, London 1975.

—— trans R. Pring Mill et al., *Apocalypse and Other Poems*, New Directions, New York 1977.

—— trans K.H. Anton, *Epigramas*, Lodestar Press, New York 1978.

—— trans D. Walsh et al, *Zero Hour and Other Documentary Poems*, New Directions, New York 1980.

—— trans T. Blackburn et al., *Psalms*, Crossroad, New York 1981.

—— trans J. Cohen, *With Walker in Nicaragua and Other Early Poems*, Wesleyan Univ. Press, Middletown, Conn. 1984.

—— trans M. Zimmerman, *Flights of Victory/Vuelos de victoria*, Orbis Books, New York 1985.

—— trans J. Cohen, *From Nicaragua with Love: Poems 1976–86*, City Lights, San Francisco 1986.

—— trans D. Livingstone, *Nicaraguan New Time*, Journeyman, London 1988.

Carrera Andrade, J. trans. H.R.Hays, *Selected Poems*, SUNY, Albany 1972.

Castellanos, Rosario, trans. M. Ahern, *Looking at the Mona Lisa*, Rivelin Equatorial, Bradford 1981.

—— trans M. Ahern, *Selected Poems of Rosario Castellanos*, Graywolf Press, St Paul's, Minn. 1988.

Castillo, Otto Rene, *Poemas*, Casa de las Americas, Havana 1971.

—— trans Roque Dalton, *Tomorrow Triumphant*, Night Horn Books, San Franciso 1984.

—— trans M. Randall, *Let's Go (Vámonos patria a caminar)*, Curbstone Press, Willimantic, Conn. 1984.

Cuadra P.A., trans Steven White, *The Birth of the Sun: Selected Poems 1933–85*, Unicorn Press, Greensboro 1988.

Cuza Male, Belkis, trans Pamela Carmell, *Belkis Cuza Malé: Woman in the Front Lines*, Unicorn Press, Greensboro 1988.

Dalton, Roque, *Poesía*, Casa de las Americas, Havana 1989.

—— *Poemas clandestinos/Clandestine Poems*, Solidarity Publications, San Francisco 1984.

—— trans Richard Schaaf, *Poemas*, Curbstone Press, Willimantic, Conn. 1984.

—— trans A. and J. Scully, *Poesía militante/militant poetry*, El Salvador Cultural Commission, London, n.d.

Darío Rubén, *Poesías completas*, Guilar, Madrid 1961.

—— trans. Lysander Kemp, *Selected Poems*, Univ. of Texas Press, Austin 1965.

Eguren, J.M. *Obras completas*, Mosca Azuk, Lima 1974.

Fernández Retamar, R., *Poesía reunida*, Bolsilibros Union, Havana 1966.

Gonzalez Leon, F., *Poesías completas*, Ed. ARS, Mexico, n.d.

Gorostiza, J., *Muerte sin fin*, Mexico 1939.

—— trans L.Villaseñor, *Death Without End*, Ark Press, New York 1972.

Guillén, Nicolás, *Obra poética*, UNEAC, Havana 1972.

—— *Poemas manuables*, UNEAC, Havana 1975.

—— *Summa poética*, Ed Catedra, Mexico, 1977.

—— trans. Langston Hughes, *Cuba libre: poems*, Ward Ritchie, Los Angeles 1948.

—— trans. Roberto Marquez, *Patria o muerte: the Great Zoo and Other Poems*, Monthly Review Press, New York 1972.

—— trans R. J. Carr, *Tengo*, Broadside Press, Detroit 1974.

Gutiérrez Najera, M., *Poesías completas*, Porrua, Mexico 1953.

Hahn, Oscar, trans. J. Hoggard, *The Art of Dying*, Latin American Review Press, Pittsburgh 1988.

Heraud, Javier, *Poemas*, Casa de las Americas, Havana 1970.

Huerta, Efrain, *Poemas prohibidos y de amor*, Siglo XXI, Mexico 1980.

Huidobro, Vicente, *Poesía y prosa*, Aguilar, Madrid 1967.

—— *Altazor*, Visor, Madrid 1973.

—— trans. W.S. Merwin et al., *The Selected Poetry of Vicente Huidobro*, New Directions, NewYork 1981.

—— trans. E. Weinberger, *Altazor or a Voyage in a Parachute*, Graywolf Press, St Paul's, Minn. 1988.

Juarroz, Roberto, trans. W.S. Merwin, *Vertical Poetry*, North Point Press, Berkeley 1988.

Lihn, Enrique, *Poesía de paso*, Casa de las Americas, Havana 1966.

—— trans. W. Witherup et al., *This Endless Malice*, Lillaburlero Press, Northwood Narrows 1969.

—— trans. D. Oliphant, *If Poetry is to be Written Right: Poems*, Texas Portfolio Press, Texas City 1977.

—— trans. J. Cohen et al., *The Dark Room and Other Poems*, New Directions, New York 1978.

Lopez Velarde, R., *Poesías completas*, Porrua, Mexico 1953.

Lugones, Leopoldo, *Obras poéticas completas*, Aguilar, Madrid 1959.

—— *Antología poética*, Austral, Buenos Aires 1965.

Martí, José, trans. Elinor Randall, *Major Poems: A Bilingual Edition*, Holmes and Meir, New York 1982.

Mejia Godoy, L.E. and Julio Valle Castillo, trans. D. Livingstone, *The Nicaraguan Epic*, Katabasis, London 1990.

Mistral Gabriela, *Antología* Ed. Zig Zag, Santiago 1957.

—— trans. Langston Hughes, *Selected Poems of Gabriela Mistral*, Indiana Univ. Press, Bloomington 1957.

—— trans. D. Dana, *Selected Poems of Gabriela Mistral*, Johns Hopkins Univ. Press, Baltimore 1971.

Morejon, Nancy, *Where the Island Sleeps like a Wing*, Black Scholar Press, San Francisco 1985.

Moro, César, trans. P. Ward, *The Scandalous Life of César Moro*, Oleander Press, Cambridge 1976.

Murillo, Rosario, *Un deber de cantar*, Ministerio de Cultura, Managua 1981.

—— *Amar es combatir*, Managua 1985.

—— *En las espléndidas ciudades*, Ed Nueva Nicaragua, Managua 1985.

Neruda, Pablo, *Obras completas*, Losada, Buenos Aires 1968/1973.

—— ed. R. Pring Mill, *Pablo Neruda: A Basic Anthology*, Dolphin, Oxford 1975.

—— *Memoirs*, Penguin Books, Harmondsworth 1978.

—— trans. M. Sayers Peden, *Selected Odes*, Univ. of California Press, Berkeley 1990.

—— trans Jack Schmitt, *Canto general*, Univ. of California Press, Berkeley 1991.

Nervo, Amado, *Plenitud*, Austral, Mexico 1963.

Pacheco, José Emilio, *Tarde o temprano*, FCE, Mexico 1980.

—— trans. Alastair Reid, *Don't Ask Me How The Time Goes By: Poems 1964–68*, Columbia Univ. Press, New York 1978.

—— trans. T. Hoeksema, *Signals from the Flames*, Latin American Review Press, Pittsburgh 1980.

—— trans. G. McWhirter et al., *Selected Poems*, New Directions, New York 1987.

Padilla, Heberto, trans. F. Calzon et al., *Poetry and Politics*, Georgetown Univ. Press, Washington 1977.

—— trans. Alastair Reid et al., *Legacies: Selected Poems*, Faber and Faber, London 1982.

Parra, I, *El libro mayor de Violeta Parra*, Ed Michay, Madrid 1975.

Parra, Nicanor, *Antipoemas*, Seix Barral, Barcelona 1976.

—— trans. L. Ferlinghetti et al., *Antipoems New and Selected*, New Directions, New York 1985.

Paz, Octavio, *Libertad bajo palabra*, FCE, Mexico 1968.

—— *Poemas 1935–75*, Seix Barral, Barcelona 1978.

—— ed. and trans. C. Tomlinson, *Octavio Paz: Selected Poems*, Penguin Books, Harmondsworth 1979.

—— ed. and trans. E. Weinberger, *The Collected Poems 1957–87*, Paladin, London 1987.

Rojas, Gonzalo, *Contra la muerte*, Ed. Universitaria, Santiago 1964.

Rugama, Leonel, trans. Sara Miles et al., *The Earth is a Satellite of the Moon*, Curbstone Press, Willimantic 1985.

Silva, José Asunción, *Obras completas*, Bogota 1965.

Sosa, Roberto, trans. Jim Lindsey, *The Difficult Days*, Princeton Univ. Press, 1983.

Storni, Alfonsina, *Poesías*, SEL, Buenos Aires 1971.

—— ed. F. Williams Talamantes, *Alfonsina Storni: Argentina's Feminist Poet*.

(The poetry in Spanish with English translations), San Marcos, Los Cerillos 1975.

—— trans. M. Freeman et al., *Selected Poems*, White Pine Press, New York 1987.

Tablada, J.J., *Obras I: Poesía*, UNAM, Mexico 1971.

Torres Bodet, J., trans S. Karsen; *Selected Poems*, Indiana Univ. Press, Bloomington 1964.

Urtecho, José Coronel, *Pal-la D'AnantaKatanta*, UNAN, Managua 1970.

Vallejo, César, *Obra poetica completa*, Alianza Editorial, Madrid 1983.

Zurita, Raul, *Purgatorio*, Ed Universitaria, Santiago 1979.

—— *Canto a su amor desaparecido*, Ed. Universitaria, Santiago 1987.

—— trans J. Jacobson, *Purgatorio 1970–77*, LA Literary Review Press, Pittsburgh 1985.

—— trans. J. Schmidt, *Anteparadise*, Univ. of California Press, Berkeley 1987.

2. Anthologies

Ahern, M. and D. Tipton, *Peru: The New Poetry*, Red Dust, New York 1977.

Ara, G., *Suma de poesía argentina 1538–1968*, Ed. Guadalupe, Buenos Aires 1970.

Arellano, J.E., *Panorama de la literatura nicaragüense*, Ed. Nueva Nicaragua, Managua 1982.

Argueta, M., *Poesía de El Salvador*, EDUCA, San José 1983.

Arkin, M. and B. Schollar, *Longman Anthology of World Literature by Women 1875–1975*, Longman, New York 1989.

Armand, O., *Towards an Image of Latin American Poetry: A Bilingual Anthology*, Longbridge Rhodes, Durango Col. 1982.

Armijo, R. and R. Paredes, *Poesía contemporánea de Centroamérica*, Libros de la Frontera, Barcelona 1983.

Baciú, S., *Antología de la poesía surrealista latinoamericana*, Joaquin Mortiz, Mexico 1974.

Benedetti, M., *Poesía trunca: poesía latinoamericana revolucionaria*, Visor, Madrid 1980.

—— trans. C. Alegría and D. Flakoll, *Unstill Life: An Introduction to the Spanish Poetry of Latin America*, Harcourt Brace, New York 1969.

Bold, Alan, *Penguin Book of Socialist Verse*, Penguin Books, Harmondsworth 1970.

Brotherston G., *Spanish American Modernista Poets*, Pergamon, London 1968.

Cardenal E., *Poesía nicaragüense*, Ed. Nueva Nicaragua, Managua 1981.

Carlisle, C., *Beyond the Rivers: An Anthology of 20th Century Paraguayan Poetry*, Thorp Springs Press, Berkeley 1977.

Carraciolo Trejo, E., *Penguin Book of Latin American Verse*, Penguin, Harmondsworth 1971.

Crow, John A., *An Anthology of Spanish Poetry*, Louisiana State Univ. Press, Baton Rouge 1979.

Crow, Mary, *Woman who has Sprouted Wings: Poems by Contemporary Latin American Women Poets*, LA Literary Review Press, Pittsburgh 1984.

Cuadra Downing, O., *Nueva poesía nicaragüense*, Ed. Escelicer, Madrid 1949.

Cunningham, V, *The Penguin Book of Spanish Civil War Verse*, Penguin, Harmondsworth 1980.

Debicki, A., *Poetas hispanoamericanos contemporáneos*, Ed. Gredos, Madrid 1978.

—— *Antología de la poesía mexicana moderna*, Tamesis Books, London 1979.

Dorn, E. and G. Brotherston, *Our Word: Guerrilla Poems from Latin America*, Cape Goliard, London 1968.

Escalona-Escalona, J.A., *Muestra de la poesía hispanoamericana del siglo XX*, (2 vols), Biblioteca Ayacucho, Caracas 1985.

Fernandez, F. de Asis, *Poesía política nicaragüense*, Ministerio de Cultura, Managua 1986.

Fitts, Dudley, *Anthology of Contemporary Latin American Poetry*, New Directions, Norfolk Conn. 1974.

Garcia, Aller A. and A. Garcia Rodriguez, *Antología de poetas hispanoamericanos*, Ed. Nebrija, Leon Argentina 1979.

Grupo de Escritores Latinoamericanos, *Anthology of Latin American Poets in London*, London 1988.

Guillén, O., *Hombres como madrugadas: la poesía de El Salvador*, Ed. Anthropos, Madrid 1985.

Hopkinson, Amanda, *Lovers and Comrades*, Women's Press, London 1989.

Horno, Delgado A. et al., *Breaking Boundaries*, Umass Press, Amherst 1989.

Jacquez, Wieser N., *Open to the Sun*, Perivale Press, Van Nuys 1977.

Jimenez, J.O., *Antología de la poesía hispanoamericana contemporánea 1914–1970*, Alianza Editorial, Madrid 1971.

Lamadrid, E. and M. del Valle, *Un ojo en el muro/an eye through the wall: Mexican poetry 1970–85*, Tooth of Time Books, Santa Fé 1986.

Lyons, J. (trans. and ed.) *Poemas de amor y revolución/Poems of love and revolution*, Nicaragua Solidarity Campaign, London 1983.

Marquez, R., *Latin American Revolutionary Poetry/Poesía revolucionaria latinoamericana*, Monthly Review Press, New York 1974.

Marzan, J., *Inventing A Word*, Columbia Univ. Press, New York 1980.

Molina, Alfonso, *Poesia revolucionaria del Perú*, Eds America Latina, Lima 1966.

Murguia, A. and B. Paschke, *Volcan: Poetry from El Salvador, Guatemala, Honduras and Nicaragua*, City Lights, San Francisco 1983.

Pacheco, J.E., *Antología del modernismo 1884–1921*, UNAM, Mexico 1970.

Padilla, H. and L. Suardiaz, *Cuban Poetry 1959–1966*, Instituto del Libro, La Habana 1967.

Panorámica de la literatura joven de Nicaragua, Ed. Juventud, Managua 1986.

Paz, O. et al., *Poesía en movimiento*, Siglo XXI, Mexico 1966.

—— and Samuel Beckett (trans.), *An Anthology of Mexican Poetry*, Indiana Univ. Press, Bloomington 1966.

—— and D. Justice et al. (trans.), *New Poetry of Mexico*, Secker and Warburg, London 1972.

Poesia atlántica; Ministerio de Cultura, Managua, 1980.

Poesia de la resistencia chilena/Poems of the Chilean Resistance, Chile Democratico, London 1989.

Prentice R. and J.M. Kirk, *A Fist and the Letter: Revolutionary Poems of Latin America*, Pulp Press, Vancouver 1977.

Ramos, Garcia Luis and E. O'Hara, *The Newest Peruvian Poetry in Translation*, Studia Hispanica, Austin 1979.

Randall, M., *Breaking the Silence*, Pulp Press, Vancouver 1982.

Rodriguez, Padron J., *Antología de la poesía hispanoamericana 1915–1960*, Espasa Calpe, Madrid 1984.

Romano, James, *Poética de la población marginal*, Ed. Prisma, Minneapolis 1987.

Rosenbaum, Sidonia, *Modern Women Poets of Spanish America*, Hispanic Institute in the US, New York 1945.

Scheer, L. and M. Flores Ramirez, *Poetry of Transition: Mexican Poetry of 1960 and 1970*, Translation Press, Ann Arbor 1984.

Shand, W., *Contemporary Argentine Poetry*, Fundación Argentina para la Poesía, Buenos Aires 1969.

Sherwin, J., *Poetry as Witness*, Amnesty Publications, London 1982.

Tarn, Nathaniel, *Con Cuba: An Anthology of Cuban Poetry of the Last Ten Years*, Grossman, New York 1969.

White, Steven, *Poets of Chile: A Bilingual Anthology*, Unicorn Press, Greensboro 1986.

Yanes, G. et al., *Mirrors of War: Literature and Revolution in El Salvador*, Zed Books, London 1985.

Young, A.V., *The Image of Black Women in 20th Century South American Poetry*, Three Continents, Washington 1987.

Zaid, G., *Omnibus de poesía mexicana*, Siglo XXI, Mexico 1971.

3. Studies

Abril, Xavier, *César Vallejo o la teoría política*, Taurus, Madrid 1962.

Agosin, M., *Pablo Neruda*, Twayne, Boston 1986.

Alazraki, J., *Jorge Luis Borges: el escritor y la crítica*, Taurus, Madrid 1976.

Alegria, F., *Walt Whitman en Hispanoamérica*, Col. Stadium, Mexico 1954.

Ara, G., *Leopoldo Lugones*, Mandragora, Buenos Aires 1958.

Arce de Vazquez, M., *Gabriela Mistral*, NYU Press, New York 1964.

Arrellano, J., *Panorama de la literatura nicaragüense*, Ed. Nueva Nicaragua, Managua 1982.

Augier, Angel, *Acción y poesia en José Martí*, Letras Cubanas, La Habana 1982.

—— *Nicolás Guillén* (2 vols), Univ. de las Villas, La Habana 1962.

Aznar, Solet M. and L.M. Schneider, *II Congreso Internacional de escritores Antifascistas* (3 vols), Laia, Barcelona 1979.

Bassnett, Susan (ed.), *Knives and Angels*, Zed Books, London 1990.

Beltran Guerrero, L., *Modernismo y modernistas*, Acad Nacional de la Historia, Caracas 1978.

Beverley, J. and M. Zimmerman, *Literature and Politics in the Central American Revolutions*, Univ. of Texas Press, Austin 1990.

Bizzatro, S., *Pablo Neruda: All the Poets the Poet*, Scarecrow Press, Metuchen, N.J. 1979.

Boneo, M.A., *Poesía argentina: ensayos*, Inst. Amigos del Libro Argentino, Buenos Aires 1968.

Borges, J.L., *Leopoldo Lugones*, Trocquel, Buenos Aires, 1955.

Borgeson, Paul W., *Hacia el hombre nuevo: poesía y pensamiento de Ernesto Cardenal*, Tamesis Books, London 1984.

Brotherston, G., *Latin American Poetry*, CUP, Cambridge 1975.

Capdevila, A., *Alfonsina: época dolor y poesía de la poetisa Alfonsina Storni*, Ed. Centurion, Buenos Aires 1948.

Carter Boyd, G., *Las revistas literarias en Hispanoamérica*, Ed. de Andrea, Mexico 1959.

Casal, Lourdes, *El caso Padilla: literatura y revolución en Cuba*, Ed. Nueva Atlantida, New York 1972.

Chiles, F., *Octavio Paz*, Peter Lang, New York/Berne 1987.

Collazos, O., *Los vanguardismos en América latin*, E. peninsula, Barcelona 1977.

—— et al., *Literatura en la revolución y revolución en la literatura*, Siglo XXI, Mexico 1979.

Concha, Jaime, *Gabriela Mistral*, Jucas, Madrid 1987.

Cortinez, C. (ed.), *Borges el poeta*, Univ. of Arkansas Press, Fayetteville 1986.

Corvalan, O., *El posmodernismo*, Las Americas, New York 1961.

Coyne, Andre, *César Vallejo*, Ed. Nueva Vision, Buenos Aires 1968.

Craven, D., *The New Concept of Art and Popular Culture in Nicaragua*, Edwin Mellin Press, Lewiston 1989.

Dauster, F., *The Double Strand: Five Mexican Poets*, Univ. of Kentucky Press, Lexington 1987.

De Costa, R., *Vicente Huidobro: the Careers of a Poet*, Clarendon, Oxford 1984.

De Torre, G., *Literaturas europeas de vanguardia*, Caro Reggio, Madrid 1925.

Dromundo, B., *Vida y pasión de Ramón López Velarde*, Ed. Guarania, Mexico 1950.

Duran, M. and M. Saifur, *Earth Tones: The Poetry of Pablo Neruda*, Indiana UP, Bloomington 1989.

Ellis, Keith, *Cuba's Nicolás Guillén*, Univ. of Toronto Press, Toronto 1983.

Escudero, Alfonso, *Rubén Darío el modernismo y otras páginas*, Ed. Nascimento, Sanitago 1985.

Fein, John M., *Towards Octavio Paz: A Reading of his Major Poems 1957–76*, Kentucky UP, Lexington 1986.

Fernandez, Moreno C., *La realidad y los papeles*, Aguilar, Madrid 1967.

Fernández Retamar, R., *Calibán y otros ensayos*: Ed. Diogenes, Mexico 1974.

Ferrari, A., *El universo poético de César Vallejo*, Monte Avila, Caracas 1972.

Finn, Julio, *Voices of Negritude*, Quartet Books, London 1988.

Flores, Angel (ed.), *Aproximaciones a César Vallejo*, Las Americas, New York 1971.

Foster, Merlin H., *Los contemporáneos*, Ed. de Andrea, Mexico 1964.

Franco, Jean, *An Introduction to Spanish American Literature*, CUP, Cambridge 1969.

—— *César Vallejo: The Dialectics of Poetry and Silence*, CUP, Cambridge 1976.

Fuente, C. de la (ed.), *López Velarde: su mundo intelectual y afectivo*, FEM, Mexico 1971.

Gracia J.E. (ed.), *Philosophy and Literature in Latin America*, SUNY, New York 1989.

Grossman, E., *The Antipoetry of Nicanor Parra*, NYU Press, New York 1979.

Guirao, R., *Orbita de la poesía negra afrocubana*, Ucar Garcia, La Habana 1938.

Gullon, R., *Direcciones del modernismo*, Ed. Gredos, Madrid 1963.

Henríquez Ureña, *Breve historia del modernismo*, FCE, Mexico 1954.

Higgins, James, *Vision del hombre y la vida en las últimas obras de César Vallejo*, Siglo XXI, Mexico 1970.

—— *The Poet in Peru*, Francis Cairns/Liverpool University, Liverpool 1982.

Irazusta, J., *Genio y figura de Leopoldo Lugones*, EUDEBA, Buenos Aires 1978.

Jitrik, Noe, *Las contradicciones del modernismo*, El Colegio de Mexico, Mexico 1978.

King, John, *Sur: A Study of the Argentine Literary Journal and its Role in the Development of a Culture*, CUP, Cambridge 1986.

Kirkpatrick, Gwen, *The Dissonant Legacy of Modernismo*, Univ. of California Press, Berkeley 1989.

List, Arzubide, *El movimiento estridentista*, Cuadernos de Lectura Popular, Mexico 1967.

Logan, C., *Rubén Darío y la búsqueda romántica de la unidad*, FCE, Mexico 1986.

Magis, C.H., *La poesía de Leopoldo Lugones*, Eds Ateneo, Mexico 1960.

Martínez, Estrada, C., *Muerte y transfiguración de Martín Fierro* (2 vols), FCE, Mexico 1958.

Masiello, F., *Languaje e ideología: las escuelas argentinas de vanguardia*, Hachette, Buenos Aires 1986.

Meyer, Doris, *Lives on the Line: The Testimony of Contemporary Latin American Authors*, Univ. of California Press, Berkeley 1988.

Morejon, Nancy (ed.), *Recopilación de textos sobre Nicolás Guillén*, Casa de las Americas, La Habana 1974.

Nobile, B. de, *El acto experimental*, Losasda, Buenos Aires 1978.

Oviedo, J.M., *Escrito al margen*, Inst. Colombiano de Cultura, Bogota 1982.

—— *Musas en guerra: arte y cultura en la nueva Nicaragua*, Mortiz, Mexico 1987.

Paz, Octavio, *Claude Lévi-Strauss o el nuevo festin de Esopo*, Siglo XXI, Mexico 1967.

—— *Posdata*, Siglo XXI, Mexico 1970.

—— *Cuadrivio*, Joaquin Mortiz, Mexico 1972.

—— *Alternating Current*, Wildwood House, London 1974.

—— *Convergences*, Harcourt Brace, San Diego/New York 1987.

—— *Mexico en la obra de Octavio Paz* (3 vols), FCE, Mexico 1987.

—— *One Earth Four or Five Worlds*, Harcourt Brace, New York 1985.

Perez, Firmat, *The Cuban Condition: Translation and Identity in Modern Cuban Literature*, Cambridge Univ. Press, Cambridge 1989.

Phillips, Rachel, *Alfonsina Storni from poetess to poet*, Tamesis Books, London 1975.

—— *The Poetic Modes of Octavio Paz*, OUP, Oxford 1972.

Rama, Angel, *Transculturación narrativa en América latina*, Siglo XXI, Mexico 1982.

—— *Literatura y clase social*, Folios, Mexico 1983.

—— *Rubén Darío y el modernismo*, Alfadil, Caracus 1985.

Randall, M., *Risking a Somersault in the Air*, Solidarity Publications, San Francisco 1984.

Reiss, Frank, *The Word and the Stone: The Poetry of Pablo Neruda*, OUP, Oxford 1972.

Rozlo, Nale and M. Marmol, *Genio y figura de Alfonsina Storni*, EUDEBA, Buenos Aires 1964.

Running, Thorpe, *Borges' Ultraista Movement and its Poets*, International Book Publishers, Michigan 1981.

Santi, E.H., *Pablo Neruda: The Poetics of Prophecy*, Cornell Univ. Press, Ithaca 1982.

Sarlo, B., *Una modernidad periférica: Buenos Aires en 1920 y 1930*, Eds Nueva Vision, Buenos Aires 1988.

—— and C. Altamirano, *Ensayos argentinos*, CEAL, Buenos Aires 1983.

Schulman, I., *Nuevos asedios al modernismo*, Taurus, Madrid 1987.

Sheridan, Guillermo, *Los contemporáneos ayer*, FCE, Mexico 1985.

Sicard, Alain, *El pensamiento poético de Pablo Neruda*, Ed. Gredos, Madrid 1981.

Sucre, G., *Borges el poeta*, Monte Avila, Caracas 1967.

Viñas, David, *Literatura argentina y realidad política*, Jorge Alvarez, Buenos Aires, 1985.

White, Steven, *Culture and Politics in Nicaragua*, Lumen Books, New York 1986.

Wilson, Jason, *An A–Z of Modern Latin American Literature in Translation*, Institute of Latin American Studies, London 1990.

—— *Octavio Paz: A Study of His Poetics*, CUP, Cambridge, 1979.

Yanover, H. (ed.), *Raul González Tuñon*, ECA, Buenos Aires 1962.

Ycaza, Tigerino J., *Las palabras y el ritmo en Rubén Darío*, Imp. tecnicas, Managua, 1987.

Yurkievich, S., *Fundadores de la nueva poesía latinoamericana: Vallejo, Huidobro, Borges, Neruda, Paz*, Barral, Barcelona 1971.

Brazil

1. Poetry

Alvim, Francisco, *Poesias reunidas 1968–1988*, Duas Cidades, São Paulo 1988.

Andrade, Carlos Drummond de, *Reunião: 10 livros de poesia de Carlos Drummond de Andrade*, José Olympio, Rio de Janeiro 1980.

Andrade, Mário de, *Obras Completas de Mário de Andrade II – Poesias Completas*, Martins, São Paulo 1966.

Andrade, Oswald de, *Obras Completas*, vol VII: *Poesias Reunidas*, Civilização Brasileira, Rio de Janeiro 1978.

—— *Do Pau-Brasil à Antropofagia e às Utopias: manifestos, teses de concursos e ensaios*, Civilização Brasileira, Rio de Janeiro 1978.

Bandeira, Manuel, *Manuel Bandeira: antologia poética*, José Olympio, Rio de Janeiro 1978.

Bilac, Olavo, *Poesias*, Edições de Ouro, Rio de Janeiro, 1978.

Bopp, Raul, *Cobra Norato e outros poemas*, Civilização Brasileira, Rio de Janeiro 1978.

Buarque de Hollanda, Heloísa (ed.), *26 poetas hoje*, Labor do Brasil, Rio de Janeiro 1976.

Cabral de Melo Neto, João, *Antologia Poética*, José Olympio, Rio de Janeiro 1979.

—— *Morte e vida severina e outros poemas em voz alta*, José Olympio, Rio de Janeiro 1980.

Campos, Augusto de, *Poesia 1949–1979*, Brasiliense, São Paulo 1986.

César, Ana Cristina, *A teus pés*, Brasiliense, São Paulo 1988.

Chamie, Mário, *Objeto Selvagem*, Quíron, São Paulo 1977.

Félix, Moacyr, *Invenção de crença e descrença*, Civilização Brasileira, Rio de Janeiro 1978.

Fontela, Orides, *Trevo (1969–1988)*, Duas Cidades, São Paulo 1988.

Freitas Filho, Armando, *À mão livre (1975–1979)*, Nova Fronteira, Rio de Janeiro 1979.

—— *Longa vida (1979–1981)*, Nova Fronteira, Rio de Janeiro 1982.

—— *3 × 4 (1981–1983)*, Nova Fronteira, Rio de Janeiro 1985.

Gullar, Ferreira, *Toda poesia (1950–1980)*, José Olympio, Rio de Janeiro 1987.

Lima, Jorge de, *Antologia Poética*, José Olympio, Rio de Janeiro 1978.

Meireles, Cecília, *Obra Poética*, José Aguilar, São Paulo, 1967.

Mendes, Murilo, *Murilo Mendes: poesia*, org. Maria Lúcia Aragão, Agir, Rio de Janeiro 1983.

Moraes, Vinicius de, *Obra Poética*, José Aguilar, Rio de Janeiro 1968.

Pignatari, Décio, *Poesia pois é Poesia 1950–1975*, Brasiliense, São Paulo 1986.

Prado, Adélia, *Bagagem*, Imago, Rio de Janeiro 1976.

Ricardo, Cassiano, *Martim Cererê (o Brasil dos meninos, dos poetas e dos heróis)*, José Olympio, Rio de Janeiro 1978.

Uchoa Leite, Sebastião, *Obra em dobras (1960–1988)*, Duas Cidades, São Paulo 1988.

Veloso, Caetano, *Caetano Veloso* (orgs Paulo Franchetti and Alcyr Pécora), Literatura Comentada, Abril Educação, São Paulo 1981.

2. Works and Anthologies in Translation

Andrade, Mário de, *Hallucinated City*, trans. Jack E. Tomlins, Vanderbilt University Press, Kingston, Tennessee 1969.

Andrade, Carlos Drummond de, *In the Middle of the Road: Selected Poems*, trans. John Nist, University of Arizona Press, Tucson 1965.

—— *The Minus Sign: a Selection from the Poetic Anthology*, trans. Virginia de Araújo, Black Swan Press, Chicago 1980; Carcanet, Manchester 1981.

—— *Travelling in the Family; Selected Poems*, trans. Thomas Colchie, Mark Strand, Elizabeth Bishop and Gregory Rabassa, Random House, New York 1986.

Bandeira, Manuel, *Recife*, trans. Eddie Flintoff, Rivelin Grapheme Press, Bradford 1984.

—— *This Earth, That Sky: Poems by Manuel Bandeira*, trans. Candace Slater, University of California Press, Berkeley 1989.

Gullar, Ferreira, *Dirty Poem: Poema Sujo by Ferreira Gullar*, trans. Leland Guyer, University Press of America, Lanham, New York, London 1990.

Lima, Jorge de, *Brazilian Psalm*, trans. Willis Wager, G. Schirmer, New York 1941.

Meireles, Cecília, *Poemas em tradução/Poems in Translation*, ed. Henry Keith and Raymond Sayers, Brazilian-American Cultural Institute, Washington DC 1977.

Moraes, Vinicius de, *The Girl from Ipanema*, trans. Merrick, Cross-Cultural Communications, New York 1982.

Bishop, Elizabeth and Brasil, Emanuel (eds.), *An Anthology of Twentieth-century Brazilian Poetry*, Wesleyan University Press, Middletown, 1972.

Brasil, Emanuel and William Jay Smith (eds.), *Brazilian Poetry (1950–1980)*, Wesleyan University Press, Middletown, 1983.

Green, J.C.R.(ed.), *Modern Brazilian Poetry*, Aquila/Phaeton Press, Isle of Skye, 1975.

Hulet, Claude L. (ed.), *Brazilian Literature 3, 1920–1960: Modernism*, Georgetown University Press, Washington 1975.

Neistein, José (ed.) and Manuel Cardoso, (trans.), *Poesia brasileira moderna: a bilingual anthology*, Brazilian-American Cultural Institute, Washington 1972.

Nist, John (ed. and trans.), *Modern Brazilian Poetry: An Anthology*, University of Texas Press, Austin 1967.

Pontiero, Giovanni (ed.), *An Anthology of Brazilian Modernist Poetry*, Pergamon Press, Oxford 1969.

Williams, Emmet (ed.), *Anthology of Concrete Poetry*, Something Else Press, New York 1967.

3. Studies

Andrade, Mário de, 'O movimiento modernista', *Aspectos da literatura brasileira*, Martins, São Paulo 1974.

Arrigucci Jr., Davi, *Humildade, paixão e morte: a poesia de Manuel Bandeira*, Companhia das Letras, São Paulo 1990.

Barata, Manoel Sarmento, *Canto melhor: uma perspectiva da poesia brasileira*, Paz e Terra, Rio de Janeiro 1969.

Bezerra de Meneses, Adélia, *Desenho mágico: poesia e política em Chico Buarque*, Hucitec, São Paulo 1982.

Buarque de Hollanda, Heloísa, *Impressões de viagem: CPC, vanguarda e desbunde: 1960/1970*, Brasiliense, São Paulo 1980.

Campos, Augusto de, Haroldo de Campos and Décio Pignatari, *Teoria da poesia concreta: textos críticos e manifestos 1950–1960*, Duas Cidades, São Paulo 1975.

Favaretto, Celso F., *Tropicália: Alegria, Alegria*, Kairós, São Paulo 1979.

Freitas Filho, Armando, 'Poesia virgula viva', *Anos 70*, eds. Armando Freitas Filho, Heloísa Buarque de Hollanda, Marcos Augusto Gonçalves, vol. 2: *Literatura*, Europa Empresa, Rio de Janeiro 1979–80.

Gledson, John, *Poesia e poética de Carlos Drummond de Andrade*, Duas Cidades, São Paulo 1981.

Johnson, John Randall, 'Tupy or not Tupy', in John King (ed.), *Modern Latin American Fiction: A survey*, Faber and Faber, London 1987.

Lafetá, João Luiz, *Figuração da intimidade: ímagens na poesia de Mário de Andrade*, Martins Fontes, São Paulo 1986.

Martins, Wilson, *The Modernist Idea: A Critical Survey of Brazilian Writing in the Twentieth Century*, Greenwood Press, Westport 1970.

Massi, Augusto (org.), *Artes e ofícios da poesia*, Artes e Ofícios, Porto Alegre 1991.

Mendonça Teles, Gilberto, *Vanguarda européia e modernismo brasileiro: apresentação dos principais poemas, manifestos, prefácios e conferências vanguardistas, de 1857 a 1972*, 10ª ed., Record, Rio de Janeiro 1987.

Moraes, Eduardo Jardim de, *A brasilidade modernista: sua dimensão filosófica*, Graal, Rio de Janeiro 1978.

Nist, John, *The Modernist Movement in Brazil: A Literary Study*, University of Texas, Austin and London 1967.

Pereira, Carlos Alberto Messeder, *Retrato de época: poesia marginal anos 70*, FUNARTE, Rio de Janeiro 1981.

Perrone, Charles A., *Masters of Contemporary Brazilian Song: MPB 1965–1985*, University of Texas, Austin 1989.

Sant'Anna, Affonso Romano de, *Música popular e moderna poesia brasileira*, Vozes, Petrópolis 1978.

Schwarz, Roberto, *Que horas são?: ensaios*, Companhia das Letras, São Paulo 1987.

Schwarz, Roberto, *Misplaced Ideas; Essays on Brazilian Culture*, Verso, London 1992.

Silva Brito, Mário da, *História do modernismo brasileiro 1 – antecedentes da Semana de Arte Moderna* 2ª ed., Civilização Brasileira, Rio de Janeiro 1964.

Solt, Mary Ellen (ed.), *Concrete Poetry: a World View*, Indiana University Press, Bloomington 1968.

Sussekind, Flora, *Literatura e vida literária: polêmicas, diários e retratos*, Jorge Zahar, Rio de Janeiro 1985.

389

General Works

Anglade, C. and Carlos Fortin, *The State and Capital Accumulation in Latin America* (2 vols), Macmillan, London 1990.

Benjamin, Walter, *Illuminations*, Jonathan Cape, London 1970.

Bennet, T., *Formalism and Marxism*, Methuen, London 1970.

Berger, John, *Selected Essays and Articles*, Penguin Books, Harmondsworth, 1971.

Berman, Marshall, *All That Is Solid Melts Into Air*, Verso, London 1983.

Bethell, Leslie (ed.), *The Cambridge History of Latin America*, CUP, Cambridge 1984.

Bisztray, G., *Marxist Models of Literary Realism*, Columbia UP, New York 1978.

Bloch, E. et al, *Aesthetics and Politics*, Verso, London 1977.

Bowra, M., *Poetry and Politics*, CUP, Cambridge, 1966.

Burns, E. Bradford, *A History of Brazil*, Columbia UP, New York 1980.

Callinicos, A., *Against Postmodernism*, Polity Press, Oxford 1989.

Clark, T.J., *The Absolute Bourgeois*, Thames & Hudson, London 1973.

Cockcroft, J.D., *Intellectual Precursors of the Mexican Revolution*, Univ. of Texas Press, Austin 1968.

Davis, H.E., *Latin American Thought*, Louisiana State UP, Baton Rouge 1972.

Dunkerley, James, *Power in the Isthmus*, Verso, London 1988.

Eagleton, Terry, *Literary Theory*, Blackwell, Oxford 1983.

Fanon, Frantz, *Black Skin White masks*, Grove Press, New York 1967.

Fraser, Ronald, *Blood of Spain*, Penguin, Harmondsworth 1981.

Galeano, Eduardo, *The Open Veins of Latin America*, Monthly Review Press, New York 1973.

Gonzalez, Casanova P., *La democracia en Mexico*, Siglo XXI, Mexico 1967.

—— (ed.), *Historia del movimiento obrero en America latina* (4 vols), Siglo XXI/ UNAM, Mexico 1984.

Habel, J., *Cuba: The Revolution in Peril*, Verso, London 1981.

Halperin, Donghi T., *Historia contemporánea de America Latina*, Alianza Editorial, Madrid 1972.

Harris, R. and C. Vilas, *Nicaragua: Revolution under Siege*, Zed Books, London 1985.

Jakobson, R., *Huit questions de poetique*, Ed. du Seuil, Paris 1977.

Knight, Alan, *The Mexican Revolution*, OUP, Oxford 1987.

Lodge, David, *The Modes of Modern Writing*, Univ. Of Chicago Press, Chicago 1977.

Mariátegui, J.C., *Seven Interpretive Essays on Peruvian Reality*, Univ. of Texas Press, Austin 1971.

Marx, K. and F. Engels, *The Communist Manifesto*, Penguin Books, Harmondsworth, 1967.

Morrow, Felix, *Revolution and Counterrevolution in Spain*, New Park, London 1983.

Needell, Jeffrey, *A Tropical Belle Epoque: Elite Culture and Society in Turn-of-the-century Rio de Janeiro*, CUP, Cambridge 1987.

Nelson, C. and L. Grossberg (eds), *Marxism and the Interpretation of Culture*, Macmillan, London 1988.

Orwell, G., *Homage to Catalonia*, Penguin, Harmondsworth 1970.

Pearce, Jenny, *Under the Eagle*, Latin America Bureau, London 1981.

—— *Promised Land*, Latin America Bureau, London 1986.

Petras, J. and M. Morley, *U.S. Hegemony under Siege*, Verso, London 1990.

Rock, David, *Politics in Argentina 1880–1930: The rise and fall of Radicalism*, CUP, Cambridge, 1975.

Rowe, William and Vivien Schelling, *Memory and Modernity: Popular Culture in Latin America*, Verso, London 1991.

Sanchez, Vazquez A., *Art and Society*, Merlin, London 1973.

—— *The Philosophy of Praxis*, Merlin, London 1977.

Slaughter, C., *Marxism Ideology and Literature*, Macmillan, London 1980.

Stein, S.J. and B., *The Colonial Heritage of Latin America*, OUP, Oxford 1970.

Stern, Irwin (ed.), *Dictionary of Brazilian Literature*, Greenwood Press, New York, 1988.

Stubbs, H.J., *Cuba: The Test of Time*, Latin America Bureau, London 1989.

Trotsky, L., *Literature and Revolution*, Bookmarks, London 1991.

Vitale, Luis, *Interpretación marxista de la historia de Chile*, Prensa Latinoamericana, Santiago 1962.

Voloshinov, V.N., *Marxism and the Philosophy of Language*, Harvard UP, Cambridge 1986.

Willett, John, *The New Sobriety: Art and Politics in the Weimar Period 1917–1933*, Thames and Hudson, London 1978.

Williams, Raymond, *The Politics of Modernism*, Verso, London 1989.

Index

Veloso, Caetano 313, 314, 316, 319
Venezuela 192
verdeamarelismo xix, 93, 96, 97
Vieira Pinto, Álvaro 240
Vietnam War 311
Villa, Francisco 'Pancho' 29
Violão de Rua (Street Guitar) 30, 250,
   251, 252, 253, 254, 311, 312
Vitier, Cintio 271, 274, 277
Voloshinov, V.N. 359 n24

Week of Modern Art (1922) 69, 70,
   71, 72, 96
Whitman, Walt 287, 289
Williams, Raymond 108, 121, 355 n6,
   356 n22, 359 n25

women xvi, xvii, xviii, 34, 57, 160,
   161, 327, 328, 343, 344
working class 56, 72, 111, 137, 151,
   189, 213, 231, 233, 241, 253, 265,
   268, 272, 282, 303, 312, 328, 362 n5

Yeats, W.B. 13
Yrigoyen, Hipólito 111, 114

Zapata, Emiliano 29
Zelaya, José Santos 286
Zhdanov, V.I. 132
Zurita, Raul
   Canto a su amor desaparecido 351,
      352–3
   Purgatorio 351–2